Axelrod & Cooper's
CONCISE
GUIDE
TO WRITING

THIRD EDITION

Axelrod & Cooper's
CONCISE
GUIDE
TO WRITING

Rise B. Axelrod
UNIVERSITY OF CALIFORNIA, RIVERSIDE

Charles R. Cooper
UNIVERSITY OF CALIFORNIA, SAN DIEGO

BEDFORD/ST. MARTIN'S
Boston • New York

Senior Production-
Production Supervisor: Tina Cameron
Marketing Manager: Brian Wheel
Art Director: Lucy Krikorian
Text Design: Anna George
Cover Design: Anna George/Lucy Krikorian
Composition: Stratford Publishing Services, Inc.
Printing and Binding: R. R. Donnelley & Sons Company

President: Charles H. Christensen
Editorial Director: Joan E. Feinberg
Editor in Chief: Nancy Perry
Director of Marketing: Karen R. Melton
Director of Editing, Design, and Production: Marcia Cohen
Managing Editor: Erica T. Appel

For information, write: Bedford/St. Martin's, 75 Arlington Street, Boston, MA 02116
(617-399-4000)

ISBN: 0-312-39083-1

Acknowledgments

(Acknowledgments and copyrights appear at the back of the book on page 424, which constitutes an extension of the copyright page.)

To the Instructor

Axelrod & Cooper's Concise Guide to Writing, Third Edition, aims to show students how writing works and how written texts are shaped by the writing situations in which they arise. Through six essay assignment chapters, students experience four fundamentally different writing situations: reflecting on past events, presenting firsthand observations, explaining information, and arguing—taking a position, proposing a solution, or justifying an evaluation. Students see how the kinds of thinking and writing required by these situations are important for them as college students, workers, and citizens. We also aim to show students that reading like a writer, planning essays systematically, getting and giving critical comments on rough drafts, revising thoughtfully, and thinking critically about their learning can improve their writing and confidence as writers. The *Concise Guide* challenges students, setting high standards for them with each essay they attempt and providing the scaffolding they need to achieve more than they imagined they could.

Although this third edition will look and feel different to those who are familiar with the second edition, you will find that it retains all the features you have come to rely on. Part One remains structured around our Guides to Writing, and Part Two still supplies essential support for critical reading, writing, and research. Almost all of the readings, however, are new, and the critical apparatus supporting each essay now focuses on only one or two of the genre's basic features exemplified in that particular reading. You will find, moreover, that our research coverage has been thoroughly updated to help students navigate their electronic research environment. Students will learn not only to evaluate and document electronic sources but also to effectively integrate them with more traditional sources in their research papers.

An Overview of the Book

The *Concise Guide to Writing* has two sections, preceded by an introductory chapter. Chapter 1 explains how writing works and what it contributes to thinking and learning. The chapter also introduces students to the writing activities in Part One.

Part One, Writing Activities, presents six different essay assignments, all reflecting actual writing situations that students may encounter both in and out of college, genres of writing that they should learn to read critically and to write intelligently. The genres included are autobiography, profile, explanation, arguing a position, proposing a solution, and justifying an evaluation.

You may choose among these chapters and teach them in any sequence you wish, though they are sequenced here to move students from writing based on personal experience and firsthand observation to writing calling for the analysis and synthesis of ideas and information derived from a variety of sources.

Each chapter follows the same organizational plan:

- Six brief **scenarios** identify the genre covered in the chapter and suggest the range of occasions when such writing is done — in other courses, in the community, and in the workplace.

- A **collaborative activity** gets students working with the genre taught in that chapter.

- Three **readings,** including at least one student essay, are each accompanied by **critical apparatus** designed to help students explore connections to their culture and experience and to analyze writing strategies used in this genre.

- **Summaries** of the **purpose and audience** and the **basic features** of this genre help students make connections between what they have read and their own writing.

- A flexible **guide to writing,** tailored to the particular genre, gives the chapter's writing assignment and helps students learn the kinds of questions they need to ask themselves as they develop their ideas.

- A **critical reading guide** for peer review of drafts helps students work collaboratively and learn to read with a critical eye both their own and other's drafts.

- **Editing and proofreading guidelines** remind students to check for sentence-level problems.

- A **Reflecting on Your Writing** activity encourages students to explore what they have learned while writing the essay.

Part Two, Strategies for Writing and Research, looks at a variety of strategies that will help students at all stages of their writing and research. Writing strategies such as invention and cueing the reader are discussed in the assignment chapters and reinforced in Chapters 8 and 9. Chapter 10 focuses on a variety of critical reading strategies. Chapter 11 is devoted to such elements of argumentation as asserting a thesis, giving reasons and support, counterarguing, and understanding logical fallacies. In Chapter 12, students are introduced to the field research skills of observing and interviewing — coverage new to this edition of the *Concise Guide.* The final two chapters of the book present comprehensive guidelines for doing research both in the library and on the Internet and for using and acknowledging sources.

Noteworthy Features

The *Concise Guide to Writing* contains several special features that contribute to the book's effectiveness. Chief among these are the practical Guides to Writing, the integration of reading and writing, clear coverage of strategies for writing and critical reading, comprehensive chapters on research, and activities to promote group discussion and inquiry.

Practical Guides to Writing.   We do not merely talk about writing; we also offer practical, flexible guides that escort students through the major stages of composing, from invention through revision and self-evaluation. Thus, this book is more than just a rhetoric that students will refer to occasionally. It is a guidebook that will help them write and develop as critical thinkers. Commonsensical and easy to follow, these writing guides teach students to assess a rhetorical situation, identify the kinds of information they will need, ask probing questions and find answers, and organize their writing to achieve their purpose.

Systematic Integration of Reading and Writing.   Because we see a close relationship between the ability to read critically and the ability to write intelligently, the *Concise Guide* combines reading instruction with writing instruction. Each chapter in Part One introduces a specific genre that students are led to consider both as readers and as writers. Each reading is accompanied by carefully focused apparatus. First is a response activity, Connecting to Culture and Experience, that relates a central theme of the reading to the students' cultural knowledge and personal experience. Questions are designed to stimulate small-group discussion that helps students explore the essay's relevance to their lives as well as its broader social implications. The two sections following, Analyzing Writing Strategies and a brief Commentary, examine how each writer applies basic genre features and strategies to a particular rhetorical situation. Taken together, these analytical activities and commentaries prepare students to write an essay of their own in the genre. Finally, in Considering Topics for Your Own Essay, students are challenged to apply this new knowledge to their own writing by imagining what they could write about and how they might address their prospective readers.

Clear Coverage of Strategies for Writing and Critical Reading.   In Chapter 8, students learn how to use strategies for cueing readers, such as orienting statements, paragraphing, cohesive devices, transitions, and headings. In Chapter 9, they learn various mapping and writing strategies to discover and develop ideas. Chapter 10 catalogs important strategies for reading critically, including outlining, paraphrasing, summarizing, and evaluating the logic of an argument. These reading strategies, which students can use in their other courses as well, complement the attention given to critical reading in the writing assignment chapters.

Comprehensive Chapters on Research.   In Chapter 12, students are introduced to the field research skills of observing and interviewing, coverage new to this edition of the *Concise Guide*. The final two chapters of the book present comprehensive guidelines for doing research both in the library and on the Internet and for using and acknowledging sources. Together, these three chapters present strategies for field research, library and Internet research, and using, evaluating, and acknowledging sources that will help students address all aspects of writing research papers.

Activities to Promote Group Discussion and Inquiry.   The *Concise Guide* offers multiple opportunities for group work throughout each Part One chapter. At the start of each chapter is a collaborative activity that invites students to try out some of the thinking and planning they will be doing for the kind of writing covered in that chapter. The Connecting to Culture and Experience section that follows each reading is designed to provoke thoughtful responses about the social and political implications of the reading. The Guide to Writing contains another collaborative activity that gets students to discuss their work in progress with one another, along with a Critical Reading Guide, which keeps students focused on the genre's basic features as they read and comment on each other's drafts. Finally, a discussion activity invites students to explore the social dimensions of the genre they have been learning to write. All of these materials include questions and prompts to guide students to work productively together.

New to This Edition

More Genres to Choose from.   The third edition of the *Concise Guide* includes six assignment chapters for six genres—one more than in the last edition. In response to our reviewers' preferences, we have included a chapter on writing profiles, as we did in the first edition.

Many New Readings.   Of the eighteen essays in the *Concise Guide,* fifteen are new and half are by women writers. Several of the new essays illustrate how visual elements such as diagrams, cartoons, and screen shots can be used effectively in a particular genre.

More Content Connected to Students' Lives.   To help students connect writing to their own lives, each of the assignment chapters now begins with scenarios about "Writing in the Community" and "Writing in the Workplace" in addition to "Writing in Your Other Courses." Community and workplace connections are emphasized in the apparatus accompanying the readings and in lists that help students generate writing topics.

Up-to-Date Coverage of Electronic Research and Documentation.   Current information on evaluating and documenting Internet sources makes it easier than ever to integrate online research into the composition course—without supplanting more traditional information sources. In addition to the three research chapters toward the end of the book, the *Concise Guide to Writing* includes three student essays reflecting MLA style and one reflecting APA style. One of the MLA papers evaluates a Web site.

A Completely New Look.   The *Concise Guide* has been completely redesigned so that key sections and features are easier to find and use—for instance, the basic features in each genre are now clearly distinguished from the surrounding text, and the pages in each Guide to Writing have a screened border. In addition, each Guide to Writing opens with a one-page "menu" that serves as an overview of that section.

Ancillaries for the *Concise Guide*

Bedford/St. Martin's offers two ancillaries especially tailored for use with the *Concise Guide*. The *Instructor's Resource Manual* contains information that will benefit novice and experienced instructors alike. The first section is devoted to teaching and evaluation practices, and the second section supplies suggested course plans, strategies for teaching the major assignments, and detailed chapter plans. Even if you have taught with previous editions of the *Concise Guide*, you will find much that is new in Part Two of the *Instructor's Resource Manual*. As in the past, the manual includes a selected bibliography in composition studies. *Sticks and Stones*, Fourth Edition, is a collection of essays written by students across the nation using our Guides to Writing. For each chapter in the *Concise Guide*, there is a corresponding chapter in *Sticks and Stones*.

To order either of these ancillaries, contact your local Bedford/St. Martin's sales representative or e-mail <sales_support@bfwpub.com>.

In addition, you may wish to visit the book companion site at <www.bedford stmartins.com/conciseguide> to take advantage of links to many additional resources from Bedford/St. Martin's, including Exercise Central, an online database with editing exercises that test a wide variety of skills and provide immediate feedback on students' progress.

Contributing to the Next Edition of the *Concise Guide*

We always are looking for new student essays for the *Concise Guide* along with *The St. Martin's Guide to Writing* and the accompanying collection of student writing. Please consider encouraging your students to send us contributions for potential publication. All you need to do is fill out copies of the agreement forms (found both at the back of this student edition and in the *Instructor's Resource Manual*) and send them to *Concise Guide*, Bedford/St. Martin's, 33 Irving Place, New York, NY 10003.

In addition, we would be delighted to receive comments and suggestions for the *Concise Guide*.

Acknowledgments

Our debt grows year by year to those teachers and students who have used *The St. Martin's Guide to Writing*, on which the *Concise Guide* is based, and who have so generously encouraged and advised us.

We would like to thank reviewers who completed a detailed questionnaire and volunteered numerous suggestions for the *Concise Guide:* Irene Anders, Indiana University–Purdue University, Fort Wayne; David Bordelon, Ocean County College;

Cynthia A. Crane, Raymond Walters College; Judith Hinman, College of the Red-woods; Patricia Howard, Frostburg State University; AnnMarie Kajencki, Bismarck State College; and Jane Schreck, Bismarck State College.

We also wish to thank Leonora P. (Lee) Smith for her contributions to the *Instructor's Resource Manual* and Larry Barkley of Mt. San Jacinto College–Menifee for coediting our collection of student essays, *Sticks and Stones*. We are especially grateful as well to the student authors who have so graciously allowed us to reprint their work in *Sticks and Stones and other student essays* and in *Axelrod & Cooper's Concise Guide*.

We wish to thank many people at Bedford/St. Martin's, including developmental editors Diana Puglisi and Judy Voss and senior production editor Harold Chester. Above all, we wish to express our appreciation to Nancy Perry, editor in chief, for helping us launch *The St. Martin's Guide* successfully so many years ago and continuing to stand by us, to Chuck Christensen and Joan Feinberg for their adroit leadership of Bedford/St. Martin's, and to marketing managers Karen Melton and Brian Wheel — along with their extraordinarily talented and hardworking sales staff — for their tireless efforts on behalf of our books.

Charles acknowledges the inspiration and advice of the other writing member of his family, his daughter Susanna, associate editor for the McClachy Newspaper Corporation and member of the editorial board at the *Sacramento Bee*. Susanna is an exemplary writer-in-the-world — informed, persistent, collaborative, personally courageous, and master of her genres. Rise wishes to dedicate this edition with love to her mother, Edna Borenstein, who always told her just to do the best she could — and had faith that she would.

Rise Axelrod
Charles Cooper

Contents

Introduction

"Why should learning to write well be important to me? What is the connection between writing and thinking? How will reading help me learn to write better? How can I learn to write more effectively and efficiently?" These are some of the questions you may be asking as you begin this writing course. Read on— for *Axelrod and Cooper's Concise Guide to Writing* offers some answers to these and other questions you may have.

■ WHY WRITING IS IMPORTANT

Writing has wide-ranging implications for the way we think and learn as well as for our chances of success, our personal development, and our relationships with other people.

Writing Influences the Ways We Think

First, the very act of writing encourages us to be creative as well as organized and logical in our thinking. When we write sentences, paragraphs, and whole essays, we generate ideas and connect these ideas in systematic ways. For example, by combining words into phrases and sentences with conjunctions such as *and, but,* and *because,* we can create complex, new ideas. By grouping related ideas into paragraphs, we develop their similarities and differences, and anchor our general ideas in specific facts and concrete examples.

By writing essays for different purposes and readers, we learn to develop our thinking in different ways. For example, writing about an important event in our lives develops our ability to select significant details and organize them into a meaningful narrative. Profiling people and places develops our observation and understanding of particular situations. Writing an explanation of a concept develops analytical and categorical thinking. Proposing solutions develops problem-solving, arguing positions develops logical thinking, and justifying an evaluation develops judgment.

> Some of the things that happen to us in life seem to have no meaning, but when you write them down, you find the meanings for them....
>
> —Maxine Hong Kingston

1

Those who are learning to compose and arrange their sentences with accuracy and order are learning, at the same time, to think with accuracy and order.

—HUGH BLAIR

Writing Contributes to the Ways We Learn

Writing helps us learn by making us active, critical thinkers. When we take notes in class, for example, writing helps us identify and remember what is important. Writing in the margins as we read encourages us to question the reading's ideas and information in light of our experience and other reading. Writing in a journal frees us to explore our understanding and response to what we are learning.

Writing essays of various kinds helps us organize and present what we have learned and, in the process, to clarify and extend our own ideas. Writing an explanatory essay, for example, helps us better understand the concept or idea we are explaining. Researching a controversial issue helps us both learn from and question others' points of view.

The mere process of writing is one of the most powerful tools we have for clarifying our own thinking. I am never as clear about any matter as when I have just finished writing about it.

—JAMES VAN ALLEN

Writing keeps me from believing everything I read.

—GLORIA STEINEM

Writing Fosters Personal Development

In addition to influencing the ways we think and learn, writing can help us grow as individuals. We are led to reflect deeply on our personal experience, for example, when we write to understand the significance of a particular event in our life. Writing about a controversial issue can make us examine critically some of our most basic assumptions. Writing an evaluation requires that we think about what we value and how our values compare to those of others. Perhaps most importantly, becoming an author confers authority on us; it gives us confidence to assert our own ideas and feelings.

In a very real sense, the writer writes in order to teach himself, to understand himself, to satisfy himself....

—ALFRED KAZIN

Writing has been for a long time my major tool for self-instruction and self-development.

—TONI CADE BAMBARA

Writing Connects Us to Others

It is easier now than ever before to connect with others via email and the Internet. We can use writing to keep in touch with friends and family, take part in academic discussion, and participate actively in democratic debate and decision making. By writing about our experiences, ideas, and observations, we reach out to readers, offering them our own point of view and inviting them to share theirs in return. Writing an argument on a controversial issue, for example, we not only assert our position on the issue but also give readers an opportunity to assert theirs. Moreover, when you and others respond constructively to each other's writing, you can clarify your differences, reexamine your reasoning, and ultimately influence each other's opinions. Similarly, writing a proposal requires us to work collaboratively with others to invent new, creative ways of solving complex problems.

> Writing is the act of saying *I,* of imposing oneself upon other people, of saying *listen to me, see it my way, change your mind.*
>
> – JOAN DIDION

> I think writing is really a process of communication....It's the sense of being in contact with people who are part of a particular audience that really makes a difference to me in writing.
>
> – SHERLEY ANNE WILLIAMS

Writing Promotes Success in College and at Work

As students, you are probably most aware of the many ways writing can contribute to your success in school. Students who learn to write for different readers and purposes do well in courses throughout the curriculum. No doubt you have been able to use writing to demonstrate your knowledge as well as to add to it. Eventually, you will need to use writing to advance your career by writing persuasive application letters for jobs or graduate school admission. Many businesses and professions expect people to write effective email messages, formal letters, and reports that present clear explanations, convincing evaluations, or constructive proposals.

> The aim of school is to produce citizens who are able to communicate with each other, to defend points of view, and to criticize....
>
> – ALBERT SHANKER

> People think it's sort of funny that I went to graduate school as a biologist and then became a writer....What I learned [in science] is how to formulate or identify a new question that hasn't been asked before and then to set about solving it, to do original research to find the way to an answer. And that's what I do when I write a book.
>
> – BARBARA KINGSOLVER

■ Exercise 1.1

Think of an occasion when writing helped you accomplish something important. For example, you may recall a time when writing helped you better understand a difficult subject you were studying, when you used writing to influence someone else, when writing helped you achieve a goal, when you worked through a problem by writing, or when you used writing for some other purpose or combination of purposes.

   Write a page or so describing what happened on this particular occasion. Describe how you came to write and what you wrote about. Then explain how you used writing on this occasion and what you wanted your writing to accomplish. For example, did you use it to help you learn something, express yourself, or connect to others?

■ HOW WRITING IS LEARNED

Writing is important. But can it be learned? This question is crucial because writing traditionally has been veiled in mystery. Some people believe that writers are born, not made. They assume that people who are good at writing do not have to spend a lot of time learning to write; they just naturally know how to do so. Others may assume that if you have to spend time working on your writing—planning, rewriting, or editing— then you might as well give up and do something else. After all, "real" writers write perfectly the first time, every time, dashing off an essay with minimal effort. Their first draft is the last draft. They may need to spell-check their work, but nothing major needs to be clarified, developed, or corrected.

■ Exercise 1.2

List some of your assumptions about writers and writing. Then write a few sentences speculating about the sources of these assumptions—personal experience, teachers, textbooks, the media, and so forth.

However, writers' testimonies, together with extensive research on how people write and learn to write, show that writing can—indeed *must*—be learned. Some writers may be more skilled than others. Some may find writing easier and more satisfying. But no one is born knowing how to write. Everyone must learn how to write.

> However great a [person's] natural talent may be, the art of writing cannot be learned all at once.
>
> —JEAN JACQUES ROUSSEAU

> Learning to write well takes time and much effort, but it can be done.
>
> —MARGARET MEAD

Axelrod and Cooper's Concise Guide to Writing, now in its third edition, has helped many students learn how to become effective, confident writers. Using the *Concise Guide,* you will read and write several different kinds of essays. From reading these essays, you will learn how other writers make their texts work for their particular readers. From writing the kinds of essays you are reading, you will learn to use your process of writing constructively to develop your thinking and compose texts that work effectively for your readers. To take full advantage of what you are learning by reading and writing, the *Concise Guide* will also help you become self-reflective as a reader and writer. From thinking critically about your learning, you will be better able to remember and apply what you have learned, thereby earning a greater sense of confidence and control.

Reading

This section shows how reading texts that work well for their readers helps you learn to write texts for your own readers and how *Axelrod and Cooper's Concise Guide to Writing* supports your learning from reading.

How Written Texts Work.   How a text works depends on what and who it is written for—its purpose and audience. A text's purpose and audience can be used to define the kind of writing it is, what we call its *genre*.

You may be familiar with genres as categories for literature (novel, poem, play) or film (science fiction, western, film noir, romance). College students read and write many different genres, such as lab reports in biology, ethnographies in anthropology, literary analysis or interpretation in English, research reviews in education. Academic disciplines rely on certain genres that have become established ways of making meaning and communicating among students and specialists in the field. The same is true of writing in business (some common genres include résumés and job-application letters, marketing reports, proposals, and personnel evaluations) and the professions (lawyers, for example, write briefs, appeals, closing arguments, and wills).

As these examples show, genres are shared by groups of people with common interests. Some genres are highly specialized and technical; to understand a biologist's lab report or a lawyer's brief, readers not only have to know the terminology but also have to be able to judge the reliability of the lab report's research methods or the legal basis of the brief's arguments. Many genres, however, are widely shared and therefore do not require specialized knowledge. For example, because of our shared experience, we can all read and understand most news reports, opinion essays, autobiographies, profiles, and advertisements we encounter in general-audience publications such as newspapers, magazines, and Web sites.

Genres develop in different communities to serve particular purposes. Biologists use the lab report to inform readers interested in biology about the results of their research and to enable other researchers to duplicate their experiments. Lawyers use briefs to convince judges that certain points of law apply to their case. Reporters write about news events to inform readers. Columnists write opinion essays to convince readers to adopt their views. Advertisers write ads to persuade readers to buy their clients' products.

A text's effectiveness—how well it achieves its purpose with its readers—depends on many factors, including how well it fulfills readers' expectations for the genre. Readers expect texts within a particular genre to have distinctive features, use specific strategies, and contain certain types of content. A remembered event essay, for example, has several basic features: a well-told story about the event, a vivid presentation of the people involved in the event and of the place where it occurred, and an indication of the event's significance. Writers of such essays use strategies of narration and description to help readers imagine what happened and understand the event's significance. Readers expect the content of autobiographical writing to be about events they consider important, such as events that have had some lasting impact — changing, challenging, or complicating the writer's sense of self or connection with others.

Although individual texts within the same genre vary (no two proposals, even those arguing for the same solution, will be identical), they nonetheless follow a general pattern using distinctive basic features, strategies, and special kinds of content to accomplish their purposes. This patterning allows for a certain amount of predictability, without which communication would be difficult, if not impossible. Language — whether spoken or written — is a system of social interaction. Everyone who speaks the same language learns to recognize certain patterns — how words should be ordered to make sentences comprehensible, how sentences can be related to one another to make coherent paragraphs, how examples can be used to explain new ideas, how arguments can be supported with quotations from authorities, and so forth. These language patterns, also called *conventions,* make communication possible.

To learn to write genres for particular groups of readers, we need to pay attention to how texts work for their readers. We have to understand also that writing in a genre does not mean that writing should be mechanical or formulaic. Each genre's basic features, strategies, and kinds of content represent broad frameworks within which writers are free to be creative. Most writers, in fact, find that working within a framework allows them to be more creative, not less so. Some even blur the boundaries between genres and invent new genres for new media such as Web sites. And as groups change, developing new interests and new ways of adding to their knowledge, genre conventions also change.

> You would learn very little in this world if you were not allowed to imitate. And to repeat your imitations until some solid grounding . . . was achieved and the slight but wonderful difference — that made *you* and no one else — could assert itself.
>
> – MARY OLIVER

How the *Concise Guide* Helps You Write Texts That Work.   To learn the conventions of a particular genre, you need to read examples of that genre. At the same time, you should also practice writing in the genre.

> Read, read, read. . . . Just like a carpenter who works as an apprentice and studies the master. Read!
>
> – WILLIAM FAULKNER

Reading is crucial. As you read examples of a genre, you begin to recognize its predictable patterns as well as the possibilities for innovation. This knowledge is stored in your memory and used both when you read and when you write in that genre.

Experienced writers read and learn from positive examples as well as negative ones. Sometimes, they focus on a particular problem — how to write realistic-sounding dialogue or how to refute someone else's argument effectively, for example. They do not look for answers in a single example. Instead, they sample many texts to see how different writers work with a certain feature of the genre. This sampling is not slavish imitation, but education. Like artists and craftspeople, writers have always learned from others. The *Concise Guide* presents a variety of examples in each genre accompanied by questions and commentary to help you see how writers use the conventional features and strategies of the genre to achieve their own purposes.

> I practiced writing in every possible way that I could. I wrote a pastiche of other people. Just as a pianist runs his scales for ten years before he gives his concert: because when he gives that concert, he can't be thinking of his fingering or of his hands, he has to be thinking of his interpretation. He's thinking of what he's trying to communicate.
> – KATHERINE ANNE PORTER

■ **Exercise 1.3**

Make two lists, one of the genres you have *read* recently, such as explanations of how to do something, stories, news reports, opinion pieces, and movie reviews; and the other of the genres you have *written* recently, both for college courses and for other purposes. Then write a few sentences speculating about how your familiarity with different genres from reading influences your writing.

Writing

This section shows how your writing process can become a more productive process of *thinking and writing* and how the *Concise Guide* helps you develop a process to meet the demands of different writing situations.

How to Make Your Writing Process Work.   When you reflect on how you write, you probably think of the steps you take: First you read the writing assignment, next decide which points to cover, then begin writing the opening paragraph, and so forth. For familiar writing situations—when you know the subject well and feel confident writing in the genre for your particular readers—the process that works best may involve minimal planning and only one draft, followed by a little rewriting, spell-checking, and proofreading. But for most writing situations, you have to figure out what you can say about the subject to your particular readers and how to communicate effectively in the genre. In these situations, the writing process itself becomes a tool for discovery and not just a sequence of steps you take to produce a written text.

> I don't see writing as a communication of something already discovered, as "truths" already known. Rather, I see writing as a job of experiment. It's like any discovery job; you don't know what's going to happen until you try it.
> –WILLIAM STAFFORD

To make writing a true process of discovery, you need to recognize that the process of writing is a process of thinking—not simply a sequence of steps. Using writing as a process of discovery means that you do not think and then write, but that the writing helps you think.

Few writers begin writing with a complete understanding of a subject. Most use writing as a way to learn about the subject, recording ideas and information they have collected, exploring connections and implications, letting the writing lead them to greater understanding. As they develop ideas and plan a draft, writers set goals for their writing: goals for the whole essay (to confront readers or inspire them, for example) and goals for particular passages (to make a sentence emphatic or include details in a paragraph).

> When I start a project, the first thing I do is write down, in longhand, everything I know about the subject, every thought I've ever had on it. This may be twelve or fourteen pages. Then I read it through, for quite a few days.... then I try to find out what are the salient points that I must make. And then it begins to take shape.
>
> — MAYA ANGELOU

While writing, most writers pause occasionally to reread what they have written. They often reread with their readers in mind to see whether they can make their writing more effective. Rereading sometimes leads to further invention — filling in a gap in the logic of an argument, for example — and frequently it leads to substantial rethinking and revising — cutting, reorganizing, rewriting.

> I think the writer ought to help the reader as much as he can without damaging what he wants to say; and I don't think it ever hurts the writer to sort of stand back now and then and look at his stuff as if he were reading it instead of writing it.
>
> — JAMES JONES

> The writer must survey his work critically, coolly, as though he were a stranger to it. At the end of each revision, a manuscript may look.... worked over, torn apart, pinned together, added to, deleted from, words changed and words changed back.
>
> — ELEANOR ESTES

Rereading your own writing with a critical eye is necessary, but many writers also share their ideas and writing with others, actively seeking constructive critical comments from friends and colleagues. Playwrights, poets, and novelists often join writers' workshops to get help from other writers. F. Scott Fitzgerald depended on his editor, Maxwell Perkins. When Perkins criticized the way Gatsby's character was being introduced in an early version of the novel, Fitzgerald made significant changes in chapters 3, 4, 5, 8, and 9 and completely rewrote chapters 6 and 7.

Writers also sometimes write collaboratively. Engineers, business executives, and research scientists usually write proposals and reports in teams. Graduate students and professors in many fields do research together and co-write conference papers and journal articles. This book is the product of extensive collaboration between the coauthors and numerous composition instructors, student writers, and editors over many years. Your instructor may ask you to try some of the *Concise Guide*'s collaborative activities with other students in your class.

> [Ezra Pound] was a marvelous critic because he didn't try to turn you into an imitation of himself. He tried to see what you were trying to do.
>
> – T. S. ELIOT

> I like working collaboratively from time to time. I like fusing ideas into one vision. I like seeing that vision come to life with other people who know exactly what it took to get there.
>
> – AMY TAN

The continual shifting of attention—from setting goals to choosing words, from inventing new ideas to rereading to anticipate readers' likely objections, from adding supporting examples to reorganizing—characterizes the dynamic thinking that underlies the writing process. Although writing may seem to progress in a linear, step-by-step fashion, invention is a thought process that does not stop when drafting begins. It continues throughout drafting and revising. Most writers plan and revise their plans, draft and revise their drafts, write and read what they have written, and then write some more. This rereading and rethinking is what we mean when we describe the writing process as recursive rather than linear. Instead of progressing in a straight line from the first sentence to the last, from opening paragraph to conclusion, the experience of writing is more like taking a steep trail with frequent switchbacks; it appears that you are retracing old ground but you are really rising to new levels.

Seasoned writers depend on this recursiveness to lead them to new ideas and to develop their insights. Many writers claim that it is only by writing that they can figure out what they think.

> How do I know what I think until I see what I say?
>
> —E. M. FORSTER

> As a writer I would find out most clearly what I thought, and what I only thought I thought, when I saw it written down
>
> —ANNA QUINDLEN

Even writers who plan in their head eventually have to work out their plans by writing them down. The advantage of writing down ideas is not only that writing makes a record you can review later, but also that the process of writing itself can help you articulate and develop your ideas.

> You have to work problems out for yourself on paper. Put the stuff down and read it—to see if it works.
>
> —JOYCE CARY

Inexperienced writers or those writing in a new genre or on a difficult subject especially benefit from writing outlines of where they are and where they hope to go so that they can then focus on how to get there. But outlines should not be written in stone; they must be flexible if the writer is to benefit from the recursiveness of the writing process.

> Somebody starting to write should have a solid foundation to build on.... When I first started to write I used to do two- or three-page outlines.
>
> —LILLIAN HELLMAN

> I began [Invisible Man] with a chart of the three-part division. It was a conceptual frame with most of the ideas and some of the incidents indicated.
>
> —RALPH ELLISON

> You are always going back and forth between the outline and the writing, bringing them closer together, or just throwing out the outline and making a new one.
>
> —ANNIE DILLARD

Sometimes, the hardest part of writing is getting down to work. Writers may procrastinate, but they learn to deal with procrastination. Many writers make writing a habit by setting a time to write and trying to stick to their schedule. Most importantly, they know that the only way to make progress on a writing project is to keep at it. They work at their writing, knowing it takes time and perseverance.

> I have to write every day because, the way I work, the writing generates the writing.
>
> — E. L. DOCTOROW

> It's a matter of piling a little piece here and a little piece there, fitting them together, going on to the next part, then going back and gradually shaping the whole piece into something. . . . You don't rely on inspiration — I don't anyway, and I don't think most writers do.
>
> — DAVE BARRY

Once immersed in invention — figuring out what they want to say about the subject, contemplating what readers already think about it, and so forth — most writers find that they continue inventing even when away from their desks. Once the process is under way, taking a walk or playing a game can be a productive part of the process rather than a means of procrastinating. Diverting a tired mind and body can help writers see connections or solve problems that had stymied them earlier.

> Often I write by not writing. I assign a task to my subconscious, then take a nap or go for a walk, do errands, and let my mind work on the problem.
>
> — DONALD MURRAY

Like most creative activities, writing is a form of problem-solving. As they work on a draft, most writers continually discover and try to solve writing problems — how to bring a scene to life, how to refute others' arguments, whether to begin with this point or that. The more writers know about their subjects, genres, and readers, the better they can anticipate and solve problems as they write.

Experienced writers develop a repertoire of strategies for solving problems they are likely to encounter. These are the tools of the trade. The *Concise Guide* will provide you with a full writer's toolbox and teach you how to select the right tool for the job.

How the *Concise Guide* Helps You Develop a Writing Process That Works.   As a student learning to write, you need to develop a writing process that is flexible and yet systematic. It should be a process that neither oversimplifies nor overwhelms, one that helps you learn about a subject and write a successful essay. The Guides to Writing in Part One of this book are designed to meet this need. These guides, which you will find on the pages bordered in green, suggest what you need to think about for each different writing situation. The first few times you write in a new genre, you can rely on these guides. They provide a scaffolding to support your work until you become more familiar with each genre.

When engaging in any new and complex activity — driving, playing an instrument, skiing, or writing — we have to learn how to break down the activity into a series of manageable tasks. In learning to play tennis, for example, you can isolate lobbing from volleying or work on your backhand or serve. Similarly, in writing about an autobiographical event, you can work first on recalling what happened, imagining the scene, or reflecting on the event's significance. What is important is focusing on one aspect at a time. Dividing the process in this way enables you to tackle a complex writing project without oversimplifying it.

> You know when you think about writing a book, you think it is overwhelming. But, actually, you break it down into tiny little tasks any moron could do.
>
> —ANNIE DILLARD

■ Exercise 1.4

Write a page or so describing the process you followed the last time you wrote something that took time and effort. Do not choose something you wrote in class. Use the following questions to help you recall what you did, but feel free to write about any other aspects of your writing process that you remember.

- What initially led you to write? Who were you writing for and what was the purpose of your writing?
- What kinds of invention and planning did you do, if any, before you began writing the first draft?
- If you discussed your ideas and plans with someone, how did discussing them help you? If you had someone read your draft, how did getting a response help?
- If you rewrote, moved, added, or cut anything in your first draft, describe what you changed.

Thinking Critically

This section shows how thinking critically about your learning can help you make your writing more effective and how the *Concise Guide* helps you think critically about your reading, your writing process, and the genres you are using.

How to Think Critically about Your Learning. Thinking critically means becoming self-aware and questioning your own as well as others' thinking.

When writing, you will find that many of your decisions do not require conscious effort. You can rely on familiar strategies that usually produce effective writing for you in the genre. But there will nearly always be occasions as you write when you become aware of problems that require your full attention. Some problems may be fairly easy to remedy, such as an inappropriate word choice or a confusing sequence of events. Other problems may require considerable rethinking and writing, for example, if you discover that your readers' likely objections seriously undermine your argument.

After you have completed a final draft, reflecting on how you identified and tried to solve such problems can be a powerful aid to learning. Understanding the problem may enable you to anticipate similar problems in the future. It may also give you a firmer grip on the standards you need to apply when rereading your drafts. Most importantly, reflecting on a problem you solved should enhance your confidence as a writer, helping you realize that problems are not signs of bad writing, but that problem-solving signifies critical thinking and good writing.

> That's what a writer is: someone who sees problems a little more clearly than others.
> — EUGENE IONESCO

How the *Concise Guide* Helps You Think Critically.   Thinking critically about your reading and writing experiences is not difficult. It simply requires that you shift focus from *what* you are reading and writing to *how* you are reading and writing.

The *Concise Guide* helps you talk and write about the hows of reading and writing different genres by providing a shared vocabulary of specialized but not very technical words you can easily learn and many of which you already know. Words like *significance,* *narrating,* and *thesis,* for example, will help you identify the features and strategies of essays you are reading in different genres. Words like *invention, setting goals,* and *revising* will help you describe what you are doing as you write your own essays in these genres.

Each writing assignment chapter in Part One includes several opportunities for you to think critically about your understanding of the genre and to reflect on your writing process. For example, a section entitled Reflecting on Your Writing concludes each chapter, giving you an opportunity to look back and reflect on how you used the writing process creatively.

■ **Exercise 1.5**

Read the following quotes to see how writers use similes (writing is like _____) and metaphors (writing is _____) to describe the processes and products of writing.

> Writing is like exploring . . . as an explorer makes maps of the country he has explored, so a writer's works are maps of the country he has explored.
> — LAWRENCE OSGOOD

> Writing is manual labor of the mind: a job, like laying pipe.
> — JOHN GREGORY DUNNE

Write several similes or metaphors of your own that express aspects of your experience as a writer. Then write a page explaining and expanding on the ideas and feelings expressed in your similes and metaphors.

■ USING THIS BOOK

Axelrod and Cooper's Concise Guide to Writing is divided into two major parts.

Part One presents writing assignments for six important genres: autobiographical events, profile, explanation, position paper, proposal, and evaluation. Each of these writing assignment chapters provides readings that demonstrate how written texts of that genre work and a Guide to Writing that will help you write an effective essay in the genre for your particular purpose and audience. Each chapter also includes a discussion of possible purposes and audiences for the genre, a summary of the genre's basic features and strategies, and, as we have mentioned, a section titled Reflecting on Your Writing.

Part Two provides illustrations and practice using strategies for invention and critical reading, writing, and research. Also included are up-to-date guidelines for writing research papers using a wide range of sources (library sources, the Internet, and your own field research).

■ **Exercise 1.6**

Preview each of the writing assignments in Part One (Chapters 2–7) of the *Concise Guide*. Begin by reading the opening paragraphs of the chapter, which introduce the genre, and skimming the examples of Writing in Your Other Courses, Writing in the Community, and Writing in the Workplace. Then turn to the Guide to Writing in the chapter, read the Writing Assignment, and skim the Invention activity immediately following the assignment to see examples of possible subjects for essays in the genre, including those listed under "Identity and Community" and "Work and Career."

List the genres you would like to work on in this class. For each genre you list, write a few sentences explaining why you want to work on it.

The Part One Readings

Each Part One chapter includes readings, some written by professional writers and others by college students. All of the readings have been selected to reflect a wide range of topics and strategies. If you read these selections with a critical eye, you will see many different ways writers use a genre.

Each reading selection is accompanied by the following groups of questions, activities, and commentary to help you learn how essays in that genre work:

Connecting to Culture and Experience invites you to explore with other students an issue or question raised by the reading.

Analyzing Writing Strategies helps you examine closely the reading's basic features or writing strategies.

Commentary points out important features of the genre and strategies the writer uses in the essay.

Considering Topics for Your Own Essay suggests subjects related to the reading that you might write about in your own essay.

Most of the assignments in this book provide opportunities to explore your connections to the world. When you are choosing a topic to write about, you might consider suggestions listed under "Identity and Community" and "Work and Career" in the Guides to Writing. These topics enable you to explore your personal connections to the various communities of which you are a part, visit and learn more about places in your community, debate issues important to your community, examine your ideas and attitudes about work, and consider issues related to your future career.

The Part One Guides to Writing

Each Part One assignment chapter provides detailed suggestions for thinking about your subject and purpose as well as your readers and their expectations. These Guides to Writing will help you develop a truly recursive process of discovery that will enable you to write an effective essay in the genre for your particular purpose and audience.

To make the process manageable, the Guide to Writing is divided into sections: The Writing Assignment, Invention and Research, Planning and Drafting, a Critical Reading Guide, Revising, and Editing and Proofreading. The "menu" preceding the Writing Assignment shows you at a glance the sections and the headings under each section. But to understand how the activities in the Guide to Writing will help you do the kinds of thinking you need to do, you must look closely at the types of activities included in each section.

The Writing Assignment. Each Guide to Writing begins with an assignment that defines the general purpose and basic features of the genre you have been studying in the chapter. The assignment does not tell you what subject to write about or who your readers will be. You will have to make these decisions, guided by the invention activities in the next section.

Invention and Research. Every Guide to Writing includes invention activities and most also include suggestions for observational, library, or Internet research. The Invention and Research activities are designed to help you find a topic, discover what you already know about it, consider your purpose and audience, research the subject further to see what others have written about it, explore and develop your ideas, and compose a tentative thesis statement to guide your planning and drafting.

Remember that invention is not a part of the writing process you can skip. It is the basic, ongoing preoccupation of all writing. As writers, we cannot choose *whether* to invent; we can only decide *how*.

You can use the invention activities before, during, and after you have written a first draft. However, the sequence of invention activities can be especially helpful before drafting because it focuses systematically on the basic genre features and writing strategies. The sequence reminds you of questions you need to think about as you collect, analyze, and synthesize ideas and information in light of your particular subject, purpose, and readers. The entire sequence of invention activities takes only a couple of hours to complete. But it works best when spread over several days, giving yourself time to think. So, if at all possible, begin the invention process far enough ahead of the deadline to let your thinking develop fully. Here is some general advice to keep in mind as you do the invention activities:

Use Writing to Explore Your Ideas. You can use writing to gather your thoughts and see where they lead. The key to exploratory writing is to refrain from censoring yourself. Simply try writing for five to ten minutes. Explore your ideas freely, letting one idea lead to another. Later, you can reread what you have written and select the most promising ideas to develop.

Focus on One Issue at a Time.   Explore your topic systematically by dividing it into its component parts and exploring them one at a time. For example, instead of trying to think of your whole argument, focus on one reason and the support you would give for it, or focus on how you might refute one objection to your argument.

■ **Exercise 1.7**

Preview the Invention section of one of the Guides to Writing. First choose an assignment chapter that interests you (Chapters 2–7). Then find the Invention (or Invention and Research) section and skim it from beginning to end. Notice the headings and subheadings, but also look closely at some of the activities to see what they ask you to do and think about.

Planning and Drafting   Each Guide to Writing includes suggestions for planning to get you started writing the first draft of your essay. These suggestions help you use the recursiveness of the writing process to continue making connections and developing your ideas. You set goals and try to implement them as you plan and write the draft. While drafting, you may make notes about new ideas or additional information you need to research, but you try to keep your focus on the ideas and information you have already discovered in order to work out their meanings.

The section is divided into four parts:

Seeing What You Have involves reviewing what you have discovered about your subject, purpose, and audience.

Setting Goals helps you think about your overall purpose as well as your goals for the various parts of your essay.

Outlining suggests some of the ways you might organize your essay.

Drafting launches you on the writing of your first draft.

As you begin your first draft, keep in mind the following practical points, many of which assist professional writers as they begin drafting:

Choose the Best Time and Place.   You can write a draft anytime and anyplace. As you probably already know, people write under the most surprising or arduous conditions. Drafting is likely to go smoothly, however, if you choose a time and place ideally suited for sustained and thoughtful work. Many professional writers have a place where they can concentrate for a few hours without repeated interruptions. Writers often find one place where they write best, and they return there whenever they have to write. Try to find such a place for yourself.

Make Revision Easy.   If possible, compose your draft on a word processor. If you do not have access to one and must write out or type your text, write on only one side of the page. Leave wide margins. Write on every other line or triple-space your typing. When you arrange your text on the page in these ways, you are looking ahead to when you will need to revise the draft, leaving yourself plenty of space to change, add, cut, and rearrange material later on.

Do the Easy Parts First.   Divide your task into manageable portions and do the easy parts first. Just aim to complete a small part of the essay—one section or paragraph—at a time. Try not to agonize over difficult parts, such as the first paragraph or the right word. Start with the part you understand best.

Lower Your Expectations—for the Time Being.   Be satisfied with less than perfect writing in a first draft, and do not be overly critical of what you are getting down on paper at this stage. Remember, you are working on a draft that you will revise later. For now, try things out. Follow digressions. Let your ideas flow. Later you can go back and cross out a sentence, rework a section, or make other changes. Now and then, of course, you will want to reread what you have written, but do not reread obsessively. Return to drafting new material as soon as possible. Avoid editing or proofreading during this stage.

Take Short Breaks—and Reward Yourself.   Drafting can be hard work, and you may need to take a break to refresh yourself. But be careful not to wander off for too long or you may lose momentum. By setting small goals and rewarding yourself regularly, you will make it easier to complete the draft.

Critical Reading Guide.   Each Guide to Writing includes a Critical Reading Guide that will help you get a good critical reading of your draft as well as help you read others' drafts. Once you have finished drafting your essay, you will want to make every effort to have someone else read the draft and comment on how to improve it. Experienced writers often seek out such advice from critical readers to help them see their drafts as others do.

When you are asked to evaluate someone else's draft, you need to read it with a critical eye. You must be both positive and skeptical—positive in that you want to identify what is workable and promising in the draft, skeptical in that you need to question the writer's assumptions and decisions.

Here is some general advice on reading any draft critically:

Make a Written Record of Your Comments.   Although talking with the writer about your reading of the draft can be useful and even fun, you will be most helpful to the writer if you put your ideas down on paper. When you write down your comments and suggestions—either on the draft or on a separate sheet of paper—you leave a record that can be used later when the writer revises the material.

Read First for an Overall Impression.   On first reading, try not to be distracted by any errors in spelling, punctuation, or word choice. Look at the big issues: clear focus, compelling presentation, forcefulness of argument, novelty and quality of ideas. What seems particularly good? What problems do you see? Focus on the overall goal of the draft and how well it is met. Write just a few sentences expressing your initial reaction.

Read Again to Analyze the Draft.   For this second reading, focus on individual parts of the draft, bringing to bear what you know about the genre and the subject.

When you read the draft at this level, you must shift your attention from one aspect of the essay to another. Consider how well the opening paragraphs introduce the essay and prepare the reader for what follows. Pay attention to specific writing strategies, like narration or argument. Notice whether the parts seem logically sequenced. Look for detailing, examples, or other kinds of support.

As you analyze, you are evaluating as well as describing, but a critical reading involves more than criticism of the draft. A good critical reader helps a writer see how each part of an essay works and how all the parts work together. By describing what you see, you help the writer view the draft more objectively, a perspective that is necessary for thoughtful revising.

Offer Advice, but Do Not Rewrite.   As a critical reader, you may be tempted to rewrite the draft—to change a word here, correct an error there, add your ideas everywhere. Resist the impulse. Your role is to read carefully, to point out what you think is or is not working, to make suggestions and ask questions. Leave the revising to the writer.

In turn, the writer has a responsibility to listen to your comments but is under no obligation to do as you suggest. "Then why go to all the trouble?" you might ask. There are at least two good reasons. First, when you read someone else's draft critically, you learn more about writing—about the decisions writers make, about how a thoughtful reader reads, about the constraints of particular kinds of writing. Second, as a critical reader you embody for the writer the abstraction called "audience." By sharing your reactions with the writer, you complete the circuit of communication.

Exercise 1.8

Preview the Critical Reading Guide in the assignment chapter you chose for Exercise 1.7. Find the section and skim it. Then look closely at item 2 or 3 in the numbered list to get a sense of what you are being asked to think about when reading and responding to another writer's draft. If you have participated in draft workshops before, compare your previous experience as a reader to the experience you think you would have by following this Critical Reading Guide. Also compare the usefulness of the response you got in the past from readers of your draft to the kind of response you could expect from readers following this guide.

Revising.   Each Guide to Writing includes a Revising section to help you get an overview of your draft, chart a plan for revision, consider critical comments, and carry out the revisions.

A first draft rarely fulfills a writer's expectations. Experienced writers are not surprised or disappointed, however, because they expect revision to be necessary. They know that revising will bring them closer to the essay they really want to write. When writers read their drafts thoughtfully and critically—and perhaps reflect on the advice of critical readers—they are able to see many opportunities for improvement. They may notice sentence-level problems such as misspelled words or garbled syntax, but more important, they discover ways to delete, move, rephrase, and add material in order to develop their ideas and say what they want to say more clearly.

Here is some general advice on revising:

Reconsider Your Purpose and Audience.   Remind yourself of what you are trying to accomplish in this essay. If someone has read and responded to your draft, you may now have a better understanding of your readers' likely interests and concerns. You may also have refined your purpose. Keep your purpose and audience in mind as you reread the essay and revise in stages. Do not try to do everything at once.

Look at Major Problems First.   Identify any major problems preventing the draft from achieving its purpose. Major problems might include a lack of awareness of your audience, inadequate development of key parts, missing or incomplete sections, or the need for further invention or research. Trying to solve these major problems will probably lead to some substantial rethinking and rewriting, so do not get diverted by sentence-level problems at this time.

Focus Next on Organization and Coherence.   Look at the introductory section of the essay to see how well it prepares readers for the parts that follow. It may help to make a paragraph-by-paragraph scratch outline to help you see at a glance what each paragraph does in the essay. If you have difficulty identifying the function of any paragraph, you may need to add an appropriate transition to clarify the paragraph's connection to the previous paragraphs or write a new topic sentence that better announces the subject of the paragraph. Or you may need to do some more extensive rewriting or reorganization.

Then Consider the Details.   As the saying goes, the devil is in the details. The details have to be selected for a specific purpose, such as to convey significance, support an argument, or provide a concrete example of an abstract idea. If any details seem unrelated to your larger purpose, you need to make the connections explicit. If your essay lacks details, you can review your invention notes or do some additional research to come up with the details you need.

Editing and Proofreading.   Once you have finished revising your essay, your next step is to edit and proofread it carefully. You want to make sure that every word, phrase, and sentence is clear and correct. Using language and punctuation correctly is an essential part of good writing. Errors will distract readers and lessen your credibility as a writer.

Be sure to save editing until the end — *after* you have planned and worked out a revision. Too much editing too early in the writing process can limit, or even block, invention and drafting.

Here are some other suggestions:

Keep a List of Your Common Errors.   Note the grammatical and spelling errors you discover in your own writing. You will probably start to recognize error patterns to check for as you edit your work.

Begin Proofreading with the Last Sentence.   To focus your attention on grammar and spelling, it may help to read backwards, beginning with the last sentence. When you read backwards, it is harder to pay attention to content and thus easier to recognize grammatical and spelling errors.

Exchange Drafts with Another Student.   Because it is usually easier to see errors in someone else's writing than in your own, consider trading essays with a classmate and proofreading one another's writing.

Reflecting on Your Writing.   Each chapter in Part One concludes with a set of activities designed to help you consider how you solved problems writing that particular kind of essay. If you are compiling a portfolio of your coursework to hand in at the end of the term, these activities may help you write a reflective essay on the work you select for the portfolio.

WRITING ACTIVITIES

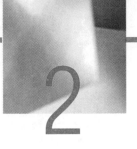

Remembering Events

When you write about remembered events in your life, you write autobiography, a popular genre of writing. Many readers love autobiographical stories because they are entertaining and informative, revealing fascinating similarities and differences between their own and others' experiences and points of view. Writers enjoy autobiography because it lets them compose vivid, dramatic stories and leads them to reflect deeply on their own lives and the forces within themselves and within society that have influenced them.

When you write about a remembered event, your purpose is to present yourself to readers by telling a story that discloses something significant about your life. Autobiographical writers do not just pour out their memories and feelings. Instead, they shape those memories into a compelling story that conveys the meaning and importance of an experience — what can be called its autobiographical significance.

Writing about your life for others to read is not the same as writing for yourself. As a writer, you must remember that autobiography is public, not private. While it requires self-presentation, it does not require you to make unwanted self-disclosures. You choose the event to write about and decide how you will portray yourself.

As you work through this chapter, you will learn to tell a story that entertains readers and lets them know something important about how you came to be the person you are now. You also will learn to describe people and places vividly so that readers can see what makes them memorable for you. As you learn to write well about a remembered event, you will be practicing two of the most basic writing strategies — narration and description. These strategies can play a role in almost every kind of writing. As you will see in Chapters 3–7, narration and description can contribute to explanatory reports and persuasive arguments, in addition to playing an essential role in the remembered event assignment for this chapter.

You will encounter writing about a remembered event in many different contexts, as the following examples suggest.

Writing in Your Other Courses

- For an assignment in a psychology course, a student tests against her own experience an idea from the developmental psychologist Erik Erikson: "[Y]oung people . . .

are sometimes preoccupied with what they appear to be in the eyes of others as compared with what they feel they are." The student recounts one event when she cared tremendously about what her peers thought about her. Then she explains how her teammates' reactions influenced her feelings and sense of self.

- For a linguistics course, a student is asked to write about current research on men's and women's conversational styles. One researcher, Deborah Tannen, has reported that women and men have different expectations when they talk about problems. Women expect to spend a lot of time talking about the problem itself, especially about their feelings. Men, in contrast, typically want to cut short the analysis of the problem and the talk about feelings; they would rather discuss solutions to the problem. Applying Tannen's findings to her own experience, the student recounts a conversation about a family problem with her brother who is one year older. She reconstructs as much of the conversation as she can remember and explains which parts constitute feelings talk and which indicate problem-solving talk. She concludes that her conversation with her brother well illustrates Tannen's findings.

Writing in the Community

- As part of a local history project in a small western ranching community, a college student volunteers to help an elderly rancher write about some of his early experiences. One experience seems especially dramatic and significant—a time in the winter of 1938 when a six-foot snowstorm isolated his family for nearly a month. The student tape-records the rancher talking about how he and his wife made preparations to survive and ensure the health of their infant sons and how he snowshoed eight miles to a logging train track, stopped the train, and gave the engineer a message to deliver to relatives in the nearest town explaining that they were going to be okay. On a second visit, the student and the rancher listen to the tape recording, and afterward talk about further details that might make the event more complete and dramatic for readers. The rancher then writes a draft of the remembered event and the student later helps him revise and edit the essay. The student copies an old snow-day photograph from the nearby town's newspaper files, and the rancher selects a photograph of his young family from a family photo album. The essay and photographs are published in a special supplement to the newspaper.

- To commemorate the retirement of the city's world-famous symphony orchestra conductor, a radio program director invites the conductor to talk about his early experiences with the orchestra. Aware of his tendency to ramble and digress in interviews, the conductor decides to write down a story about the first time he asked the orchestra members to play a never-before-performed modern composition noted for its lack of familiar tones, progressions, and rhythms. He describes how he tried to prepare the orchestra members for this experience and how they went about the hard, slow work of mastering the difficult music. The conductor expresses regret over posing this challenge so early in his experience of working with the orchestra members, but he proudly asserts that their great success with the music gave them the confidence to master any music they chose to play together.

For the radio program, he alternates reading this remembered event aloud with playing brief recorded excerpts from the orchestra's polished performance.

Writing in the Workplace

- As part of an orientation manual for new employees, the founder of a highly successful computer software company describes the day she spent with the Silicon Valley venture capitalists who lent her the money to start the company. She describes how other venture capitalists had turned her down and how desperately anxious she was for this group to fund her company. The meeting had barely begun when she spilled her coffee across the top of the gleaming conference-room table. She describes some of the questions and her answers and traces her rising and falling hopes during the discussion. She left dejected and resigned to giving up the dream of founding her own company. The next morning a member of the group who had not asked any questions at the meeting phoned her to praise her proposal and announce that his group would fund her company. He invited her to a celebratory lunch with the group at the best restaurant in town, where she was careful not to spill her vodka martini served in a long-stemmed glass.

- In the highway department offices of a large upper-midwestern state, there have been sudden increases in violence and threats of violence. One worker has killed another, and several managers have been threatened. To keynote a statewide meeting of highway department managers seeking solutions to this problem, a manager writes a speech that includes a detailed description of an incident when he was confronted in his office by an employee unhappy about an overtime assignment. The employee came into the office without knocking and would not sit down. He talked loudly, waved his arms, and threatened to harm the manager and his family. He would not leave when asked to. The manager reflects on his fear and on his frustration about not knowing what to do when the employee finally left. The department's published procedures seemed not to apply to this case. He acknowledges his reluctance to report the incident to the state office because he did not want to appear to be ineffective and indecisive.

Practice Remembering an Event: A Collaborative Activity

The preceding scenarios suggest some occasions for writing about events in one's life. Think of an event in your life that you would feel comfortable describing to others in your class. The only requirements are that you remember the event well enough to tell the story and that the story lets your classmates learn something about you. Here are some guidelines to follow:

Part 1. Consider several events and choose one you feel comfortable telling in this situation. Then, for two or three minutes, make notes about how you will tell your story.

Now, get together with two or three other students and take turns telling your stories. Be brief—each story should take only a few minutes.

Part 2. Take ten minutes or so to discuss what happened when you told about a remembered event:

- Tell each other how you chose your particular story. What did you think about when you were choosing an event? How did your purpose and audience—what you wanted your classmates to know and think about you—influence your choice?
- Review what each of you decided to include in your story. Did you plunge right into telling what happened, or did you first provide some background information? Did you decide to leave any of the action out of your story? If so, what did you leave out and why? Did you include a physical description of the scene? Did you describe any of the people, including yourself, or mention any specific dialogue? Did you tell your listeners how you felt at the time the event occurred or did you say how you feel now looking back on it?
- What was the easiest part of telling a story about a remembered event in your life? What was the most difficult part?

READINGS

The readings in this chapter illustrate the features of essays about remembered events and the strategies writers rely on to realize the features. No two essays in this genre are much alike, and yet they share defining features. The section Analyzing Writing Strategies and the Commentary following each reading touch on a few features best illustrated by that essay, capturing its special qualities and strengths. Together, the three essays cover many of the possibilities of the genre. Consequently, you will want to read as many of the essays and Commentaries as possible and, if time permits, complete the activities in Analyzing Writing Strategies. Following the last reading in the chapter, the Basic Features section offers a concise description of the features of writing about remembered events and provides examples from all of the readings.

Annie Dillard won the Pulitzer Prize for her very first book, Pilgrim at Tinker Creek *(1974). In that book, she describes herself as "no scientist," merely "a wanderer with a background in theology and a penchant for quirky facts." She has since written many other books, including collections of poetry, essays, and literary theory. Her most recent book,* For the Time Being *(1999), is a collection of essays. This selection comes from her autobiography,* An American Childhood *(1987).*

In "Handed My Own Life," we see the early stirrings of Dillard's lifelong enthusiasm for learning and fascination with nature. As you read her story, think about why she wrote it. What do you think she wants to tell readers about herself? What impression do you have of Annie Dillard from reading her story?

Handed My Own Life

Annie Dillard

After I read *The Field Book of Ponds and Streams* several times, I longed for a microscope. Everybody needed a microscope. Detectives used microscopes, both for the FBI and at Scotland Yard. Although usually I had to save my tiny allowance for things I wanted, that year for Christmas my parents gave me a microscope kit. 1

In a dark basement corner, on a white enamel table, I set up the microscope kit. I supplied a chair, a lamp, a batch of jars, a candle, and a pile of library books. The microscope kit supplied a blunt black three-speed microscope, a booklet, a scalpel, a dropper, an ingenious device for cutting thin segments of fragile tissue, a pile of clean slides and cover slips, and a dandy array of corked test tubes. 2

One of the test tubes contained "hay infusion." Hay infusion was a wee brown chip of grass blade. You added water to it, and after a week it became a jungle in a drop, full of one-celled animals. This did not work for me. All I saw in the microscope after a week was a wet chip of dried grass, much enlarged. 3

Another test tube contained "diatomaceous earth." This was, I believed, an actual pinch of the white cliffs of Dover. On my palm it was an airy, friable chalk. The booklet said it was composed of the siliceous bodies of diatoms—one-celled creatures that live in, as it were, small glass jewelry boxes with fitted lids. Diatoms, I read, come in a variety of transparent geometrical shapes. Broken and dead and dug out of geological deposits, they made chalk, and a fine abrasive used in silver polish and toothpaste. What I saw in the microscope must have been the fine abrasive—grit enlarged. It was years before I saw a recognizable, whole diatom. The kit's diatomaceous earth was a bust. 4

All that winter I played with the microscope. I prepared slides from things at hand, as the books suggested. I looked at the transparent membrane inside an onion's skin and saw the cells. I looked at a section of cork and saw the cells, and at scrapings from the inside of my cheek, ditto. I looked at my blood and saw not much; I looked at my urine and saw long iridescent crystals, for the drop had dried. 5

All this was very well, but I wanted to see the wildlife I had read about. I wanted especially to see the famous amoeba, who had eluded me. He was supposed to live in the hay infusion, but I hadn't found him there. He lived outside in warm ponds and streams, too, but I lived in Pittsburgh, and it had been a cold winter. 6

Finally, late that spring I saw an amoeba. The week before, I had gathered puddle water from Frick Park; it had been festering in a jar in the basement. This June night after dinner I figured I had waited long enough. In the basement at my microscope table I spread a scummy drop of Frick Park puddle water on a slide, peeked in, and lo, there was the famous amoeba. He was as blobby and grainy as his picture; I would have known him anywhere. 7

Before I had watched him at all, I ran upstairs. My parents were still at table, drinking 8
coffee. They, too, could see the famous amoeba. I told them, bursting, that he was all set
up, that they should hurry before his water dried. It was the chance of a lifetime.

Father had stretched out his long legs and was tilting back in his chair. Mother sat 9
with her knees crossed, in blue slacks, smoking a Chesterfield. The dessert dishes were
still on the table. My sisters were nowhere in evidence. It was a warm evening; the big
dining-room windows gave onto blooming rhododendrons.

Mother regarded me warmly. She gave me to understand that she was glad I had 10
found what I had been looking for, but that she and Father were happy to sit with their coffee, and would not be coming down.

She did not say, but I understood at once, that they had their pursuits (coffee?) and I 11
had mine. She did not say, but I began to understand then, that you do what you do out of
your private passion for the thing itself.

I had essentially been handed my own life. In subsequent years my parents would 12
praise my drawings and poems, and supply me with books, art supplies, and sports
equipment, and listen to my troubles and enthusiasms, and supervise my hours, and discuss and inform, but they would not get involved with my detective work, nor hear about
my reading, nor inquire about my homework or term papers or exams, nor visit the sala-
manders I caught, nor listen to me play the piano, nor attend my field hockey games, nor
fuss over my insect collection with me, or my poetry collection or stamp collection or rock
collection. My days and nights were my own to plan and fill.

When I left the dining room that evening and started down the dark basement stairs, 13
I had a life; I sat to my wonderful amoeba, and there he was, rolling his grains more
slowly now, extending an arc of his edge for a foot and drawing himself along by that foot,
and absorbing it again and rolling on. I gave him some more pond water.

I had hit pay dirt. For all I knew, there were paramecia, too, in that pond water, or 14
daphniae, or stentors, or any of the many other creatures I had read about and never
seen: volvox, the spherical algal colony; euglena with its one red eye; the elusive, glassy
diatom; hydra, rotifers, water bears, worms. Anything was possible. The sky was the limit.

Connecting to Culture and Experience: Coming of Age

The story Dillard tells about her experience may be seen as a coming-of-age story. In
many cultures around the world, a young person must undergo a rite of passage into
adulthood, a coming-of-age experience that often attracts autobiographers. This
experience usually tests the person's spiritual strength as well as physical prowess and
know-how. The person must pass the test alone, without the help of friends or relatives. A coming-of-age story typically includes these rites-of-passage elements.

With other students in your class, find these elements in Dillard's essay. With these
elements in mind, discuss why Dillard considers such an apparently trivial event important enough to write an essay about and pivotal enough to title "Handed My Own Life."

Analyzing Writing Strategies

1. At the beginning of this chapter, we make several assertions about remembered event essays. Consider which of these are true of Dillard's essay:

   - It tells an entertaining story.
   - It is vivid, letting readers see what makes the event as well as the people and places memorable for the writer.
   - It is purposeful, trying to give readers an understanding of why this particular event was significant in the writer's life.
   - It includes self-presentation but not unwanted self-disclosures.
   - It can lead readers to think in new ways about their own experiences or about how other people's lives differ from their own.

2. Visual description — naming objects and detailing their colors, shapes, sizes, and textures — is an important writing strategy in remembered event essays. To see how Dillard uses naming to present scenes and people, skim paragraphs 5–8, underlining the names of objects or people. These are nearly always nouns. To start, underline these names in the sentences of paragraph 5: *microscope, slides, books, membrane, skin, cells, cork, cells, scrapings, cheek, blood, urine, crystals,* and *drop.* To see how Dillard uses detailing, put brackets around all of the words and phrases that modify the nouns that name. Details help readers imagine more precisely and concretely the objects and people Dillard presents. To start, put brackets around these details in the sentences of paragraph 5: *transparent, onion's, from the inside of my cheek, long, iridescent, dried.*

   Notice first how frequently naming and detailing occur in paragraphs 5–8. Notice also how many different kinds of objects and people are named. Then consider these questions: Does naming sometimes occur without any accompanying detailing? What do you think the naming contributes to this part of Dillard's essay? What do you think the detailing contributes?

Commentary: Organizing a Well-Told Story

"Handed My Own Life" is a well-told story. It provides a dramatic structure that arouses our curiosity, builds suspense, and completes the action.

From the very first sentence of Dillard's essay — "After I read *The Field Book of Ponds and Streams* several times, I longed for a microscope" — not only do we want to know what will happen, but we also want to know more about this girl who wants a microscope. We may not share her particular enthusiasm, but we can identify with her because we have all desired something as much as she "longed for" a microscope. Identification with the writer may get us to start reading, and our curiosity makes us want to continue reading. We wonder whether the girl will get the microscope and, if she does, what will happen.

In addition to arousing our curiosity, the search for the amoeba gives Dillard's story a simple structure, like that of a mystery.

We can see this simple narrative organization in the following paragraph-by-paragraph scratch outline (for more on scratch outlining, see Chapter 10, p. 311):

1. Gives history of her desire to have a microscope and tells when she got one
2. Describes workplace and supplies
3. Tells of failed efforts to see one-celled animals in hay infusion
4. Tells of failed efforts to see diatoms—one-celled creatures—in diatomaceous earth
5. Summarizes what she saw or failed to see in microscope during the winter
6. Explains that what she wanted to see but failed repeatedly to find was the amoeba (the one-celled animal that lives in the hay infusion and elsewhere)
7. Announces that in late spring she saw the amoeba; tells what led up to her seeing the amoeba; describes the amoeba
8. Tells that as soon as she found the amoeba, she ran upstairs to tell her parents
9. Describes father and mother lounging after dinner
10. Summarizes what her mother said
11. Explains what she understood her mother to mean
12. Reflects on the significance of what she had learned from her mother by telling what happened in the years that followed this event
13. Returns to the time of the event to tell what she did that night—studied the amoeba and gave it pond water
14. Recalls looking forward to seeing many other creatures through the microscope

From the sample scratch outline, we can see that the story focuses on the evening when Dillard finally saw the elusive amoeba. This focus on a single brief incident is the hallmark of the remembered event essay. The entire essay, however, actually spans several months from before Christmas to late spring; but from these months Dillard includes only action and information that contribute to our understanding of why finding the amoeba was so significant. Her narrative follows a simple chronology, beginning some time before the amoeba sighting, pausing for the dramatic sighting of the amoeba and the significant interaction with her parents, and, at the conclusion, projecting into the future.

Also worth noting is Dillard's use of specific narrative action, a way of showing people talking, moving, and gesturing. This important strategy enables writers to present people more vividly and dramatically. For example, in paragraph 9, Dillard prepares readers for the fact that her parents will not be jumping up and rushing to the basement to see the amoeba by showing her father sitting "stretched out" and "tilting back in his chair" and her mother sitting "with her knees crossed." In paragraph 13, Dillard shows the amoeba—not a person but still an important character in the story—"rolling his grains more slowly now, extending an arc of his edge for a foot and drawing himself along by that foot, and absorbing it again and rolling on." These specific actions may heighten both our interest in and understanding of what Dillard sees in the dining room and through her microscope.

Considering Topics for Your Own Essay

List two or three occasions when you learned something important or made a significant discovery. Choose only occasions that, like Dillard's, focus on learning or discoveries that you can trace to one moment or brief time of unexpected insight. Then choose one occasion that you would be interested in writing about for readers who do not know you. What would you want them to learn about you from reading your essay?

Rick Bragg, *a domestic correspondent for the* New York Times, *lives in Atlanta, Georgia. Before coming to the* Times, *he reported for the* Los Angeles Times, St. Petersburg Times *(as Miami bureau chief),* Birmingham News, *and* Anniston (Alabama) Star. *He has received the Pulitzer Prize for his* New York Times *feature writing as well as the American Society of Newspaper Editors' Distinguished Writing Award. From 1992 to 1993, Bragg was a Nieman Fellow at Harvard University. He has also taught writing at Harvard, Boston University, and the University of South Florida. This reading is from Bragg's autobiography of his small-town Alabama upbringing in a poor family,* All Over but the Shoutin' *(1997), a best-seller and a* New York Times *Notable Book of the Year.*

As you read, notice how the metaphor of the slingshot in the opening sentence anticipates what happens in the rest of the reading.

100 Miles per Hour, Upside Down and Sideways

Rick Bragg

Since I was a boy I have searched for ways to slingshot 1
myself into the distance, faster and faster. When you turn the key on a car built for speed, when you hear that car rumble like an approaching storm and feel the steering wheel tremble in your hands from all that power barely under control, you feel like you can run away from anything, like you can turn your whole life into an insignificant speck in the rearview mirror.

In the summer of 1976, the summer before my senior year at Jacksonville High 2
School, I had the mother of all slingshots. She was a 1969 General Motors convertible muscle car with a 350 V-8 and a Holley four-barreled carburetor as long as my arm. She got about six miles to the gallon, downhill, and when you started her up she sounded like Judgment Day. She was long and low and vicious, a mad dog cyclone with orange houndstooth interior and an eight-track tape player, and looked fast just sitting in the yard under a pine tree. I owned just one tape, that I remember, *The Eagles' Greatest Hits.*

I worked two summers in the hell and heat at minimum wage to earn enough money 3
to buy her and still had to borrow money from my uncle Ed, who got her for just nineteen hundred dollars mainly because he paid in hundred-dollar bills. "You better be careful, boy," he told me. "That'un will kill you." I assured him that, Yes, Sir, I would creep around in it like an old woman.

I tell myself I loved that car because she was so pretty and so fast and because I 4
loved to rumble between the rows of pines with the blond hair of some girl who had yet to

discover she was better than me whipping in the breeze. But the truth is I loved her because she was my equalizer. She raised me up, at least in my own eyes, closer to where I wanted and needed to be. In high school, I was neither extremely popular nor one of the great number of want-to-bes. I was invited to parties with the popular kids, I had dates with pretty girls. But there was always a distance there, of my own making, usually.

That car, in a purely superficial way, closed it. People crowded around her at the Hardee's. I let only one person drive her, Patrice Curry, the prettiest girl in school, for exactly one mile.   5

That first weekend, I raced her across the long, wide parking lot of the TG&Y, an insane thing to do, seeing as how a police car could have cruised by at any minute. It was a test of nerves as well as speed, because you actually had to be slowing down, not speeding up, as you neared the finish line, because you just ran out of parking lot. I beat Lyn Johnson's Plymouth and had to slam on my brakes and swing her hard around, to keep from jumping the curb, the road and plowing into the parking lot of the Sonic Drive-In.   6

It would have lasted longer, this upraised standing, if I had pampered her. I guess I should have spent more time looking at her than racing her, but I had too much of the Bragg side of the family in me for that. I would roll her out on some lonely country road late at night, the top down, and blister down the blacktop until I knew the tires were about to lift off the ground. But they never did. She held the road, somehow, until I ran out of road or just lost my nerve. It was as if there was no limit to her, at how fast we could go, together.   7

It lasted two weeks from the day I bought her.   8

On Saturday night, late, I pulled up to the last red light in town on my way home. Kyle Smith pulled up beside me in a loud-running Chevrolet, and raced his engine. I did not squall out when the light changed—she was not that kind of car—but let her rpm's build, build and build, like winding up a top.   9

I was passing a hundred miles per hour as I neared a long sweeping turn on High-way 21 when I saw, coming toward me, the blue lights of the town's police. I cannot really remember what happened next. I just remember mashing the gas pedal down hard, halfway through that sweeping turn, and the sickening feeling as the car just seemed to lift and twist in the air, until I was doing a hundred miles per hour still, but upside down and sideways.   10

She landed across a ditch, on her top. If she had not hit the ditch in just the right way, the police later said, it would have cut my head off. I did not have on my seat belt. We never did, then. Instead of flinging me out, though, the centrifugal force—I had taken sci-ence in ninth grade—somehow held me in.   11

Instead of lying broken and bleeding on the ground beside my car, or headless, I just sat there, upside down. I always pulled the adjustable steering wheel down low, an inch or less above my thighs, and that held me in place, my head covered with mud and bro-ken glass. The radio was still blaring—it was the Eagles' "The Long Run," I believe—and I tried to find the knob in the dark to turn it off. Funny. There I was in an upside-down car, smelling the gas as it ran out of the tank, listening to the tick, tick, tick of the hot engine, thinking: "I sure do hope that gas don't get nowhere near that hot manifold," but all I did about it was try to turn down the radio.   12

I knew the police had arrived because I could hear them talking. Finally, I felt a hand 13
on my collar. A state trooper dragged me out and dragged me up the side of the ditch and
into the collective glare of the most headlights I had ever seen. There were police cars
and ambulances and traffic backed up, it seemed, all the way to Piedmont.

"The Lord was riding with you, son," the trooper said. "You should be dead." 14

My momma stood off to one side, stunned. Finally the police let her through to look 15
me over, up and down. But except for the glass in my hair and a sore neck, I was fine.
Thankfully, I was too old for her to go cut a hickory and stripe my legs with it, but I am sure
it crossed her mind.

The trooper and the Jacksonville police had a private talk off to one side, trying to 16
decide whether or not to put me in prison for the rest of my life. Finally, they informed my
momma that I had suffered enough, to take me home. As we drove away, I looked back
over my shoulder as the wrecker dragged my car out of the ditch and, with the help of
several strong men, flipped it back over, right-side up. It looked like a white sheet of paper
someone had crumpled up and tossed in the ditch from a passing car.

"The Lord was riding with that boy," Carliss Slaughts, the wrecker operator, told my 17
uncle Ed. With so many people saying that, I thought the front page of the *Anniston Star*
the next day would read: LORD RIDES WITH BOY, WRECKS ANYWAY.

I was famous for a while. No one, no one, flips a convertible at a hundred miles per 18
hour, without a seat belt on, and walks away, undamaged. People said I had a charmed
life. My momma, like the trooper and Mr. Slaughts, just figured God was my copilot.

The craftsmen at Slaughts' Body Shop put her back together, over four months. My 19
uncle Ed loaned me the money to fix her, and took it out of my check. The body and
fender man made her pretty again, but she was never the same. She was fast but not real
fast, as if some little part of her was still broken deep inside. Finally, someone backed into
her in the parking lot of the Piggly Wiggly, and I was so disgusted I sold her for fourteen
hundred dollars to a preacher's son, who drove the speed limit.

Connecting to Culture and Experience: Social Status

Bragg worked hard and saved his money for two years when he was a teenager in high
school in order to buy the convertible. Probably he had several motives for doing so;
but after he started driving the car, he came to think of it as "my equalizer" that
"closed" the distance between the most popular students and himself and gave him
immediate "upraised standing."

With other students, discuss this concern with standing or status in high school.
Was it a concern of yours personally? If not, speculate about the reasons. If so, what
did you try to do, if anything, to raise your status? Why do you think you made
this effort? How did other students you knew well respond to the concern about
status? Does this concern with status seem to you to be realistic preparation for college and life after college, or does it strike you as a distortion of typical adult human
relationships?

Analyzing Writing Strategies

1. One important strategy used for describing people, places, and objects in auto-biographical writing is comparing—using similes and metaphors to help readers imagine what happened. Similes are explicit comparisons. For example, in paragraph 1, Bragg writes, "you hear that car rumble like an approaching storm." As in this example, the word *like* or *as* introduces a simile. Metaphors are implied comparisons. For example, Bragg opens his essay by writing, "Since I was a boy I have searched for ways to slingshot myself into the distance, faster and faster." Here he implies a comparison between himself and a stone launched from a hand-held slingshot; the stone speeds into space as Bragg hopes to speed into the future, to get to any place other than the place he is in now.

   There are several comparisons in paragraph 1 and one each in paragraphs 3, 7, 9, 13, and 16. Locate and underline the comparisons in these paragraphs. Which one is most vivid for you—that is, most helps you imagine the events Bragg describes? For you as one reader, what do the comparisons as a group add to this particular essay? They should not, of course, be merely decorative but highly substantive and functional. Comparisons are not a requirement of success-ful remembered event essays, but they can contribute to readers' experience.

2. To learn more about how Bragg tells his story, begin by marking off the three main parts of the essay: the context (paragraphs 1–8), the incident (9–16), and the conclusion (17–19). Notice how much time passes in each main section. How does the context prepare you for the incident, and does it do so adequately? What are the particular elements of the conclusion, and how do they help bring the story to a satisfactory close?

   In the central incident (9–16), the defining element of a remembered event essay, Bragg narrates a compelling story. To understand more fully how Bragg organizes the incident, make a paragraph scratch outline of it. Does the order of events make sense? Are there further details you need to know in order to fol-low easily what happens? What does Bragg do to arouse your curiosity and build suspense?

   For an example of a paragraph scratch outline, turn to the Commentary fol-lowing Annie Dillard's essay on p. 30. For more information on scratch outlining, see Chapter 10, p. 311.)

Commentary: Autobiographical Significance

Bragg's essay illustrates the two main ways writers convey the autobiographical signif-icance of a remembered event: showing and telling. Bragg shows the event's signifi-cance through details and action. For example, he shows us how the car raised his status by describing its power and imposing appearance and the blond-haired girls he took for rides in it. He shows the importance of the car by recounting how terribly hard he worked to buy it and then to have it repaired after the wreck. He reveals per-haps his resigned acceptance that the car would not change his life by selling it deci-sively when it was dented in a parking lot. The least Bragg must do to succeed is to show consistently through details and action what the remembered event meant to him. This showing of significance, sometimes referred to as creating a dominant impression, gives readers a consistent impression throughout the essay of what the autobiographical significance might be.

Bragg also tells readers what he believes the autobiographical significance might be, and he does so in two ways: by relating his remembered thoughts and feelings from the time of the event as well as by giving his present perspective on the event.

Bragg's remembered thoughts and feelings frame his essay. In the first paragraph, he remembers thinking that owning a powerful car makes "you feel like you can run away from anything, like you can turn your whole life into an insignificant speck in the rearview mirror." In the final paragraphs, he remembers his temporary fame for surviving the accident and his disgust when someone damaged his car in a parking lot. These remembered thoughts and feelings reveal perhaps a change of values, from materialism to some yet-to-be-defined values, from Bragg's relying on a car for status to his parting with it readily for far less money than he had invested in it.

Bragg's present perspectives on this remembered event occur in paragraphs 4–7, between the time he bought the car and had the accident. From his perspective in his mid-thirties, as he was writing *All Over but the Shoutin'*, Bragg writes, "I tell myself I loved that car because she was so pretty and so fast.... But the truth is I loved her because she was my equalizer." He now recognizes, "It would have lasted longer, this upraised standing, if I had pampered her.... [B]ut I had too much of the Bragg side of the family in me for that." He also acknowledges that racing in the parking lot was "an insane thing to do." Although Bragg devotes relatively little space in the essay to telling us what he believes the significance of the incident to be, he balances his remembered thoughts and feelings with his present perspectives.

Considering Topics for Your Own Essay

Bragg has focused on a particular incident that conveys something about himself both as an adolescent and as the man he would become by his mid-thirties. Think of incidents early in your life (before you were eleven or twelve years old) that are particularly revealing about you, both as a child and as a person of your present age. You might try to think of incidents that tested or challenged you, or incidents in which you behaved either typically or atypically in relation to the way you remember yourself to have been or think of yourself now. Perhaps you experienced a dreadful disappointment or an unexpected delight. Perhaps you were in danger or you accomplished something you now think you were unprepared for.

Jean Brandt wrote this essay as a first-year college student. In it she tells about a memorable event that occurred when she was thirteen. Reflecting on how she felt at the time, Brandt writes, "I was afraid, embarrassed, worried, mad." As you read, look for places where these tumultuous and contradictory remembered feelings are expressed.

Calling Home

Jean Brandt

As we all piled into the car, I knew it was going to be a fab-   1
ulous day. My grandmother was visiting for the holidays;
and she and I, along with my older brother and sister,
Louis and Susan, were setting off for a day of last-minute
Christmas shopping. On the way to the mall, we sang Christmas carols, chattered, and
laughed. With Christmas only two days away, we were caught up with holiday spirit. I felt
light-headed and full of joy. I loved shopping — especially at Christmas.

The shopping center was swarming with frantic last-minute shoppers like ourselves.   2
We went first to the General Store, my favorite. It carried mostly knickknacks and other
useless items which nobody needs but buys anyway. I was thirteen years old at the time,
and things like buttons and calendars and posters would catch my fancy. This day was no
different. The object of my desire was a 75-cent Snoopy button. Snoopy was the latest. If
you owned anything with the Peanuts on it, you were "in." But since I was supposed to be
shopping for gifts for other people and not myself, I couldn't decide what to do. I went in
search of my sister for her opinion. I pushed my way through throngs of people to the
back of the store where I found Susan. I asked her if she thought I should buy the button.
She said it was cute and if I wanted it to go ahead and buy it.

When I got back to the Snoopy section, I took one look at the lines at the cashiers   3
and knew I didn't want to wait thirty minutes to buy an item worth less than one dollar. I
walked back to the basket where I found the button and was about to drop it when suddenly, instead, I took a quick glance around, assured myself no one could see, and
slipped the button into the pocket of my sweatshirt. I hesitated for a moment, but once the
item was in my pocket, there was no turning back. I had never before stolen anything; but
what was done was done. A few seconds later, my sister appeared and asked, "So, did
you decide to buy the button?"

"No, I guess not." I hoped my voice didn't quaver. As we headed for the entrance, my   4
heart began to race. I just had to get out of that store. Only a few more yards to go and I'd
be safe. As we crossed the threshold, I heaved a sigh of relief. I was home free. I thought
about how sly I had been and I felt proud of my accomplishment.

An unexpected tap on my shoulder startled me. I whirled around to find a middle-aged   5
man, dressed in street clothes, flashing some type of badge and politely asking me to
empty my pockets. Where did this man come from? How did he know? I was so sure that no
one had seen me! On the verge of panicking, I told myself that all I had to do was give this
man his button back, say I was sorry, and go on my way. After all, it was only a 75-cent item.

Next thing I knew, he was talking about calling the police and having me arrested
and thrown in jail, as if he had just nabbed a professional thief instead of a terrified kid. I   6
couldn't believe what he was saying.

"Jean, what's going on?"   7

The sound of my sister's voice eased the pressure a bit. She always managed to get   8
me out of trouble. She would come through this time too.

"Excuse me. Are you a relative of this young girl?"   9

"Yes, I'm her sister. What's the problem?"   10

"Well, I just caught her shoplifting and I'm afraid I'll have to call the police."   11

"What did she take?" 12

"This button." 13

"A button? You are having a thirteen-year-old arrested for stealing a button?" 14

"I'm sorry, but she broke the law." 15

The man led us through the store and into an office, where we waited for the police officers to arrive. Susan had found my grandmother and brother, who, still shocked, didn't say a word. The thought of going to jail terrified me, not because of jail itself, but because of the encounter with my parents afterward. Not more than ten minutes later, two officers arrived and placed me under arrest. They said that I was to be taken to the station alone. Then, they handcuffed me and led me out of the store. I felt alone and scared. I had counted on my sister being with me, but now I had to muster up the courage to face this ordeal all by myself. 16

As the officers led me through the mall, I sensed a hundred pairs of eyes staring at me. My face flushed and I broke out in a sweat. Now everyone knew I was a criminal. In their eyes I was a juvenile delinquent, and thank God the cops were getting me off the streets. The worst part was thinking my grandmother might be having the same thoughts. The humiliation at that moment was overwhelming. I felt like Hester Prynne being put on public display for everyone to ridicule. 17

That short walk through the mall seemed to take hours. But once we reached the squad car, time raced by. I was read my rights and questioned. We were at the police station within minutes. Everything happened so fast I didn't have a chance to feel remorse for my crime. Instead, I viewed what was happening to me as if it were a movie. Being searched, although embarrassing, somehow seemed to be exciting. All the movies and television programs I had seen were actually coming to life. This is what it was really like. But why were criminals always portrayed as frightened and regretful? I was having fun. I thought I had nothing to fear—until I was allowed my one phone call. I was trembling as I dialed home. I didn't know what I was going to say to my parents, especially my mother. 18

"Hi, Dad, this is Jean." 19

"We've been waiting for you to call." 20

"Did Susie tell you what happened?" 21

"Yeah, but we haven't told your mother. I think you should tell her what you did and where you are." 22

"You mean she doesn't even know where I am?" 23

"No, I want you to explain it to her." 24

There was a pause as he called my mother to the phone. For the first time that night, I was close to tears. I wished I had never stolen that stupid pin. I wanted to give the phone to one of the officers because I was too ashamed to tell my mother the truth, but I had no choice. 25

"Jean, where are you?" 26

"I'm, umm, in jail." 27

"Why? What for?" 28

"Shoplifting." 29

"Oh no, Jean. Why? Why did you do it?" 30

"I don't know. No reason. I just did it." 31

"I don't understand. What did you take? Why did you do it? You had plenty of money   32
with you."

"I know but I just did it. I can't explain why. Mom, I'm sorry."   33

"I'm afraid sorry isn't enough. I'm horribly disappointed in you."   34

Long after we got off the phone, while I sat in an empty jail cell, waiting for my par-   35
ents to pick me up, I could still distinctly hear the disappointment and hurt in my mother's
voice. I cried. The tears weren't for me but for her and the pain I had put her through. I felt
like a terrible human being. I would rather have stayed in jail than confront my mom right
then. I dreaded each passing minute that brought our encounter closer. When the officer
came to release me, I hesitated, actually not wanting to leave. We went to the front desk,
where I had to sign a form to retrieve my belongings. I saw my parents a few yards away
and my heart raced. A large knot formed in my stomach. I fought back the tears.

Not a word was spoken as we walked to the car. Slowly, I sank into the back seat   36
anticipating the scolding. Expecting harsh tones, I was relieved to hear almost the opposite from my father.

"I'm not going to punish you and I'll tell you why. Although I think what you did was   37
wrong, I think what the police did was more wrong. There's no excuse for locking a thirteen-
year-old behind bars. That doesn't mean I condone what you did, but I think you've been
punished enough already."

As I looked from my father's eyes to my mother's, I knew this ordeal was over.   38
Although it would never be forgotten, the incident was not mentioned again.

Connecting to Culture and Experience: Shame

In paragraph 17, Brandt gives us a vivid portrait of how excruciating the feeling of
shame can be: "I sensed a hundred pairs of eyes staring at me. My face flushed and I
broke out in a sweat." Shame, as this description indicates, involves a desire for the
community's approval or a dread of its disapproval. (The words *shame* and *guilt* are
often used interchangeably, but they have different connotations: *Shame* involves anxiety about social acceptance, whereas *guilt* is a more private, inward-looking emotion
associated with morality.)

Identify one occasion when you felt ashamed. With other students, take turns
briefly explaining what happened and why you were ashamed. In whose eyes did you
feel the most shame? (Note that Brandt, for example, feels shame at being thought of
as a criminal by strangers in the shopping mall, but she feels even more ashamed with
her grandmother and perhaps most ashamed with her mother.)

Analyzing Writing Strategies

1. Reread the essay, paying particular attention to Brandt's use of dialogue —
   reconstructed conversation from the time of the event. What do you learn about
   the author from what she says and how she says it? What do you learn about her
   relationship with her parents?

2. The story begins and ends in a car, with the two car rides framing the story. Framing, a narrative device, echoes something from the beginning in the ending. Review what happens in each car ride. The writer assumes you might think of the beginning as you are reading the ending. What effect might this awareness have on your response to the ending car ride?

Commentary: A Vivid Presentation of Places and People

To present the people involved in the event and especially to dramatize her relationship with her parents, Brandt depends on dialogue. We can see from her use of dialogue the two ways writers typically present remembered conversations: quoting and summarizing. Compare the two examples that follow. In the first example, Brandt quotes a brief exchange between herself and her sister as they were leaving the store (paragraphs 3 and 4):

> A few seconds later, my sister appeared and asked, "So, did you decide to buy the button?"
> "No, I guess not." I hoped my voice didn't quaver.

In this second example, Brandt summarizes what the store manager said to her as she left the store (5 and 6):

> An unexpected tap on my shoulder startled me. I whirled around to find a middle-aged man, dressed in street clothes, flashing some type of badge and politely asking me to empty my pockets. . . .
> Next thing I knew, he was talking about calling the police and having me arrested. . . .

As these examples indicate, writers usually summarize rather than quote when they need to give only the gist of what was said. Brandt apparently decides that the manager's actual words and way of speaking are not important for her purpose. However, presenting her response to her sister's question is important because it shows how she felt at the time. When you write a remembered event essay, you too will have to decide what to summarize and what to quote in light of your overall purpose.

While we are looking at Brandt's quoted dialogue, you should note a few of the conventions readers expect writers to follow when quoting dialogue. Use quotation marks for quoted dialogue but not for summarized dialogue. If you include one or two exact words in a summarized dialogue and want to call attention to the fact that they were actually spoken, put quotes only around those particular words. Indicate each change of speaker with a new paragraph. Put a concluding period, question mark, or exclamation point that is part of the quotation inside the quotation marks; otherwise, place it after the closing quotation marks. Do not conclude a sentence with one punctuation mark inside the quotation marks and a second one outside the marks.

Considering Topics for Your Own Essay

Think of a few occasions when you did something uncharacteristic. Perhaps you acted on impulse or took a chance you would not ordinarily take. The events do not have to be reckless, dangerous, or illegal; they could be quite harmless or even pleasant. Pick one occasion you might like to write about. What would you want your readers to recognize about you on the basis of reading your story?

■ PURPOSE AND AUDIENCE

Writers have various reasons for writing about their experiences. Reminiscing makes it possible for writers to relive moments of pleasure and pain, but it also helps them gain insight, to learn who they are now by examining who they used to be and the forces that shaped them. Reflecting on the past can lead a writer to significant self-discovery. Nevertheless, writing about personal experience is public, not private. The autobiographer writes to be read and is therefore as much concerned with self-presentation as with self-discovery. Writers present themselves to readers in the way they want to be perceived. The rest they keep hidden, though readers may read between the lines.

We read about others' experiences for much the same reason that we write about our own—to learn how to live our lives. Reading autobiography can validate our sense of ourselves, particularly when we see our own experience reflected in another's life. Reading about others' lives can also challenge our complacency and help us appreciate other points of view. It can enlarge our sympathies by awakening our humanity. When we read about other people's lives, we are invited to empathize with their values and feelings and thus break the shell of our own isolation.

BASIC FEATURES: REMEMBERING EVENTS

A Well-Told Story

An essay about a remembered event should tell an interesting story. Whatever else the writer may attempt to do, he or she must shape the experience into a story that is entertaining and memorable. This is done primarily by building suspense, leading readers to wonder, for example, whether Annie Dillard will find the amoeba or Jean Brandt will get caught for shoplifting. In addition, writers use time markers or temporal transitions to cue readers and move the narrative through time, as when Rick Bragg begins paragraphs with "In the summer of 1976," "That first weekend," and "On Saturday night." Finally, writers often use dialogue to convey immediacy and drama, as Brandt does to dramatize her confrontation with her mother on the phone.

A Vivid Presentation of Places and People

Instead of giving a generalized impression, skillful writers attempt to re-create the place where the event occurred and let us hear what people say. Vivid language and specific details make the writing memorable. By moving in close, a writer can name specific objects at a place, such as when Brandt catalogs the store's knickknacks, calendars, and buttons. A writer may also provide details about some of the objects, as when Brandt describes the coveted "75-cent Snoopy button." Finally, writers use similes and metaphors to draw comparisons and thereby help readers understand the point. For example, when Brandt says she felt "like Hester Prynne being put on public display," readers familiar with *The Scarlet Letter* can imagine how embarrassed Brandt must have felt.

To present people who played an important role in a remembered event, autobiographers often provide some descriptive details and a snatch of dialogue. They may detail the person's appearance, as Annie Dillard does by describing her mother sitting "with her knees crossed, in blue slacks, smoking a Chesterfield." They may also reveal people through their postures movements, or gestures, as Dillard does when she shows her father "tilting back in his chair" and her mother "with her knees crossed." Dialogue can be an especially effective way of giving readers a vivid impression of someone. Brandt, for example, reconstructs the conversation she had with her parents when she telephoned them from the police station, and her parents' responses—"Oh, no," "Why did you do it?" and "I'm horribly disappointed in you"—communicate their values and expectations.

An Indication of the Event's Significance

There are two ways a writer can communicate an event's autobiographical significance: by showing us that the event was important or by telling us directly what it meant. Most writers do both. Showing is necessary because the event must be dramatized for readers to appreciate its importance and understand the writer's feelings about it. Seeing the important scenes and people from the writer's point of view naturally leads readers to identify with the writer. We can well imagine what that "unexpected tap on [the] shoulder" must have felt like for Brandt, how Dillard felt running upstairs to tell her parents about her great discovery, and what Bragg was thinking as he hung upside down in his overturned car.

Telling also contributes to a reader's understanding, so most writers comment on the event's meaning and importance. Readers expect to understand the significance of the event, but they do not expect the essay to begin with the kind of thesis statement typical of argumentative writing. Instead, as the story moves along, writers tell us how they felt at the time or how they feel now as they look back on the experience. Often writers do both. Bragg, for example, tells us some of his remembered feelings when he recalls feeling "the steering wheel tremble in your hands." He also tells us what he thinks looking back on the experience: "[Y]ou feel like you can run away from anything, like you can turn your whole life into an insignificant speck in the rearview mirror." Telling is the main way that writers interpret the event for readers, but skillful writers are careful not to append these reflections artificially, like a moral tagged on to a fable.

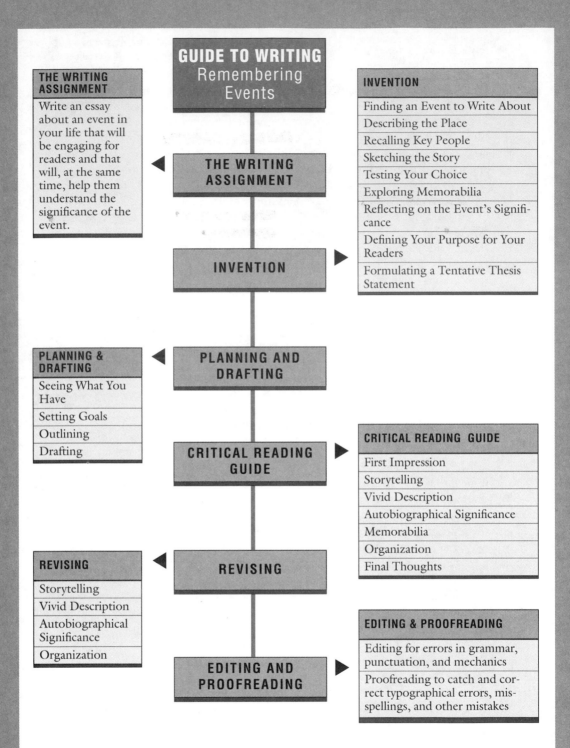

GUIDE TO WRITING
Remembering Events

THE WRITING ASSIGNMENT

Write an essay about an event in your life that will be engaging for readers and that will, at the same time, help them understand the significance of the event.

THE WRITING ASSIGNMENT

INVENTION

Finding an Event to Write About

Describing the Place

Recalling Key People

Sketching the Story

Testing Your Choice

Exploring Memorabilia

Reflecting on the Event's Significance

Defining Your Purpose for Your Readers

Formulating a Tentative Thesis Statement

INVENTION

PLANNING & DRAFTING

Seeing What You Have

Setting Goals

Outlining

Drafting

PLANNING AND DRAFTING

CRITICAL READING GUIDE

CRITICAL READING GUIDE

First Impression

Storytelling

Vivid Description

Autobiographical Significance

Memorabilia

Organization

Final Thoughts

REVISING

Storytelling

Vivid Description

Autobiographical Significance

Organization

REVISING

EDITING & PROOFREADING

Editing for errors in grammar, punctuation, and mechanics

Proofreading to catch and correct typographical errors, misspellings, and other mistakes

EDITING AND PROOFREADING

GUIDE TO WRITING

■ THE WRITING ASSIGNMENT

Write an essay about an event in your life that will be engaging for readers and that will, at the same time, help them understand the significance of the event. Tell your story dramatically and vividly.

■ INVENTION

The following invention activities will help you choose an appropriate event, recall specific details, sketch out the story, test your choice, and explore the event's autobiographical significance. Each activity is easy to do and takes only a few minutes. If you can spread out the activities over several days, it will be easier for you to recall details and to reflect deeply on the event's meaning in your life. Keep a written record of your invention work to use when you draft the essay and later when you revise it.

Finding an Event to Write About

To find the best possible event to write about, consider several possibilities rather than choosing the first event that comes to mind.

Listing Remembered Events. *Make a list of significant events from your past.* Include only those events about which you can recall details, people, and activities. Begin your list now and add to it over the next few days. Include possibilities suggested by the Considering Topics for Your Own Essay activities following each reading in this chapter. Make your list as complete as you can. The following categories may give you some more ideas:

- An occasion when you realized you had a special skill, ambition, or problem
- A time when you became aware of injustice, selflessness, heroism, sexism, racism
- A difficult situation, such as when you had to make a tough choice, when someone you admired let you down (or you let someone else down), or when you struggled to learn or understand something hard
- An occasion when things did not turn out as expected, such as when you expected to be praised but were criticized or ignored, or when you were convinced you would fail but succeeded
- An incident charged with strong emotion, such as love, fear, anger, embarrassment, guilt, frustration, hurt, pride, happiness, or joy
- An incident that you find yourself thinking about frequently or occasionally or one you know you will never forget

Listing Events Related to Identity and Community.   Whenever you write about events in your life, you are likely to reveal important aspects of your sense of identity and your relationships with others. The suggestions that follow, however, will help you recall events that are particularly revealing of your efforts to know yourself and to discover your place in the communities to which you belong.

- An event that shaped you in a particular way or revealed an aspect of your personality you had not seen before, such as your independence, insecurity, ambitiousness, or jealousy
- An incident that made you reexamine one of your basic values or beliefs, such as when you were expected to do something that went against your better judgment or when your values conflicted with someone else's values
- An occasion when others' actions led you to consider seriously a new idea or point of view
- An incident that made you feel the need to identify yourself with a particular community, such as an ethnic group, a political or religious group, or a group of co-workers
- An event that made you realize that the role you were playing did not conform to what was expected of you as a student, as a male or female, as a parent or sibling, as a believer in a particular religious faith, or as a member of a particular community
- An incident in which a single encounter with another person changed the way you view yourself or changed your ideas about how you fit into a particular community

Listing Events Related to Work and Career.   The following suggestions will help you think of events involving your work experiences as well as your career aspirations.

- An event that made you aware of your capacity for or interest in a particular kind of work or career, or an event that convinced you that you were not cut out for a particular kind of work or career
- An incident of harassment or mistreatment at work
- An event that revealed to you other people's assumptions, attitudes, or prejudices about you as a worker, your fitness for a particular job, or your career goals
- An incident of conflict or serious misunderstanding with a customer, fellow employee, supervisor, or someone you supervised

Choosing an Event.   *Look over your list of possibilities and choose one event that you think will make an interesting story.* You should be eager to explore the significance of the event and comfortable about sharing the event with your instructors and classmates, who will be your first readers. You may find the choice easy to make, or you may have several equally promising possibilities from which to choose.

It may help you in choosing an event if you tentatively identify your ultimate readers, the people with whom you most want to share the story. They could include, for example, your personal friends, members of your family, people you work with, members of a group with which you identify or of an organization to which you belong, your classmates, an instructor, or even the public at large.

Make the best choice you can now. If this event does not work out, you can try a different one later.

Describing the Place

The following activities will help you decide which places are important to your story and what you remember about them. Take the time now to explore your memory and imagination. This exploration will yield descriptive language you can use in your essay.

Listing Key Places. *Make a list of all the places where the event occurred, skipping a few lines after each entry on your list.* Your event may have occurred in one or more places. For now, list all the places you remember without worrying about whether they should be included in your story.

Describing Key Places. *In the space after each entry on your list, make some notes describing each place.* As you remember each place, what do you see (excluding people for the moment)? What objects stand out? Are they large or small, green or brown, square or oblong? What sounds do you hear? Do you detect any smells? Does any taste come to mind? Do you recall anything soft or hard, smooth or rough?

Recalling Key People

These activities will help you remember the people who played a role in the event—what they looked like, did, and said.

Listing Key People. *List the people who played more than a casual role in the event.* You may have only one person to list or you may have several.

Describing Key People. *Write a brief description of the people who played major roles in the event.* For each person, name and detail a few distinctive physical features or items of dress. Describe the person's way of talking or gesturing.

Re-Creating Conversations. *Reconstruct any important conversations you had during the event.* Also try to recall any especially memorable comments, any unusual choice of words, or any telling remarks that you made or were made to you. You may not remember exactly what was said during an entire conversation, but try to re-create it so that readers will be able to imagine what was going on.

Sketching the Story

Write for a few minutes, telling what happened. You may find it easier to outline what happened rather than writing complete sentences and paragraphs. Any way you can put the main action on paper is fine. Over the next few days you may want to add to this rough sketch.

Testing Your Choice

Now you need to decide whether you recall enough detail to write a good story about this particular event. Reread your invention notes to see whether your initial memories seem promising. If you can recall clearly what happened and what the important scenes and people were like, then you have probably made a good choice. If at any point you lose confidence in your choice, return to your list and choose another event.

Testing Your Choice: A Collaborative Activity

At this point, you will find it useful to get together with two or three other students to try out your story. Their reactions to your story will help you determine whether you have chosen an event you can present in an interesting way.

Storytellers: Take turns telling your story briefly. Try to make your story dramatic (by piquing your listeners' curiosity and building suspense) and vivid (by briefly describing the place and key people).

Listeners: Briefly tell each storyteller what you found most intriguing about the story. For example, were you eager to know how the story would turn out? Were you curious about any of the people? Were you able to identify with the story-teller? Could you imagine the place? Could you understand why the event is so memorable and significant for the storyteller?

Exploring Memorabilia

Memorabilia are visual images, sounds, and objects that can help you remember details and understand the significance of an event. Examples include photographs, newspaper or magazine clippings, recordings of popular music, souvenirs, medals or trophies, and even items not necessarily designated as mementoes (restaurant menus and movie, theater, or concert stubs). *If you can easily obtain access to relevant memorabilia, take time to do so now. Add to your invention notes any details about the period, places, or people the memorabilia suggest. Consider using one or more pieces of memorabilia in your essay.*

Reflecting on the Event's Significance

You should now feel fairly confident that you can tell an interesting story about the event you have chosen. The following activities will help you understand the meaning the event holds in your life and develop ways to convey this significance to your readers.

Recalling Your Remembered Feelings and Thoughts. *Write for a few minutes about your feelings and thoughts during and immediately after the event.* The following questions may help stimulate your memory:

- What were my expectations before the event?
- What was my first reaction to the event as it was happening and right after it ended?
- How did I show my feelings? What did I say?
- What did I want the people involved to think of me? Why did I care what they thought of me?
- What did I think of myself at the time?
- How long did these initial feelings last?
- What were the immediate consequences of the event for me personally?

Pause now to reread what you have written. *Then write another sentence or two about the event's significance at the time it occurred.*

Exploring Your Present Perspective. *Write for a few minutes about your current feelings and thoughts as you look back on the event.* These questions may help you get started:

- Looking back, how do I feel about this event? If I understand it differently now than I did then, what is the difference?
- What do my actions at the time of the event say about the kind of person I was then? How would I respond to the same event if it occurred today?
- Can looking at the event historically or culturally help explain what happened? For example, did I upset gender expectations? Did I feel torn between two cultures or ethnic identities? Did I feel out of place?
- Do I now see that there was a conflict underlying the event? For example, did I struggle with contradictory desires within myself? Did I feel pressured by others or by society in general? Were my desires and rights in conflict with someone else's? Was the event about power or responsibility?

Pause now to reflect on what you have written about your present perspective. *Then write another sentence or two, commenting on the event's significance as you look back on it.*

Defining Your Purpose for Your Readers

Write a few sentences, defining your purpose in writing about this particular event for your readers. Use these questions to focus your thoughts:

- Who are my readers? (Remember that in choosing an event, you considered several possible readers: your personal friends, members of your family, people you work with, members of a group with which you identify or of an organization to which you belong, your classmates, an instructor, even the public at large.)

- What do my readers know about me?
- What do my readers expect when they read autobiography?
- How do I expect my readers to understand or react to the event?
- How do I want my readers to feel about what happened? What is the dominant impression or mood I want my story to create?
- What specifically do I want my readers to think of me? What do I expect or fear they might think?

It is unlikely, but you may decide at this point that you feel uncomfortable disclosing this event. If so, choose another event to write about.

Formulating a Tentative Thesis Statement

Review what you wrote for Reflecting on the Event's Significance and add another two or three sentences, not necessarily summarizing what you already have written but extending your insights into the significance of the event, what it meant to you at the time, and what it means now. These sentences must necessarily be speculative and tentative because you may never fully understand the event's significance in your life.

Keep in mind that readers do not expect you to begin your essay with the kind of explicit thesis statement typical of argumentative or explanatory writing. If you do decide to tell readers explicitly why the event was meaningful or significant, you will most likely do so as you tell the story, by commenting on or evaluating what happened, instead of announcing it at the beginning. Keep in mind that you are not obliged to tell readers the significance, but you should show it through the way you tell the story.

■ PLANNING AND DRAFTING

This section will help you review your invention writing and get started on your first draft.

Seeing What You Have

You have now done a lot of thinking and writing about the basic elements of a remembered event essay: what happened, where it happened, who was involved, what was said, and how you felt. You have also begun to develop your understanding of why the event is so important to you. Reread what you have written so far to see what you have. Watch for specific narrative actions, vivid descriptive details, choice bits of dialogue. Note also any language that resonates with feeling or that seems especially insightful. Highlight any writing you think could be used in your draft. Then ask yourself the following questions:

- Do I remember enough specific details about the event to describe it vividly?
- Do I understand how the event was significant to me?
- Does my invention material provide what I need to convey that significance to my readers?
- Does my present perspective on this event seem clear to me?
- Does the dominant impression I want to create in my essay seem relevant?

If you find little that seems promising, you are not likely to be able to write a good draft. Consider starting over with another event.

If, however, your invention writing offers some promising material, the following activities may help you develop more:

- To remember more of what actually happened, discuss the event with someone who was there or who remembers having heard about it at the time.
- To recall additional details about a person who played an important role in the event, look at any available photographs or letters, talk with the person, or talk with someone who remembers the person. If that is impossible, you might imagine having a conversation with the person today about the event: What would you say? How do you think the person would respond?
- To remember how you felt at the time of the event, try to recall what else was happening in your life during that period. What music, television shows, movies, sports, books, and magazines did you like? What concerns did you have at home, school, work, play?
- To develop your present perspective on the event, try viewing your experience as a historical event. If you were writing a news story or documentary about the event, what would you want people to know?
- To decide on the dominant impression you want your story to have on readers, imagine that you are making a film based on this event. What would your film look like? What mood or atmosphere would you try to create? Alternatively, imagine writing a song or poem about the event. Think of an appropriate image or refrain. What kind of song would you write — blues, hip-hop, country, ranchera, rock?

Setting Goals

Before starting to draft, set goals that will help you make decisions and solve problems as you draft and revise. Here are some questions that will help you set your goals:

Your Purpose and Readers

- What do I want my readers to think of me and my experience? Should I tell them how I felt and what I thought at the time of the event? Should I tell them how my perspective has changed, as Bragg does?

- If my readers are likely to have had a similar experience, how can I convey the uniqueness of my experience or its special importance in my life? Should I tell them more about my background or the particular context of the event, as Bragg does? Should I give them a glimpse, as Dillard does, of its impact years later?
- If my readers are not likely to have had a similar experience, how can I help them understand what happened and appreciate its importance? Should I reveal the cultural influences acting on me, as Bragg does?

The Beginning

- What can I do in the opening sentences to arouse readers' curiosity? Should I begin with a surprising announcement, as Dillard does, or should I establish the setting and situation, as Brandt does?
- How can I get my readers to identify with me? Should I tell them a few things about myself, as Bragg does?
- Should I do something unusual, such as begin in the middle of the action or with a funny bit of dialogue?

The Story

- What should be the climax of my story, the point readers anticipate with trepidation or eagerness?
- What specific narrative actions or dialogue would intensify the drama of the story?
- Should I follow strict chronological order? Or would flashback (referring to an event that occurred earlier) or flashforward (referring to an event that will occur later) make the narrative more interesting?
- How can I use vivid descriptive detail to dramatize the story?

The Ending

- If I conclude with some reflections on the meaning of the experience, how can I avoid tagging on a moral or being too sentimental?
- If I want readers to think well of me, should I conclude with a philosophical statement? Should I be satirical? Should I be self-critical to avoid seeming smug?
- If I want to underscore the event's continuing significance in my life, can I show that the conflict was never fully resolved, as Brandt does? Could I contrast my remembered and current feelings and thoughts?
- Should I frame the essay by echoing something from the beginning to give readers at least a superficial sense of closure, as Brandt does by setting the last scene, like the first, in a car?

Outlining

The goals you have set should help you draft your essay, but first you might want to make a quick scratch outline to refocus on the basic story line. List the main actions in order. You could also note on your outline where you plan to describe the place, introduce particular people, present dialogue, and insert remembered or current feelings and thoughts. Use this outline to guide your drafting, but do not feel tied to it. As you draft, you may find a better way to sequence the action and integrate these features. (For an example of a paragraph scratch outline, turn to the Commentary following Annie Dillard's essay on p. 30. For more information on scratch outlining, see Chapter 9, p. 292.)

Drafting

Start drafting your essay, keeping in mind the goals you have set for yourself, especially the goal of telling the story dramatically. Refer to your outline to help you sequence the action. If you get stuck while drafting, either make a note of what you need to fill in later or see if you can use something from your invention writing.

As you read over your first draft, you may see places where you can add new material to make the story dramatic. Or you may even decide that after this first draft you can finally see the story you want to write and set out to do so in a second draft.

CRITICAL READING GUIDE
Now is the time to get a good critical reading of your draft. Your instructor may schedule readings of drafts as part of your coursework. If not, ask a classmate, friend, or family member to read your draft. You could also seek comments from a tutor at your campus writing center. The guidelines in this section can be used by *anyone* reviewing an essay about a remembered event. (If you are unable to have someone read your draft, turn ahead to the Revising section, where you will find guidelines for reading your own draft critically.)

If You Are the Writer. In order to provide focused, helpful comments, your reader must know your essay's intended audience, your purpose, and a problem in the draft that you need help solving. Briefly write out this information at the top of your draft.

- *Readers.* Identify the intended readers of your essay.
- *Purpose.* What do you hope to achieve in writing this remembered event essay? What features of your story do you hope will most interest readers? What do you want to disclose about yourself?
- *Problem.* Ask your reader to help you solve the single most important problem with your draft. Describe this problem briefly.

If You Are the Reader. Use the following guidelines to help you give critical comments to others on remembered event essays.

1. *Read for a First Impression.* Begin by reading the draft quickly, to enjoy the story and to get a sense of its significance. Then, in just a few sentences, describe your first impression. If you have any insights about the meaning or importance of the event, share your thoughts.

    Next, consider the problem the writer identified. If the problem will be covered by one of the other questions, deal with it there. Otherwise, respond to the writer's concerns now.

2. *Analyze the Effectiveness of the Storytelling.* Review the story, looking at the way the suspense builds and resolves itself. Point to any places where the drama loses intensity—perhaps where the suspense slackens, where specific narrative action is sparse or action verbs are needed, where narrative transitions would help readers, or where dialogue could be added to dramatize people's interactions.

3. *Consider How Vividly the Places and People Are Described.* Point to any descriptive details, similes, or metaphors that are especially effective. Note any places or people that need more specific description. Also indicate any descriptive details that seem unnecessary. Identify any quoted dialogue that might be summarized instead or any dialogue that does not seem relevant.

4. *Assess Whether the Autobiographical Significance Is Clear.* Explain briefly what you think makes this event significant for the writer. Point out any places in the draft where the significance might seem to the intended readers so overstated as to be sentimental or so understated as to be insignificant. If the event lacks significance, speculate about what you think the significance could be. Then point to one place in the draft where you think the significance could be brought forth by telling the story more fully or dramatically or by stating the significance.

5. *Assess the Use of Memorabilia.* If the writer makes use of memorabilia, evaluate how successfully each item is used. How is it relevant? Does it seem integrated into the event or merely appended? Is it placed in the most appropriate location? Does it make a meaningful contribution to the essay?

6. *Analyze the Effectiveness of the Organization.* Consider the *overall plan,* perhaps by making a scratch outline. Pay special attention to narrative transitions and verb tense markers so that you can identify any places where the order of the action is unclear. Also indicate any places where you think the description or background information interrupts the action. If you can, suggest other locations for this material.

- Look at the *beginning*. If it does not arouse curiosity, point to language elsewhere in the essay that might serve as a better opening—for example, a bit of dialogue, a striking image, or a remembered feeling.

- Look at the *ending*. Indicate whether the conflict in the story is too neatly resolved at the end, whether the writer has tagged on a moral, or whether the essay abruptly stops without really coming to a conclusion. If there is a problem with the ending, try to suggest an alternative ending, such as framing the story with a reference to something from the beginning or projecting into the future.

7. *Give the Writer Your Final Thoughts.* What is the draft's strongest part? What part is most in need of further work?

■ REVISING

Now you have the opportunity to revise your essay. Your instructor or other students may have given you advice. You may have begun to realize that your draft requires not so much revising as rethinking. For example, you may recognize that the story you told is not the story you meant to tell. Or maybe you realize only now why the incident is important to you. Consequently, you may need to reshape your story radically or draft a new version of it, instead of working to improve the various parts of your first draft. Many students—and professional writers—find themselves in this situation. Often a writer produces a draft or two and gets advice on them from others and only then begins to see what might be achieved.

However, if instead you feel satisfied that your draft achieves what you set out to do, you can focus on refining the various parts of it. Very likely you have thought of ways to improve your draft, and you may even have begun revising it. This section will help you get an overview of your draft and revise it accordingly.

Getting an Overview

Consider the draft as a whole, following these two steps:

1. *Reread.* If at all possible, put the draft aside for a day or two. When you do reread it, start by reconsidering your purpose. Then read the draft straight through, trying to see it as your intended readers will.

2. *Outline.* Make a quick scratch outline. (For more on scratch outlines, see Chapter 9, pp. 292–93.)

Charting a Plan for Revision.   Once you have an overview of your draft, you may want to make a double-column chart to keep track of any problems you need to solve. In the left-hand column, list the basic features of writing about remembered events.

(Turn to pp. 40–41 to review the basic features.) As you analyze your draft and study any comments received from others, note the problems you want to solve in the right-hand column. Here is an example:

Basic Features	*Problems to Solve*
A well-told story	
A vivid presentation of places and people	
An indication of the event's significance	
The organization	

Analyzing the Basic Features of Your Own Draft.   Turn to the Critical Reading Guide on the preceding pages. Using this guide, identify problems you now see in your draft. Note the problems on your chart.

Studying Critical Comments.   Review all of the comments you have received from other readers. For each comment, refer to the draft to see what might have led the reader to make that particular point. Try to be objective about any criticism. Ideally, these comments will help you to see your draft as others see it (rather than as you hoped it would be) and to identify specific problems.

Carrying Out Revisions

Having identified problems in your draft, you now need to figure out solutions and — most important — to carry them out. Basically, there are three ways to find solutions:

1. Review your invention and planning notes for material you can add to your draft.
2. Do additional invention writing to provide material you or your readers think is needed.
3. Look back at the readings in this chapter to see how other writers have solved similar problems.

The following suggestions, which are organized according to the basic features on your revision chart, will get you started solving some common writing problems.

A Well-Told Story

- *Is the climax difficult to identify?* Check to be sure your story has a climax. Perhaps it is the point when you get what you were striving for (Dillard), when something frightening happens (Bragg), or when you get caught (Brandt). If you cannot find a climax in your story or reconstruct your story so that it has one, then you may have a major problem. If this is the case, you should discuss with your instructor the possibility of starting over with another event.

- *Does the suspense slacken instead of building to the climax?* Try showing people moving or gesturing, adding narrative transitions to propel the action, or substituting quoted dialogue for summarized dialogue.

A Vivid Presentation of Places and People

- *Do any places or people need more specific description?* Try naming objects and adding sensory details to help readers imagine what the objects look, feel, smell, taste, or sound like. For people, describe a physical feature or mannerism that shows the role the person plays in your story.

- *Does any dialogue seem irrelevant or poorly written?* Eliminate any unnecessary dialogue or summarize quoted dialogue that has no distinctive language or dramatic purpose. Liven up quoted dialogue with faster repartee to make it more dramatic. Instead of introducing each comment with the dialogue cue "he said," describe the speaker's attitude or personality with phrases like "she gasped" or "he jokingly replied."

- *Do any descriptions weaken the dominant impression?* Omit extraneous details or reconsider the impression you want to make. Add similes and metaphors that strengthen the dominant impression you want your story to have.

- *Do readers question any visuals you used?* Might you move a visual to a more appropriate place? Could you make clear the relevance of a visual by mentioning it in your text? Consider replacing an ineffective visual with a more appropriate one.

An Indication of the Event's Significance

- *Are readers getting a different image of you from the one you want to make?* Look closely at the language you use to express your feelings and thoughts. If you project an aspect of yourself you did not intend to, reconsider what the story reveals about you. Ask yourself again why the event stands out in your memory. What do you want readers to know about you from reading this essay?

- *Are your remembered or current feelings and thoughts about the event coming across clearly and eloquently?* If not, look in your invention writing for more expressive language. If your writing seems too sentimental, try to express your feelings more directly and simply. Let yourself show ambivalence or uncertainty.

- *Do readers appreciate the event's uniqueness or special importance in your life?* If not, consider giving them more insight into your background or cultural heritage. Also consider whether they need to know what has happened since the event took place to appreciate why it is so memorable for you.

The Organization

- *Is the overall plan ineffective or the story hard to follow?* Look carefully at the way the action unfolds. Fill in any gaps. Eliminate unnecessary digressions. Add or clarify narrative transitions. Fix confusing verb tense markers.

- *Does description or other information disrupt the flow of the narrative?* Try integrating this material by adding smoother transitions. Or consider removing the disruptive parts or placing them elsewhere.

- *Is the beginning weak?* See whether there is a better way to start. Review the draft and your notes for an image, a bit of dialogue, or a remembered feeling that might catch readers' attention or spark their curiosity.

- *Does the ending work?* If not, think about a better way to end—with a memorable image, perhaps, or a provocative assertion. Consider whether you can frame the essay by referring back to something in the beginning.

■ EDITING AND PROOFREADING

Now is the time to check your revised draft for connections between sentences and for errors in grammar, punctuation, and mechanics. As you reread, ask yourself whether the connection from one sentence to the next is logical and easy for readers to follow. If you sense a gap or disconnection that would cause a reader to stumble or become confused, try revising one or both sentences so that gap is closed. Notice whether you shift from one word to another unnecessarily in one sentence to the next, and, if you do, consider repeating the same word instead. Look for sentences that might be combined to allow readers to follow the narrative more easily or to imagine the people and their interactions more readily. Look as well for long or garbled sentences that might be divided into two or three sentences.

As you work on your sentences, look for errors in spelling, capitalization, punctuation, usage, and grammar. Consult a writer's handbook for advice about how to correct any errors you cannot confidently correct on your own. Ask a friend or classmate to read over your draft, looking for errors.

Before you hand in your revised essay, proofread it carefully and run it through a spell-checker. Your goal is to hand in an error-free essay.

REFLECTING ON YOUR WRITING

Now that you have worked extensively in autobiography—reading it, talking about it, writing it—take some time for reflection. Reflecting on your writing process will help you gain a greater understanding of what you learned about solving the problems you encountered writing about an event.

Write a page or so telling your instructor about a problem you encountered in writing your essay and how you solved it. Before you begin, gather all of your writing—

invention and planning notes, outlines, drafts, critical comments, revision plans, and final revision. Review these materials as you complete this writing task.

1. *Identify one problem you needed to solve as you wrote about a remembered event.* Do not be concerned with grammar and punctuation; concentrate on problems unique to writing a story about your experience. For example: Did you puzzle over how to present a particular place or person? Was it difficult to structure the narrative so it held readers' interest? Did you find it hard (or uncomfortable) to convey the event's autobiographical significance?

2. *Determine how you came to recognize the problem.* When did you first discover it? What called it to your attention? Did you notice it yourself, or did another reader point it out? Can you now see hints of it in your invention writing, your planning notes, or an earlier draft? If so, where specifically?

3. *Reflect on how you went about solving the problem.* Did you work on a particular passage, cut or add details, or reorganize the essay? Did you reread one of the essays in the chapter to see how another writer handled similar material? Did you look back at the invention guidelines? Did you discuss the problem with another student, a tutor, or your instructor? If so, how did talking about it help, and how useful was the advice you got?

4. *Write a brief explanation of the problem and your solution.* Be as specific as possible in reconstructing your efforts. Quote from your invention notes or early drafts, from readers' comments, from your revision plan, and from your final revision to show the various changes your writing underwent as you worked to solve the problem. Taking the time now to think about how you recognized and solved a real writing problem will help you become more aware of what works and does not work, making you a more confident writer.

3

Writing Profiles

Much of what we know about people and the world we learn from profiles based on firsthand observation and interviews. Profiles tell about people, places, and activities. Some profiles give us a glimpse of the inner workings of familiar places. Others introduce us to the exotic — peculiar hobbies, unusual professions, bizarre personalities.

Whatever their subject, profile writers strive first and foremost to enable readers to visualize the person, place, or activity that is the focus of the profile. Writers succeed only by presenting many concrete details: how the person dresses, gestures, and talks; what the place looks, sounds, and smells like; what the activity involves and how it progresses. Not only must the details be vivid, but they also must help to convey the subject's significance — what makes the subject interesting and meaningful.

Because profiles share many features with essays about remembered events — such as narration, description, dialogue, and significance — you may use many of the strategies learned in Chapter 2 when you write your profile. Yet profiles differ from writing that reflects on personal experience in that profiles present newly acquired knowledge. To write a profile, you need to learn new strategies for researching, analyzing, synthesizing, and presenting information. Taking a questioning approach to even the most familiar subjects, you practice the field research methods of observing, interviewing, and notetaking. These research activities, combined with thoughtful analysis and imaginative synthesis, form the basic strategies of learning in many areas of study, including anthropology, sociology, and psychology.

The scope of your profile may be large or small, depending on your assignment and your subject. You could attend a single event such as a parade or tournament and write up your observations of the place, people, and activities. Or you might conduct an interview with a person who has an unusual occupation and write up a profile based on your interview notes. If you have the time to do more extensive research, you might write a full-blown profile based on several observations and interviews with various people.

You will encounter profiles in many different contexts, as the following examples suggest.

Writing in Your Other Courses

- For a research essay in an education course, a student who has been studying collaborative learning principles incorporates a profile of a group of sixth-grade students working together on an Internet project. The college student observes and takes extensive notes on the collaboration, and to learn what the sixth graders think about working together, she interviews them individually and as a group. She also talks with the classroom teacher about how students were prepared to do this kind of work and how their collaboration will be evaluated.

- For an anthropology assignment, a student plans to research and write an ethnography about football at the local high school. He models his project on Clifford Geertz's groundbreaking research on Balinese cockfighting. Like Geertz, he writes a "thick description" that alternates observational details with his own ideas about what football means to this particular high school community. He focuses his profile on the way football confers status on the players, their parents, and friends.

Writing in the Community

- An art history student profiles a local artist recently commissioned to paint an outdoor mural for the city. The student visits the artist's studio and talks with him about the process of painting murals. The artist invites the student to spend the following day with a team of local art students and neighborhood volunteers working on the mural under his direction. This firsthand experience helps the student describe the process of mural painting almost from an insider's point of view. She organizes her profile around the main stages of this collaborative mural project, from conception to completion. As she describes each stage, she weaves in details about the artist, his helpers, and the site of their work, seeking to capture the civic spirit that pervades the mural project.

- For a small-town newspaper, a writer profiles a community activist who appears regularly at city council meetings to speak on various problems in the neighborhood. The writer interviews the activist as well as two of the council members. He also observes the activist speaking at one particular council meeting on the problem of trash being dumped in unauthorized areas. At this meeting, the activist describes an all-night vigil he made to capture on videotape a flagrant act of illegal dumping in an empty lot near his home. The writer uses the activist's appearance at this meeting as a narrative framework for the profile; he also integrates details of the activist's public life along with images from the videotape.

Writing in the Workplace

- A social worker preparing to write a probation report on a teenager convicted of a crime interviews the teenager and his parents and observes the interactions among the family members. Her report describes in detail what she saw and heard, concluding with a recommendation that the teenager return to his parents' home.

- For a company newsletter, a personnel officer writes a day-in-the-life type of profile of the new CEO. He follows the CEO from meeting to meeting, interviewing her between meetings about her management philosophy and her plans for handling the challenges facing the company. The CEO, who adopts a personal management style, invites the writer to visit her at home and meet her family. The profile is illustrated by two photographs—one showing the CEO in an intense business conference, and the other showing her at home with her family.

Practice Choosing a Profile Subject: A Collaborative Activity

The preceding scenarios suggest some occasions for writing profiles. Imagine that you have been assigned to write a profile of a person, a place, or an activity on your campus, in your community, or at your workplace. Think of subjects that you would like to know more about.

Part 1. List several subjects. Consider interesting people (store owner, distinguished teacher, newspaper columnist, public defender, CEO, radio talk show host), places (student health center, research center, machine shop, police department, student newspaper office, day-care center, exercise or sports facility, women's resource center, campus tour office, office of telecommunications services), and businesses or activities (comic-book store, auto wrecking company, motorcycle dealer, commercial fishing boat, local brewery or winery, eating disorder treatment center, building contractor, dance studio, private tutoring service, dog kennel).

Now get together with two or three other students and take turns reading your lists of subjects to one another. The other group members will tell you which item on your list they personally find most interesting and discuss with you briefly any questions they have about it.

Part 2. After you have all read your lists and received responses, discuss these questions as a group:

- Are you surprised by which items on your list the other members of the group find most interesting?
- Are you surprised by any of their questions about this subject?
- How might these questions influence your approach to the subject?

READINGS

The readings in this chapter illustrate the features of profiles and the strategies writers rely on to realize the features. No two essays in this genre are much alike, and yet they share defining features. The section Analyzing Writing Strategies and the Commentary following each reading touch on a few features best illustrated by that essay, capturing its special qualities and strengths. Together, the three essays cover many of the possibilities of the genre. Consequently, you will want to read as many of the essays and Commentaries as possible and, if time permits, complete the activities in Analyzing Writing Strategies. Following the last reading in the chapter, the Basic Features section offers a concise description of the features of writing about remembered events and provides examples from all of the readings.

"Soup" is an unsigned profile that initially appeared in the "Talk of the Town" section of the New Yorker *magazine (January 1989). The* New Yorker *regularly features brief, anonymous profiles like this one, whose subject is the fast-talking owner/chef of a takeout restaurant specializing in soup. In 1995, Albert Yeganeh, the subject of this profile, also inspired an episode of the television series* Seinfeld. *As you read, notice the prominence given to dialogue.*

Soup

The New Yorker

When Albert Yeganeh says "Soup is my lifeblood," he means it. And when he says "I am extremely hard to please," he means that, too. Working like a demon alchemist in a tiny storefront kitchen at 259-A West Fifty-fifth Street, Mr. Yeganeh creates anywhere from eight to seventeen soups every weekday. His concoctions are so popular that a wait of half an hour at the lunchtime peak is not uncommon, although there are strict rules for conduct in line. But more on that later.

"I am psychologically kind of a health freak," Mr. Yeganeh said the other day, in a lisping staccato of Armenian origin. "And I know that soup is the greatest meal in the world. It's very good for your digestive system. And I use only the best, the freshest ingredients. I am a perfectionist. When I make a clam soup, I use three different kinds of clams. Every other place uses canned clams. I'm called crazy. I am not crazy. People don't realize why I get so upset. It's because if the soup is not perfect and I'm still selling it, it's a torture. It's *my* soup, and that's why I'm so upset. First you clean and then you cook. I don't believe that ninety-nine per cent of the restaurants in New York know how to clean a tomato. I tell my crew to wash the parsley *eight* times. If they wash it five or six times, I scare them. I tell them they'll go to jail if there is sand in the parsley. One time, I found a mushroom on the floor, and I fired the guy who left it there." He spread his arms, and added, "This place is the only one like it in...in...the whole earth! One day, I hope to learn something from the other places, but so far I haven't. For example, the other day I went to a very fancy restaurant

1

2

and had borscht. I had to send it back. It was *junk*. I could see all the chemicals in it. I never use chemicals. Last weekend, I had lobster bisque in Brooklyn, a very well-known place. It was *junk*. When I make a lobster bisque, I use a whole lobster. You know, I never advertise. I don't have to. All the big-shot chefs and the kings of the hotels come here to see what *I'm* doing."

As you approach Mr. Yeganeh's Soup Kitchen International from a distance, the first 3
thing you notice about it is the awning, which proclaims "Homemade Hot, Cold, Diet Soups." The second thing you notice is an aroma so delicious that it makes you want to take a bite out of the air. The third thing you notice, in front of the kitchen, is an electric signboard that flashes, say, "Today's Soups... Chicken Vegetable... Mexican Beef Chili... Cream of Watercress... Italian Sausage... Clam Bisque... Beef Barley... Due to Cold Weather... For Most Efficient and Fastest Service the Line Must... Be Kept Moving... Please... Have Your Money... Ready... Pick the Soup of Your Choice... Move to Your Extreme... Left After Ordering."

"I am not prejudiced against color or religion," Mr. Yeganeh told us, and he jabbed an 4
index finger at the flashing sign. "Whoever follows that I treat very well. My regular customers don't say anything. They are very intelligent and well educated. They know I'm just trying to move the line. The New York cop is very smart—he sees everything but says nothing. But the young girl who wants to stop and tell you how nice you look and hold everyone up—*yah!*" He made a guillotining motion with his hand. "I tell you, I hate to work with the public. They treat me like a slave. My philosophy is: The customer is always wrong and I'm always right. I raised my prices to try to get rid of some of these people, but it didn't work."

The other day, Mr. Yeganeh was dressed in chefs' whites with orange smears across 5
his chest, which may have been some of the carrot soup cooking in a huge pot on a little stove in one corner. A three-foot-long handheld mixer from France sat on the sink, looking like an overgrown gardening tool. Mr. Yeganeh spoke to two young helpers in a twisted Armenian-Spanish barrage, then said to us, "I have no overhead, no trained waitresses, and I have the cashier here." He pointed to himself theatrically. Beside the doorway, a glass case with fresh green celery, red and yellow peppers, and purple eggplant was topped by five big gray soup urns. According to a piece of cardboard taped to the door, you can buy Mr. Yeganeh's soups in three sizes, costing from four to fifteen dollars. The order of any well-behaved customer is accompanied by little waxpaper packets of bread, fresh vegetables (such as scallions and radishes), fresh fruit (such as cherries or an orange), a chocolate mint, and a plastic spoon. No coffee, tea, or other drinks are served.

"I get my recipes from books and theories and my own taste," Mr. Yeganeh said. "At 6
home, I have several hundreds of books. When I do research, I find that I don't know anything. Like cabbage is a cancer fighter, and some fish is good for your heart but some is bad. Every day, I should have one sweet, one spicy, one cream, one vegetable soup— and they *must* change, they should always taste a little different." He added that he wasn't sure how extensive his repertoire was, but that it probably includes at least eighty soups,

among them African peanut butter, Greek moussaka, hamburger, Reuben, B.L.T., asparagus and caviar, Japanese shrimp miso, chicken chili, Irish corned beef and cabbage, Swiss chocolate, French calf's brain, Korean beef ball, Italian shrimp and eggplant Parmesan, buffalo, ham and egg, short rib, Russian beef Stroganoff, turkey cacciatore, and Indian mulligatawny. "The chicken and the seafood are an addiction, and when I have French garlic soup I let people have only one small container each," he said. "The doctors and nurses love that one."

A lunch line of thirty people stretched down the block from Mr. Yeganeh's doorway.   7
Behind a construction worker was a man in expensive leather, who was in front of a woman in a fur hat. Few people spoke. Most had their money out and their orders ready.

At the front of the line, a woman in a brown coat couldn't decide which soup to get   8
and started to complain about the prices.

"You talk too much, dear," Mr. Yeganeh said, and motioned to her to move to the left.   9
"Next!"

"Just don't talk. Do what he says," a man huddled in a blue parka warned.   10

"He's downright rude," said a blond woman in a blue coat. "Even abusive. But you   11
can't deny it, his soup is the best."

Connecting to Culture and Experience: Standards of Excellence

A popular book urged American business executives to "search for excellence," claiming that profit will follow. Albert Yeganeh is a prime example of this philosophy.

Discuss with two or three other students your experiences with excellence as a worker and student. How have your work values been shaped by the situations in which you have worked? On the job, for example, what kinds of attitudes encourage — or discourage — high-quality work? In school, what has inspired you to do your best work or prevented or discouraged you from doing it? Focus on specific examples of school and work experiences.

Analyzing Writing Strategies

1. At the beginning of this chapter, we make several generalizations about profile essays. Consider which of these assertions are true of "Soup":

    • It is based on a writer's newly acquired observations.

    • It takes readers behind the scenes of familiar places or introduces them to unusual places and people.

    • It is informative and entertaining.

    • It presents scenes and people vividly through description, action, and dialogue.

    • It conveys the subject's significance — what makes it interesting and meaningful.

2. In addition to profiling a person, "Soup" describes a place of business. Reread paragraphs 1, 3, and 5, underlining details that describe the soup restaurant itself, inside and outside. For example, in paragraph 3, you would underline *awning* as well as what is written on the awning: *"Homemade Hot, Cold, Diet Soups."* You need not worry about whether you are underlining too many or too few details. Try to catch every detail that expands your image of the place.

Commentary: A Specific Focus and Informative Plan

A profile focuses on a person, place, or activity. Often, as in "Soup," a profile focuses on one element—a person—while also presenting a good deal of information about the place and activity associated with the person. "Soup" begins and ends with Albert Yeganeh, the creative and rather demanding owner/chef of a small restaurant called Soup Kitchen International. Much of what we learn about him—his attitudes, ideas, and business methods—comes from Mr. Yeganeh himself, through the comments he made during interviews with the *New Yorker* writer. In addition, we are given the writer's firsthand observations and a few comments from customers.

Profile writers not only need to focus their observations, but they also need to plan how best to present the bits and pieces of information they accumulate from observations and interviews. Most profiles are organized in one of two ways: chronologically, as a story, or topically, as groups of related information. "Soup" is organized topically. (You will see an example of chronological organization in the following profile, "The Daily Grind," by Peggy Orenstein.)

The following scratch outline of "Soup" shows at a glance the topics the writer has chosen and how they are sequenced:

Introduction to Yeganeh and his soup kitchen (paragraph 1)

Yeganeh's perfectionism (2)

An outside view of the soup kitchen (3)

Yeganeh's attitudes toward customers (4)

Yeganeh at work and his rules of the house (5)

Yeganeh's soup-making repertoire (6)

Customers and their interactions with Yeganeh (7–11)

This plan alternates interview segments with observations of the soup kitchen. There are three interview topics: perfectionism (paragraph 2), attitudes toward customers (4), and soup-making repertoire (6). Observational topics present the soup kitchen from three different vantage points: outside, approaching from a distance (3); inside the kitchen (5); and within the line of customers waiting to be served (7–11). Instead of organizing the information chronologically by telling a story of one visit to the soup kitchen, the writer reports topic by topic what is learned on several visits. The writer probably first grouped related topics and then came up with a sensible plan of alternating them, perhaps assuming that readers would remain more engaged if the relatively large blocks of quoted material alternated with descriptions of the soup kitchen. When you plan your profile essay, you will have to decide whether to organize your first draft topically or chronologically.

Considering Topics for Your Own Essay

List three to five unusual people or places on campus or in your community that you could profile. Then think of a few questions you or your readers might want answered about each of these possible subjects. Finally, choose the subject you think would be most interesting to research. What makes this choice interesting for you?

Peggy Orenstein has been a managing editor of Mother Jones, *a founding editor of the award-winning magazine* 7 days, *and an editor of* Esquire *and* Manhattan, inc. *Her own essays have appeared in the* New York Times Magazine, The New Yorker, Vogue, *and other nationally known publications. Her most recent book is* Flux. Women on Sex, Work, Kids, Love, and Life in a Half-Changed World *(2000). The following profile, which takes place primarily in Mrs. Richter's math class, comes from the opening chapter of her book* School Girls: Young Women, Self-Esteem, and the Confidence Gap *(1994), a winner of the* New York Times Notable Book of the Year Award. Orenstein undertook the extensive research for this book after reading a study conducted by the American Association of University Women in 1991, which identified a gender gap between male and female students in America. Her research "concentrated on the ways in which the educational system—often unwittingly—inhibits, restricts, diminishes, and denies girls' experience." As you read the profile, think about whether the story it tells is one you have witnessed firsthand.*

The Daily Grind: Lessons in the Hidden Curriculum

Peggy Orenstein

Amy Wilkinson has looked forward to being an eighth grader forever—at least for the last two years, which, when you're thirteen, seems like the same thing. By the second week of September she's settled comfortably into her role as one of the school's reigning elite. Each morning before class, she lounges with a group of about twenty other eighth-grade girls and boys in the most visible spot on campus: at the base of the schoolyard, between one of the portable classrooms that was constructed in the late 1970s and the old oak tree in the overflow parking lot. The group trades gossip, flirts, or simply stands around, basking in its own importance and killing time before the morning bell. 1

At 8:15 on Tuesday the crowd has already convened, and Amy is standing among a knot of girls, laughing. She is fuller-figured than she'd like to be, wide-hipped and heavy-limbed with curly, blond hair, cornflower-blue eyes, and a sharply upturned nose. With the help of her mother, who is a drama coach, she has become the school's star actress: last year she played Eliza in Weston's production of *My Fair Lady*. Although she earns solid 2 grades in all of her subjects—she'll make the honor roll this fall—drama is her passion, she says, because "I love entertaining people, and I love putting on characters."

Also, no doubt, because she loves the spotlight: this morning, when she mentions a   3
boy I haven't met, Amy turns, puts her hands on her hips, anchors her feet shoulder width apart, and bellows across the schoolyard, "Greg! Get over here! You have to meet Peggy."

She smiles wryly as Greg, looking startled, begins to make his way across the   4
schoolyard for an introduction. "I'm not exactly shy," she says, her hands still on her hips. "I'm *bold.*"

Amy is bold. And brassy, and strong-willed. Like any teenager, she tries on and dis-   5
cards different selves as if they were so many pairs of Girbaud jeans, searching ruth-lessly for a perfect fit. During a morning chat just before the school year began, she told me that her parents tried to coach her on how to respond to my questions. "They told me to tell you that they want me to be my own person," she complained. "My mother *told* me to tell you that. I do want to be my own person, but it's like, you're interviewing me about who *I* am and she's telling me what to say—that's not my own person, is it?"

When the morning bell rings, Amy and her friends cut off their conversations, scoop   6
up their books, and jostle toward the school's entrance. Inside, Weston's hallways smell chalky, papery, and a little sweaty from gym class. The wood-railed staircases at either end of the two-story main building are worn thin in the middle from the scuffle of hundreds of pairs of sneakers pounding them at forty-eight-minute intervals for nearly seventy-five years. Amy's mother, Sharon, and her grandmother both attended this school. So will her two younger sisters. Her father, a mechanic who works on big rigs, is a more recent Weston recruit: he grew up in Georgia and came here after he and Sharon were married.

Amy grabs my hand, pulling me along like a small child or a slightly addled new stu-   7
dent: within three minutes we have threaded our way through the dull-yellow hallways to her locker and then upstairs to room 238, Mrs. Richter's math class.

The twenty-two students that stream through the door with us run the gamut of phys-   8
ical maturity. Some of the boys are as small and compact as fourth graders, their legs sticking out of their shorts like pipe cleaners. A few are trapped in the agony of a growth spurt, and still others cultivate downy beards. The girls' physiques are less extreme: most are nearly their full height, and all but a few have already weathered the brunt of puberty. They wear topknots or ponytails, and their shirts are tucked neatly into their jeans.

Mrs. Richter, a ruddy, athletic woman with a powerful voice, has arranged the chairs   9
in a three-sided square, two rows deep. Amy walks to the far side of the room and, as she takes her seat, falls into a typically feminine pose: she crosses her legs, folds her arms across her chest, and hunches forward toward her desk, seeming to shrink into herself. The sauciness of the playground disappears, and, in fact, she says hardly a word during class. Meanwhile, the boys, especially those who are more physically mature, sprawl in their chairs, stretching their legs long, expanding into the available space.

Nate, a gawky, sanguine boy who has shaved his head except for a small thatch   10
that's hidden under an Oakland A's cap, leans his chair back on two legs and, although the bell has already rung, begins a noisy conversation with his friend, Kyle.

Mrs. Richter turns to him, "What's all the discussion about, Nate?" she asks.   11

"*He's* talking to *me*," Nate answers, pointing to Kyle. Mrs. Richter writes Nate's name on the chalkboard as a warning toward detention and he yells out in protest. They begin to quibble over the justice of her decision, their first—but certainly not their last—power struggle of the day. As they argue, Allison, a tall, angular girl who once told me, "My goal is to be the best wife and mother I can be," raises her hand to ask a question. Mrs. Richter, finishing up with Nate, doesn't notice. 12

"Get your homework out, everyone!" the teacher booms, and walks among the students, checking to make sure no one has shirked on her or his assignment. Allison, who sits in the front row nearest both the blackboard and the teacher, waits patiently for another moment, then, realizing she's not getting results, puts her hand down. When Mrs. Richter walks toward her, Allison tries another tack, calling out her question. Still, she gets no response, so she gives up. 13

As a homework assignment, the students have divided their papers into one hundred squares, color-coding each square prime or composite—prime being those numbers which are divisible only by one and themselves, and composite being everything else. Mrs. Richter asks them to call out the prime numbers they've found, starting with the tens. 14

Nate is the first to shout, "Eleven!" The rest of the class chimes in a second later. As they move through the twenties and thirties, Nate, Kyle, and Kevin, who sit near one another at the back of the class, call out louder and louder, casually competing for both quickest response and the highest decibel level. Mrs. Richter lets the boys' behavior slide, although they are intimidating other students. 15

"Okay," Mrs. Richter says when they've reached one hundred. "Now, what do you think of one hundred and three? Prime or composite?" 16

Kyle, who is skinny and a little pop-eyed, yells out, "Prime!" but Mrs. Richter turns away from him to give someone else a turn. Unlike Allison, who gave up when she was ignored, Kyle isn't willing to cede his teacher's attention. He begins to bounce in his chair and chant, *"Prime! Prime! Prime!"* Then, when he turns out to be right, he rebukes the teacher, saying, *"See,* I told you." 17

When the girls in Mrs. Richter's class do speak, they follow the rules. When Allison has another question, she raises her hand again and waits her turn; this time, the teacher responds. When Amy volunteers her sole answer of the period, she raises her hand, too. She gives the wrong answer to an easy multiplication problem, turns crimson, and flips her head forward so her hair falls over her face. 18

Occasionally, the girls shout out answers, but generally they are to the easiest, lowest-risk questions, such as the factors of four or six. And their stabs at public recognition depend on the boys' largesse: when the girls venture responses to more complex questions the boys quickly become territorial, shouting them down with their own answers. Nate and Kyle are particularly adept at overpowering Renee, who, I've been told by the teacher, is the brightest girl in the class. (On a subsequent visit, I will see her lay her head on her desk when Nate overwhelms her and mutter, "I hate this class.") 19

Mrs. Richter doesn't say anything to condone the boys' aggressiveness, but she doesn't have to: they insist on—and receive—her attention even when she consciously tries to shift it elsewhere in order to make the class more equitable. 20

After the previous day's homework is corrected, Mrs. Richter begins a new lesson, on the use of exponents. 21

"What does three to the third power mean?" she asks the class. 22

"I know!" shouts Kyle. 23

Instead of calling on Kyle, who has already answered more than his share of questions, the teacher turns to Dawn, a somewhat more voluble girl who has plucked her eyebrows down to a few hairs. 24

"Do you know, Dawn?" 25

Dawn hesitates, and begins "Well, you count the number of threes and. . . ." 26

"But I know!" interrupts Kyle. *"I know!"* 27

Mrs. Richter deliberately ignores him, but Dawn is rattled: she never finishes her sentence, she just stops. 28

"I know! ME!" Kyle shouts again, and then before Dawn recovers herself he blurts, *"It's three times three times three!"* 29

At this point, Mrs. Richter gives in. She turns away from Dawn, who is staring blankly, and nods at Kyle. "Yes," she says. "Three times three times three. Does everyone get it?" 30

"YES!" shouts Kyle; Dawn says nothing. 31

Mrs. Richter picks up the chalk. "Let's do some others," she says. 32

"Let me!" says Kyle. 33

"I'll pick on whoever raises their hand," she tells him. 34

Nate, Kyle, and two other boys immediately shoot up their hands, fingers squeezed tight and straight in what looks like a salute. 35

"Don't you want to wait and hear the problem first?" she asks, laughing. 36

They drop their hands briefly. She writes 8^4 on the board. "Okay, what would that look like written out?" 37

Although a third of the class raises their hands to answer—including a number of students who haven't yet said a word—she calls on Kyle anyway. 38

"Eight times eight times eight times eight," he says triumphantly, as the other students drop their hands. 39

When the bell rings, I ask Amy about the mistake she made in class and the embarrassment it caused her. She blushes again. 40

"Oh yeah," she says. "That's about the only time I ever talked in there. I'll never do that again." 41

Connecting to Culture and Experience: Gender Equality

The "hidden curriculum," according to Orenstein, teaches girls that boys have more power and authority than they do. Discuss your own experience and observation to see whether you agree with Orenstein about gender inequality in middle school and high school. Also consider whether school culture fosters other kinds of inequality — for example, based on money, cultural background, success in sports or academics.

Analyzing Writing Strategies

1. What do you think is the focus of Orenstein's observations — a person, a place, or an activity? This profile (like most profiles) includes all three elements, but which one seems to be at the center of Orenstein's attention? Consider how you know. What in the essay, for example, enables you to identify the primary focus of the observations?

2. Whereas the author of "Soup" organizes the information topically, Orenstein organizes her profile chronologically. Reread the essay and underline the time markers: calendar time ("By the second week of September" [paragraph 1]) and clock time ("At 8:15" [2]), as well as temporal transitions ("when" [6]). Then reflect on how well these time markers help you follow the profile's chronological organization.

Commentary: Significance

Profiles, like essays about remembered events, do more than merely present information; they also indicate what is significant or interesting about the person, place, or activity that is the focus of the profile. To convey this significance, profile writers either tell what they think or try to show it through description, action, and dialogue.

In "The Daily Grind," Orenstein relies predominantly on showing. She uses the strategies of comparison and contrast to show how girls like Amy Wilkinson fail to thrive in classrooms like Mrs. Richter's. The opening paragraphs present Amy as a confident, outgoing teenager: She is "one of the school's reigning elite" (paragraph 1) and the "school's star actress" (2). Not only do we hear Amy describe herself as "bold" (4), but we also see her acting boldly toward Greg. Here Orenstein also uses specific narrative actions to show Amy's movements: "Amy turns, puts her hands on her hips, anchors her feet shoulder width apart, and bellows across the schoolyard, 'Greg! Get over here!'" (3). This image of Amy, however, contrasts sharply with the image we get of her in math class, where she appears shy and retiring, sitting on the "far side of the room" (9). Her posture and movements seem anything but bold: "she crosses her legs, folds her arms across her chest, and hunches forward toward her desk, *seeming to shrink into herself*" (9). Here Orenstein says directly what she thinks Amy's body language means when she labels Amy's pose "typically feminine." To support her interpretation, Orenstein lets us see what happens when Amy gives a wrong answer (18) and, at the end, hear what Amy has to say about her mistake (41).

In addition to contrasting the two sides of Amy, Orenstein contrasts the behavior of the boys and girls in the math class. Whereas Amy seems to shrink into herself, for example, the boys "sprawl . . . expanding into the available space" (9). While the girls raise their hands, the boys shout out their answers louder and louder (15). Orenstein points out that when the girls do shout out questions or answers, they are not recognized by the teacher, allowed by the boys to respond only to easy questions, or shouted down by the boys. These contrasts between the boys and girls and between the self-confident and self-effacing Amy help to convey to readers Orenstein's ideas without her having to explain at length what she thinks.

Considering Topics for Your Own Essay

Consider profiling a group of people who interact with each other for a specific purpose—such as a teacher and students interacting in a classroom, a group of actors rehearsing for a play, a basketball team practicing for an upcoming game, employees working collaboratively on a project, or a family celebrating a birthday.

Brian Cable wrote the following selection when he was a first-year college student. Cable's profile of a mortuary combines both seriousness and humor. He lets readers know his feelings as he presents information about the mortuary and the people working there. As you read, notice in particular the way Cable uses his visit to the mortuary as an occasion to reflect on death.

The Last Stop
Brian Cable

> Let us endeavor so to live that when we come to die even the undertaker will be sorry.
>
> —MARK TWAIN

Death is a subject largely ignored by the living. We don't discuss it much, not as children (when Grandpa dies, he is said to be "going away"), not as adults, not even as senior citizens. Throughout our lives, death remains intensely private. The death of a loved one can be very painful, partly because of the sense of loss, but also because someone else's mortality reminds us all too vividly of our own. 1

Thus did I notice more than a few people avert their eyes as they walked past the dusty-pink building that houses the Goodbody Mortuaries. It looked a bit like a church—tall, with gothic arches and stained glass—and somewhat like an apartment complex—low, with many windows stamped out of red brick. 2

It wasn't at all what I had expected. I thought it would be more like Forest Lawn, serene with lush green lawns and meticulously groomed gardens, a place set apart from the hustle of day-to-day life. Here instead was an odd pink structure set in the middle of a business district. On top of the Goodbody Mortuaries sign was a large electric clock. What the hell, I thought, mortuaries are concerned with time, too. 3

I was apprehensive as I climbed the stone steps to the entrance. I feared rejection or, worse, an invitation to come and stay. The door was massive, yet it swung open easily on well-oiled hinges. "Come in," said the sign. "We're always open." Inside was a cool and quiet reception room. Curtains were drawn against the outside glare, cutting the light down to a soft glow. 4

I found the funeral director in the main lobby, adjacent to the reception room. Like most people, I had preconceptions about what an undertaker looked like. Mr. Deaver fulfilled my expectations entirely. Tall and thin, he even had beady eyes and a bony face. A low, slanted forehead gave way to a beaked nose. His skin, scrubbed of all color, contrasted sharply with his jet black hair. He was wearing a starched white shirt, gray pants, and black shoes. Indeed, he looked like death on two legs. 5

He proved an amiable sort, however, and was easy to talk to. As funeral director, Mr.   6
Deaver ("call me Howard") was responsible for a wide range of services. Goodbody Mortuaries, upon notification of someone's death, will remove the remains from the hospital
or home. They then prepare the body for viewing, whereupon features distorted by illness
or accident are restored to their natural condition. The body is embalmed and then
placed in a casket selected by the family of the deceased. Services are held in one of
three chapels at the mortuary, and afterward the casket is placed in a "visitation room,"
where family and friends can pay their last respects. Goodbody also makes arrangements for the purchase of a burial site and transports the body there for burial.

All this information Howard related in a well-practiced, professional manner. It was   7
obvious he was used to explaining the specifics of his profession. We sat alone in the
lobby. His desk was bone clean, no pencils or paper, nothing—just a telephone. He did
all his paperwork at home; as it turned out, he and his wife lived right upstairs. The phone
rang. As he listened, he bit his lips and squeezed his Adam's apple somewhat nervously.

"I think we'll be able to get him in by Friday. No, no, the family wants him cremated."   8

His tone was that of a broker conferring on the Dow Jones. Directly behind him was a   9
sign announcing "Visa and Master Charge Welcome Here." It was tacked to the wall, right
next to a crucifix.

"Some people have the idea that we are bereavement specialists, that we can handle   10
the emotional problems which follow a death: Only a trained therapist can do that. We
provide services for the dead, not counseling for the living."

Physical comfort was the one thing they did provide for the living. The lobby was   11
modestly but comfortably furnished. There were several couches, in colors ranging from
earth brown to pastel blue, and a coffee table in front of each one. On one table lay some
magazines and a vase of flowers. Another supported an aquarium. Paintings of pastoral
scenes hung on every wall. The lobby looked more or less like that of an old hotel. Nothing seemed to match, but it had a homey, lived-in look.

"The last time the Goodbodies decorated was in '59, I believe. It still makes people   12
feel welcome."

And so "Goodbody" was not a name made up to attract customers but the owners'   13
family name. The Goodbody family started the business way back in 1915. Today, they do
over five hundred services a year.

"We're in *Ripley's Believe It or Not,* along with another funeral home whose owners'   14
names are Baggit and Sackit," Howard told me, without cracking a smile.

I followed him through an arched doorway into a chapel that smelled musty and old.   15
The only illumination came from sunlight filtered through a stained glass ceiling. Ahead of
us lay a casket. I could see that it contained a man dressed in a black suit. Wooden
benches ran on either side of an aisle that led to the body. I got no closer. From the red
roses across the dead man's chest, it was apparent that services had already been held.

"It was a large service," remarked Howard. "Look at that casket—a beautiful work of   16
craftsmanship."

I guess it was. Death may be the great leveler, but one's coffin quickly reestablishes   17
one's status.

We passed into a bright, fluorescent-lit "display room." Inside were thirty coffins, lids   18
open, patiently awaiting inspection. Like new cars on the showroom floor, they gleamed
with high-gloss finishes.

"We have models for every price range."   19

Indeed, there was a wide variety. They came in all colors and various materials.   20
Some were little more than cloth-covered cardboard boxes, others were made of wood,
and a few were made of steel, copper, or bronze. Prices started at $400 and averaged
about $1,800. Howard motioned toward the center of the room: "The top of the line."

This was a solid bronze casket, its seams electronically welded to resist corrosion.   21
Moisture-proof and air-tight, it could be hermetically sealed off from all outside elements.
Its handles were plated with 14-karat gold. The price: a cool $5,000.

A proper funeral remains a measure of respect for the deceased. But it is expensive.   22
In the United States the amount spent annually on funerals is about $2 billion. Among
ceremonial expenditures, funerals are second only to weddings. As a result, practices
are changing. Howard has been in this business for forty years. He remembers a time
when everyone was buried. Nowadays, with burials costing $2,000 a shot, people often
opt instead for cremation—as Howard put it, "a cheap, quick, and easy means of dis-
posal." In some areas of the country, the cremation rate is now over 60 percent. Observing this trend, one might wonder whether burials are becoming obsolete. Do burials serve
an important role in society?

For Tim, Goodbody's licensed mortician, the answer is very definitely yes. Burials   23
will remain in common practice, according to the slender embalmer with the disarming
smile, because they allow family and friends to view the deceased. Painful as it may be,
such an experience brings home the finality of death. "Something deep within us
demands a confrontation with death," Tim explained. "A last look assures us that the person we loved is, indeed, gone forever."

Apparently, we also need to be assured that the body will be laid to rest in comfort   24
and peace. The average casket, with its inner-spring mattress and pleated satin lining, is
surprisingly roomy and luxurious. Perhaps such an air of comfort makes it easier for the
family to give up their loved one. In addition, the burial site fixes the deceased in the survivors' memory, like a new address. Cremation provides none of these comforts.

Tim started out as a clerk in a funeral home but then studied to become a mortician.   25
"It was a profession I could live with," he told me with a sly grin. Mortuary science might
be described as a cross between pre-med and cosmetology, with courses in anatomy
and embalming as well as in restorative art.

Tim let me see the preparation, or embalming, room, a white-walled chamber about   26
the size of an operating room. Against the wall was a large sink with elbow taps and a
draining board. In the center of the room stood a table with equipment for preparing the
arterial embalming fluid, which consists primarily of formaldehyde, a preservative, and
phenol, a disinfectant. This mixture sanitizes and also gives better color to the skin. Facial
features can then be "set" to achieve a restful expression. Missing eyes, ears, and even
noses can be replaced.

I asked Tim if his job ever depressed him. He bridled at the question: "No, it doesn't   27 depress me at all. I do what I can for people and take satisfaction in enabling relatives to see their loved ones as they were in life." He said that he felt people were becoming more aware of the public service his profession provides. Grade-school classes now visit funeral homes as often as they do police stations and museums. The mortician is no longer regarded as a minister of death.

Before leaving, I wanted to see a body up close. I thought I could be indifferent after all I had seen and heard, but I wasn't sure. Cautiously, I reached out and touched the skin. It felt cold and firm, not unlike clay. As I walked out, I felt glad to have satisfied my curiosity about dead bodies, but all too happy to let someone else handle them.   28

Connecting to Culture and Experience: Death

"Death," Cable announces in the opening sentence, "is a subject largely ignored by the living. We don't discuss it much, not as children (when Grandpa dies, he is said to be 'going away'), not as adults, not even as senior citizens." Yet when a family member dies, every family is forced to mark death in some way.

Discuss with other students the various ways your families and friends prepare for and arrange a memorial or funeral service. Think of a funeral you attended or ask a family member to describe how your family traditionally marks the death of a loved one. Consider the following questions, for example: Is there a formal service? If so, where does it take place — in a house of worship, a funeral home, a private home, a cemetery, or somewhere else? Who typically attends? Do people dress formally or informally? Who speaks and what kinds of things are said? What kind of music, if any, is played? Is the body cremated or buried? Is there usually a gathering after the formal service? If so, what is its purpose compared to the formal service?

Compare the different family traditions described by the members of your group. What do you think the service accomplishes for each family? If you have attended a service yourself, what did it accomplish for you?

Analyzing Writing Strategies

1. How does the opening quotation from Mark Twain shape your expectations as a reader? Compare Cable's opening (the quotation and paragraphs 1 and 2) with the openings of the two other profile essays in this chapter. What can you conclude about the opening strategies of these profile writers? Given each writer's subject, materials, and purpose, which opening do you find most effective and why?

2. During his visit to the mortuary, Cable focuses on four rooms: the lobby (paragraph 11), the chapel where funeral services are conducted (15), the casket display room (18–21), and the embalming room (26). Reread Cable's descriptions of these four rooms, and then underline the details he uses to describe each room. What impression do you get of each room? What does Cable gain by contrasting

them so sharply? How do these descriptions work together to convey Cable's ideas about the mortuary, what we call its significance?

Commentary: Significance and Vivid Presentation

By organizing the profile essay as a narrative of his tour of the mortuary, Cable can present himself directly (using the first-person pronoun *I*) and tell readers what he thinks and feels about the mortuary and the people who work there. He begins with some general ideas about death and how people tend to deal with death basically by ignoring it. Then, in paragraphs 3 and 4, he discusses his expectations and confesses his apprehensions about the initial visit.

Cable reports what he learned from Howard and Tim, describing them and commenting on what they said as he quotes and summarizes their words. His descriptions and comments express his judgments about these people and the kinds of work they do. Look at paragraphs 5–10, for example, where Cable introduces Howard Deaver, the funeral director. He begins by comparing Deaver to his "preconceptions about what an undertaker looked like." Then he describes Deaver, no doubt emphasizing his stereotypical features:

> Tall and thin, he even had beady eyes and a bony face. A low, slanted forehead gave way to a beaked nose. His skin, scrubbed of all color, contrasted sharply with his jet black hair. He was wearing a starched white shirt, gray pants, and black shoes. Indeed, he looked like death on two legs. (5)

In this example, Cable uses all of the describing strategies: naming features (such as "eyes" and "face"), detailing the features ("beady" and "bony"), and comparing ("he looked like death on two legs"). The description creates an image that reinforces the stereotype of an undertaker. But Cable quickly replaces this stereotype with a different one when he describes Howard's tone on the telephone with a client as "that of a broker conferring on the Dow Jones" (paragraph 9). To make sure readers get the idea that mortuaries are a big business, Cable points out that on the wall directly behind Howard "was a sign announcing 'Visa and Master Charge Welcome Here.'"

Considering Topics for Your Own Essay

Think of a place or an activity about which you have strong preconceptions. Then imagine how you would go about writing a profile about that place or activity. What would you choose to tell about? How might you use your preconceptions to capture readers' attention?

■ PURPOSE AND AUDIENCE

A profile writer's primary purpose is to inform readers about the subject of the profile. Readers expect a profile to present information in an engaging way, however. Whether profiling people (a soup kitchen owner, an eighth-grade student), places (a mortuary), or activities, the writer must engage as well as inform readers. Readers of profiles expect to be surprised by unusual subjects. If the subject is familiar, they expect it to be presented from an unusual perspective. When writing a profile, you will have an immediate advantage if your subject is a place, an activity, or a person that is likely to surprise and intrigue your readers. For example, the writer of "Soup" has the double advantage of both a colorful person and an unusual place. Even when your subject is very familiar, however, you can still engage your readers by presenting it in a way they have never before considered.

A profile writer has one further concern: to be sensitive to readers' knowledge of a subject. Since readers must imagine the subject profiled and understand the new information offered about it, the writer must carefully assess what readers are likely to have seen and to know. Profiling girls' experiences in a math class, the writer can assume that nearly all readers have been students in math classes. If the writer decides to focus on one of the less familiar or more modern math concepts taken up in the class, however, then the writer may have to explain the concepts to readers so that they can understand the interactions between the teacher and students and among the students themselves. For example, Orenstein need not tell her readers what math is or that it is studied in a room big enough for two or three dozen students. At the same time, she seems to have decided that at least some of her readers may not readily recall how physically mature eighth-grade girls are, relative to most eighth-grade boys, and how much the boys differ among themselves in physical maturity. Or perhaps Orenstein details these physical differences in order to sharpen the paradox that though the girls in class are on average more physically mature than most of the boys, they appear to be no match for the most vocal boys in terms of math knowledge and self-confidence. Finally, because Orenstein suspects that few of her readers will know the concepts "prime" and "composite," she offers a brief definition of each concept: "prime being those numbers which are divisible only by one and themselves, and composite being everything else." Later in the profile, however, she seems to assume that her readers will be familiar with the concept "exponent," which she does not define, or that her readers can infer its meaning from the students' comments. Orenstein makes decisions like these continuously, sentence by sentence. If, on the one hand, she underestimates readers' knowledge, she risks boring or insulting them. If, on the other hand, she overestimates readers' knowledge, she risks confusing them or failing to convey to them important aspects of her observations.

BASIC FEATURES: PROFILES

A Specific Focus

The focus of a profile is typically a specific person, place, or activity. In this chapter, the *New Yorker* writer shows us Albert Yeganeh, soup cook extraordinaire; Peggy Orenstein shows us two sides of eighth-grader Amy Wilkinson; and Brian Cable describes a place of business, Goodbody Mortuaries.

Although they focus on a person or a place, all of these profiles contain all three elements: certain people performing a specific activity at a particular place.

Whatever they examine, profile writers try to bring attention to the uniqueness of their subject, showing what is remarkable about it. In "Soup" and "The Daily Grind," we are shown something familiar in a new light. "The Last Stop" takes a behind-the-scenes look at an activity and a place few of us have explored.

A Vivid Presentation

A profile particularizes its subject—one student's life, an opinionated chef, a mortuary—rather than generalizing about the subject. Because profile writers are interested more in presenting individual cases than in making generalizations, they present the subject vividly and in detail.

Successful profile writers master the strategies of description—naming, detailing, and comparing. The profiles in this chapter, for example, evoke all the senses: sight (a "dusty-pink building" that "looked a bit like a church—tall, with gothic arches and stained glass—and somewhat like an apartment complex—low, with many windows stamped out of red brick"), touch, ("Cautiously, I reached out and touched the skin. It felt cold and firm, not unlike clay"), smell ("Weston's hallways smell chalky, papery, and a little sweaty from gym class"), and sound ("a lisping staccato of Armenian origin"). Similes ("their legs sticking out of their shorts like pipe cleaners") and metaphors ("Soup is my lifeblood") also abound.

Profile writers often describe people in graphic detail ("Nate, a gawky, sanguine boy who has shaved his head except for a small thatch that's hidden under an Oakland A's cap"). They reveal personal habits and characteristic poses ("As he listened, he bit his lips and squeezed his Adam's apple somewhat nervously"). They use dialogue to reveal character ("He spread his arms and added, 'This place is the only one like it in . . . in . . . the whole earth! One day, I hope to learn something from the other places, but so far I haven't'"). Dialogue also helps to dramatize power struggles and other relationships:

> Kyle . . . yells out, "Prime!" but Mrs. Richter turns away from him to give someone else a turn. . . . Kyle isn't willing to cede his teacher's attention. He begins to bounce in his chair and chant, *"Prime! Prime! Prime!"* Then, when he turns out to be right, he rebukes the teacher, saying "*See,* I told you."

An Indication of the Significance

Profile writers do not simply present their observations of a subject; they also convey what they think is significant or interesting about the person, place, or activity being profiled. After having spent time observing and interviewing people, profile writers formulate ideas and insights about the subject. Brian Cable, for example, shares his realization that Americans seem to capitalize on death as a way of coping with it. Profile writers may also make evaluations, as the writer of "Soup" does in expressing admiration for Mr. Yeganeh, and as Peggy Orenstein does in expressing concern for Amy.

Profile writers may show their ideas, interpretations, and evaluations through such means as detail, actions, dialogue, and contrast, or they may tell readers directly what they think. Readers expect to understand the profile's significance, but do not expect the essay to begin with the kind of explicit thesis statement typical of argumentative writing. Some writers, like Cable and the author of "Soup," begin their essays with statements about significance, but these statements tell only part of what they have to say. The rest comes in the writers' comments and evaluations as they describe people, places, and activities.

An Engaging, Informative Plan

Successful profile writers know that if they are to maintain their readers' attention, they must engage as well as inform. For this reason, they tell their stories dramatically, describe people and places vividly, and also control the flow of unfamiliar information carefully. Whether the overall plan is topical or chronological, writers give much thought to where unfamiliar information is introduced and how it is introduced.

Profiles present a lot of factual detail about their subject. Cable provides many facts about the Goodbody Mortuary and the services it offers, from the process of embalming and source of the company name, to the variety and prices of caskets, costs of a funeral, and trend toward cremation. But this information is woven into the essay in bits and pieces—conveyed in dialogue, interspersed throughout the narrative, given in description—rather than presented in one large chunk.

Parceling out information in this way enables readers to master one part of the information before going on to the next. Perhaps even more important, such control injects a degree of surprise and thus makes readers curious to know what will come next. Controlling the information flow may, in fact, keep readers reading, especially when the essay is organized topically, as it is in "Soup." Profiles organized chronologically tend to be easier to follow. Some even read like stories. Orenstein and Cable organize their profiles as narratives, using suspense and drama to maintain readers' interest.

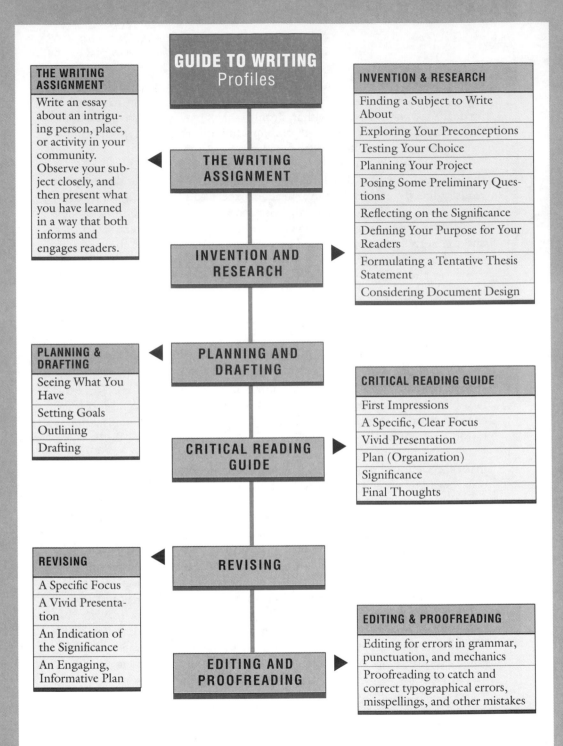

GUIDE TO WRITING
Profiles

THE WRITING ASSIGNMENT

Write an essay about an intriguing person, place, or activity in your community. Observe your subject closely, and then present what you have learned in a way that both informs and engages readers.

THE WRITING ASSIGNMENT

INVENTION AND RESEARCH

INVENTION & RESEARCH

| Finding a Subject to Write About |
| Exploring Your Preconceptions |
| Testing Your Choice |
| Planning Your Project |
| Posing Some Preliminary Questions |
| Reflecting on the Significance |
| Defining Your Purpose for Your Readers |
| Formulating a Tentative Thesis Statement |
| Considering Document Design |

PLANNING & DRAFTING

| Seeing What You Have |
| Setting Goals |
| Outlining |
| Drafting |

PLANNING AND DRAFTING

CRITICAL READING GUIDE

CRITICAL READING GUIDE

| First Impressions |
| A Specific, Clear Focus |
| Vivid Presentation |
| Plan (Organization) |
| Significance |
| Final Thoughts |

REVISING

| A Specific Focus |
| A Vivid Presentation |
| An Indication of the Significance |
| An Engaging, Informative Plan |

REVISING

EDITING AND PROOFREADING

EDITING & PROOFREADING

| Editing for errors in grammar, punctuation, and mechanics |
| Proofreading to catch and correct typographical errors, misspellings, and other mistakes |

GUIDE TO WRITING

■ THE WRITING ASSIGNMENT

Write an essay about an intriguing person, place, or activity in your community. Observe your subject closely, and then present what you have learned in a way that both informs and engages readers.

■ INVENTION AND RESEARCH

Preparing to write a profile involves several activities, such as finding a subject, exploring your preconceptions about it, planning your project, posing some preliminary questions, and reflecting on the significance of the subject. Each step takes no more than a few minutes, yet together these activities will enable you to anticipate problems likely to arise in a complex project like a profile, arrange and schedule your interviews wisely, and take notes and gather materials in a productive way. There is much to learn about observing, interviewing, and writing about what you have learned, and these activities will support your learning.

Finding a Subject to Write About

When you choose a subject, you consider various possibilities, select a promising one, and check that particular subject's accessibility.

Listing Subjects.   *Make a list of subjects to consider for your essay.* Even if you already have a subject in mind for your profile, take a few minutes to consider some other possible subjects. The more possibilities you consider, the more confident you can be about your choice. Do not overlook the subjects suggested by the Considering Topics for Your Own Essay activities following each reading in this chapter.

Before you list possible subjects, consider realistically the time you have available and the amount of observing and interviewing you will be able to accomplish. Whether you have a week to plan and write up one observational visit or interview or a month to develop a full profile will determine what kinds of subjects will be appropriate for you. Consult with your instructor if you need help defining the scope of your profile project.

Here we present some ideas you might use as starting points for a list of subjects. Try to extend your list to ten or twelve possibilities. Consider every subject you can think of, even unlikely ones. People like to read about the unusual.

People

- Anyone with an unusual or intriguing job or hobby—a private detective, beekeeper, classic-car owner, dog trainer

- A prominent local personality—a parent of the year, labor organizer, politician, consumer advocate, television or radio personality, community activist
- A campus personality—an ombudsman, coach, distinguished teacher
- Someone recently recognized for outstanding service or achievement—a volunteer, mentor, therapist

Places

- A weight-reduction clinic, martial arts or body-building gym, health spa
- A small-claims court, juvenile court, consumer fraud office
- A used-car lot, old movie house, used-book store, antique shop, historic site, auction hall, flower or gun show, farmers' or flea market
- A hospital emergency room, hospice, birthing center, psychiatric unit
- A local diner; the oldest, biggest, or quickest restaurant in town; a coffeehouse
- A campus radio station, computer center, agricultural research facility, student center, faculty club, museum, newspaper office, health center
- A book, newspaper, or Internet publisher; florist shop, nursery, or greenhouse; pawnshop; boatyard; automobile restorer or wrecking yard
- A recycling center; fire station; airport control tower; theater, opera, or symphony office; refugee center; orphanage; convent or monastery

Activities

- A citizens' volunteer program—a voter registration service, public television auction, meals-on-wheels project, tutoring program, election campaign
- A sports event—a marathon, Frisbee tournament, chess match, wrestling or boxing meet
- A hobby—folk dancing, roller blading, rock climbing, poetry reading

Listing Subjects Related to Identity and Community.   Writing a profile about a person or a place in your community can help you learn more about particular individuals in your community and about institutions and activities fundamental to community life. By "community" we mean both geographic communities, such as towns and neighborhoods, and institutional and temporary communities, such as religious congregations, college students majoring in the same subject, volunteer organizations, and sports teams. The following suggestions will enable you to list several possible subjects.

People

- Someone who has made or is currently making an important contribution to a community

- Someone who, as a prominent member of one of the communities you belong to, can help you define and understand that community
- Someone in a community who is generally not liked or respected but tolerated, such as a homeless person, gruff store owner, or unorthodox church member, or someone who has been or is in danger of being shunned or exiled from a community
- Someone who has built a successful business, succeeded in overcoming a disability or setback, supported a worthy cause, served as a role model, won respect from co-workers or neighbors

Places

- A facility that provides a needed service in a community, such as a legal advice bureau, child-care center, medical clinic, mission or shelter offering free meals
- A place where people of different ages, genders, ethnic groups, or some other attribute have formed a kind of ongoing community, such as a chess table in the park, political or social action headquarters, computer class, local coffeehouse, barber or beauty shop
- A place where people come together because they are of the same age, gender, or ethnic group, such as a seniors-only housing complex, a boathouse for a men's crew team, a campus women's center, an African American or Asian American student center
- An Internet site where people form a virtual community, such as a chat room, game parlor, or bulletin board

Activities

- A team practicing a sport or other activity (one you can observe as an outsider, not as a participant)
- A community improvement project, such as graffiti cleaning, tree planting, house repairing, church painting, highway litter pickup
- A group of researchers working collaboratively on a project

Listing Subjects Related to Work and Career. The following categories will help you consider work- and career-related subjects. Writing a profile on one of these possibilities can help you learn more about your attitudes toward your own work and career goals by examining how others do their work and pursue their careers.

People

- A college senior or graduate student in a major you are considering
- Someone working in the career you are thinking of pursuing
- Someone who trains people to do the kind of work you would like to do

Places

- A place on campus where students work — the library, computer center, cafeteria, bookstore, office, tutoring or learning center
- A place where you could learn more about the kind of career you would like to pursue — a law office, medical center, veterinary hospital, research institute, television station, newspaper, school, software manufacturer, engineering firm
- A place where people do a kind of work you would like to know more about — a clothing factory, coal mine, dairy farm, racetrack, restaurant, bakery, commercial fishing boat, gardening nursery, nursing home, delicatessen
- A place where people are trained for a certain kind of work or career — a police academy, cosmetology program, video repair course, truck drivers' school

Activities

- The actual activities performed by someone doing a kind of work represented on television, such as that of a police detective, judge, attorney, newspaper reporter, taxi driver, novelist, or emergency room doctor
- The activities involved in preparing for a particular kind of work, such as a boxer preparing for a fight, an attorney preparing for a trial, a teacher or professor preparing a course, an actor rehearsing a role, or a musician practicing for a concert

Choosing a Subject.   *Look over your list of possibilities and choose a subject that you find you want to know more about and that your readers will find interesting.*

Note, too, that most profile writers report the greatest satisfaction and the best results when they profile an unfamiliar person, place, or activity. If you choose a subject with which you are somewhat familiar, try to study it in an unfamiliar setting. For example, if you are a rock climber and decide to write a profile on rock climbing, do not rely exclusively on your own knowledge of and authority on the subject. Seek out other rock-climbing enthusiasts, even interview some critics of the sport to get another perspective, or visit a rock-climbing event or training class where you could observe without participating. By adopting an outsider's perspective on a familiar subject, you can make writing your profile a process of discovery for yourself as well as for your readers.

Stop now to focus your thoughts. *In a sentence or two, identify the subject you have chosen and explain why you think it is a good choice for you and your readers.*

Checking on Accessibility.   *Take steps to ensure that your subject will be accessible to you.* Having chosen a subject, you need to be certain you will be able to make observations and conduct interviews to learn more about it. Find out who might be able to give you information by making some preliminary phone calls. Explain that you need information for a school research project. You will be surprised how helpful people can be when they have the time. If you are unable to contact knowledgeable people or get access to the place you need to observe, you may not be able to write on this subject. Therefore, try to make these initial contacts early.

Exploring Your Preconceptions

Explore your initial thoughts and feelings about your subject in writing before you begin observing or interviewing. Take ten minutes to write about your thoughts, using the following questions as a guide:

What I already know about this subject

- How can I define or describe it?
- What are its chief qualities or parts?
- Do I associate anyone or anything with it?
- What is its purpose or function?
- How does it compare with other, similar subjects?

My attitude toward this subject

- Why do I consider it intriguing?
- What about it most interests me?
- Do I like it? Respect it? Understand it?

My own and my readers' expectations

- How do my preconceptions of this subject compare with my readers'?
- What might be unique about my preconceptions?
- What attitudes about this subject do I share with my readers?
- How is this subject represented in the media?
- What values and ideas are associated with subjects of this kind?

Testing Your Choice: A Collaborative Activity

At this point, you will find it useful to get together with two or three other students and describe the subject you have chosen to profile. This collaborative activity will help you decide whether you have chosen a good subject to write about, one that will allow you to proceed confidently as you develop your profile.

Presenters: Take turns identifying your subjects. Explain your interest in the subject and speculate about why you think it will interest your readers.

Listeners: Briefly tell each presenter what you already know about his or her subject, if anything, and what would make it interesting to readers.

Planning Your Project

Set up a tentative schedule for your observational and interview visits. Whatever the scope of your project—a single observation, an interview with follow-up, or multiple observations and interviews—you will want to get the most out of your time with your subject. Chapter 12 offers guidance in observing and interviewing and will give you an idea of how much time you will need to plan, carry out, and write up an observation or interview.

Take time now to consult Chapter 12. Figure out first the amount of time you have to complete your essay; then decide what visits you will need to make, whom you will need to interview, and what library or Internet research you might want to do, if any. Estimate the time necessary for each. You might use a chart like the following one:

Date	Time Needed	Purpose	Preparation
10/23	1 hour	Observe	Bring map, directions, paper
10/25	2 hours	Library research	Bring references, change or copycard for copy machine
10/26	45 minutes	Interview	Read brochure and prepare questions
10/30	3 hours	Observe and interview	Confirm appointment; bring questions and extra pen

You will probably have to modify your plan once you actually begin work, but it is a good idea to keep some sort of schedule in writing.

If you are developing a full profile, your first goal is to get your bearings. Some writers begin by observing; others start with an interview. Many read up on the subject before doing anything else, to get a sense of its main elements. You may also want to read about other subjects similar to the one you have chosen. Save your notes.

Posing Some Preliminary Questions

Write questions to prepare for your first visit. Before beginning your observations and interviews, try writing some questions for which you would like to find answers. These questions will orient you and allow you to focus your visits. As you work, you will find answers to many of these questions. Add to this list as new questions occur to you, and delete any that come to seem irrelevant.

Each subject invites its own special questions, and every writer has particular concerns. Consider, for example, how one student writing a profile on a local center of the Women's Health Initiative, a nationwide fifteen-year study of women's health, goes about preparing interview questions. After reading about the study in her local newspaper, she calls the local center to get further information. The center administrator faxes her a fact sheet on the study and the local center's special part in it. The student knows that she will need to report on the study within her profile of the local center and key people who work there. She also hopes to interview women who come to the center to participate in the research. Consequently, she devises these questions to launch her research and prepare for her first visit to the center to interview the director:

- Why has so little research been done until now on women's health?
- How did the study come about, and what is the role of the National Institutes of Health?
- Why does the study focus only on women between the ages of fifty and eighty?
- Will women from all income levels be involved?
- Why will it take fifteen years to complete the study?
- When was this center established, and what role does it play in the national study?
- Does the center simply coordinate the study, or does it also provide health and medical advice to women participating in the study?
- Who works at the center, and what are their qualifications to work there?
- Will I be able to interview women who come to the center to participate in the research?
- Will I be permitted to take photographs of the location?
- Would it be appropriate to take photographs of the researchers and participants, if they give their consent?

For more on interviewing techniques, see Chapter 12, pp. 316–49.

Reflecting on the Significance

Write for five to ten minutes, reflecting on what you now think is interesting and mean-ingful about the person, place, or activity you have chosen for your profile. Consider how you would answer these questions about your subject:

- What visual or other sensory impression is most memorable?
- What does this impression tell me about the person, place, or activity?
- What mood do I associate with my subject?
- What about my subject is most striking and likely to surprise or interest my readers?
- What is the most important thing I have learned about my subject? Why is it important?
- If I could find out the answer to one more question about my subject, what would that question be? Why is this question important?
- What about my subject says something larger about our culture and times?
- Which of my ideas, interpretations, or judgments do I most want to share with readers?

Defining Your Purpose for Your Readers

Write a few sentences, defining your purpose in writing about this particular person, place, or activity for your readers. Use these questions to focus your thoughts:

- Who are my readers? Apart from my instructors and classmates, who would be interested in reading an essay about this particular subject? If I were to try to publish my essay, what magazine, newspaper, newsletter, or Web site might want a profile on this particular subject? Would people who work in a particular kind of business or who pursue certain kinds of hobbies or sports be interested in the essay?

- What do I want my readers to learn about the person, place, or activity from reading my essay?

- What do I want my readers to understand about the significance I see in this particular person, place, or activity?

Formulating a Tentative Thesis Statement

Review what you wrote for Reflecting on the Significance and add another two or three sentences that will help you tell readers what you understand about the person, place, or activity on which you are focusing. Try to write sentences that do not summarize what you have already written, but that extend your insights and interpretations.

Keep in mind that readers do not expect you to begin a profile essay with the kind of explicit thesis statement typical of argumentative essays. If you do decide to tell readers why the person, place, or activity is significant, you will most likely do so through interpretive or evaluative comments as you describe people and places, present dialogue, and narrate what you observed. You are not obliged to tell readers the significance, but you should show it through the way you profile the subject.

Considering Document Design

Think about whether visual or audio elements—photographs, postcards, menus, or snippets from films, television programs, or songs—would strengthen your profile. These are not at all a requirement of an effective profile, but they could be helpful. Consider also whether your readers might benefit from design features such as headings, bulleted or numbered lists, or other typographic elements that can make an essay easier to follow.

■ PLANNING AND DRAFTING

This section will help you review your invention writing and research notes and get started on your first draft.

Seeing What You Have

Read over your invention materials to see what you have. You probably have a great deal of material—notes from observational and interview visits or from library research; some idea of your preconceptions; a list of questions, perhaps with some answers. You should also have a tentative interpretation. Your goals at this point are to digest all of the information you have gathered; to pick out the promising facts, details, anecdotes, and quotations; and to see how it all might come together to present your subject and your interpretation of it to readers.

As you sort through your material, try asking yourself the following questions to help clarify your focus and interpretation:

- How do my preconceptions of the subject contrast with my findings about it?
- Can I compare or contrast what different people say about my subject? Do I see any discrepancies between people's words and their behavior?
- How do my reactions compare with those of the people directly involved?
- How could I consider the place's appearance in light of the activity that occurs there?
- If I examine my subject as an anthropologist or archaeologist would, what evidence could explain its role in society at large?
- Could I use an illustration to complement the text?

Setting Goals

The following questions will help you establish goals for your first draft. Consider each item briefly now, and then return to the questions as necessary as you draft and revise.

Your Purpose and Readers

- Are my readers likely to be familiar with my subject? If not, what details do I need to provide to help them understand and visualize it?
- If my readers are familiar with my subject, how can I present it to them in a new and engaging way? What information do I have that is likely to be unfamiliar or entertaining to them?
- What design elements might make my writing more interesting or easier for readers to understand?

The Beginning

The opening is especially important in a profile. Because readers are unlikely to have any particular reason to read a profile, the writer must arouse their curiosity and interest. The best beginnings are surprising and specific; the worst are abstract. Here are some strategies you might consider:

- Should I open with an emphatic statement, as Orenstein does, or an intriguing epigraph, as Cable does?

- Do I have any dialogue to open with, as in "Soup"?

- Can I start with an amazing fact, anecdote, question, or striking image that would catch readers' attention?

A Vivid Presentation

- Where might I use naming and detailing to give readers a strong visual image of people and places?

- Can I think of a simile or metaphor that would help me present an evocative image?

- Which bits of dialogue would convey information about my subject as well as a vivid impression of the speaker?

- What specific narrative actions can I include to show people and activities?

An Informative Plan

Profile writers use two basic methods of organizing information, arranging it chronologically in a narrative or topically by grouping related materials.

If You Use a Chronological Plan

- How can I make the narrative interesting, perhaps even dramatic?

- What information should I present through dialogue and what information should I interrupt the narrative to present?

- How much space should I devote to describing people and places and to showing what happened?

- Can I set up comparisons or contrasts that would dramatize the significance?

- If I have the option of including design elements, how might I use them effectively: perhaps to clarify the chronology, highlight a dramatic part of the narrative, illustrate how the people and places in the profile changed over time?

If You Use a Topical Plan

- Which topics will best inform my readers and hold their interest?

- How can I sequence the topics to bring out significant comparisons or contrasts?

- What transitions will help readers make connections between topics?

- Where and how should I describe the subject vividly?

- If I have the option of including design elements, are there ways I can use them effectively to reinforce the topical organization?

The Ending

- Should I try to frame the essay by repeating an image or phrase from the beginning or by completing an action begun earlier in the profile?
- Would it be effective to end by stating or restating my interpretation or evaluation?
- Should I end with a telling image, anecdote, or bit of dialogue, or with a provocative question or connection?

Outlining

If you plan to arrange your material chronologically, plot the key events on a timeline. If you plan to arrange your material topically, you might use clustering or topic outlining to help you divide and group related information. (To learn about these mapping strategies, see Chapter 9, pp. 290–94.)

The following outline suggests one possible way to organize a chronological profile of a place:

> Begin by describing the place from the outside.
>
> Present background information.
>
> Describe what you see as you enter.
>
> Introduce the people and activities.
>
> Tour the place, describing what you see as you move from room to room.
>
> Fill in information and comment about the place or the people.
>
> Conclude with reflections on what you have learned about the place.

Here is a suggested outline for a topical profile about a person:

> Begin with a vivid image of the person in action.
>
> Use dialogue to present the first topic.
>
> Narrate an anecdote or a procedure to illustrate the first topic.
>
> Present the second topic.
>
> Describe something related to it.
>
> Evaluate or interpret what you have observed.
>
> Present the third topic.
>
> Conclude with a bit of action or dialogue.

All of the material for these hypothetical essays would come from observations, interviews, and background reading. The plan you choose should reflect the possibilities in your material as well as your purpose and readers. At this point, your decisions must be tentative. As you begin drafting, you will almost certainly discover new ways of organizing your material. Once you have written a first draft, you and others may see better ways to organize the material for your particular audience.

Drafting

Start drafting your essay, keeping in mind the goals you set while you were planning. As you write, try to describe your subject in a way that makes its significance clear to your readers. If you get stuck while drafting, explore the problem by using some of the writing activities in the Invention and Research section of this chapter or by reviewing the general advice on planning and drafting in Chapter 1, pp. 15–17.

As you read over your first draft, you may see places where you can add new material to reveal more about the person, place, or activity. You may even decide that after this first draft, you can finally understand the complexity of your subject, and set out to convey it more fully in a second draft.

CRITICAL READING GUIDE   Now is the time to get a good critical reading of your draft. Writers usually find it helpful to have someone else read and comment on their drafts, and all writers know how much they learn about writing when they read other writers' drafts. Your instructor may schedule readings of drafts as part of your coursework. If not, you can ask a classmate, friend, or family member to read your draft. You could also seek comments from a tutor at your campus writing center. The guidelines in this section can be used by *anyone* reviewing a profile. (If you are unable to have someone else read your draft, turn ahead to the Revising section, where you will find guidelines for reading your own draft critically.)

If You Are the Writer. In order to provide focused, helpful comments, your reader must know your essay's intended audience, your purpose, and a problem in the draft that you need help solving. Briefly write out this information at the top of your draft:

- *Readers.* Identify the intended readers of your essay. How do you assume they will react to your writing?
- *Purpose.* What effect do you want your profile to have on readers? What do you want them to discover?
- *Problem.* Ask your reader to help you solve the single most important problem you see with your draft. Describe this problem briefly.

If You Are the Reader. Use the following guidelines to help you give critical comments to others on profile essays.

1. *Read for a First Impression.* Begin by reading the draft straight through to get a general impression. Read for enjoyment, ignoring spelling, punctuation, and sentence problems for now. When you have finished this first quick

reading, write a few sentences about what seems most interesting to you about the person, place, or activity that is the focus of the profile. If you have any insights or questions about the subject, write down these thoughts as well. Next, consider the problem the writer identified. If the problem will be covered by one of the other questions below, deal with it there. Otherwise, respond to the writer's concerns now.

2. *Consider Whether the Focus Is Specific and Clear.* Consider whether the essay clearly focuses on a particular person, place, or activity. Point to any passages where the focus seems to shift to something else. Also let the writer know if the essay seems too much about the writer's general ideas and not enough about the specific person, place, or activity.

3. *Assess the Vividness of the Presentation.* Find the descriptions of people, places, and activities and let the writer know if any need enlivening. Point to passages where additional features could be named and detailed, or where the sense of smell or touch could be added to the visual description. Also indicate if you have difficulty seeing people in action or imagining what is involved in the activity.

4. *Evaluate the Plan.* Point out any places where you feel bogged down or overwhelmed with information or where information is not clearly presented or is inadequate. If the profile is organized chronologically, point out any places where the narrative seems to drag as well as where it seems most compelling. If the profile is organized topically, note whether the writer presents too little or too much material for a topic and whether topics might be sequenced differently or connected more clearly.

- Look at the *opening* to see if it captures your attention. If not, is there a quotation, a fact, or an anecdote elsewhere in the draft that might make a better opening?

- Look at the *ending* to see if it leaves you hanging, seems too abrupt, or oversimplifies the material. If it does, suggest another way of ending, possibly by moving a passage or a quotation from elsewhere in the essay.

- Assess the *design features.* Comment on the contribution of any design features such as photographs, song lyrics, or headings. Help the writer think of design features that could be added.

5. *Consider Whether the Significance Is Clear.* Point to any comments, judgments, interpretations, or ideas that seem vague or unrelated to what you are shown in the profile. Tell the writer what you take to be significant and most interesting about the person, place, or activity that is the focus of the profile. Indicate any details that seem especially meaningful and explain why you think so.

6. *Give the Writer Your Final Thoughts.* What is the draft's strongest part? What part is most memorable? What part is weak or most in need of further work?

■ REVISING

This section will help you get an overview of your draft and revise it accordingly.

Getting an Overview

Consider your draft as a whole, following these two steps:

1. *Reread.* If at all possible, put the draft aside for a day or two. When you do reread it, start by reconsidering your purpose. Then read the draft straight through, trying to see it as your intended readers will.

2. *Outline.* Make a quick scratch outline, indicating the basic features as they appear in the draft. (For more on scratch outlines, see Chapter 9, pp. 292–93.)

Charting a Plan for Revision.   Preparing a two-column list is a good way to start plotting out the course of your revision. In the left-hand column list the basic features of profiles; in the right-hand column list any problems that you or other readers identified with that feature. (Turn to pp. 75–77 to review the basic features.)

Basic Features   *Problems to Solve*

A specific focus

A vivid presentation

An indication of the significance

An engaging, informative plan

Analyzing the Basic Features of Your Own Draft.   Turn to the Critical Reading Guide on the preceding pages. Using this guide, identify problems you now see in your draft. Note the problems on the chart.

Studying Critical Comments.   Review all of the comments you have received from other readers. For each comment, look at the draft to determine what might have led the reader to make that particular point. Try to be objective about any criticism. Ideally, these comments will help you see your draft as others see it (rather than as you hoped it would be) and to identify specific problems.

Carrying Out Revisions

Having identified problems in your draft, you now need to figure out solutions and — most important — to carry them out. Basically, you have three options for finding solutions:

1. Review your observation or interview notes for other information and ideas.

2. Do additional observations or interviews to answer questions you or other readers raised.

3. Look back at the readings in this chapter to see how other writers have solved similar problems.

The following suggestions, which are organized according to the basic features on your revision chart, will get you started solving some problems common to profiles.

A Specific Focus

- *Does the essay fail to focus clearly on a particular person, place, or activity?* Make explicit the focus of your profile. Add more description or bring the description together in one paragraph closer to the beginning of the essay.

- *Does the essay seem too general?* Break up long stretches of commentary. Interweave your ideas, interpretations, and evaluations into your presentation of the person, place, or activity. Try to present background information through dialogue rather than through your own comments.

A Vivid Presentation

- *Can the description of the person who is the focus of the profile be improved?* Add details to help readers see the person. Think, for example, of Orenstein's description of Amy's "curly, blond hair, cornflower-blue eyes, and [. . .] sharply upturned nose." Consider adding a vivid comparison, as the *New Yorker* writer does to describe Mr. Yeganeh as "working like a demon alchemist." Insert specific narrative actions to show the person's gestures and mannerisms. Recall, for example, how after giving a wrong answer Amy "turns crimson, and flips her head forward so her hair falls over her face."

- *Should other people be described briefly?* Consider naming and detailing a few physical features of each person. Recall, for example, Orenstein's quick descriptive phrases: "Kyle, who is skinny and a little pop-eyed" and "Mrs. Richter, a ruddy, athletic woman with a powerful voice." Add comparisons, as Cable does when he says Howard Deaver "looked like death on two legs." Also consider adding specific narrative action. Think of Howard again on the phone: "As he listened, he bit his lips and squeezed his Adam's apple."

- *Can you enliven the description of the place?* Add to visual description other senses. Recall, for example, these sensory descriptions from the readings: sound ("a lisping staccato of Armenian origin"), texture ("downy beards"), smell ("chalky, papery, and a little sweaty"), and taste ("one sweet, one spicy").

- *Do readers have difficulty seeing people in action or imagining what is involved in the activity?* Add specific narrative actions to show people moving, gesturing, or talking. For example, recall how, in Orenstein's profile, Amy introduces her friend Greg: she "turns, puts her hands on her hips, anchors her feet shoulder width apart, and bellows across the schoolyard, 'Greg! Get over here! You have to meet Peggy.'" Explain a procedure or use dialogue to narrate what an activity involves.

An Indication of the Significance

- *Do any comments seem vague or unrelated to what is being profiled?* Try stating your ideas more directly. Be sure that the dominant impression you create through descriptive and narrative details reinforces the significance you want to convey.

- *Do your readers have different ideas about the person, place, or activity being profiled?* Consider whether you can incorporate any of their ideas into your essay or use them to develop your own ideas.

- *Do critical readers point to any details that seem especially meaningful?* Consider what these details suggest about the significance of the person, place, or activity.

An Engaging, Informative Plan

- *Do readers feel bogged down by information?* Look for ways to reduce information or to break up long blocks of informational text with description of scenes or people, narration of events, lists, or other design elements. Consider presenting information through dialogue, as the "Soup" author and Cable do.

- *Does your chronologically arranged essay seem to drag or ramble?* Try adding drama through dialogue or specific narrative action. Try using comparison and contrast, as Orenstein does.

- *Does your topically arranged essay seem disorganized or out of balance?* Try rearranging topics to see if another order makes more sense. Add clearer, more explicit transitions or topic sentences. Move or condense information to restore balance.

- *Does the opening fail to engage readers' attention?* Consider alternatives. Think of questions you could open with, or look for an engaging image or dialogue later in the essay to move to the beginning. Go back to your observation or interview notes for other ideas. Recall how the writers in this chapter open their profile essays: the "Soup" author begins with an arresting quotation, Orenstein tells us how Amy felt, and Cable combines a quote by Mark Twain with comments about how people try to ignore death.

- *Are transitions between stages in the narrative or between topics confusing or abrupt?* Add appropriate words or phrases or revise sentences to make transitions clearer or smoother.

- *Does the ending seem weak?* Consider ending at an earlier point or moving something striking to the end. Review your invention and research notes to see if you overlooked something that would make for a strong ending. Consider ending your essay with a quotation, as some of the writers in this chapter do.

- *Are the design features effective?* Consider adding textual references to any visual elements in your essay or positioning visuals more effectively. Think of other possible design features you might incorporate to enhance your profile.

■ EDITING AND PROOFREADING

Now is the time to check your revised draft for connections between sentences and for errors in grammar, punctuation, and mechanics. As you reread, ask yourself whether the connection from one sentence to the next is logical and easy for readers to follow. If you sense a gap or disconnection that would cause a reader to stumble or become confused, try revising one or both sentences so that the gap is closed. Notice whether you shift from one word to another unnecessarily in one sentence to the next, and, if you do, consider repeating the same word instead. Look for sentences that might be combined to allow readers to follow the observations more easily. Look as well for long or garbled sentences that might be divided into two or three sentences.

As you work on your sentences, look for errors in spelling, capitalization, punctuation, usage, and grammar. Consult a writer's handbook for advice about how to correct any errors you cannot confidently correct on your own. Ask a friend or classmate to read over your draft, looking for errors.

Before you hand in your revised essay, proofread it carefully and run it through a spell-checker. Your goal is to hand in an error-free essay.

REFLECTING ON YOUR WRITING

Now that you have spent at least several days discussing profiles and writing one of your own, take some time for reflection. Reflecting on your writing process will help you gain a greater understanding of what you learned about solving the problems you encountered.

Write a one-page explanation, telling your instructor about a problem you encountered in writing your profile and how you solved it. Before you begin, gather all of your writing — invention material, planning and interview notes, drafts, critical comments, revision notes and plans, and final revision. Review these materials as you complete this writing task.

1. *Identify one writing problem you needed to solve as you worked on your profile.* Do not be concerned with grammar or punctuation; concentrate instead on problems unique to developing a profile. For example: Did you puzzle over how to organize your diverse observations into a coherent essay? Was it difficult to convey the significance? Did you have any concerns about presenting your subject vividly or controlling the flow of information?

2. *Determine how you came to recognize the problem.* When did you first discover it? What called it to your attention? If someone else pointed out the problem to you, can you now see hints of it in your invention writings? If so, where specifically? When you first recognized the problem, how did you respond?

3. *Reflect on how you went about solving the problem.* Did you work on the wording of a passage, cut or add details about your subject, or move paragraphs or sentences around? Did you reread one of the essays in this chapter to see how another writer handled a similar problem, or did you look back at the invention suggestions? If you talked about the problem with another student, a tutor, or your instructor, did talking about it help? How useful was the advice you received?

4. *Write a brief explanation of the problem and your solution.* Reconstruct your efforts as specifically as possible. Quote from your invention notes or draft essay, others' critical comments, your revision plan, and your revised essay to show the various changes your writing underwent as you tried to solve the problem. When you have finished, consider how explaining what you have learned about solving this writing problem can help you solve future writing problems.

Explaining a Concept

Explanatory writing serves to inform readers. In general, it does not feature its writers' experiences or feelings, as autobiography does (see Chapter 2). Instead, successful explanatory writing presents information, confidently and efficiently, with the purpose of educating the reader about a subject. This type of writing, required almost every day in nearly every profession, may be based on firsthand observation (Chapter 3), but it always moves beyond describing specific objects and events to explain general principles and patterns of behavior. Since it deals almost exclusively with established information, explanatory writing tends not to present an argument but to present information as if everyone assumes it were true. It does not aspire to be more than it is: a way for readers to find out about a particular subject. Much of what we find in newspapers, encyclopedias, instruction manuals, reference books, and research reports is explanatory writing.

This chapter focuses on one important kind of explanatory writing, explanations of concepts. The chapter readings explain the concepts "love," "Internet addiction," and "cannibalism." These concepts name processes and phenomena under study. Scientists in various fields have studied the body's chemistry during both new romances and long-term relationships to create a "neurochemistry of love." Psychologists have borrowed the concept of "addiction" from their studies of other compulsive behaviors like alcohol and drug addiction to understand why some Internet users spend many hours every day online. Anthropologists continue to learn more about the situations and cultural practices that lead humans to eat other humans, a phenomenon known as "cannibalism."

Every field of study has its concepts: physics has "entropy," "mass," and "fission"; literature has "irony," "romanticism," and "bildungsroman"; music has "harmony"; art has "perspective"; mathematics has "probability"; and so on. You can see from this brief list that concepts are central to the understanding of virtually every subject. Moreover, when you enter a new field, you are expected to learn a new set of concepts. That is why introductory courses and their textbooks teach a whole new vocabulary of technical terms and specialized jargon. When you read the opening chapter of this textbook, for example, you were introduced to many concepts important to the study of writing, such as "genre," "writing process," "invention," and "revision."

Learning to explain a concept is especially important to you as a college student. It will help you read textbooks (which themselves exist to explain concepts); it will prepare you to write a common type of exam and paper assignment; and it will acquaint you with the basic strategies common to all types of explanatory writing—definition, classification, comparison and contrast, cause and effect, and process narration.

You will encounter writing that explains concepts in many different contexts, as the following examples suggest.

Writing in Your Other Courses

- For a linguistics course, a student writes a term paper tracing children's gradual control of sentences (or syntax, as linguists say) from about eighteen months to five or six years of age. The student first explains how researchers go about studying children's syntax, using several well-known studies as examples. Then he presents the widely accepted classification of stages that children go through as they gain control of snytax. As he presents each stage, he gives examples of children's syntax in both their spoken monologues and their conversations in different situations, examples chosen from many possibilities in the published research studies. Even though he writes for his instructor, who is an expert in child language development, he carefully defines key terms to show that he understands what he is writing about.

- For a history of religion course, a student writes a term paper on religious fundamentalism. To explain this concept, she relies primarily on a book by a noted religious scholar. She follows the scholar in classifying the ways fundamentalist religious groups are similar and organizes her paper around these similarities, which include a sense of threat and an organized reaction to the threat, a reliance on authoritative texts, a resistance to ambiguity and ambivalence, an inclination to behave aggressively toward unbelievers, an allegiance to a grand past, and a belief in a bright future. She illustrates each of these features of fundamentalism with examples from the beliefs and histories of fundamentalist groups around the world. She concludes by pointing out that religious fundamentalism has become a major political force at the beginning of the twenty-first century.

Writing in the Community

- "Community policing" has just been adopted by the police department in a mid-sized city, and a writer in the department's public relations division has been assigned the task of writing and producing a brochure explaining the new approach. The brochure will be mailed to all homes in the city. The writer designs a small, fold-out, six-panel, two-sided brochure that will feature both text and photographs. The text explains briefly the major features of community policing; for example, neighborhood-focused crime control and prevention, neighborhood involvement in deciding on crime-control priorities, the long-term assignment of officers to neighborhoods, increased reliance on foot and bicycle patrols and decreased reliance on car patrols, and the establishment of neighborhood mini-police stations. Working with a photographer, the writer arranges to get photographs taken that represent the different features of community policing explained in the text.

- As part of her firm's plan to encourage managers to volunteer in the community for a few hours each month, the manager at a marketing research firm has been tutoring fifth-grade students in math. Learning of the manager's expertise in surveys, the teacher encourages the manager to plan a presentation to the class about surveying, a concept and important research method in the social sciences. The manager agrees to do so and begins her lesson by having students fill out a brief questionnaire on their television-watching habits. She explains that she is not collecting data for marketing purposes, but rather introducing them to surveys. With the students helping, she tabulates the results on a computer, separating the results by sex, time of week (weekdays or weekends), and kinds of television shows. Using a PowerPoint program, she projects the data onto a large screen so that everyone can see how the tables represent the survey results. The manager first guides a brief discussion of the survey and the results, helping students understand its purpose, form, and graphic representation. Then she shows them on the screen examples of questions from other surveys and explains who gives such surveys, what they hope to learn, and how they report and use the results. She explains that the state tests the students take every year are a form of survey. Finally, she passes out a short-answer quiz so that she and each student can find out how much has been learned about surveys.

Writing in the Workplace

- Returning from a small invitational seminar on the national security implications of satellite photography, the CEO of a space-imaging company prepares a report to his employees on the international debate about symmetrical transparency, the concept of using satellite photography to make everything on the planet visible to everyone on the planet at one-meter resolution—enough detail to reveal individual cars in parking lots, small airplanes on runways, backyard swimming pools, and individual shrubs and trees planted in parks. Aware of the financial implications for his company of the outcome of the debate, the executive carefully organizes his information and prepares a written text to read aloud to his employees, a one-page handout that lists key issues in the debate, and a transparency to project on a large screen during his presentation. He begins by reminding employees that the company's cameras already provide high-resolution images to government and corporate purchasers. Addressing the question of whether symmetrical transparency and the multinational monitoring it makes possible compromise national security—or promise greater worldwide security and peace—the CEO gives a brief overview of key issues in the debate. These issues include differing impacts on closed societies (like those of North Korea and Iraq) and more open ones, whether global terrorism will be reduced or become more prevalent or more effective, and whether the chance of a nuclear standoff will be lessened. He concludes by pointing out that the big question for the U.S. government to answer soon is whether it must attempt to control space or insist that it be open to everyone.

- Legislation in a western state defines a new concept in tourism—agri-tourism. In one area where farmers, vineyard owners, and ranchers might be most affected, a university-extension farm adviser calls a meeting to explain the concept as defined in the legislation. To prepare for the meeting, he writes a four-page summary of the legislation and prepares a one-page list of the main points in his presentation for everyone to pick up and read before the meeting begins. Assuming his listeners have all visited a bed and breakfast, the farm adviser compares the rules in the new law with the rules governing bed and breakfasts. He emphasizes that in agri-tourism, guests must be able to tour the farm or ranch and even participate in carefully supervised chores. Whoever prepares and serves the meals, which must be offered three times a day, has to be certified through coursework at a community college. He also explains that the greatest beneficiaries of agri-tourism will be small and middle-sized farms and ranches, where income is relatively low and varies greatly from year to year.

Practice Explaining a Concept: A Collaborative Activity

The preceding scenarios suggest some occasions for writing about concepts. Think of concepts you are currently studying or have recently studied or concepts connected to a sport or hobby you know a lot about. Here are some possibilities: "squeeze play," "creativity," "friendship," "success," "hypertext," "interval training," "job satisfaction," "photosynthesis," "maturity," "community," "civil rights," "manifest destiny."

Part 1. Choose one concept to explain to two or three other students. When you have chosen your concept, think about what others in the group are likely to know about it and how you can inform them about it in two or three minutes. Consider how you will define the concept and what other strategies you might use—description, comparison, and so on—to explain it in an interesting, memorable way.

Get together with two or three other students and explain your concepts to one another. You might begin by indicating where you learned the concept and in what area of study or work or leisure it is usually used.

Part 2. When all group members have explained their concepts, discuss what you learned from the experience of explaining a concept. Begin by asking one another a question or two that would elicit further information you need to understand each concept more fully. Then, consider these questions:

- How did you decide what to include in your explanation and what to leave out?
- How successfully did you estimate listeners' prior knowledge of your concept?
- If you were to repeat your explanation to a similar group of listeners, what would you add, subtract, or change?

READINGS

The readings in this chapter illustrate the features of essays that explain concepts and the strategies writers rely on to realize the features. No two essays in this genre are much alike, and yet they share defining features. The Analyzing Writing Strategies and the Commentary following each reading touch on a few features best illustrated by that essay, capturing its special qualities and strengths. Together, the three essays cover many of the possibilities of explanatory writing. Consequently, you will want to read as many of the essays and Commentaries as possible and, if time permits, complete the activities in Analyzing Writing Strategies. Following the last reading in the chapter, the Basic Features section offers a concise description of the features of concept explanations and provides examples from all of the readings.

Anastasia Toufexis, *a senior editor at* Discover *magazine, was for many years an associate editor at* Time, *where she wrote major reports for nearly every section of the magazine: medicine, health and fitness, law, environment, education, science, and national and world news. Toufexis received her bachelor's degree in premedicine from Smith College in 1967 and spent several years reporting for medical and pharmaceutical magazines. She has won a number of awards for her work at* Time *and has lectured on newsmagazine journalism and science writing at Columbia University, the University of North Carolina, and the School of Visual Arts in New York. In 2000 she was Ocean Science Writing Fellow at the Woods Hole Oceanographic Institute. The following essay was originally published in a 1993 issue of* Time. *As you read, notice how Toufexis brings together a variety of sources of information to present a neurochemical perspective on love.*

Love: The Right Chemistry

Anastasia Toufexis

Love is a romantic designation for a most ordinary biological — or, shall we say, chemical? — process. A lot of nonsense is talked and written about it.

— Greta Garbo to Melvyn Douglas in *Ninotchka*

O.K., let's cut out all this nonsense about romantic love. 1
Let's bring some scientific precision to the party. Let's put love under a microscope.

When rigorous people with Ph.D.s after their names do that, what they see is not some 2
silly, senseless thing. No, their probe reveals that love rests firmly on the foundations of

evolution, biology and chemistry. What seems on the surface to be irrational, intoxicated behavior is in fact part of nature's master strategy—a vital force that has helped humans survive, thrive and multiply through thousands of years. Says Michael Mills, a psychology professor at Loyola Marymount University in Los Angeles: "Love is our ancestors whispering in our ears."

It was on the plains of Africa about 4 million years ago, in the early days of the human species, that the notion of romantic love probably first began to blossom—or at least that the first cascades of neurochemicals began flowing from the brain to the bloodstream to produce goofy grins and sweaty palms as men and women gazed deeply into each other's eyes. When mankind graduated from scuttling around on all fours to walking on two legs, this change made the whole person visible to fellow human beings for the first time. Sexual organs were in full display, as were other characteristics, from the color of eyes to the span of shoulders. As never before, each individual had a unique allure. 3

When the sparks flew, new ways of making love enabled sex to become a romantic encounter, not just a reproductive act. Although mounting mates from the rear was, and still is, the method favored among most animals, humans began to enjoy face-to-face couplings; both looks and personal attraction became a much greater part of the equation. 4

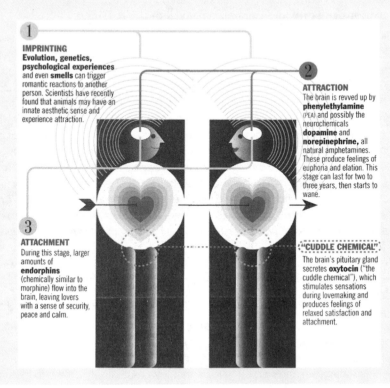

1 IMPRINTING
Evolution, genetics, psychological experiences and even **smells** can trigger romantic reactions to another person. Scientists have recently found that animals may have an innate aesthetic sense and experience attraction.

2 ATTRACTION
The brain is revved up by **phenylethylamine** (PEA) and possibly the neurochemicals **dopamine** and **norepinephrine,** all natural amphetamines. These produce feelings of euphoria and elation. This stage can last for two to three years, then starts to wane.

3 ATTACHMENT
During this stage, larger amounts of **endorphins** (chemically similar to morphine) flow into the brain, leaving lovers with a sense of security, peace and calm.

"CUDDLE CHEMICAL"
The brain's pituitary gland secretes **oxytocin** ("the cuddle chemical"), which stimulates sensations during lovemaking and produces feelings of relaxed satisfaction and attachment.

Romance served the evolutionary purpose of pulling males and females into long-term partnership, which was essential to child rearing. On open grasslands, one parent would have a hard—and dangerous—time handling a child while foraging for food. "If a woman was carrying the equivalent of a 20-lb. bowling ball in one arm and a pile of sticks in the other, it was ecologically critical to pair up with a mate to rear the young," explains anthropologist Helen Fisher, author of *Anatomy of Love*.

While Western culture holds fast to the idea that true love flames forever (the movie *Bram Stoker's Dracula* has the Count carrying the torch beyond the grave), nature apparently meant passions to sputter out in something like four years. Primitive pairs stayed together just "long enough to rear one child through infancy," says Fisher. Then each would find a new partner and start all over again.

What Fisher calls the "four-year itch" shows up unmistakably in today's divorce statistics. In most of the 62 cultures she has studied, divorce rates peak around the fourth year of marriage. Additional youngsters help keep pairs together longer. If, say, a couple have another child three years after the first, as often occurs, then their union can be expected to last about four more years. That makes them ripe for the more familiar phenomenon portrayed in the Marilyn Monroe classic *The Seven-Year Itch*.

If, in nature's design, romantic love is not eternal, neither is it exclusive. Less than 5% of mammals form rigorously faithful pairs. From the earliest days, contends Fisher, the human pattern has been "monogamy with clandestine adultery." Occasional flings upped the chances that new combinations of genes would be passed on to the next generation. Men who sought new partners had more children. Contrary to common assumptions, women were just as likely to stray. "As long as prehistoric females were secretive about their extramarital affairs," argues Fisher, "they could garner extra resources, life insurance, better genes and more varied DNA for their biological futures. . . ."

Lovers often claim that they feel as if they are being swept away. They're not mistaken; they are literally flooded by chemicals, research suggests. A meeting of eyes, a touch of hands or a whiff of scent sets off a flood that starts in the brain and races along the nerves and through the blood. The results are familiar: flushed skin, sweaty palms, heavy breathing. If love looks suspiciously like stress, the reason is simple: the chemical pathways are identical.

Above all, there is the sheer euphoria of falling in love—a not-so-surprising reaction, considering that many of the substances swamping the newly smitten are chemical cousins of amphetamines. They include dopamine, norepinephrine and especially phenylethylamine (PEA). Cole Porter knew what he was talking about when he wrote, "I get a kick out of you." "Love is a natural high," observes Anthony Walsh, author of *The Science of Love: Understanding Love and Its Effects on Mind and Body*. "PEA gives you that silly smile that you flash at strangers. When we meet someone who is attractive to us, the whistle blows at the PEA factory."

But phenylethylamine highs don't last forever, a fact that lends support to arguments that passionate romantic love is short-lived. As with any amphetamine, the body builds up a tolerance to PEA; thus it takes more and more of the substance to produce love's special kick. After two to three years, the body simply can't crank up the needed amount of PEA. And chewing on chocolate doesn't help, despite popular belief. The candy is high in PEA, but it fails to boost the body's supply.

Fizzling chemicals spell the end of delirious passion; for many people that marks the   12
end of the liaison as well. It is particularly true for those whom Dr. Michael Liebowitz of the New York State Psychiatric Institute terms "attraction junkies." They crave the intoxication of falling in love so much that they move frantically from affair to affair just as soon as the first rush of infatuation fades.

Still, many romances clearly endure beyond the first years. What accounts for that?   13
Another set of chemicals, of course. The continued presence of a partner gradually steps up production in the brain of endorphins. Unlike the fizzy amphetamines, these are soothing substances. Natural pain-killers, they give lovers a sense of security, peace and calm. "That is one reason why it feels so horrible when we're abandoned or a lover dies," notes Fisher. "We don't have our daily hit of narcotics."

Researchers see a contrast between the heated infatuation induced by PEA, along   14
with other amphetamine-like chemicals, and the more intimate attachment fostered and prolonged by endorphins. "Early love is when you love the way the other person makes you feel," explains psychiatrist Mark Goulston of the University of California, Los Angeles. "Mature love is when you love the person as he or she is." It is the difference between passionate and compassionate love, observes Walsh, a psychobiologist at Boise State University in Idaho. "It's Bon Jovi vs. Beethoven."

Oxytocin is another chemical that has recently been implicated in love. Produced by   15
the brain, it sensitizes nerves and stimulates muscle contraction. In women it helps uterine contractions during childbirth as well as production of breast milk, and seems to inspire mothers to nuzzle their infants. Scientists speculate that oxytocin might encourage similar cuddling between adult women and men. The versatile chemical may also enhance orgasms. In one study of men, oxytocin increased to three to five times its normal level during climax, and it may soar even higher in women. . . .

Chemicals may help explain (at least to scientists) the feelings of passion and com-   16
passion, but why do people tend to fall in love with one partner rather than a myriad of others? Once again, it's partly a function of evolution and biology. "Men are looking for maximal fertility in a mate," says Loyola Marymount's Mills. "That is in large part why females in the prime childbearing ages of 17 to 28 are so desirable." Men can size up youth and vitality in a glance, and studies indeed show that men fall in love quite rapidly. Women tumble more slowly, to a large degree because their requirements are more complex; they need more time to check the guy out. "Age is not vital," notes Mills, "but the ability to provide security, father children, share resources and hold a high status in society are all key factors."

Still, that does not explain why the way Mary walks and laughs makes Bill dizzy with   17
desire while Marcia's gait and giggle leave him cold. "Nature has wired us for one special person," suggests Walsh, romantically. He rejects the idea that a woman or a man can be in love with two people at the same time. Each person carries in his or her mind a unique subliminal guide to the ideal partner, a "love map," to borrow a term coined by sexologist John Money of Johns Hopkins University.

Drawn from the people and experiences of childhood, the map is a record of what-   18
ever we found enticing and exciting—or disturbing and disgusting. Small feet, curly hair.
The way our mothers patted our head or how our fathers told a joke. A fireman's uniform,
a doctor's stethoscope. All the information gathered while growing up is imprinted in the
brain's circuitry by adolescence. Partners never meet each and every requirement, but a
sufficient number of matches can light up the wires and signal, "It's love." Not every partner will be like the last one, since lovers may have different combinations of the characteristics favored by the map.

O.K., that's the scientific point of view. Satisfied? Probably not. To most people—   19
with or without Ph.D.s—love will always be more than the sum of its natural parts. It's a
commingling of body and soul, reality and imagination, poetry and phenylethylamine. In
our deepest hearts, most of us harbor the hope that love will never fully yield up its
secrets, that it will always elude our grasp.

Connecting to Culture and Experience: Love Maps

The chemistry of love is easily summarized: Amphetamines fuel romance; endorphins
and oxytocin sustain lasting relationships. As Toufexis makes clear, however, these
chemical reactions do not explain why people are initially attracted to each other.
Toufexis observes that an initial attraction occurs because each of us carries a "unique
subliminal guide" or "love map" that leads us unerringly to a partner. Moreover, she
explains that in heterosexual pairing, men look for maximal fertility, whereas women
look for security, resources, status, and a willingness to father children.

Discuss these explanations for attraction between the sexes. Consider where your
love map comes from and how much it may be influenced by factors such as age, economic class, sexual orientation, family, ethnicity, or images in the media or advertising.

Analyzing Writing Strategies

1. At the beginning of this chapter, we make several generalizations about essays
   explaining concepts. Consider which of these assertions are true of Toufexis's essay:
   - It seeks to inform readers about a specific subject.
   - It presents information confidently and efficiently.
   - It relies almost exclusively on established information.
   - It does not feature its writer's experiences or feelings.
   - It tends not to argue for its points.
2. To explain a concept, you have to classify the information; that is, group or divide
   it into meaningful categories. Otherwise, you struggle to write about a jumble of
   information, and your readers quickly give up trying to make sense of it. For

example, a writer setting out to explain testing in American colleges to a college student in Thailand would first try to classify the subject by dividing it into categories like the following: short-answer, essay, multiple-choice, lab demonstration, artistic performance. To understand more about how Toufexis divides her information, make a scratch outline of paragraphs 9–15, where she presents the centrally important information on specific chemicals. How is the information divided and sequenced in these paragraphs? What cues does Toufexis provide to help you follow the sequence? What do you find most and least successful about the division? (For illustrations of scratch outlining, turn to Chapter 10, pp. 311–12 and to the Commentary following Linh Kieu Ngo's essay in this chapter.)

Commentary: A Focused Concept and Careful Use of Sources

Unless they are writing an entire book on the subject, writers explaining concepts must focus their attention on some particular aspect of the concept. A relatively brief essay or magazine article offers limited space for approaching a concept from several different angles or attempting to survey everything known about it. Consequently, after getting an overview of what is known about a concept, writers must choose a focus and select information related only to that focus. For instance, Toufexis focuses on the chemistry of love between adult human mates. She excludes parents' love for their children, dogs' love for their masters, views on love by the Catholic church, the history of romance as revealed in literature, courtship rituals in the United States in the 1990s, and dozens of other possible subjects related to love. Toufexis holds to her chemical focus throughout the essay, except for a brief but relevant digression about "love maps" toward the end. When they finish the essay, readers have learned nothing new about love in general, but they are well informed about the neurochemistry of love. By keeping to this narrow focus Toufexis is able to present information that is likely to be new to most readers, and therefore has a better chance of holding readers' attention.

Besides holding to a well-chosen concept focus, concept explanations rely on authoritative, expert sources, on established material gleaned from reputable publications or interviews. Toufexis uses both these kinds of sources. She apparently arranged telephone or in-person interviews with six different professors specializing in diverse academic disciplines: psychology, anthropology, psychiatry, and sexology. (She does not immediately identify the discipline of one professor—Walsh, in paragraph 10— but from the title of his book, we might guess that he is a biochemist, and in paragraph 14 we are not surprised to learn that he is a psychobiologist.) We assume that Toufexis read at least parts of the two books she names in paragraphs 5 and 10, and perhaps she also read other sources, which may have led her to some of the professors she interviewed.

What is obvious about Toufexis's use of sources is that she does not indicate precisely where she obtained all the information she includes. For example, she does not cite the source of the anthropological information in paragraphs 3–5, although a reader might guess that she summarized it from *Anatomy of Love,* cited at the end of paragraph 5. We cannot be certain whether the quote at the end of paragraph 5 comes from the book or from an interview with its author. These liberties in citing sources are acceptable in newspapers and magazines, including the leading ones educated readers count on to keep them up to date on developments in various fields. Experienced readers know that reporters, who write about surprisingly diverse topics as part of their jobs, rely entirely on sources for their articles and essays. They understand that Toufexis is not an expert on the neurochemistry of love; they accept her role as synthesizer and summarizer of authoritative sources. In most college writing situations, however, you will be expected to cite formally all of your sources.

Observing an important requirement of essays explaining concepts, Toufexis provides several different kinds of cues to keep readers on track. In addition to paragraph-opening transitions, Toufexis carefully forecasts the topics and direction of her essay in her second paragraph: "their probe reveals that love rests firmly on the foundations of evolution, biology and chemistry." This forecast helps readers anticipate the types of scientific information Toufexis has selected for her special focus on love and the sequence in which she will introduce them.

Considering Topics for Your Own Essay

Like Toufexis, you could write an essay about love or romance, but with a different focus: on its history (how and when did it develop as an idea in the West?), its cultural characteristics (how is love regarded presently among different American ethnic groups or world cultures?), its excesses or extremes, its expression between parent and child, or the phases of falling in and out of love. Also consider writing about other concepts involving personal relationships, such as "jealousy," "codependency," "idealization," "stereotyping," or "homophobia."

Carol Potera, *a freelance writer living in Great Falls, Montana, writes about topics and issues in medicine and science for WebMD, Shape magazine, and other publications. She has worked as a researcher and writer in the Department of Human Oncology, University of Wisconsin, Madison, and at the Eleanor Roosevelt Institute for Cancer Research in Denver. Her awards include a 1990 Deems Taylor Award sponsored by the American Society of Composers, Authors, and Publishers for a profile of an academic chemist who studies the materials and sound qualities of the famous Stradivarius violins and a 1999 science writing fellowship at the Molecular Biological Laboratory, Woods Hole, Massachusetts. In this 1998 essay from Psychology Today, Potera explains a relatively new concept—Internet addiction. She identifies an addict as someone who spends around forty hours a week on the Internet, most of it in chat rooms or at interactive game sites, and who is experiencing personal, social, academic, or occupational problems as a result. Like all the authors in this chapter, Potera relies on experts for the information she needs. As you read, think about your own use of the Internet. How much of it is for academic or personal purposes and how much for diversion or entertainment?*

Internet Addiction

Carol Potera

Frustration with the sluggish speed of a browser is about the most serious psychological pitfall that most of us face when surfing the World Wide Web. But for as many as five million Americans, experts say, the Internet has become a destructive force, its remarkable benefits overshadowed by its potential to disrupt the lives of those who can't resist the lure of round-the-clock social opportunities, entertainment, and information. For such people, work, friends, family, and sleep are replaced by a virtual world of chat rooms and games.

Take Judy and Bob, a Seattle couple who were saving to buy their first house — until monthly credit card bills started arriving with $350 charges for online services. Bob was "pissing away all our money on the Internet," says Judy. And soon he was doing likewise to their marriage. Every evening Bob came home from work and headed straight for the computer; he stopped joining Judy for dinner or helping with household chores. At 10 P.M. each night Judy hit the sack, while Bob stumbled to bed some five hours later. Before long he was sucked into cyberspace 40 or 50 hours a week. When it became clear after six months that Bob had chosen his online world over his real one, Judy left.

Such tales became increasingly common in the early 1990s, when the growing popularity of commercial providers made the Internet affordable and accessible to anyone with a personal computer, modem, and phone. Only recently, however, have psychologists begun devising strategies to wean online addicts from their endless browsing and chatting. And while it's too soon to say how successful their efforts have been, their hope is that the extent of the problem will be recognized before it becomes even more widespread.

Cybertrouble

One of the first experts to notice that some people were spending an unhealthy amount of time on the Internet was Kimberly Young, Ph.D., an assistant professor of psychology at the University of Pittsburgh, Bradford. In 1994, Young launched the first major study of the problem, surveying nearly 500 avid Internet users about their online habits. Because there was no formal definition for the disorder — which she quickly christened "Internet addiction" — Young classified study participants as "dependent" or "nondependent" Internet users based on their answers to seven questions she adapted from those used to diagnose pathological gambling. (Sample question: Do you experience withdrawal symptoms — depression, agitation, moodiness — when not online?) Those who answered "yes" to three or more questions were classified as dependent.

On average, Young found, dependents spent an astonishing 38 hours a week online, compared with just five hours a week for nondependents. And usually they were not cruising the information highway to enrich their knowledge of El Niño or the Russian space station. Instead, dependents sought contact with other people: their favorite activities were chat rooms (35 percent) and Multi User Dungeon games (28 percent), while nondependents were most likely to use the Internet for electronic mail (30 percent) and searching the World Wide Web (25 percent). Similarly, a 1996 survey of 530 college students by

Kathy Scherer, Ph.D., a psychologist at the University of Texas at Austin, found that dependents and nondependents spent similar amounts of time exchanging email and searching the Web, but dependents spent twice as much time in chat rooms and playing games.

None of the nondependents in Young's study reported academic, personal, financial, or occupational problems caused by their Internet use. But about half of dependents reported problems in all of these areas. Yet many dependents insisted they couldn't give up the Internet; a few even tossed out their modems, but their Internet cravings led them to buy a new one to get their cyberspace fix. In fact, the smokers in the study reported that their cravings for the Internet were stronger than the urge to light up a cigarette.   6

Who's at Risk?

Most Internet users don't become addicted. Among people who gamble or drink alcohol, about 5 to 10 percent develop problem behaviors, and Young believes that the figures are similar for pathological Internet behavior. With an estimated 47 million people currently online, as many as two to five million could be addicted. Especially vulnerable, Young believes, are those who are lonely, bored, depressed, introverted, lack self-esteem, or have a history of addictions.   7

Perhaps the most surprising—and widely reported—finding in Young's original study was that the majority (60 percent) of dependent users were middle-aged women, particularly housewives, not young male computer geeks. But this has not held up in later studies, which give men a slight edge. Young suspects a bias occurred in her first study, perhaps because women are more likely to admit and talk about their problems. Still, she understands the appeal that chat rooms hold for these women and others in her sample. "You never worry about how you look or how nice a house you have, and you talk to people all over the world. It's instant gratification without having to reveal yourself." Lonely housewives or shy sophomores can feel like exciting people when online. "It's novel and unique, and they get attached to the people they meet online," Young says.   8

Indeed, like alcoholics with favorite drinking buddies, Internet addicts form close bonds that fuel their compulsions. Dan, a college student, earned a 3.2 grade point average his freshman year. Then he moved in with roommates who played an interactive Multi User Dungeon computer game as a team from separate computers, and soon began logging on 50 to 60 hours a week. Dan's grade point average nose-dived to 1.6. His fiancée began to complain that he spent too much time with his computer friends; they, in turn, griped when he signed off to spend time with her. Faced with the reality that he might not graduate or get married, Dan tried to cut back, a goal that grew easier after his roommates graduated. A year later, his use was down to 10 hours per week. "I still get high on the Internet," he admits, "but I'm in control."   9

Get high? Internet addiction? Time was when the word "addiction" referred to drug and alcohol problems—period. Today, so-called addictions are everywhere: sex, exercise, work, chocolate, TV, shopping, and now the Internet. Have we been, well, abusing the word?   10

An Addiction? Really?

"Addiction," notes Young, "is a layman's term, not a clinical one." In fact, the DSM-IV[1] 11
doesn't even mention the word. Young chose the label "Internet addiction" because it's
readily understandable by the public. When writing for clinical journals, however, she refers
to "pathological Internet use," modeling the term after that for pathological gambling in the
DSM-IV.

Other experts shun the term addiction altogether because it means too many things 12
to too many people. "It's a sloppy word," says pharmacologist Carlton Erickson, Ph.D.,
head of the Addiction Science Research and Education Center at the University of Texas
at Austin. In the drug abuse field, he notes, "dependence" has replaced "addiction." "In
dependence, people can't stop because they have developed a brain chemistry that
does not allow them to stop," explains Erickson. Excessive behavior that hasn't quite
reached full-fledged dependency, meanwhile, is called "abuse." If Internet abusers cannot stop for a month, suggests Erickson, then "Internet dependence" would be the appropriate term. Others believe that the problem is best described as a compulsion,
suggesting the phrase "compulsive Internet use." And many psychologists question
whether excessive Internet use should be pathologized at all: John Grohol, Ph.D., who
directs the Web site "Mental Health Net," says that by the same logic, bookworms should
be diagnosed with "book addiction disorder."

Perhaps the controversy will be definitively resolved when researchers determine 13
whether behaviors like pathological gambling or Internet addiction produce chemical
changes in the brain similar to those found in drug abusers. In the meantime, Young
believes that the often severe personal consequences of Internet addiction justify popular
use of the term. "Internet addiction does not cause the same physical problems as other
addictions," she says, "but the social problems parallel those of established addictions."

Treatments for Internet addiction are beginning to emerge. Trouble is, not all mental 14
health specialists recognize the problem or know how to treat it. Internet dependents
have been told by uninformed therapists to simply "turn off the computer." That's like
telling a heroin addict to just say no to drugs—and just as unsuccessful. What's more,
HMOs and insurance companies do not pay for Internet addiction therapy because it's
not recognized by the DSM-IV.

Among those developing treatments for the problem is Maressa Hecht Orzack, Ph.D., 15
a psychologist at Harvard University's McLean Hospital in Belmont, Massachusetts. Orzack
founded Harvard's Computer Addiction Services in Fall 1996, after seeing firsthand the fall-
out from Internet-related problems: divorce, child neglect, job termination, debt, flunking out
of school, legal trouble. One client, she says, had separated from his wife but couldn't afford
to move out because he spent so much money on computer services. He moved his bed
into the computer room and started an affair with an online sweetheart.

---

[1] The *Diagnostic and Statistical Manual of Mental Disorders: DSM-IV,* used by medical professionals

A cognitive therapist, Orzack likens Internet addiction to such impulse control disorders as pathological gambling and kleptomania. However, "gamblers have a choice to gamble or not," she notes. "People addicted to the Internet often do not have that choice, since so many activities require people to use a computer." 16

Like Binge-Eating

So the best approach for excessive Internet use, Orzack believes, will be to treat it like binge eating, where the individual frequently engages in the activity to be restricted. She treats both by teaching clients how to set limits, balance activities, and schedule time, without having to go cold turkey. "People often change in six or eight sessions," she says. 17

Unfortunately, the afflicted rarely admit to the problem, and it usually takes a crisis with a job, relationship, or school to spur an Internet addict to seek treatment. More often, it's loved ones who turn to the experts. "Families notice things and call me," says Orzack. And she receives letters like this: "We got divorced one year after we got the computer. My wife was in chat rooms all the time and ignored our young daughter. She spent hundreds of dollars on phone bills . . . [and] had an affair online that turned into a real affair. . . . Then she left. I don't know what to do. Please help." Now lawyers and family courts call Orzack and Young wanting them to testify about Internet addiction in divorce and custody battles. (In October, a Florida woman lost custody of her kids when her ex-husband convinced a judge that the woman was addicted to the Internet and thus incapable of properly caring for their children.) 18

College students are often vulnerable to Internet addiction because many universities provide free, unlimited access. At the University of Texas Counseling and Mental Health Center at Austin, Scherer and her computer scientist husband Jacob Kornerup created a workshop, called It's 4 A.M. and I Can't—Uh, Won't—Log Off, to help students recognize harmful Internet habits. Scherer and Kornerup recommend keeping a chart sorting weekly Internet time into academic/professional and leisure/personal use. If a large part of your leisure time is spent on the Internet, she says, ask what you get out of it, what you're giving up, and why you're finding online time so much more pleasurable than other activities. Take note if your personal relationships are suffering. 19

Next, set a goal of how many hours a week you want to use the Internet. If your actual usage exceeds it, remind yourself to log off after a period of time. Set a kitchen timer and turn off the computer—no excuses—when it rings. 20

It's particularly important to separate work and play when online, says Jane Morgan Bost, Ph.D., assistant director of the University of Texas Counseling and Mental Health Center. Stay focused, visit only sites needed to complete work, and don't detour. Also, she says, cut back mailing list memberships and sort play e-mail from work e-mail. 21

None of the experts *Psychology Today* spoke with demonize the Internet; they use it extensively themselves and applaud the benefits of rapid communication and information exchange. But, they add, the Internet is here to stay, and problems with excessive use need to be addressed. . . . 22

Are You Addicted to the Internet?

Psychologist Kimberly Young, Ph.D., has identified several warning signs of excessive   23
Internet use. Behaviors that signal concern include:

- Staying online longer than you intended
- Admitting that you can't stop from signing on
- Neglecting loved ones, chores, sleep, reading, television, friends, exercise, hobbies, sex, or social events because of the Internet
- Spending 38 hours or more a week online
- Failing to cut down on time online
- Feeling anxious, bored, sad, lonely, angry, or stressed before going online, but feeling happy, excited, loved, calmed, or confident while on the Internet
- Favoring chat rooms, games, and Multi User Dungeons over other Internet activities

Connecting to Culture and Experience: Wasting Time Online

From researcher Kimberly Young's definition of nondependent Internet users, readers might infer that nondependents are always purposeful and efficient when they are online. Our own experience, however, tells us that it is nearly impossible to avoid wasting any time on the Internet, given the ease of writing email notes to friends, checking out advertised products, playing games, following more tangents at a site than are necessary to fulfill our purpose researching some subject, checking out sites that promise entertainment and diversion, and so on. Is there an Internet saint somewhere who has never wasted a moment on the Internet? Probably not. As Potera points out, unlike gambling addiction, which requires that you drive or get other transportation to a casino, Internet addiction is easily satisfied by a push of a button—the one that powers up your ever-present personal computer. Computers with Internet access have become as much a part of daily life as a toothbrush. How do you manage this new electronic element of your life?

Discuss the features of the Internet that seem to make occasional time-wasting inevitable. Tell about one or two recent instances when you relied on the Internet for diversion. What was the situation? Did you go online looking for diversion, or did you pursue it while doing research, seeking information, or responding to messages that called for a reply? How long did the diversion last? Did you have the feeling you had unwisely spent too much time online? How do these experiences help you understand Internet addiction, as Potera and the researchers define it?

Analyzing Writing Strategies

1. Like the other writers in this chapter, Potera relies on sources for the information she needs to explain her subject, and, like Anastasia Toufexis, she acknowledges those sources informally within the sentences of her essay. Skim the essay and list all of the experts she relies on (text, interview, and Internet sources). Write down

the last name of each expert, along with brief phrases identifying that person's primary academic focus (for example, psychology) and key professional qualification. Include the paragraph numbers where each expert is mentioned. Some will be mentioned only one time, others more than one time.

Then consider these questions: How many different experts and academic specialties does Potera refer to? Given her purpose and readers, does Potera refer to enough experts? Too many? How does Potera establish the authority of each professional? Given the facts Potera presents about each expert, do you think they all seem equally well qualified? Do any seem unqualified or clearly less qualified than the others? Does one expert stand out as better qualified than the others? Which one does Potera most rely on — and why? Is there an expert you would like to have heard more from? If so, explain why briefly. (For more information on evaluating sources with a critical eye, see Chapter 13, pp. 384–87.)

2. Potera makes good use of causes and effects to explain Internet addiction. Given her focus on Internet addiction as a problem needing a solution, it is appropriate and even essential for her to rely on these two strategies: She wants readers to know what causes this addiction and what its effects are on those addicted. Potera presents the effects through both cases (paragraphs 2 and 9) and explanation (4–6). She presents the causes of Internet addiction in paragraphs 7 and 8.

In these paragraphs, underline specific effects and causes. Then consider whether Potera presents enough effects and causes to explain Internet addiction to readers unfamiliar with it. Can you think of any effects or causes she has overlooked? Why do you think she uses both personal anecdotes (paragraphs 2 and 9) and research findings (4–6) to present effects? Given her purpose and readers, how well do you think she covers possible causes for the addiction?

Commentary: Defining an Emerging Phenomenon

Definitions are important to an essay explaining a concept. Even though a concept can be examined and illustrated in various ways, at some point it must be defined. With an emerging phenomenon — one that researchers and writers are trying to understand fully — there may not yet be agreement on how to define it and what to call it. Nevertheless, if the concept is to become widely understood, it has to have an agreed-upon name. Potera's essay well illustrates the struggle to name a new phenomenon. She reports on the struggle, but at the same time she selects a favorite name for the concept and defines it clearly.

Potera reports that experts are divided over what to call a behavior that occupies forty or more hours a week and usually results in personal problems of various kinds (paragraphs 10–16). One expert, psychologist Kimberly Young, prefers the term "Internet addiction" when writing for the general public but relies on the term "pathological Internet use" when writing for academic journals in her field. Pharmacologist Carlton Erickson prefers the term "Internet dependence," making a distinction between dependency and "abuse," which he would use to identify behavior that "hasn't quite reached full-fledged dependency." Other specialists Potera does not identify prefer the term "compulsion," leading her to suggest the term "compulsive Internet disorder." Psychologist Maressa Orzack likes the term "impulse control disorder." For readers, Potera's explanation of the experts' division over what to call this new Internet-related behavior provides important information. It also allows Potera to demonstrate near-universal agreement among experts that the phenomenon exists and should be taken seriously. It even allows her to quote one expert who says, in effect, if we are not worried about people reading too much, why should we be worried about people being online too much? This expert would say that the phenomenon is none of the above.

Potera would lose authority with readers if she took sides in this dispute, and yet in order to explain her subject, she must settle on a name for it. Her subject is not the dispute itself but the phenomenon, whatever it may eventually be called by the experts and the general public. She uses Kimberly Young to resolve this problem, quoting Young as saying that for now the most sensible term to use is "Internet addiction," the term that best suggests "the often severe personal consequences" and "the social problems" of alcohol and drug addiction.

Potera relies on two anecdotes (in paragraphs 2 and 9) and the research findings of Young and psychologist Kathy Scherer to define Internet addiction. Instead of attempting a one- or two-sentence definition, she provides in paragraphs 1–9 a full profile of the Internet addict.

Toward the end of her essay, Potera focuses on treatments for Internet addiction. She does not, however, describe any one treatment at length or argue that one treatment is more effective than the others. Therefore, she does not propose a solution to the problem of Internet addiction. Instead, she merely surveys briefly several approaches to treatment that reflect the different approaches to understanding Internet addiction she has presented earlier in her essay.

Considering Topics for Your Own Essay

Consider writing an essay that would explain and help you learn about another type of addictive behavior or illness that can strain interpersonal relationships, such as drug or alcohol abuse or dependence, binge-eating, pathological gambling, domestic violence, hypochondriasis, mood disorders, or phobic behaviors. You can find introductions to these conditions in professional reference books such as the *Diagnostic and Statistical Manual of Mental Disorders: DSM-IV.* You would also want to look for current research on your topic. Notice that an essay on drug addiction appears in this book on pp. 146–47.

Linh Kieu Ngo wrote this essay as a first-year college student. In it, he defines a concept of importance in anthropology and of wide general interest—cannibalism, the eating of human flesh by other humans. Most Americans know about survival cannibalism but few may know *about the importance historically of dietary and ritual cannibalism. Ngo explains all of these types in his essay. As you read, notice how he relies on examples to illustrate the types.*

Cannibalism: It Still Exists

Linh Kieu Ngo

Fifty-five Vietnamese refugees fled to Malaysia on a small   1
fishing boat to escape communist rule in their country following the Vietnam War. During their escape attempt, the
captain was shot by the coast guard. The boat and its passengers managed to outrun the coast guard to the open
sea, but they had lost the only person who knew the way to Malaysia, the captain.

The men onboard tried to navigate the boat, but after a week fuel ran out and they   2
drifted farther out to sea. Their supply of food and water was gone; people were starving,
and some of the elderly were near death. The men managed to produce a small amount
of drinking water by boiling salt water, using dispensable wood from the boat to create a
small fire near the stern. They also tried to fish, but had little success.

A month went by, and the old and weak died. At first, the crew threw the dead over   3
board, but later, out of desperation, the crew turned to human flesh as a source of food.
Some people vomited as they attempted to eat it, while others refused to resort to cannibalism and see the bodies of their loved ones sacrificed for food. Those who did not eat
died of starvation, and their bodies in turn became food for others. Human flesh was cut
out, washed in salt water, and hung to dry for preservation. The liquids inside the cranium
were eaten to quench thirst. The livers, kidneys, heart, stomach, and intestines were
boiled and eaten.

Five months passed before a whaling vessel discovered the drifting boat, looking like   4
a graveyard of bones. There was only one survivor.

Cannibalism, the act of human beings eating human flesh (Sagan 2), has a long his-   5
tory and continues to hold interest and create controversy. Many books and research
reports offer examples of cannibalism, but a few scholars have questioned whether cannibalism was ever practiced anywhere, except in cases of ensuring survival in times of
famine or isolation (Askenasy 43–54). Recently, some scholars have tried to understand
why people in the West have been so eager to attribute cannibalism to non-westerners
(Barker, Hulme, and Iversen). Cannibalism has long been a part of American popular culture. For example, Mark Twain's "Cannibalism in the Cars" tells a humorous story about
cannibalism by well-to-do travelers on a train stranded in a snowstorm, and cannibalism
is still a popular subject for jokes ("Cannibal Jokes").

If we assume there is some reality to the reports about cannibalism, how can we   6
best understand this concept? Cannibalism can be broken down into two main categories: exocannibalism, the eating of outsiders or foreigners, and endocannibalism, the
eating of members of one's own social group (Shipman 70). Within these categories are
several functional types of cannibalism, three of the most common being survival cannibalism, dietary cannibalism, and religious and ritual cannibalism.

Survival cannibalism occurs when people trapped without food have to decide   7
"whether to starve or eat fellow humans" (Shipman 70). In the case of the Vietnamese
refugees, the crew and passengers on the boat ate human flesh to stay alive. They did

not kill people to get human flesh for nourishment, but instead waited until the people had died. Even after human carcasses were sacrificed as food, the boat people ate only enough to survive. Another case of survival cannibalism occured in 1945, when General Douglas MacArthur's forces cut supply lines to Japanese troops stationed in the Pacific Islands. In one incident, Japanese troops were reported to have sacrificed the Arapesh people of northeastern New Guinea for food in order to avoid death by starvation (Tuzin 63). The most famous example of survival cannibalism in American history comes from the diaries, letters, and interviews of survivors of the California-bound Donner Party, who in the winter of 1846 were snowbound in the Sierra Nevada Mountains for five months. Thirty-five of eighty-seven adults and children died, and some of them were eaten (Hart 116–17; Johnson).

Unlike survival cannibalism, in which human flesh is eaten as a last resort after a person has died, in dietary cannibalism, humans are purchased or trapped for food and then eaten as a part of a culture's traditions. In addition, survival cannibalism often involves people eating other people of the same origins, whereas dietary cannibalism usually involves people eating foreigners.   8

In the Miyanmin society of the west Sepik interior of Papua, New Guinea, villagers do not value human flesh over that of pigs or marsupials because human flesh is part of their diet (Poole 17). The Miyanmin people observe no differences in "gender, kinship, ritual status, and bodily substance"; they eat anyone, even their own dead. In this respect, then, they practice both endocannibalism and exocannibalism; and to ensure a constant supply of human flesh for food, they raid neighboring tribes and drag their victims back to their village to be eaten (Poole 11). Perhaps, in the history of this society, there was at one time a shortage of wild game to be hunted for food, and because people were more plentiful than fish, deer, rabbits, pigs, or cows, survival cannibalism was adopted as a last resort. Then, as their culture developed, the Miyanmin may have retained the practice of dietary cannibalism, which has endured as a part of their culture.   9

Similar to the Miyanmin, the people of the Leopard and Alligator societies in South America eat human flesh as part of their cultural tradition. Practicing dietary exocannibalism, the Leopard people hunt in groups, with one member wearing the skin of a leopard to conceal the face. They ambush their victims in the forest and carry their victims back to their village to be eaten. The Alligator people also hunt in groups, but they hide themselves under a canoelike submarine that resembles an alligator, then swim close to a fisherman's or trader's canoe to overturn it and catch their victims (MacCormack 54).   10

Religious or ritual cannibalism is different from survival and dietary cannibalism in that it has a ceremonial purpose rather than one of nourishment. Sometimes only a single victim is sacrificed in a ritual, while at other times many are sacrificed. For example, the Bangala tribe of the Congo River in central Africa honors a deceased chief or leader by purchasing, sacrificing, and feasting on slaves (Sagan 53). The number of slaves sacrificed is determined by how highly the tribe members revered the deceased leader.   11

Ritual cannibalism among South American Indians often serves as revenge for the dead. Like the Bangalas, some South American tribes kill their victims to be served as part of funeral rituals, with human sacrifices denoting that the deceased was held in high   12 honor. Also like the Bangalas, these tribes use outsiders as victims. Unlike the Bangalas, however, the Indians sacrifice only one victim instead of many in a single ritual. For example, when a warrior of a tribe is killed in battle, the family of the warrior forces a victim to take the identity of the warrior. The family adorns the victim with the deceased warrior's belongings and may even force him to marry the deceased warrior's wives. But once the family believes the victim has assumed the spiritual identity of the deceased warrior, the family kills him. The children in the tribe soak their hands in the victim's blood to symbolize their revenge of the warrior's death. Elderly women from the tribe drink the victim's blood and then cut up his body for roasting and eating (Sagan 53–54). By sacrificing a victim, the people of the tribe believe that the death of the warrior has been avenged and the soul of the deceased can rest in peace.

In the villages of certain African tribes, only a small part of a dead body is used in ritual cannibalism. In these tribes, where the childbearing capacity of women is highly valued, women are obligated to eat small, raw fragments of genital parts during fertility rites. Elders of the tribe supervise this ritual to ensure that the women will be fertile. In the Bimin-Kuskusmin tribe, for instance, a widow eats a small, raw fragment of flesh from the penis of her deceased husband in order to enhance her future fertility and reproductive capacity. Similarly, a widower may eat a raw fragment of flesh from his deceased wife's vagina along with a piece of her bone marrow; by eating her flesh, he hopes to strengthen the fertility capacity of his daughters borne by his dead wife, and by eating her bone marrow, he honors her reproductive capacity. Also, when an elder woman of the village who has shown great reproductive capacity dies, her uterus and the interior parts of her vagina are eaten by other women who hope to further benefit from her reproductive power (Poole 16–17). 13

Members of developed societies in general practice none of these forms of cannibalism, with the occasional exception of survival cannibalism when the only alternative is starvation. It is possible, however, that our distant-past ancestors were cannibals who through the eons turned away from the practice. We are, after all, descended from the same ancestors as the Miyanmin, the Alligator, and the Leopard people, and survival cannibalism shows that people are capable of eating human flesh when they have no other choice. 14

Works Cited

Askenasy, Hans. *Cannibalism: From Sacrifice to Survival.* Amherst, NY: Prometheus, 1994.

Barker, Francis, Peter Hulme, and Margaret Iversen, eds. *Cannibalism and the New World.* Cambridge: Cambridge UP, 1998.

Brown, Paula, and Donald Tuzin, eds. *The Ethnography of Cannibalism.* Washington: Society of Psychological Anthropology, 1983.

"Cannibal Jokes." The Loonie Bin of Jokes. 22 Sept. 1999 <http://www.looniebin.mb.ca/cannibal.html>.

Hart, James D. *A Companion to California.* Berkeley: U of California P, 1987.

Johnson, Kristin. "New Light on the Donner Party." 28 Sept. 1999 <http://www.metrogourmet.com/crossroads.KJhome.htm>.

MacCormack, Carol. "Human Leopard and Crocodile." Brown and Tuzin 54–55.

Poole, Fitz John Porter. "Cannibals, Tricksters, and Witches." Brown and Tuzin, 11, 16–17.

Sagan, Eli. *Cannibalism.* New York: Harper, 1976.

Shipman, Pat. "The Myths and Perturbing Realities of Cannibalism." *Discover* Mar. 1987: 70+.

Tuzin, Donald. "Cannibalism and Arapesh Cosmology." Brown and Tuzin 61–63.

Twain, Mark. "Cannibalism in the Cars." *The Complete Short Stories of Mark Twain.* Ed. Charles Neider. New York: Doubleday, 1957. 9–16.

Connecting to Culture and Experience: Taboos

The author of a respected book on the Donner Party has this to say about the fact that some members of the party ate other members after they had died:

> Surely the necessity, starvation itself, had forced them to all they did, and surely no just man would ever have pointed at them in scorn, or assumed his own superiority.... Even the seemingly ghoulish actions involved in the story may be rationally explained. To open the bodies first for the heart and liver, and to saw apart the skulls for the brain were not acts of perversion. We must remember that these people had been living for months upon the hides and lean meat of half-starved work oxen; their diet was lacking not only in mere quantity, but also in all sorts of necessary vitamins and mineral constituents, even in common salt. Almost uncontrollable cravings must have assailed them, cravings which represented a real deficiency in diet to be supplied in some degree at least by the organs mentioned.
>
> —GEORGE R. STEWART, *Ordeal by Hunger*

With other students, discuss this author's argument and his unwillingness to pass judgment on the Donner Party's cannibalism. Individually, are you inclined to agree or disagree with the author? Give reasons for your views. Keep in mind that no one, perhaps with one exception toward the very end of the Donner Party's isolation, was murdered in order to be eaten. Therefore, the issue is not murder but humans' eating other humans' flesh and body parts in order to remain alive. Humans do eat many other animals' flesh and body parts for nourishment. Where do you think the taboo against human cannibalism comes from in our society? Do you believe it should be observed in all circumstances? Do you think the taboo should be extended to the consumption of animal flesh?

Analyzing Writing Strategies

1. Ngo organizes his explanation around two categories and three types of cannibalism. Review this classification in paragraph 6. Then analyze how Ngo defines the five terms of the classification. Begin by underlining the definitions in paragraphs

6–8 and 12. Some definitions are given in a single phrase, and others are made up of several phrases, not always contiguous. Exclude the examples from your underlining. Then look over the definitions you have underlined with the following questions in mind: What makes these definitions easy or hard for you to understand? In what ways does the example that begins the essay (paragraphs 1–4) prepare you to understand the definitions? How do the examples that follow the definitions help you understand each concise definition?

2. As he explains the different types of cannibalism, Ngo makes good use of examples in paragraphs 7–13. Choose *one* of the longer examples in paragraph 9, 12, or 13, and analyze how it is put together and how effective it is. How many sentences long is the example? What kinds of information does it offer? What sources does the writer rely on? What seems most memorable or surprising to you in the example? How does it help you understand the type of cannibalism being illustrated? In general, how effective does it seem to you as an example of the concept?

Commentary: A Logical Plan

Writers face special challenges in planning essays that explain concepts. First they gather a lot of information about a concept. Then they find a focus for the explanation. With the focus in mind, they research the concept further, looking just for information to develop the focus. At this point they have to find a way to collect the information into logically related topics. This process is known formally as classifying. Sometimes, as in Ngo's research, one of the sources provides the classification, but sometimes the writer has to create it. This borrowing or creation allows writers to plan their essays—to identify the topics in the order in which they will present them. Ngo's explanation of cannibalism well illustrates the importance of a logical plan. (For more on scratch outlines, see Chapter 10, p. 311.) The following topical scratch outline of the essay will help you see Ngo's classification and plan:

- Narration of a specific recent incident of cannibalism (paragraphs 1–4)
- Context for the concept (5)
- Definition of cannibalism and introduction of its two main categories and three types (6)
- Definition of survival cannibalism, with two brief examples (7)
- Definition of dietary cannibalism (8)
- Two extended examples of dietary cannibalism (9 and 10)
- Definition of ritual cannibalism, with one brief example (11)
- Two extended examples of ritual cannibalism (12 and 13)
- Conclusion (14)

Ngo presents the classification in paragraph 6. It has two levels. In the first level the information is divided into exocannibalism and endocannibalism. In the second level each of the first two divisions is divided into three parts: survival, dietary, and ritual cannibalism. That is, in each of these three types of cannibalism, either outsiders or members of one's own group can be eaten. Ngo relies on the three types of cannibalism to create a plan for his essay. First he explains survival cannibalism, then dietary cannibalism, and finally, ritual cannibalism. This plan may be considered logical in at least two ways: it moves from most to least familiar and from least to most complex. Perhaps Ngo assumes his readers will know about the Donner Party, an unfortunate group of 1846 immigrants to California who were trapped high in the Sierra Nevada Mountains by early, heavy snowstorms and ended up practicing survival endocannibalism. Therefore, Ngo explains this type of cannibalism first and then moves on to the less-familiar types. It seems that these two less-familiar types are also the most complex in that their practice takes different forms around the world. Ngo devotes two or three times more space to explaining dietary and ritual cannibalism than he does to explaining survival cannibalism, and he presents the examples in more detail.

Ngo does more than adopt a classification and put it to use to plan his essay. He helps readers anticipate and follow the plan by forecasting it and then providing obvious cues to the steps in the plan. At the end of paragraph 6, Ngo forecasts the types of cannibalism he will focus on: "survival cannibalism, dietary cannibalism, and religious and ritual cannibalism." It is considered a forecast because it introduces the names or terms Ngo will use consistently throughout the explanation and because Ngo presents these types of cannibalism in the order he lists them here. Readers are thereby prepared for the step-by-step plan of the explanation. (For more about forecasting, see p. 275 in Chapter 8.)

Ngo lets readers know when he is leaving one type of cannibalism and addressing the next type by constructing visible transitions at the beginnings of paragraphs. Here are the three key transition sentences:

Survival cannibalism occurs when people trapped without food have to decide "whether to starve or eat fellow humans. . . ." (paragraph 7)

Unlike survival cannibalism, in which human flesh is eaten as a last resort after a person has died, in dietary cannibalism, humans are purchased or trapped for food and then eaten as a part of a culture's traditions. (8)

Religious or ritual cannibalism is different from survival and dietary cannibalism in that it has a ceremonial purpose rather than one of nourishment. (11)

(For more about transitions, turn to pp. 277–78 in Chapter 8.)

You can feature these types of cues—forecasts and transitions—in your essay explaining a concept. Whereas forecasting is optional, transitions are essential; without them, your readers will either stumble along resentfully or throw up their hands in confusion and irritation.

Considering Topics for Your Own Essay

Consider writing about some other cultural taboo or practice such as ostracism, incest, pedophilia, murder, circumcision, celibacy or virginity, caste systems, a particular religion's dietary restrictions, adultery, stealing, gourmandism, or divorce.

■ PURPOSE AND AUDIENCE

Though it often seeks to engage readers' interests, explanatory writing gives prominence to the facts about its subject. It aims at readers' intellect rather than their imagination, determined to instruct rather than entertain or argue.

To set out to teach readers about a concept is no small undertaking. To succeed, you must know the concept so well that you can explain it simply, without jargon or other confusing language. You must be authoritative without showing off or talking down. You must also estimate what your readers already know about the concept in order to decide which information will be truly new to them. You want to define unfamiliar words and pace the information carefully so that your readers are neither bored nor overwhelmed.

This assignment requires a willingness to cast yourself in the role of expert, which may not come naturally to you at this stage in your development as a writer. Students are most often asked to explain things in writing to readers who know more than they do — their instructors. When you plan and draft this essay, however, you will be aiming at readers who know less — maybe much less — than you do about the concept you will explain. Like Toufexis and Potera, you could write for a general audience of adults who regularly read a newspaper and subscribe to a few magazines. Even though some of them may be highly educated, you can readily and confidently assume the role of expert after a couple of hours of research into your concept. Your purpose may be to deepen your readers' understanding of a concept they may already be familiar with. You could also write for upper elementary or secondary school students, introducing them to an unfamiliar concept, or for your classmates, demonstrating to them that a concept in an academic discipline they find forbidding can actually be made both understandable and interesting. Even if you are told to consider your instructor your sole reader, you can assume that your instructor is eager to be informed about nearly any concept you choose.

You have spent many years in school reading explanations of concepts: Your textbooks in every subject have been full of concept explanations. Now, instead of receiving these explanations, you will be delivering one. To succeed, you will have to accept your role of expert. Your readers will expect you to be authoritative and well informed; they will also expect that you have limited the focus of your explanation but that you have not excluded anything essential to their understanding.

BASIC FEATURES: EXPLAINING CONCEPTS

A Focused Concept

The primary purpose for explaining a concept is to inform readers, but writers of explanatory essays do not hope to say everything there is to say about a concept. Instead, they make choices about what to include, what to emphasize, and what to omit. Most writers focus on one aspect of the concept. Anastasia Toufexis, for example, focuses on the neurochemistry of love, and Linh Kieu Ngo focuses on types of cannibalism.

An Appeal to Readers' Interests

Most people read explanations of concepts for work or study. Consequently, they do not expect the writing to be entertaining, but simply informative. Yet readers appreciate explanations that both make clear the concept's importance and keep them awake with lively writing and vivid detail. The essays in this chapter show some of the ways in which writers may appeal to readers — for example, by using humor and unaffected, everyday language; by giving readers reasons for learning about the concept; or by showing how the concept might apply personally to them.

A Logical Plan

Since concept explanations present information that is new to readers and can therefore be hard to understand, writers need to develop a plan that presents new material step by step in a logical order. The most effective explanations are carefully organized and give readers all the obvious cues they need, such as forecasting statements, topic sentences, transitions, and summaries. In addition, the writer may try to frame the essay for readers by relating the ending to the beginning. We have seen these features repeatedly in the readings in this chapter. For example, Toufexis frames her essay with references to Ph.D.s, forecasts the three sciences from which she has gleaned her information about the neurochemistry of love, and begins nearly all of her paragraphs with a transition sentence.

Good writers never forget that their readers need clear signals. Because writers already know the information and are aware of how their essays are organized, it can be difficult for them to see the essay the way someone reading it for the first time would. That is precisely how it should be seen, however, to be sure that the essay includes all the necessary cues.

Clear Definitions

Essays explaining concepts depend on clear definitions. To relate information clearly, a writer must be sensitive to readers' knowledge; any key terms that are likely to be unfamiliar or misunderstood must be explicitly defined. Toufexis defines *attraction junkies* (paragraph 12) and *endorphins* (13), and Ngo defines the *categories* of cannibalism (6) and *types* of cannibalism (at the beginnings of paragraphs where he illustrates them). In a sense, all the readings in this chapter are extended definitions of concepts, and all the authors offer relatively concise, clear definitions of their concepts at some point in their essays.

Appropriate Writing Strategies

Many writing strategies are useful for presenting information. The strategies a writer uses are determined by the way he or she focuses the essay and the kind of information available. The following strategies are particularly useful in explaining concepts.

Classification. One way of presenting information is to divide it into groups and discuss the groups one by one. For example, Toufexis divides the chemicals she discusses into those associated with falling in love and those associated with lasting relationships.

Process Narration. Process narration typically explains how something is done. Many concepts involve processes that unfold over time, such as the geologic scale, or over both time and space, such as bird migration. Process narration involves some of the basic storytelling strategies covered in Chapter 2: narrative time signals, actors and action, and connectives showing temporal relationships. For example, Ngo briefly narrates one process of ritual cannibalism (paragraph 12).

Comparison and Contrast. The comparison-and-contrast strategy is especially useful for explaining concepts because it helps readers understand something new by showing how it is similar to or different from things they already know. Every essayist in this chapter makes use of comparison and contrast. For example, Potera contrasts dependent with nondependent Internet users.

Cause and Effect. Another useful strategy for explaining a concept is to report its causes or effects. Toufexis explains the evolutionary benefits of romantic love, and Potera explores both the causes and effects of Internet addiction.

Note that writers of explanatory essays ordinarily either report established causes or effects or report others' speculated causes or effects as if they were established facts. They usually do not themselves speculate about possible causes or effects.

Careful Use of Sources

To explain concepts, writers usually draw on information from many different sources. Although they often draw on their own experience and observation, they almost always do additional research into what others have to say about their subject. Referring to expert sources always lends authority to an explanation.

How writers treat sources depends on the writing situation. Certain formal situations, such as college assignments or scholarly papers, have rules for citing and documenting sources. Students and scholars are expected to cite their sources formally because readers judge their writing in part by what they have read and how they have used their reading. For more informal writing—magazine articles, for example—readers do not expect page references or publication information, but they do expect sources to be identified; this identification often appears within the text of the article.

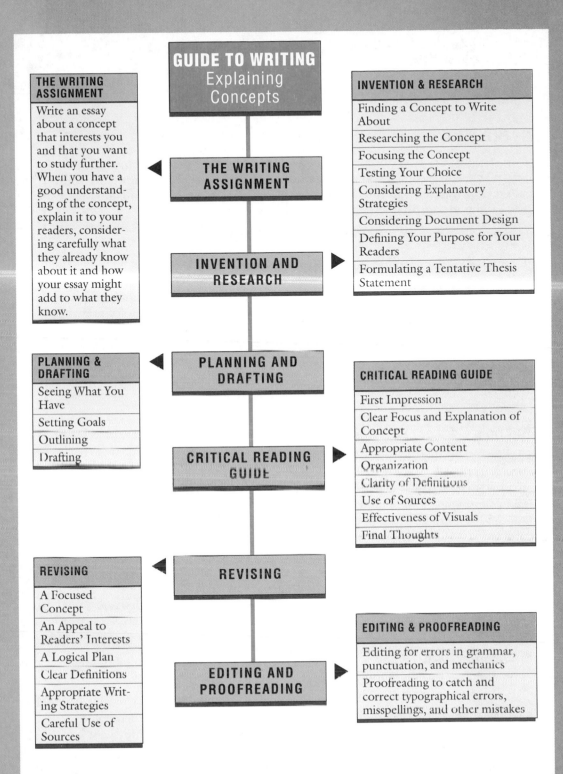

GUIDE TO WRITING
Explaining Concepts

THE WRITING ASSIGNMENT

Write an essay about a concept that interests you and that you want to study further. When you have a good understanding of the concept, explain it to your readers, considering carefully what they already know about it and how your essay might add to what they know.

THE WRITING ASSIGNMENT

INVENTION AND RESEARCH

INVENTION & RESEARCH

Finding a Concept to Write About

Researching the Concept

Focusing the Concept

Testing Your Choice

Considering Explanatory Strategies

Considering Document Design

Defining Your Purpose for Your Readers

Formulating a Tentative Thesis Statement

PLANNING & DRAFTING

Seeing What You Have

Setting Goals

Outlining

Drafting

PLANNING AND DRAFTING

CRITICAL READING GUIDE

CRITICAL READING GUIDE

First Impression

Clear Focus and Explanation of Concept

Appropriate Content

Organization

Clarity of Definitions

Use of Sources

Effectiveness of Visuals

Final Thoughts

REVISING

A Focused Concept

An Appeal to Readers' Interests

A Logical Plan

Clear Definitions

Appropriate Writing Strategies

Careful Use of Sources

REVISING

EDITING AND PROOFREADING

EDITING & PROOFREADING

Editing for errors in grammar, punctuation, and mechanics

Proofreading to catch and correct typographical errors, misspellings, and other mistakes

GUIDE TO WRITING

■ THE WRITING ASSIGNMENT

Write an essay about a concept that interests you and that you want to study further. When you have a good understanding of the concept, explain it to your readers, considering carefully what they already know about it and how your essay might add to what they know.

■ INVENTION AND RESEARCH

The following guidelines will help you find a concept, understand it fully, select a focus appropriate for your readers, test your choice, and devise strategies for presenting what you have discovered in a way that will be truly informative for your particular readers. Each activity is easy to do and takes only a few minutes. If you can spread out the activities over several days, you will have adequate time to understand the concept and decide how to present it. Keep a written record of your invention work to use when you draft the essay and later when you revise it.

Finding a Concept to Write About

Even if you already have a concept in mind, completing the following activities will help you to be certain of your choice.

Listing Concepts.   *Make a list of concepts you could write about.* The longer your list, the more likely you are to find just the right concept for you. And should your first choice not work out, you will have a ready list of alternatives. Include concepts you already know something about as well as some you know only slightly and would like to research further. Also include concepts suggested by the Considering Topics for Your Own Essay activities following each reading in this chapter.

Your courses provide many concepts you will want to consider. Here are some typical concepts from a number of academic and other subjects. Your class notes or textbooks will suggest many others.

- *Literature:* hero, antihero, picaresque, the absurd, canon, representation, figurative language, modernism
- *Philosophy:* existentialism, nihilism, logical positivism, determinism
- *Business management:* autonomous work group, quality circle, cybernetic control system, management by objectives, zero-based budgeting, liquidity gap
- *Psychology:* Hawthorne effect, assimilation/accommodation, social cognition, moratorium, intelligence, divergent/convergent thinking, operant conditioning, short-term memory, tip-of-the-tongue phenomenon, sleep paralysis

- *Government:* majority rule, minority rights, federalism, popular consent, exclusionary rule, political party, political machine, interest group, political action committee
- *Biology:* photosynthesis, morphogenesis, ecosystem, electron transport, plasmolysis, phagocytosis, homozygosity, diffusion
- *Art:* cubism, Dadaism, surrealism, expressionism
- *Math:* polynomials, boundedness, null space, permutations and combinations, factoring, Rolle's theorem, continuity, derivative, indefinite integral
- *Physical sciences:* matter, mass, weight, energy, gravity, atomic theory, law of definite proportions, osmotic pressure, first law of thermodynamics, entropy
- *Public health:* alcoholism, seasonal affective disorder, contraception, lead poisoning, prenatal care
- *Environmental studies:* acid rain, recycling, ozone depletion, toxic waste, endangered species
- *Sports:* squeeze play, hit and run (baseball); power play (hockey); nickel defense, wishbone offense (football); serve and volley offense (tennis); setup (volleyball); pick and roll, inside game (basketball)
- *Personal finance:* mortgage, budget, insurance, deduction, revolving credit
- *Law:* tort, contract, garnishment, double indemnity, liability, reasonable doubt
- *Sociology:* norm, deviance, role conflict, ethnocentrism, class, social stratification, conflict theory, functionalist theory

Listing Concepts Related to Identity and Community.   Many concepts are important in understanding identity and community. As you consider the following concepts, try to think of others in this category: self-esteem, character, personality, autonomy, individuation, narcissism, multiculturalism, ethnicity, race, racism, social contract, communitarianism, community policing, Social Darwinism, identity politics, special-interest groups, diaspora, colonialism, public space, the other, agency, difference, yuppie, generation X.

Listing Concepts Related to Work and Career.   Concepts like the following enable you to gain a deeper understanding of your work experiences and career aspirations: free enterprise, minimum wage, affirmative action, stock option, sweatshop, glass ceiling, downsizing, collective bargaining, service sector, market, entrepreneur, bourgeoisie, underclass, working class, middle class, division of labor, monopoly, automation, robotics, management style, deregulation, multinational corporation.

Choosing a Concept.   *Look over your list of possibilities and select one concept to explore.* Pick a concept that interests you, one you feel eager to learn more about. Consider also whether it might interest others. You may know very little about the concept now, but the guidelines that follow will help you research it and understand it fully.

Researching the Concept

Considering What You Already Know.   *Take a few minutes to write out whatever you know about the concept.* Also say why you have chosen the concept and why you find it interesting and worth knowing about. Write quickly, without planning or organizing. Write phrases or lists as well as sentences. You might also want to make drawings or charts. Ask questions that you hope to answer.

Gathering Information.   *Learn more about your concept by taking notes or making copies of relevant material and keeping careful records of your sources.* Check any materials you already have at hand that explain your concept. If you are considering a concept from one of your academic courses, you will find explanatory material in your textbook or lecture notes.

To acquire a comprehensive, up-to-date understanding of your concept and to write authoritatively about it, you may also need to know how experts other than your textbook writer and instructor define and illustrate the concept. To find this information, you might locate relevant articles or books in the library, search for resources or make inquiries on the Internet, or consult experts on campus or in the community. (For more on search strategies and specific sources for researching your concept, see Chapter 13.)

As you get a better understanding of the concept and decide which aspect of it you will focus your essay on, you may need to do additional research to get answers to specific questions.

If you can, make photocopies or print out information you download from CD-ROMs or the Internet. If you must rely on notes, be sure to copy the language exactly so that later you can quote sources accurately.

Since you do not know what information you will ultimately use, keep a careful record of the author, title, publication date, and page numbers for all the source material you gather. Check with your instructor about whether you should follow the Modern Language Association (MLA) or American Psychological Association (APA) style of acknowledging sources. In this chapter, the Ngo essay follows the MLA style. (For MLA and APA guidelines, see Chapter 14, pp. 397–422.)

Focusing the Concept

Once you have done some research on your concept, you must choose a way to focus your essay. Because more is known about most concepts than you can include in an essay and concepts can be approached from so many perspectives (for example, history, definition, significance), you must limit your explanation. Doing so will help you avoid the common problem of trying to explain too much.

Because the focus must reflect both your special interest in the concept and your readers' likely knowledge and interest, you will want to explore both.

Exploring Your Own Interests.   *Make a list of different aspects of the concept that could become a focus for your essay, and evaluate what you know about each aspect.* To consider which aspect of the concept most interests you, review what you know about the concept. As you review this information, make a list of different aspects of the concept, skipping a few lines after each item in the list.

Under each item in your list, indicate whether you know enough to begin writing about that aspect of the concept, what additional questions you would need to answer, and what is important or interesting to you about that particular aspect.

Analyzing Your Readers. *Take a few minutes to analyze your readers in writing.* To decide what aspect of the concept to focus on, you also need to think about who your prospective readers are likely to be and to speculate about their knowledge of and interest in the concept. Even if you are writing only for your instructor, you should give some thought to what he or she knows and thinks about the concept.

The following questions are designed to help you with your analysis:

- Who are my readers, and what are they likely to know about this concept?
- What, if anything, might they know about the field of study to which this concept applies?
- What could I point out that would be useful for them to know about this concept, perhaps something that could relate to their life or work?
- What connections could I make between this concept and others that my readers are likely to be familiar with?

Choosing a Focus. *With your interests and those of your readers in mind, choose an aspect of your concept on which to focus, and write a sentence justifying its appropriateness.*

Testing Your Choice

Pause now to test whether you have chosen a workable concept and focused it appropriately. As painful as it may be to consider, starting fresh with a new concept is better than continuing with an unworkable one. The following questions can help you test your choice:

- Do I understand my concept well enough to explain it?
- Have I discovered a focus for writing about this concept?
- Have I found enough information for an essay with such a focus?
- Do I see possibilities for engaging my readers' interest in this aspect of my subject?

If you cannot answer yes to all four questions, consider choosing another focus or selecting another concept to write about.

Testing Your Choice: A Collaborative Activity

Get together with two or three other students to find out what your readers are likely to know about your subject and what might interest them about it.

Presenters: Take turns briefly explaining your concept, describing your intended readers, and identifying the aspect of the concept you will focus on.

Listeners: Briefly tell the presenter whether the focus sounds appropriate and interesting for the intended readers. Share what you think readers are likely to know about the concept and what might be especially interesting and informative for them to learn about.

Considering Explanatory Strategies

Before you move on to plan and draft your essay, consider some possible ways of presenting the concept. Try to answer each of the following questions in a sentence or two. Questions that you can answer readily may identify strategies that can help you explain your concept.

- What term is used to name the concept, and what does it mean? (definition)
- How is this concept like or unlike related concepts? (comparison and contrast)
- How can an explanation of this concept be divided into parts? (classification)
- How does this concept happen, or how does one go about doing it? (process narration)
- What are this concept's known causes or effects? (cause and effect)

Considering Document Design

Think about whether visual elements—tables, graphs, drawings, photographs—would make your explanation clearer. These are not at all a requirement of an essay explaining a concept, but they could be helpful. Consider also whether your readers might benefit from design features such as headings, bulleted or numbered lists, or other elements that would present information efficiently or make your explanation easier to follow. You could construct your own graphic elements, download materials from the Internet, copy images from television or other sources, or scan into your document visuals from books and magazines. Be sure to cite the source of any visuals you use.

Defining Your Purpose for Your Readers

Write a few sentences, defining your purpose in writing about this particular concept for your readers. Remember that you have already identified and analyzed your readers, and you have begun to research and develop your explanation with these readers in mind. Given these readers, try now to define your purpose in explaining the concept to them. Use these questions to focus your thoughts:

- Are my readers familiar with the concept? If not, how can I overcome their resistance or puzzlement? Or, if so, will my chosen focus allow my readers to see the familiar concept in a new light?

- If I suspect that my readers have misconceptions about the concept, how can I correct the misconceptions without offending readers?

- Do I want to arouse readers' interest in information that may seem at first to be less than engaging?

- Do I want to get readers to see that the information I have to report is relevant to their lives, families, communities, work, or studies?

Formulating a Tentative Thesis Statement

Write one or more sentences that could serve as a thesis statement. State your concept and focus. You might also want to forecast the topics you will use to explain the concept.

Anastasia Toufexis begins her essay with this thesis statement:

> O.K., let's cut out all this nonsense about romantic love. Let's bring some scientific precision to the party. Let's put love under a microscope.
>
> When rigorous people with Ph.D.s after their names do that, what they see is not some silly, senseless thing. No, their probe reveals that love rests firmly on the foundations of evolution, biology and chemistry.

Toufexis's concept is love, and her focus is the scientific explanation of love, specifically the evolution, biology, and chemistry of love. In announcing her focus, she forecasts the order in which she will present information from the three most relevant academic disciplines—anthropology (which includes the study of human evolution), biology, and chemistry. These discipline names become her topics.

In his essay on cannibalism, Linh Kieu Ngo offers his thesis statement in paragraph 6:

> Cannibalism can be broken down into two main categories: exocannibalism, the eating of outsiders or foreigners, and endocannibalism, the eating of members of one's own social group (Shipman 70). Within these categories are several functional types of cannibalism, three of the most common being survival cannibalism, dietary cannibalism, and religious and ritual cannibalism.

Ngo's concept is cannibalism, and his focus is three common types of cannibalism. He carefully forecasts how he will divide the information to create topics and the order in which he will explain each of the topics, the common types of cannibalism.

As you draft your own tentative thesis statement, take care to make the language clear and unambiguous. Although you may want to revise your thesis statement as you draft your essay, trying to state it now will give your planning and drafting more focus and direction. Keep in mind that the thesis in an explanatory essay merely announces the subject; it never asserts a position that requires an argument to defend it.

■ PLANNING AND DRAFTING

The following guidelines will help you get the most out of your invention notes, determine specific goals for your essay, and write a first draft.

Seeing What You Have

Reread everything you have written so far. This is a critically important time for reflection and evaluation. Before beginning the actual draft, you must decide whether your subject is worthwhile and whether you have sufficient information for a successful essay.

It may help, as you read, to annotate your invention writings. Look for details that will help you explain the concept in a way that your readers can grasp. Underline or circle key words, phrases, or sentences; make marginal notes. Your goal is to identify the important elements in what you have written so far.

Be realistic. If at this point your notes do not look promising, you may want to choose a different focus for your concept or select a different concept to write about. If your notes seem thin but promising, do further research to find more information before continuing.

Setting Goals

Successful writers are always looking beyond the next sentence to larger goals. Indeed, the next sentence is easier to write if you keep larger goals in mind. The following questions can help you set these goals. Consider each one now, and then return to them as necessary while you write.

Your Purpose and Readers

- How can I build on my readers' knowledge?
- What new information can I present to them?
- How can I organize my essay so that my readers can follow it easily?
- What tone would be most appropriate? Would an informal tone like Toufexis's or a formal one like Ngo's be more appropriate to my purpose?

The Beginning

- How shall I begin? Should I open with a provocative quotation, as Toufexis does? With an incident illustrating the concept, as Ngo does? With a question?

- How can I best forecast the plan my explanation will follow? Should I offer a detailed forecast, as Toufexis and Ngo do? Or should I begin with general statements, as Potera does?

Writing Strategies

- What terms do I need to define? Can I rely on brief sentence definitions, or will I need to write extended definitions?
- Are there ways to categorize the information?
- What examples can I use to make the explanation more concrete?
- Would any comparisons or contrasts help readers understand the information?
- Do I need to explain any processes or known causes or effects?

The Ending

- Should I frame the essay by relating the ending to the beginning, as Toufexis does?
- Should I offer leads to further relevant information?
- Should I end with a speculation about the past, as Ngo does?
- Should I end with a prediction about the future?

Outlining

An essay explaining a concept is made up of four basic parts:

1. An attempt to engage readers' interest in the explanation
2. The thesis statement, announcing the concept, its focus, and its topics
3. An orientation to the concept, which may include a description or definition of the concept
4. Information about the concept

These parts nearly always appear in the order listed above. Parts 1, 2, and 3 are relatively brief, sometimes no more than two or three paragraphs.

Here is a possible outline for an essay explaining a concept:

An attempt to gain readers' interest in the concept

Thesis statement

Definition of the concept

Topic 1 with illustration

Topic 2 with illustration

(etc.)

Conclusion

An attempt to gain readers' interest could take as little space as two or three sentences or as much as four or five paragraphs. The thesis statement and definition are usually quite brief, sometimes only a few sentences. A topic illustration may occupy one or several paragraphs, and there can be few or many topics, depending on how the information has been divided up. A conclusion might summarize the information presented, give advice about how to use or apply the information, or speculate about the future of the concept.

Consider tentative any outlining you do before you begin drafting. Never be a slave to an outline. As you draft, you will usually see ways to improve on your original plan. Be ready to revise your outline, shift parts around, or drop or add parts as you draft.

Drafting

Begin drafting your essay, keeping your focus in mind. Remember also the needs and expectations of your readers; organize, define, and explain with them in mind. Work to increase readers' understanding of your concept. You may want to review the general advice on drafting in Chapter 1, pp. 15–17.

CRITICAL READING GUIDE

Now is the time to get a good critical reading of your draft. Your instructor may arrange such a reading as part of your coursework. If not, you can ask a classmate, friend, or family member to read your draft using this guide. If your campus has a writing center, you might ask a tutor there to read and comment on your draft. (If you are unable to have someone else review your draft, turn ahead to the Revision section for help reading your own draft with a critical eye.)

If You Are the Writer. In order to provide focused, helpful comments, your reader must know your essay's intended audience, your purpose, and a problem in the draft that you need help solving. Briefly write out this information at the top of your draft.

- *Readers.* To whom are you directing your concept explanation? What do you assume they know about the concept? How do you plan to engage and hold their interest?

- *Purpose.* What do you hope to achieve with your readers?

- *Problem.* Ask your reader to help you solve the single most important problem you see in the draft. Describe this problem briefly.

If You Are the Reader. Use the following guidelines to help you give constructive, helpful comments to others on essays explaining concepts.

1. ***Read for a First Impression.*** Read first to get a sense of the concept. Then briefly write out your impressions. What in the draft do you think will especially interest the intended readers? Where might they have difficulty in following the explanation? Next, consider the problem the writer identified. If the problem will be covered by one of the other questions below, deal with it there. Otherwise, respond to the writer's concerns now.

2. ***Assess Whether the Concept Is Clearly Explained and Focused.*** Restate, in one sentence, what you understand the concept to mean. Indicate any confusion or uncertainty you have about its meaning. Given the concept, does the focus seem appropriate, too broad, or too narrow for the intended readers? Can you think of a more interesting aspect of the concept on which to focus the explanation?

3. ***Consider Whether the Content Is Appropriate for the Intended Readers.*** Does it tell them all that they are likely to want to know about the concept? Can you suggest additional information that should be included? What unanswered questions might readers have about the concept? Point out any information that seems either superfluous or too predictable.

4. ***Evaluate the Organization.*** Look at the way the essay is organized by making a scratch outline. (For an illustration of scratch outlining, see Chapter 10, pp. 311–12.) Does the information seem to be logically divided? If not, suggest a better way to divide it. Also consider the order or sequence of information. Can you suggest a better way of sequencing it?

   - Look at the *beginning*. Does it pull readers into the essay and make them want to continue? Does it adequately forecast the direction of the essay? If possible, suggest a better way to begin.

   - Look for obvious *transitions* in the draft. Tell the writer how they are helpful or unhelpful. Try to improve one or two of them. Look for additional places where transitions would be helpful.

   - Look at the *ending*. Explain what makes it particularly effective or less effective than it might be, in your opinion. If you can, suggest a better way to end.

5. ***Assess the Clarity of Definitions.*** Point out any definitions that may be unclear or confusing to readers. Identify any other terms that may need to be defined for the intended readers.

6. ***Evaluate the Use of Sources.*** If the writer has used sources, review the list of sources cited. Given the purpose, readers, and focus of the essay, does the list seem balanced, and are the selections appropriate? Try to suggest concerns or questions about sources that readers knowledgeable about the concept might raise. Then consider the use of sources within the text of the essay. Are there places where summary or paraphrase would be preferable to quoted material or vice versa? Note any places where the writer has placed quotations awkwardly into the text, and recommend ways to smooth them out.

7. *Evaluate the Effectiveness of Visuals.* If charts, graphs, tables, or other visuals are included, let the writer know if they help you understand the concept or if you find them confusing. Suggest ideas you have for changing, adding, moving, or deleting visuals.

8. *Give the Writer Your Final Thoughts.* Which part needs the most work? What do you think the intended readers will find most informative or memorable? What do you like best about the draft essay?

■ REVISING

Now you are ready to revise your essay. Your instructor or other students may have given you advice on improving your draft. Nevertheless, you may have begun to realize that your draft requires not so much revision as rethinking. For example, you may recognize that the focus you chose is too broad to be explained adequately in a few pages, that you need to make the information more engaging or interesting for your intended readers, or that you need substantially more information to present the concept adequately. Consequently, instead of working to improve parts of the draft, you may need to write a new draft that radically reenvisions your explanation. It is not unusual for students—and professional writers—to find themselves in this situation. Seek your instructor's advice if you must plan a radical revision.

On the other hand, you may feel quite satisfied that your draft achieves most, if not all, of your goals. In that case, you can focus on refining specific parts of your draft. Very likely you have thought of ways to improve your draft, and you may even have begun improving it. This section will help you get an overview of your draft and revise it accordingly.

Getting an Overview

Consider your draft as a whole. It may help to do so in two steps:

1. *Reread.* If at all possible, put the draft aside for a day or two before rereading it. When you return to it, start by reconsidering your readers and purpose. Then read the draft straight through, trying to see it as your intended readers will.

2. *Outline.* Make a scratch outline to get an overview of the essay's development. (For an illustration of scratch outlining, turn to the Commentary following Linh Kieu Ngo's essay in this chapter. For more information on making a scratch outline, see Chapter 9, pp. 292–93.)

Charting a Plan for Revision.   After you gain an overview of your draft, you may want to make a two-column chart like the following one to keep track of the work you need to do as you revise. In the left-hand column, list the basic features of concept explanations, skipping several lines between each feature. As you analyze your draft and study any comments from other readers, note any problems you need to solve in the right-hand column. (Turn to pp. 122–24 to review the basic features.)

Basic Features	*Problems to Solve*
A focused concept	
An appeal to readers' interests	
A logical plan	
Clear definitions	
Appropriate writing strategies	
Careful use of sources	

Analyzing the Basic Features of Your Own Draft. Using the Critical Reading Guide on the preceding pages, reread the draft to identify problems you need to solve. Note the problems on your revision chart.

Studying Critical Comments. Review all of the comments you have received from other readers, and add to your chart any commentary that you intend to act on. Try not to react defensively. For each comment, look at the draft to determine what might have led the reader to make the comment. By letting you see how others respond to your draft, these comments provide valuable information about how you might improve it.

Carrying Out Revisions

Having identified problems in your draft, you now need to come up with solutions and—most important—to carry them out. Basically, there are three ways to find solutions:

1. Review your invention and planning notes and your sources for information and ideas to add to the draft.
2. Do further invention or research to answer questions your readers raised.
3. Look back at the readings in this chapter to see how other writers have solved similar problems.

The following suggestions, which are organized according to the basic features on your revision chart, will get you started solving some writing problems common to explanatory essays.

A Focused Concept

- **Is the focus too broad?** Consider limiting it further so that you can explain one part of the concept in more depth. If readers were uninterested in the aspect you focused on, consider focusing on some other aspect of the concept.

- *Is the focus too narrow?* You may have isolated too minor an aspect. Go back to your invention and research notes and look for larger or more significant aspects.

An Appeal to Readers' Interests

- *Do you fail to connect to readers' interests and engage their attention throughout the essay?* Help readers see the significance of the information to them personally. Eliminate superfluous or too-predictable content. Open with an unusual piece of information that will catch readers' interest.

- *Do you think readers will have unanswered questions?* Review your invention writing and sources for further information to satisfy your readers' needs or answer their concerns and questions.

A Logical Plan

- *Does the beginning successfully orient readers to your purpose and plan?* Try making your focus obvious immediately. Forecast the plan of your essay.

- *Is the explanation difficult to follow?* Look for a way to reorder the parts so that the essay is easier to follow. Try constructing an alternative outline. Add transitions or summaries to help keep readers on track. Or consider ways you might classify and divide the information to make it easier to understand or provide a more interesting perspective on the topic.

- *Is the ending inconclusive?* Consider moving important information there. Try summarizing highlights of the essay or framing it by referring to something in the beginning. Or you might speculate about the future of the concept or assert its usefulness.

Clear Definitions

- *Do readers need a clearer or fuller definition of the concept?* Add a concise definition early in your essay, or consider adding a brief summary that defines the concept later in the essay (in the middle or at the end). Remove any information that may blur readers' understanding of the concept.

- *Are other key terms inadequately defined?* Supply clear definitions, searching your sources or checking a dictionary if necessary.

Appropriate Writing Strategies

- *Does the content seem thin or the definition of the concept blurred?* Consider whether any other writing strategies would improve the presentation.
  - Try comparing or contrasting the concept with a related one that is more familiar to readers.
  - Add some information about its known causes or effects.
  - See whether adding examples enlivens or clarifies your explanation.

- Tell more about how the concept works or what people do with it.
- Add design features such as charts, headings, drafts, drawings, photographs.

Careful Use of Sources

- *Do readers find your sources inadequate?* Return to the library or the Internet to find additional ones. Consider dropping weak or less reliable sources. Make sure that your sources provide coverage in a comprehensive, balanced way.

- *Do you rely too much on quoting, summarizing, or paraphrasing?* Change some of your quotations to summaries or paraphrases, or vice versa.

- *Does quoted material need to be more smoothly integrated into your own text?* Revise to make it so. (See Chapter 14, pp. 390–92, for advice on integrating quotations into your text.)

- *Are there discrepancies between your in-text citations and list of sources?* Compare each in-text citation against the examples of your chosen citation style given in Chapter 14. Be sure that all of the citations and sources follow the style you are using exactly. Check to see that your list of sources has an entry for each in-text citation.

■ EDITING AND PROOFREADING

Now is the time to check your revised draft for connections between sentences and for errors in grammar, punctuation, and mechanics. As you reread, ask yourself whether the connection from one sentence to the next is logical and easy for readers to follow. If you sense a gap or disconnection that would cause a reader to stumble or become confused, try revising one or both sentences so that the gap is closed. Notice whether you shift from one word to another unnecessarily in one sentence to the next, and, if you do, consider repeating the same word instead. Look for sentences that might be combined to allow readers to follow the observations more easily. Look as well for long or garbled sentences that might be divided into two or three sentences.

As you work on your sentences, look for errors in spelling, capitalization, punctuation, usage, and grammar. Consult a writer's handbook for advice about how to correct any errors you cannot confidently correct on your own. Ask a friend or classmate to read over your draft, looking for errors.

Before you hand in your revised essay, proofread it carefully and run it through a spell-checker. Your goal is to hand in an error free essay.

REFLECTING ON YOUR WRITING

Now that you have read and discussed several essays that explain concepts and written one of your own, take some time for reflection. Reflecting on your writing process will help you gain a greater understanding of what you learned about solving the problems you encountered explaining a concept.

Write a one-page explanation, telling your instructor about a problem you encountered in writing your essay and how you solved it. Before you begin, gather all of your writing—invention and planning notes, drafts, critical comments, revision notes and plans, and final revision. Review these materials and refer to them as you complete this writing task.

1. *Identify one writing problem you had to solve as you worked to explain the concept in your essay.* Do not be concerned with grammar and punctuation; concentrate instead on problems unique to developing a concept explanation. For example: Did you puzzle over how to focus your explanation? Did you worry about how to appeal to your readers' interests or how to identify and define the terms your readers would need explained? Did you have trouble integrating sources smoothly?

2. *Determine how you came to recognize the problem.* When did you first discover it? What called it to your attention? If you did not become aware of the problem until someone else pointed it out, can you now see hints of it in your invention writings? If so, where specifically? How did you respond when you first recognized the problem?

3. *Reflect on how you went about solving the problem.* Did you work on the wording of a particular passage, cut or add information, move paragraphs or sentences around, add transitions or forecasting statements, experiment with different writing strategies? Did you reread one of the essays in this chapter to see how another writer handled the problem, or did you look back at the invention suggestions? If you talked about the writing problem with another student, a tutor, or your instructor, did talking about it help? How useful was the advice you received?

4. *Write a brief explanation of how you identified the problem and how you solved it.* Be as specific as possible in reconstructing your efforts. Quote from your invention notes and draft essay, others' critical comments, your revision plan, and your revised essay to show the various changes your writing underwent as you tried to solve the problem. If you are still uncertain about your solution, say so. Thinking in detail about how you identified a particular problem, how you went about solving it, and what you learned from this experience can help you solve future writing problems more easily.

5

Arguing a Position

You may associate arguing with quarreling or with the in-your-face debating we hear so often on radio and television talk shows. These ways of arguing may let us vent strong feelings, but they seldom lead us to consider seriously other points of view, let alone to look critically at our own thinking or learn anything new.

This chapter presents a more deliberative way of arguing that we call *reasoned argument* because it depends on giving reasons rather than raising voices. It expects positions to be supported rather than merely asserted. It also demands respect for the right of others to disagree with you as you may disagree with them. Reasoned argument requires more critical thinking than quarreling, but no less passion or commitment, as you will see when you read the essays in this chapter arguing about controversial issues.

Controversial issues are, by definition, issues about which people feel strongly and sometimes disagree vehemently. The issue may involve a practice that has been accepted for some time, like fraternity hazing, or it may concern a newly proposed or recently instituted policy, like the "Peacekeeper" school program. People may agree about goals but disagree about the best way to achieve them, as in the perennial debate over how to guarantee adequate health care for all citizens. Or they may disagree about fundamental values and beliefs, as in the debate over euthanasia.

As you can see from these examples, controversial issues have no obvious "right" answer, no truth that everyone accepts, no single authority on which everyone relies. Writers cannot offer absolute proof in debates about controversial issues because they are matters of opinion and judgment. Simply gathering information—finding the facts or learning from experts—will not settle disputes like these, although the more that is known about an issue, the more informed the positions will be. To some extent, people decide such matters by considering factual evidence, their own experience, and the opinions of people they trust, but they also base their positions on less objective factors such as values and principles, assumptions and preconceptions about how the world works and how it should work.

Although it is not possible to prove that a position on a controversial issue is right or wrong, it is possible through argument to convince others to accept or reject a particular position. To be convincing, not only must an argument present plausible reasons and solid support for its position, but it also should anticipate readers' likely

141

objections and opposing arguments, conceding those that are reasonable and refuting those that are not. Vigorous debate that sets forth arguments and counterarguments on all sides of an issue can advance everyone's thinking.

Learning to make reasoned arguments on controversial issues and to think critically about our own as well as others' arguments is not a luxury; it is a necessity if our increasingly diverse society is to survive and flourish. As citizens in a democracy, we have a special duty to inform ourselves about pressing issues and to participate constructively in the public debate. Honing our thinking and arguing skills also has practical advantages in school, where we are often judged by our ability to write convincingly, and in the workplace, where we often need to recommend or defend controversial decisions. You will encounter writing that argues a position in many different contexts, as the following examples suggest.

Writing in Your Other Courses

- For a sociology class, a student writes an essay on surrogate mothering. She finds several newspaper and magazine articles and checks the Internet for surrogate mothering Web sites. In her essay, she acknowledges that using *in vitro* fertilization and a surrogate may be the only way some couples can have their own biological children. Although she respects this desire, she argues that from a sociological perspective surrogate mothering does more harm than good. She gives two reasons — that the practice has serious emotional consequences for the surrogates and their families, and that it exploits poor women by creating a class of professional breeders. She supports her argument with anecdotes from surrogates and their families as well as with quotations from sociologists and psychologists who have studied surrogate mothering.

- For a business course, a student writes an essay arguing that the "glass ceiling" that prevents women from advancing up the corporate ladder still exists at the highest executive levels. She acknowledges that in the twenty years since the phrase "glass ceiling" was coined by a writer at the *Wall Street Journal,* the percentage of corporate officers who are women has grown. Nevertheless, she argues, the statistics are misleading. Because it is good business to claim gender equity, many companies define to their own advantage the positions counted as corporate officers. The student cites statistics from the Catalyst research group indicating that only 7 percent of the corporate officers in "line" positions — those responsible for the bottom line and therefore most likely to be promoted to chief executive positions — are women.

Writing in the Community

- For the campus newspaper, a student writes an editorial condemning the practice of fraternity hazing. He acknowledges that most hazing is harmless but argues that hazing can get out of hand and even be lethal. He refers specifically to two incidents reported in the national news in which one student died of alcohol poisoning after being forced to drink too much liquor and another student had a heart attack after being made to run too many laps. To show that the potential for a similar tragedy exists on his college campus, the writer recounts several anecdotes told to him by students about their experiences pledging for campus fraternities. He concludes with a plea to the fraternities on campus to curtail—or at least, radically change—their hazing practices before someone is seriously hurt or killed.

- In a letter to the school board, parents protest a new "Peacekeepers" program being implemented at the local middle school. The writers acknowledge that the aim of the program—to teach students to avoid conflict—is worthwhile. But they argue that the program's methods unduly restrict students' freedoms. Moreover, they claim that the program teaches children to become passive rather than thinking adults ready to fight for what is right. To support their argument, they list some of the rules that have been instituted: students must wear uniforms to school, must keep their hands clasped behind their backs when walking down the halls, are not permitted to raise their voices in anger or to use obscenities, and cannot play aggressive games like dodgeball or contact sports like basketball and football.

Writing in the Workplace

- For a business magazine, a corporate executive writes an essay arguing that protecting the environment is not only good citizenship, but also good business. She supports her position with examples of two companies that became successful by developing innovative methods of reducing hazardous wastes. She also reminds readers of the decisive action taken in the late 1980s by established corporations to help solve the problem of ozone depletion, such as DuPont's decision to discontinue production of chlorofluorocarbons (CFCs) and McDonald's elimination of styrofoam cartons. Finally, she points out that *Fortune* magazine agrees with her position, noting that its annual ranking of "America's Most Admired Corporations" includes "community and environmental responsibility" alongside "financial soundness" among the eight deciding factors.

- In a memo to the director of personnel, a loan company manager argues that written communication skills should be a more important factor in hiring. He acknowledges that math skills are necessary, but tries to convince the director that mistakes in writing are too costly to ignore. To support his argument, he cites examples when bad writing in letters and memos cost the company money and time. For additional examples and suggestions on solving the problem, he refers the personnel director to an ongoing discussion about writing on a listserv to which the manager subscribes.

Practice Arguing a Position: A Collaborative Activity

The preceding scenarios suggest some occasions for arguing a position. To construct an effective argument, you must assert a position and offer support for it. This activity gives you a chance to practice constructing an argument with other students.

Part 1. Get together with two to three other students and choose an issue. You do not have to be an expert on the issue, but you should be familiar with some of the arguments people typically make about it. If you do not have an issue in mind, the following list might help you think of possibilities.

- Should all students be required to wear uniforms in school?
- Should college athletes be paid a portion of the money the school gains from sports events?
- Should community service be a requirement for graduation from high school or college?

In your group, spend two to three minutes quickly exchanging your opinions and then agree together to argue for the same position on the issue, whether you personally agree with the position or not. Also decide who you would want to read your argument and what you expect these readers to think about the issue. Choose someone in the group to write down the results of your discussion like this:

Issue: Should grades in college be abolished?

Position: Grades should be abolished.

Readers: Teachers who think grades measure learning accurately and efficiently.

Take another ten to fifteen minutes to construct an argument for your position, giving several reasons and noting the kinds of support you would need. Also try to anticipate one or two objections you would expect from readers who disagree with your position. Write down what you discover under the following headings: *Reasons, Support Needed*, and *Likely Objections*. Following is an example of this work for the position that grades should be abolished.

Reasons

1. Tests are not always the best way to judge students' knowledge because some students do poorly on tests even though they know the material.
2. Tests often evaluate only what is easily measurable, such as whether students remember facts, rather than whether students can use facts to support their ideas.

Support Needed

1. Research on testing anxiety
2. Anecdotes from students' experience with testing anxiety

3. Teachers' comments on why they rely on tests and how they feel about alternatives to testing (such as group projects)

Likely Objections

1. Tests are efficient—for teachers and for students, especially in comparison with research papers.
2. Tests are evaluated strictly on what students have learned about the subject, not on how well they write or how well a group collaborates.

Part 2. Discuss for about five minutes what you did as a group to construct an argument:

Reasons: What did you learn about giving reasons? If you thought of more reasons than you needed, how did you choose? If you had difficulty thinking of reasons, what could you do?

Support: What did you learn about supporting an argument? How many different kinds of support (such as quotations, examples, or anecdotes) did you consider? Which reasons seemed the easiest to support? Which the hardest?

Objections: What did you learn about anticipating objections to your argument? How did you come up with these objections? Given your designated readers, was it easy or hard to think of their likely objections? How could you learn more about your readers' likely objections?

READINGS

The readings in this chapter illustrate the features of essays that argue a position on a controversial issue and the strategies writers rely on to realize the features. No two essays in this genre are much alike, and yet they share defining features. The section Analyzing Writing Strategies and the Commentary following each reading touch on a few features best illustrated by that essay, capturing its special qualities and strengths. Together, the three essays cover many of the possibilities of writing that argues a position. Consequently, you will want to read as many of the essays and Commentaries as possible and, if time permits, complete the activities in Analyzing Writing Strategies. Following the last reading in the chapter, the Basic Features section offers a concise description of the features of writing that argues a position and gives examples from all of the readings.

Alan I. Leshner is the director of the National Institute on Drug Abuse (NIDA), one of the National Institutes of Health (NIH). NIDA supports worldwide research on drug abuse, prevention, and treatment. In addition to his administrative duties, Leshner advises the president and Congress on drug policy and informs the public about policy issues and research developments. Before coming to NIDA, Leshner was acting director of the National Institute of Mental Health and served at the National Science Foundation. A former professor of psychology, Leshner's scientific research has focused on the biological bases of behavior. He has received many awards for his national leadership in substance abuse and addiction, science education, and mental health. In 1996, President Clinton gave him the Presidential Distinguished Executive Rank Award, the highest recognition for federal service.

In his role as NIDA director, Leshner writes and speaks to a wide range of audiences, from research scientists to schoolchildren. As this reading demonstrates, he also writes syndicated newspaper columns intended to influence public opinion. "Why Shouldn't Society Treat Substance Abusers?" first appeared in the Los Angeles Times *(June 11, 1999). As you read, notice that Leshner refers to scientific research but, following newspaper convention, does not cite specific sources.*

Why Shouldn't Society Treat Substance Abusers?

Alan I. Leshner

Imagine a debilitating disease for which there are effective treatments. Imagine that this treatable disease costs society $110 billion a year. Can you imagine not using the treatments? It seems unfathomable, but that often is the case with the treatment of drug addiction.   1

Addicts are frequently denied treatment that would not only improve their lives, but also would improve our own lives — by cutting crime, reducing disease and improving the productivity of employees and the economy.   2

People are polarized on the issue of treatment: They are either strong advocates for treating addiction or they hate the idea. People debate with passion whether treatment works or not, which approaches are best and whether treatments such as methadone simply substitute one addiction for another.   3

From my observation post, the core of the issue cannot be simply whether drug treatments are effective or not, since there already is abundant scientific data showing that they are. In fact, research shows that drug treatments are as, or more, effective than treatments for other chronic disorders, such as forms of heart disease, diabetes and some mental illness.   4

The central issue for many people is whether addicts should be treated at all. I frequently hear people ask: Do they really deserve to be treated? Didn't they just do it to themselves? Why should we coddle people who cause so much societal disruption? Shouldn't they be punished, rather than treated? Even many people who recognize addiction as a disease still get hung up on whether it is a "no-fault" illness.   5

Science has brought us to a point where we should no longer focus the drug treatment question simply on these kinds of unanswerable moral dilemmas. From a practical perspective, benefits to society must be included in the decision equations. The very   6 same body of scientific data that demonstrates the effectiveness of treatments in reducing an individual's drug use also shows the enormous benefits that drug treatment can have for the patient's family and the community.

A variety of studies from the National Institutes of Health, Columbia University, the University of Pennsylvania and other institutions all have shown that drug treatment reduces use by 50% to 60%, and arrests for violent and nonviolent criminal acts by 40% or more. Drug abuse treatment reduces the risk of HIV infection, and interventions to prevent HIV are much less costly than treating AIDS. Treatment tied to vocational services improves the prospects for employment, with 40% to 60% more individuals employed after treatment. 7

The case is just as dramatic for prison and jail inmates, 60% to 80% of whom have serious substance abuse problems. Science shows that appropriately treating addicts in prison reduces their later drug use by 50% to 70% and their later criminality and resulting arrests by 50% to 60%. These data make the case against warehousing addicts in prison without attending to their addictions. 8

Successful drug treatment takes a person who is now seen as only a drain on a community's resources and returns the individual to productive membership in society. Best estimates are that for every $1 spent on drug treatment, there is a $4 to $7 return in cost savings to society. This means that dwelling on moralistic questions, such as who deserves what kind of help, blocks both the individual and society from receiving the economic and societal benefits that can be achieved from treating addicts. 9

It is true that the individual initially made the voluntary decision to use drugs. But once addicted, it is no longer a simple matter of choice. Prolonged drug use changes the brain in long-lasting and fundamental ways that result in truly compulsive, often uncontrollable, drug craving, seeking and use, which is the essence of addiction. Once addicted, it is almost impossible for most people to stop using drugs without treatment. 10

It is clearly in everyone's interest to rise above our moral outrage that addiction results from a voluntary behavior. If we are ever going to significantly reduce the tremendous price that drug addiction exacts from every aspect of our society, drug treatment for all who need it must be a core element of our society's strategies. 11

Connecting to Culture and Experience: Addiction

In this essay, Leshner focuses on drug addiction, but if you read Carol Potera's essay on Internet addiction in Chapter 4 (pp. 108–112), you know there are other kinds of addiction—such as addiction to chocolate, exercise, work, shopping. For many of us, the word *addiction* carries negative connotations because of its association with drug and alcohol abuse. But some addictions may not be bad for us, and it is possible that certain addictions actually might be good. Before making judgments, we need to determine what we mean by addiction, and whether we should distinguish among kinds or intensities of addiction. For example, would playing poker every Friday night qualify as an addiction? Is a sports fan who goes to every game of his favorite team addicted? Is a person who attends city council meetings as a self-appointed public watchdog addicted?

With two or three other students, begin exploring your understanding of addiction by taking turns either telling about your own experience with addiction or about the experience of someone you know. Or if you have no personal experience, describe the image you have of someone with an addiction and where you think that image comes from.

Then, as a group, try to define *addiction* based on your experiences as well as on popular cultural images and stereotypes. Do you think some addictions are socially acceptable and should be encouraged?

Analyzing Writing Strategies

1. At the beginning of this chapter, we discuss several features of essays that argue a position. Consider which of these is true of Leshner's essay:

- It presents a controversial issue.

- It asserts a clear position on the issue.

- It argues for the position by presenting plausible reasons and support.

- It anticipates readers' objections and arguments, either conceding or refuting them.

2. In paragraph 3, Leshner anticipates objections and questions that readers might raise about the effectiveness of different treatments for drug addiction. Reread paragraph 4, where he responds to these objections. Decide whether he responds by acknowledging, conceding, or refuting the objections. Then consider how convincing his response is likely to be for his audience of newspaper readers.

Commentary: Convincing Support

For an argument to succeed with readers, it must not only give reasons but also provide support. Examples, statistics, authorities, and anecdotes are some of the main kinds of support writers use. Examples may be used as support on all types of arguments. Leshner, for instance, uses hypothetical examples or scenarios in paragraph 1 to suggest that our society's reluctance toward treating drug addicts is wasteful and unjust. To support his argument in paragraphs 7–9 that drug treatment can not only help drug users but also benefit the community, Leshner uses a combination of statistics and authorities. In paragraph 7, for example, he cites statistics on the effects of treatment on reducing drug use and crime and of increasing the prospects for employment. In paragraph 8, he uses much the same strategy in discussing inmates. And in paragraph 9, he uses statistics to show how much society would save from treating drug addicts.

For this statistical support to be convincing, Leshner's readers must accept it as fact. But most critical readers are appropriately skeptical about statistics. They need to know whether the statistics come from reliable sources and whether they are current, relevant, and accurate. Leshner, as we pointed out in the headnote, wrote his essay for a newspaper, so he cannot document it as he would a research report. To overcome this difficulty, he uses authorities to bolster the credibility of his statistics. He tries to establish the authority of his sources in three ways: by invoking the authority of the research institutions where the studies were conducted, by invoking his own authority, and by invoking the authority of science itself. He begins by simply naming the institutions, two respected research universities most readers will have heard of, and his own National Institutes of Health (paragraph 7). He tries to establish his own authority both by displaying his wide knowledge of the subject and by letting readers know his credentials, which appeared originally in a box at the end of the essay. Finally, Leshner invokes the authority of science itself in sentences that begin like this: "Science has brought us to a point" and "Science shows" (6 and 8). Some readers may question the ultimate authority of science, but since Leshner is a researcher himself and director of an institute that, according to his own Director's Page at the NIDA Web site, "supports 85% of the World's research on the health aspects of drug abuse and addiction," it is not surprising that he expects readers to have faith in scientists and scientific research.

Leshner, as we said, is prevented by newspaper convention from citing his sources. The NIDA Web site at < http://www.nida.nih.gov > contains links to various research studies, so we can infer that, in another context, it would have been easy for Leshner to support his statistics by referring to specific reports.

The next two essays in this chapter, an excerpt from a book by Mariah Burton Nelson and an academic essay by Jessica Statsky, illustrate two different citation styles. The style used in the excerpt from Nelson is based on the *Chicago Manual of Style* (often used in books published for general audiences), whereas Statsky uses the Modern Language Association (MLA) style (often used in academic writing). These two systems use different types of citations in the text and different formats for the references collected in a list at the end. (For guidance on using and acknowledging sources, see Chapter 14.)

Considering Topics for Your Own Essay

Consider other controversial issues that involve public policy. For example, should individuals be able to sell videotapes they have copied from commercial broadcasts? Should prime-time television programs be permitted to show nudity? Should store owners be prohibited from selling recordings with "Parental Advisory" stickers to people under eighteen? Should there be censorship on the Internet? Select one issue on which you have a position; then consider how you would construct a reasoned argument for your position.

Mariah Burton Nelson is a sports reporter and writer who has written extensively on sports and gender. As a former Stanford University star athlete and professional basketball player, Nelson is highly critical of the unequal funding of men's and women's college sports programs, the issue addressed in this reading from her controversial book, The Stronger Women Get, the More Men Love Football: Sexism and the American Culture of Sports *(1994). Another of her books on sports and gender is* Embracing Victory: Life Lessons in Competition and Compassion (1999). *Nelson's most recent book, on a new subject, is* The Unburdened Heart: Five Keys to Forgiveness and Freedom *(2000).*

As you read this excerpt from The Stronger Women Get, the More Men Love Football, *which we have titled "Adventures in Equality" after the cartoon from her book, consider whether the problem that Nelson identifies of a "disparity between male and female college sports opportunities" (paragraph 3) applies to your college or your high school.*

Adventures in Equality

Mariah Burton Nelson

In the early 1990s, as female athletes and coaches sued dozens of universities for equal opportunities and as judges consistently ruled in favor of the women, football coaches and administrators waged what one woman called "an offensive" against athletic feminists, claiming that women were attacking the sacred football cow. [1]

Women weren't, in fact, attacking football. They just wanted to swim, row, play soccer, play tennis, or golf, and to coach and direct programs, as men do. They just wanted equal salaries, uniforms, travel schedules, scholarships, and facilities. [2]

In fact, football—or, rather, male support of football and lack of support of women's sports—is responsible for much of the disparity between male and female college sports opportunities. Football "requires" oodles of athletes (108, on average, in Division I), scores of scholarships (75, on average), excessive coaching salaries ($81,574 is the average "base"), and exorbitant operating expenses (more than for all other women's and men's sports combined). [3]

Inevitably, if women are to have half of all sports allocations, as they are entitled to by law, football will have to change. Some schools will trim football's bloated budgets. Others will drop football altogether, as the University of Wisconsin, Superior; Wichita State; the University of Southern Colorado; and Northeastern Illinois University have already done. Others will leave football alone and add several large-squad women's sports, market women's programs to increase revenue, or find other creative ways to stop discriminating. But football defenders fear that their glory days are limited, and they blame women. [4]

"What I'm afraid of is that somebody is trying to put a bull's eye on football's chest," said Oregon Athletic Director Bill Byrne, former president of the National Association of Collegiate Directors of Athletics. [1] [5]

The Reverend Edmund P. Joyce, former executive vice-president at the University of Notre Dame, accused "militant women" of waging a "strident, irresponsible, and irrational campaign" against football. "Never have our football programs been in such jeopardy as they are today," Joyce said. "I think we are fighting for our lives and had better act accordingly." [2] [6]

The fight for college football's life includes arguing that football is the cash cow upon which all the women's programs suckle, even though this is a lie. "Revenue producing"— a term often used to justify discriminatory football and men's basketball programs—is not synonymous with "profit producing." Football programs that earn money almost always spend more—not on women's sports, but on football. In 91 percent of all col- [7]

leges, the football program does not make enough money to pay for itself.[3] Even in the big, football-dominated universities (Division I-A), 45 percent of the football programs lose money. In the other three divisions (I-AA, II, and III), between 94 and 99 percent of the schools lose money on football.[4]

Besides, judges have ruled that "financial considerations cannot justify gender discrimination."   8

The fight for football's life includes arguing that football should be exempt from gender-discrimination calculations. Thomas Hearn, president of Wake Forest University, defended his school to Representative Cardiss Collins of Illinois during a congressional hearing by saying, "At Wake Forest, our athletic scholarship awards without football would approach parity, with 60 percent going to men and 40 percent to women."   9

University of New Haven football coach Mark Whipple has said, "Football shouldn't have anything to do with gender equity. If you don't count football, I think everyone would be happy."[5]   10

"I don't think football players are a third sex," Women's Sports Foundation executive director Donna Lopiano responded. The courts have agreed.   11

The fight for football's life includes arguing that women are being unAmerican, even communist, by depriving young men of their right to play football. Auburn University football coach Pat Dye has said, "To tell a kid he can't come out for college football as a walk-on because it creates a numbers problem with the women in another area, I mean that's almost like communism. That (isn't) what this country was built on, or what it stands for."[6]   12

University of Iowa women's athletic director Christine Grant's response: "Schools   13
have had twenty years to think about this. It's unfortunate for the young men who get cut,
but it's even more unfortunate for the millions of young women who have missed out for
100 years."[7]

The fight for football's life includes redefining "gender equity" to mean men get 60   14
percent, women get 40 percent. In what was hailed as a bold move, the Big Ten Conference recently approved a "gender equity" plan requiring 40 percent of its athletes to be
women by 1997. Only the University of Iowa committed itself to a 50–50 split, which will
make it the only Big Ten school to comply, finally, with the 1972 law.

The fight for football's life includes arguing that "progress" toward Title IX compliance is   15
being made. In fact, if athletic directors had wanted to end discrimination during the wealthy
eighties, they could have added women's programs while holding men's programs steady.
Instead, over the ten-year period between the 1981–1982 season and the 1991–1992
season, for every two female participation slots created, 1.5 male slots were created.[8]

Representative Cardiss Collins has introduced a House bill called the "Equity in Ath-   16
letics Disclosure Act" that would require school administrators to disclose participation
rates and expenditures for male and female athletes. Football coaches and male athletic
directors testified against the bill.

The fight for football's life includes contending that few women want to play sports.   17
This is a last-ditch effort to deny women their rights based on a Title IX interpretation that
allows unequal allocations if "the program fully and effectively accommodates the interests and abilities" of both sexes. Big Ten Commissioner Jim Delaney told me, "Not as
many women are interested in playing sports as men. Look at field hockey versus football. Hundreds of men go out for football. It carries more status."

Collins's response: "Lower participation rates are the *result* of discrimination, and   18
not an *excuse* for continued inequities."[9]

At the Division I-A level, only one out of 107 schools complies with Title IX. This is   19
Washington State University (WSU), which was forced to do so by its own Supreme
Court. In response to a class action suit filed by fifty-three female coaches and players, a
judge ruled in 1982 that the number of WSU scholarships must be proportional to the
ratio of women and men in the undergraduate student body. However, he exempted football from the count. But in 1987, the Supreme Court of Washington overruled the football
exemption. The number of female athletes at WSU is now 44 percent, up from 29 percent
in 1987. The female undergraduate student population is 46 percent.

"We were dragged kicking and screaming into the forefront," recalls Harold C. Gibson,   20
Washington State's associate athletic director. People "thought the sky was falling."[10]

They still seem to think so. The College Football Association's Charles Neinas   21
recently launched a public relations campaign with the slogan, "College football: More
than just a game."[11]

In a surprisingly frank speech to his fellow football coaches and athletic directors,   22
Neinas said, "Football may be the last bastion of male domination."[12]

Which explains a lot.   23

Notes

1. Ben Brown, "Law Gives Women Their Fair Share," *USA Today,* 9 June 1992, p. C1.

2. Buck Turnbull, "Notre Dame's Joyce Says Future of Game on Line vs. Militant Women," *USA Today,* 7 June 1993, p. 12C.

3. Mitchell H. Raiborn, "Revenues and Expenses of Intercollegiate Athletics Programs: Analysis of Financial Trends and Relationships 1985–89" (Mission, Kansas: National Collegiate Athletic Association, 1990). This data refers to NCAA member institutions, which includes most colleges and universities.

4. Ibid.

5. Woody Anderson, Greg Garber, and Lori Riley, "At Last, Title IX Gets Serious Look," *The Hartford Courant,* p. D4.

6. Pat Dye, quoted in the *Birmingham Post–Herald,* cited in "Fundamentals Apply in Education," *NCAA News,* 19 August 1992, p. 4.

7. Chris Grant, *Chicago Tribune,* cited in "Coaches Question Baseball Use of RPI," *NCAA News,* 23 June 1993, p. 4.

8. National Collegiate Athletic Association, 1993, cited in Donna Lopiano, "Statement Before the Subcommittee on Commerce, Consumer Protection, and Competitiveness" (Washington, D.C.: U.S. House of Representatives, 17 February 1993).

9. Cardiss Collins, "Opening Statement," Subcommittee on Commerce, Consumer Protection, and Competitiveness (Washington, D.C.: U.S. House of Representatives, 17 February 1993).

10. Mary Jordan, "Only One School Meets Gender Equity Goal," *Washington Post,* 21 June 1992, p. D1.

11. Debra E. Blum, "Officials of Big-Time College Football See Threat In Moves to Cut Costs and Provide Equity for Women," *The Chronicle of Higher Education,* 16 June 1993, p. A35.

12. Brown, 1992, p. C2.

Connecting to Culture and Experience: Equity

Nelson bases her argument on a fundamental value most Americans share: "equity." As she explains in paragraph 2, "[Women] just wanted to swim, row, play soccer, play tennis, or golf, and to coach and direct programs, as men do. They just wanted equal salaries, uniforms, travel schedules, scholarships, and facilities." She makes equity sound so simple, and yet legislation and court rulings requiring colleges to comply with fairness guidelines have not had much effect. If equity is such a treasured American value, why do you suppose compliance with the Title IX law has been so hard to achieve?

Discuss this question with two or three other students in your class. Begin by exchanging your views on the issue. What values most concern you in regard to college sports? Is gender equity your highest priority, or do other competing values matter more to you than equal opportunity in sports for men and women? How do you think Americans traditionally decide between competing values on issues like this? How do you think Americans should decide?

Analyzing Writing Strategies

1. To examine how Nelson presents the issue, reread the first four paragraphs and note in the margin what she does to demonstrate to readers that the issue exists and is important. To get started, notice that she opens paragraph 1 with a brief history ("In the early 1990s..."). How does she use this history lesson to explain the issue? What else does she do, in paragraphs 1–4, to help her readers understand and appreciate what is at stake?

2. One of the ways Nelson supports her argument is by quoting authorities. Skim the essay and put brackets around each quotation. Some of the sources Nelson quotes share her opinion, while others take a different stand on the issue. Look at what Nelson tells readers in the text and in the list of references at the end about each source she quotes (such as the name, credentials, and affiliations); then consider how readers can use this information to help evaluate what the sources are saying.

Commentary: Anticipating Opposing Positions

Successfully arguing a position usually requires the writer to be aware of widely held positions others have taken on the issue and to respond in some way to their most likely arguments. Writers have three options for counterarguing: merely acknowledging other positions, conceding valid points by accommodating or making room for them in their own argument, or trying to refute them.

How writers choose to counterargue depends on their readers and purpose. Nelson probably had two kinds of readers in mind: those who know very little about the debate, and those who already know about the debate and basically agree with her. Nelson's purpose in addressing the less knowledgeable readers is primarily to convince them that there is no reason to delay implementing the Title IX law requiring gender equity in spending for college sports. For her more knowledgable readers, Nelson may have had two aims: to remind them of the outrageous and unfounded reasons advanced by the opposition, and to inspire them to continue the fight for gender equity in collegiate sports.

The bulk of Nelson's essay (twelve of twenty-three paragraphs) is organized as a refutation in which she systematically describes and critiques six common reasons for the opposing position:

1. Gender equity should not be imposed on football programs because football supports other sports programs, including women's sports (paragraphs 7–8).

2. Gender equity should not be imposed on football programs because football is special and should not be included in gender-discrimination calculations (9–11).

3. Gender equity should not be imposed on football programs because college men in America have the "right" to play football (12–13).

4. Gender equity should not be imposed on football programs because a 50–50 split is an unfair goal (14).

5. Gender equity should not be imposed on football programs because "progress" is being made (15–16).

6. Gender equity should not be imposed on football programs because "few women want to play sports" anyway (17–18).

Nelson attempts to refute each of these points, supporting her counterargument with information, examples, statistics, and quotations from experts.

You probably noticed that Nelson repeats the same language ("The fight for football's life includes. . . .") to announce each new point she refutes. This repetition has two purposes. Repeating an introductory phrase in this way enhances cohesion by making it easy for readers to follow the thread of the argument. It also may serve a rhetorical purpose by creating the impression that her opponents are desperately fighting for football's life, grasping at straws in search of any argument that will postpone the inevitable, and suggesting that women themselves had better continue fighting until funding equity is assured.

Considering Topics for Your Own Essay

Think of a political issue on which you could write an essay. You might consider a local campus issue (such as whether a particular instructor should get tenure or be fired, whether funds should be used for computer labs or parking spaces, or whether student athletes should be required to maintain a certain grade point average to participate in sports) or a local community issue (such as whether a new shelter for abused women and children should be opened, whether parents should be held responsible legally and financially for crimes committed by their children under age eighteen, or whether skateboarding should be permitted in a park). Choose an issue and then think about how you would go about getting information to support your argument.

Jessica Statsky wrote the following essay about children's competitive sports for her college composition course. Before reading, recall your own experiences as an elementary student playing competitive sports, either in or out of school. If you were not actively involved yourself, did you know anyone who was? Looking back, do you think that winning was unduly emphasized? What value was placed on having a good time? On learning to get along with others? On developing athletic skills and confidence?

Children Need to Play, Not Compete

Jessica Statsky

Over the past three decades, organized sports for children have increased dramatically in the United States. And though many adults regard Little League Baseball and Peewee Football as a basic part of childhood, the games are not always joyous ones. When overzealous parents and coaches impose adult standards on children's sports, the result can be activities that are neither satisfying nor beneficial to children.

I am concerned about all organized sports activities for children between the ages of six and twelve. The damage I see results from noncontact as well as contact sports, from sports organized locally as well as those organized nationally. Highly organized competitive sports such as Peewee Football and Little League Baseball are too often played to adult standards, which are developmentally inappropriate for children and can be both physically and psychologically harmful. Furthermore, because they eliminate many children from organized sports before they are ready to compete, they are actually counterproductive for developing either future players or fans. Finally, because they emphasize competition and winning, they unfortunately provide occasions for some parents and coaches to place their own fantasies and needs ahead of children's welfare.

One readily understandable danger of overly competitive sports is that they entice children into physical actions that are bad for growing bodies. Although the official *Little League Online* Web site acknowledges that children do risk injury playing baseball, it insists that severe injuries are infrequent, "far less than the risk of riding a skateboard, a bicycle, or even the school bus" ("What about My Child"). Nevertheless, Leonard Koppett in *Sports Illusion, Sports Reality* claims that a twelve-year-old trying to throw a curve ball, for example, may put abnormal strain on developing arm and shoulder muscles, sometimes resulting in lifelong injuries (294). Contact sports like football can be even more hazardous. Thomas Tutko, a psychology professor at San Jose State University and coauthor of the book *Winning is Everything and Other American Myths,* writes:

> I am strongly opposed to young kids playing tackle football. It is not the right stage of development for them to be taught to crash into other kids. Kids under the age of fourteen are not by nature physical. Their main concern is self-preservation. They don't want to meet head on and slam into each other. But tackle football absolutely requires that they try to hit each other as hard as they can. And it is too traumatic for young kids. (qtd. in Tosches A1)

As Tutko indicates, even when children are not injured, fear of being hurt detracts from their enjoyment of the sport. *Little League Online* ranks fear of injury as the seventh of seven reasons children quit ("What about My Child"). One mother of an eight-year-old Peewee Football player explained, "The kids get so scared. They get hit once and they don't want anything to do with football anymore. They'll sit on the bench and pretend their leg hurts..." (qtd. in Tosches A1). Some children are driven to even more desperate measures. For example, in one Peewee Football game, a reporter watched the following scene as a player took himself out of the game:

"Coach, my tummy hurts. I can't play," he said. The coach told the player to get back onto the field. "There's nothing wrong with your stomach," he said. When the coach turned his head the seven-year-old stuck a finger down his throat and made himself vomit. When the coach turned back, the boy pointed to the ground and told him, "Yes there is, coach. See?" (Tosches A33)

Besides physical hazards and anxieties, competitive sports pose psychological dangers for children. Martin Rablovsky, a former sports editor for the *New York Times,* says that in all his years of watching young children play organized sports, he has noticed very few of them smiling. "I've seen children enjoying a spontaneous pre-practice scrimmage become somber and serious when the coach's whistle blows," Rablovsky says. "The spirit of play suddenly disappears, and sport becomes joblike" (qtd. in Coakley 94). The primary goal of a professional athlete—winning—is not appropriate for children. Their goals should be having fun, learning, and being with friends. Although winning does add to the fun, too many adults lose sight of what matters and make winning the most important goal. Several studies have shown that when children are asked whether they would rather be warming the bench on a winning team or playing regularly on a losing team, about 90 percent choose the latter (Smith, Smith, and Smoll 11).

Winning and losing may be an inevitable part of adult life, but they should not be part of childhood. Too much competition too early in life can affect a child's development. Children are easily influenced, and when they sense that their competence and worth are based on their ability to live up to their parents' and coaches' high expectations—and on their ability to win—they can become discouraged and depressed. Little League advises parents to "keep winning in perspective" (*Little League Online,* "Your Role"), noting that the most common reasons children give for quitting, aside from change in interest, are lack of playing time, failure and fear of failure, disapproval by significant others, and psychological stress (*Little League Online,* "What about My Child"). According to Dr. Glyn C. Roberts, a professor of kinesiology at the Institute of Child Behavior and Development at the University of Illinois, 80 to 90 percent of children who play competitive sports at a young age drop out by sixteen (Kutner C8).

This statistic illustrates another reason I oppose competitive sports for children: because they are so highly selective, very few children get to participate. Far too soon, a few children are singled out for their athletic promise, while many others, who may be on the verge of developing the necessary strength and ability, are screened out and discouraged from trying out again. Like adults, children fear failure, and so even those with good physical skills may stay away because they lack self-confidence. Consequently, teams lose many promising players who with some encouragement and experience might have become stars. The problem is that many parent-sponsored, out-of-school programs give more importance to having a winning team than to developing children's physical skills and self-esteem.

Indeed, it is no secret that too often scorekeeping, league standings, and the drive to win bring out the worst in adults who are more absorbed in living out their own fantasies than in enhancing the quality of the experience for children (Smith, Smith, and Smoll 9).

Recent newspaper articles on children's sports contain plenty of horror stories. *Los Angeles Times* reporter Rich Tosches, for example, tells the story of a brawl among seventy-five parents following a Peewee Football game (A33). As a result of the brawl, which began when a parent from one team confronted a player from the other team, the teams are now thinking of hiring security guards for future games. Another example is provided by an *L.A. Times* editorial about a Little League manager who intimidated the opposing team by setting fire to one of their team's jerseys on the pitching mound before the game began. As the editorial writer commented, the manager showed his young team that "intimidation could substitute for playing well" ("The Bad News" B6).

Although not all parents or coaches behave so inappropriately, the seriousness of   9
the problem is illustrated by the fact that Adelphi University in Garden City, New York, offers a sports psychology workshop for Little League coaches, designed to balance their "animal instincts" with "educational theory" in hopes of reducing the "screaming and hollering," in the words of Harold Weisman, manager of sixteen Little Leagues in New York City (Schmitt B2). In a three-and-one-half-hour Sunday morning workshop, coaches learn how to make practices more fun, treat injuries, deal with irate parents, and be "more sensitive to their young players' fears, emotional frailties, and need for recognition." Little League is to be credited with recognizing the need for such workshops.

Some parents would no doubt argue that children cannot start too soon preparing to   10
live in a competitive free-market economy. After all, secondary schools and colleges require students to compete for grades, and college admission is extremely competitive. And it is perfectly obvious how important competitive skills are in finding a job. Yet the ability to cooperate is also important for success in life. Before children are psychologically ready for competition, maybe we should emphasize cooperation and individual performance in team sports rather than winning.

Many people are ready for such an emphasis. In 1988, one New York Little League   11
official who had attended the Adelphi workshop tried to ban scoring from six- to eight-year-olds' games — but parents wouldn't support him (Schmitt B2). An innovative children's sports program in New York City, City Sports for Kids, emphasizes fitness, self-esteem, and sportsmanship. In this program's basketball games, every member on a team plays at least two of six eight-minute periods. The basket is seven feet from the floor, rather than ten feet, and a player can score a point just by hitting the rim (Bloch C12). I believe this kind of local program should replace overly competitive programs like Peewee Football and Little League Baseball. As one coach explains, significant improvements can result from a few simple rule changes, such as including every player in the batting order and giving every player, regardless of age or ability, the opportunity to play at least four innings a game (Frank).

Authorities have clearly documented the excesses and dangers of many competitive   12
sports programs for children. It would seem that few children benefit from these programs and that those who do would benefit even more from programs emphasizing fitness, cooperation, sportsmanship, and individual performance. Thirteen- and fourteen-year-olds may be eager for competition, but few younger children are. These younger children deserve sports programs designed specifically for their needs and abilities.

Works Cited

Bloch, Gordon B. "Thrill of Victory Is Secondary to Fun." *New York Times* 2 Apr. 1990, late ed.: C12.

"The Bad News Pyromaniacs?" Editorial. *Los Angeles Times* 16 June 1990: B6.

Coakley, Jay J. *Sport in Society: Issues and Controversies.* St. Louis: Mosby, 1982.

Frank, L. "Contributions from Parents and Coaches." Online posting. 8 July 1997. CYB Message Board. 14 May 1999 <http://members.aol.com/JohnHoelter/b-parent.html>.

Koppett, Leonard. *Sports Illusion, Sports Reality.* Boston: Houghton, 1981.

Kutner, Lawrence. "Athletics, through a Child's Eyes." *New York Times* 23 Mar. 1989, late ed.: C8.

Little League Online. "Your Role as a Little League Parent." Little League Baseball, Incorporated 1999. 30 June 1999 <http://www.littleleague.org/about/parents/yourrole.htm>.

———. "What about My Child." Little League Baseball, Incorporated 1999. 30 June 1999 <http://www.littleleague.org/about/parents/yourchild.htm>.

Schmitt, Eric. "Psychologists Take Seat on Little League Bench." *New York Times* 14 Mar. 1988, late ed.: B2.

Smith, Nathan, Ronald Smith, and Frank Smoll. *Kidsports: A Survival Guide for Parents.* Reading: Addison, 1983.

Tosches, Rich. "Peewee Football: Is It Time to Blow the Whistle?" *Los Angeles Times* 3 Dec. 1988: A1+.

Connecting to Culture and Experience: Competition versus Cooperation

Statsky makes the point that competition is highly valued in our culture, whereas cooperation tends to be downplayed. Discuss some of the ways in which our society encourages competition, especially among children and through sports or other forms of play. Consider also how cooperation is encouraged. Think about whether, in your own experience, the educational system has encouraged one more than the other.

Then expand your discussion to include the influence of cultural forces such as advertising, television, and movies. Which of the two, competition or cooperation, seems to be valued more highly in these areas? If you believe there is a cultural preference for competition or cooperation, reflect on who in society might benefit most from such a preference. Consider such factors as gender, age, ethnicity, class, and religion. Who loses most?

Analyzing Writing Strategies

1. Anecdotes can provide convincing support if they are clearly relevant to the point they support, believable, and vivid enough to enable readers to imagine what

happened. In paragraph 4, Statsky presents one fully developed anecdote that includes dialogue and a detailed narrative. In paragraph 8, she offers two brief anecdotes that summarize rather than detail the events: one is about a brawl among parents and the other about a team manager who set fire to a jersey of the opposing team. Locate and reread these anecdotes in order to find out what each one contributes to Statsky's argument and to judge how convincing they are likely to be for her readers.

2. To support her argument, Statsky repeatedly quotes authorities, experts who agree with her position. Skim the essay, underlining each authority she cites. Note where she quotes whole sentences or individual words and phrases. Also try to determine where she summarizes the source instead of quoting it verbatim. Then pick one source you think adds something important to her argument, and briefly explain what it adds.

3. Statsky also makes effective use of examples. Reread paragraphs 8 and 11. Notice that the first sentence in each paragraph states the claim Statsky hopes to support with examples. Then identify each of the separate examples, some merely mentioned, others developed. What does each example contribute to Statsky's argument? How convincing do you think each example will be for Statsky's readers, parents with children participating—or who may soon want to participate—in organized competitive sports?

Commentary: A Clear Position

Writers arguing a position must state their opinion clearly, but they also try not to overstate it. By avoiding absolute, unconditional language and carefully qualifying her position, Statsky makes clear her concerns without making enthusiasts overly defensive. Throughout the essay, she temporizes with words like *not always, can, maybe,* and *it would seem*—words that potentially have a major effect on readers, making Statsky's position seem reasonable without making her seem indecisive. Similarly, Statsky qualifies her position by focusing on a particular age group. To ensure that readers know the particular kind of sports she is talking about, she gives two familiar examples: Peewee Football and Little League Baseball.

Statsky's unambiguous word choice and appropriate qualification satisfy two of the three standards of an effective thesis. (For more on asserting a thesis, see Chapter 11, pp. 327–30.) The third criterion, that the position be arguable, is indicated clearly in paragraph 2, where Statsky forecasts the three reasons for opposing organized competitive sports for young children developed later in the essay:

Such sports are "physically and psychologically harmful" (developed in paragraphs 3–6)

They are "counterproductive for developing either future players or fans" (developed in paragraph 7)

They "emphasize competition and winning" (developed in paragraphs 8–9)

(For more on forecasting, see Chapter 8, p. 275.)

Inexperienced writers are sometimes reluctant to state their thesis and forecast their reasons as clearly and directly as Statsky does. They fear that being explicit would oversimplify or give away the whole argument. But we can see from Statsky's essay that the effectiveness of her argument is enhanced, not diminished, by her directness. Nor does explicitness prevent her from advancing a complex and thoughtful argument on an issue that is certain to arouse strong feelings in many readers.

Considering Topics for Your Own Essay

Make a list of issues related to childhood and adolescence. For example, should elementary and secondary schools be on a year-round schedule? Should children have the right to "divorce" their parents? Should adolescents who commit serious crimes be tried as adults? Then choose an issue that you think you could write about. What position would you take?

■ PURPOSE AND AUDIENCE

Purpose and audience are closely linked when you write an essay arguing a position. In defining your purpose, you also need to anticipate your readers. Most writers compose essays arguing for a position because they care deeply about the issue. As they develop an argument with their readers in mind, however, writers usually feel challenged to think critically about their own as well as their readers' feelings and thoughts about the issue.

Writers with strong convictions seek to influence their readers. Assuming that logical argument will prevail over prejudice, they try to change readers' minds by presenting compelling reasons and support based on shared values and principles. Nevertheless, they also recognize that in cases where disagreement is profound, it is highly unlikely that a single essay will be able to change readers' minds, no matter how well written it is. Addressing an audience that is completely opposed to their position, most writers are satisfied if they can simply win their readers' respect for their different point of view. Often, however, all that can be done is to sharpen the differences.

BASIC FEATURES: ARGUING POSITIONS

A Focused Presentation of the Issue

Writers use a variety of strategies to present the issue and prepare readers for their argument. For current, hotly debated issues, the title may be enough to identify the issue. Leshner, for example, frames the issue as a question ("Why Shouldn't Society Treat Substance Abusers?"), Leshner states explicitly that "people are polarized on the issue," and Statsky gives a brief history of the debate about competitive sports for children. Many writers provide concrete examples early on to make sure that readers can understand the issue. Statsky mentions Peewee Football and Little League Baseball as examples of the kind of organized sports she opposes. Leshner opens his essay with a hypothetical example, a scenario in which readers are asked to imagine a situation like the one he is writing about.

How writers present the issue depends on what they assume readers already know and what they want readers to think about the issue. Therefore, they try to define the issue in a way that promotes their position. Leshner, for example, presents the issue of treating drug addiction in terms of its practical impact on society.

A Clear Position

Very often writers declare their position in a thesis statement early in the essay. This strategy has the advantage of letting readers know right away where the writer stands. Statsky places her thesis in the opening paragraph, whereas Leshner and Nelson put it in the second paragraph. Moreover, they all restate the thesis at places in the argument where readers could lose sight of the central point. And they reiterate the thesis at the end.

In composing a thesis statement, writers try to make their position unambiguous, appropriately qualified, and clearly arguable. For example, Statsky uses unambiguous language in her thesis statement: "When overzealous parents and coaches impose adult standards on children's sports, the result can be activities that are neither satisfying nor beneficial to children." It is clear that Statsky is not opposed to children's sports, but only to "adult standards" imposed on children's sports. Because some readers may be envisioning teenaged players and wondering what is wrong with the standards used in secondary school competitions, Statsky further qualifies her thesis by stating that she is concerned about children at a certain stage of physical and psychological maturity, "between the ages of six and twelve." In addition, Statsky makes her position arguable by asserting that the adults' emphasis on winning "can" cause problems for children, rather than making a blanket statement that it always does so. Later in the essay she supports this by conceding "not all parents or coaches behave so inappropriately."

Plausible Reasons and Convincing Support

To argue for a position, writers must give reasons. Even in relatively brief essays, writers usually give more than one reason and make their reasons explicit. Leshner, for instance, supports treating drug addicts for four reasons: doing so will improve lives, cut crime, reduce disease, and improve productivity.

Moreover, to make their reasons seem plausible to readers, writers try to logically connect each reason to the position it backs. This logical connection can be understood in terms of an "if...then" relationship. For example, if readers believe Leshner's argument that treatments for drug addiction are effective and that treating drug addicts will improve lives, cut crime, reduce disease, and enhance productivity, then readers will be more inclined to "rise above" their "moral outrage that addiction results from a voluntary behavior," as Leshner urges in the final paragraph. In other words, logic dictates that if the reason is true, then the position is also likely to be true. The truth of the reason, of course, depends on how convincing the support seems to individual readers.

Writers know they cannot simply assert their reasons. They must support them with examples, statistics, authorities, or anecdotes. We have seen all of these kinds of support used in this chapter. For instance, Statsky uses all of them in her essay — giving examples of common sports injuries children may incur, citing statistics indicating the percentage of children who prefer not to play on their team, quoting authorities on the physical and psychological hazards of competitive sports for young children, and relating an anecdote of a child vomiting to show the enormous psychological pressure competitive sports put on some children.

Anticipating Opposing Positions and Objections

Writers also try to anticipate other widely held positions on the issue as well as objections and questions readers might raise to their argument. The writers in this chapter counterargue by either accommodating or refuting opposing positions and objections. Nelson, for instance, takes up six different reasons often presented by opponents of Title IX gender equity requirements and devotes most of her argument to refuting them. For each, she first presents the opposing argument, summarizing and quoting what others have said or written. Then she counterargues briefly, often quoting an authority or citing statistics to undermine the argument.

Anticipating readers' positions and objections can enhance the writer's credibility and strengthen the argument. When readers holding an opposing position recognize that the writer takes their position seriously, they are more likely to listen to what the writer has to say. It can also reassure readers that they share certain important values and attitudes with the writer, building a bridge of common concerns among people who have been separated by difference and antagonism.

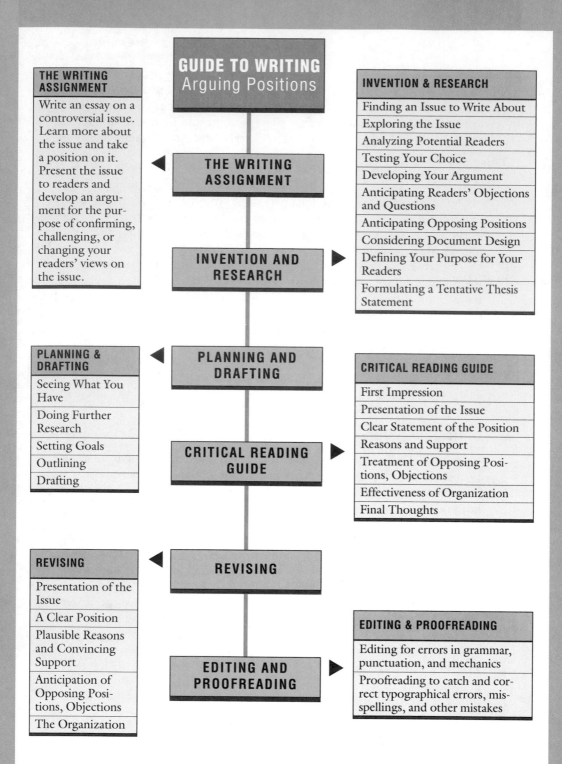

GUIDE TO WRITING
Arguing Positions

THE WRITING ASSIGNMENT

Write an essay on a controversial issue. Learn more about the issue and take a position on it. Present the issue to readers and develop an argument for the purpose of confirming, challenging, or changing your readers' views on the issue.

THE WRITING ASSIGNMENT

INVENTION & RESEARCH

Finding an Issue to Write About

Exploring the Issue

Analyzing Potential Readers

Testing Your Choice

Developing Your Argument

Anticipating Readers' Objections and Questions

Anticipating Opposing Positions

Considering Document Design

Defining Your Purpose for Your Readers

Formulating a Tentative Thesis Statement

INVENTION AND RESEARCH

PLANNING & DRAFTING

Seeing What You Have

Doing Further Research

Setting Goals

Outlining

Drafting

PLANNING AND DRAFTING

CRITICAL READING GUIDE

First Impression

Presentation of the Issue

Clear Statement of the Position

Reasons and Support

Treatment of Opposing Positions, Objections

Effectiveness of Organization

Final Thoughts

CRITICAL READING GUIDE

REVISING

Presentation of the Issue

A Clear Position

Plausible Reasons and Convincing Support

Anticipation of Opposing Positions, Objections

The Organization

REVISING

EDITING & PROOFREADING

Editing for errors in grammar, punctuation, and mechanics

Proofreading to catch and correct typographical errors, misspellings, and other mistakes

EDITING AND PROOFREADING

GUIDE TO WRITING

■ THE WRITING ASSIGNMENT

Write an essay on a controversial issue. Learn more about the issue and take a position on it. Present the issue to readers and develop an argument for the purpose of confirming, challenging, or changing your readers' views on the issue.

■ INVENTION AND RESEARCH

The following activities will help you find an issue, explore what you know about it, and do any necessary research to develop an argument and counterargument. Each activity is easy to do and in most cases takes only a few minutes. Spreading the activities over several days will help you think critically about your own as well as other people's positions on the issue. Keep a written record of your invention and research to use when you draft and revise your essay.

Finding an Issue to Write About

To find the best possible issue for your essay, list as many possibilities as you can. The following activities will help you make a good choice.

Listing Issues. *Make a list of issues you might consider writing about.* Begin your list now, and add to it over the next few days. Include issues on which you already have a position and ones you do not know much about but would like to explore further. Do not overlook the issues suggested by the Considering Topics for Your Own Essay activities following each reading in this chapter.

Put the issues in the form of questions, like the following examples:

- Should local school boards be allowed to ban books (like *The Adventures of Huckleberry Finn* and *Of Mice and Men*) from school libraries?
- Should teenagers be required to get their parents' permission to obtain birth-control information and contraceptives?
- Should public libraries and schools be allowed to block access to selected Internet sites?
- Should undercover police officers be permitted to pose as high school students in order to identify sellers and users of drugs?
- Should training in music performance or art (drawing, painting, sculpting) be required of all high school students?
- Should college admission be based solely on academic achievement in high school?

- Should colleges be required to provide child-care facilities for children of students taking classes?
- Should students attending public colleges be required to pay higher tuition fees if they do not graduate within four years?
- Should sports officials rely on instant replay to settle disputed calls?
- Should elected state or national representatives vote primarily on the basis of their individual conscience, their constituents' interests, or the general welfare?
- Should scientists attempt to clone human beings as they have done with animals?

Listing Issues Related to Identity and Community.   As the following suggestions indicate, many controversial issues will enable you to explore your understanding of identity and community. List issues that interest you.

- Can self-esteem be increased by workshops or counseling?
- Should students choose a college or courses that would confirm or challenge their beliefs and values?
- Should our schools continue to emphasize the history, philosophy, literature, and art of western European civilization, or should they give equal time to other cultural traditions (such as Native American, African, Asian, and Latin) that contribute to American civilization?
- Should high schools or colleges require students to perform community service as a condition for graduation?
- Should children of immigrants who do not speak English be taught in their native language while they are learning English?
- Should all materials related to voting, driving, and income-tax reporting be written only in English or in other languages read by members of the community?
- Should the racial, ethnic, or gender makeup of a police force parallel the makeup of the community it serves?

Listing Issues Related to Work and Career.   Many current controversial issues will allow you to explore work and career topics. Identify issues that you would consider writing about.

- Should businesses remain loyal to their communities, or should they move to wherever labor costs, taxes, or other conditions are more favorable?
- Should companies be free to replace workers who go on strike for better wages or working conditions, or should they be required to negotiate with workers?
- When they choose careers, should people look primarily for jobs that are well paid or for jobs that are personally fulfilling, morally correct, or socially responsible?
- Should the state or federal government provide job training, temporary employment, or financial aid to people who are unemployed and willing to work?

- Should the primary purpose of a college education be job training?
- Should drug testing be mandatory for people in high-risk jobs such as bus drivers, heavy-equipment operators, and airplane pilots?

Choosing an Interesting Issue.   *Select an issue from your list that you think would be interesting to explore further.* You may already have an opinion on the issue, or you may have chosen it because you want to learn more about it.

Your choice may be influenced by whether you have time for research or whether your instructor requires you to do research. Issues that have been written about extensively make excellent topics for extended research projects. In contrast, you may feel confident writing about a local community or campus issue without doing much, if any, research. It also may help you in choosing an issue to identify your readers tentatively and to think about the kinds of arguments people usually make when debating the issue.

Exploring the Issue

To explore the issue, you need to define it, determine whether you need to do research, and decide tentatively on your position.

Defining the Issue.   *To begin thinking about the issue, write for a few minutes explaining how you currently understand it.* If you have strong feelings about the issue, briefly explain why, but do not present your argument at this time. Focus on clarifying the issue by considering questions like these:

- Who has taken a position on this issue, and what positions have they taken?
- How does the issue affect different groups of people? What is at stake for them?
- What is the issue's history? How long has it been an issue? Has it changed over time? What makes it important now?
- How broad is the issue? What other issues are related to it? In what category (or categories) might the issue fit?

Doing Research.   *If you do not know very much about the issue or the different views people have taken on it, do some research before continuing.* You can gather information by talking to others and by reading what others have written. (Refer to Chapter 12 for advice on interviewing an expert or surveying opinion and to Chapter 13 for guidelines on doing library and Internet research.)

If you do not have time for research and lack confidence in your knowledge of the issue, you should switch to another issue about which you are better informed. Return to your list of possible issues and start over.

Exploring Your Opinion.   *Write for a few minutes exploring your current thinking on the issue.* What is your current position? Why do you hold this position? What other positions on the issue do you know about? As you develop your argument and learn more about the issue, you may change your mind. Your aim now is merely to record your thinking as of this moment.

Analyzing Potential Readers

Write several sentences describing the readers to whom you will be addressing your argument. Begin by briefly identifying your readers; then use the following questions to help you describe them.

- What position or positions will my readers take on this issue? How entrenched are these positions likely to be?

- What do my readers know about the issue? In what contexts are they likely to have encountered it? In what ways might the issue affect them personally or professionally?

- How far apart on the issue are my readers and I likely to be? What fundamental differences in worldview or experience might keep us from agreeing? Which of my readers' values might most influence their view of the issue?

- Why would I want to present my argument to these particular readers? What could I realistically hope to achieve — convincing them to adopt my point of view, getting them to reconsider their own position, confirming or challenging some of their underlying beliefs and values?

Testing Your Choice

Decide whether you should proceed with this particular issue. Review your invention notes to see whether you understand the issue well enough to continue working with it and whether you can feel confident that you will be able to construct a convincing argument for your prospective readers. To make these decisions, ask yourself the following questions:

- Have I begun to understand the issue and my own position well enough to begin constructing a well-reasoned, well-supported argument?

- Do I have a good enough sense of how my readers view this issue to begin formulating an argument that is appropriate for them?

- Do I now know enough about the issue or can I learn what I need to know in the time I have remaining?

If you cannot answer these questions affirmatively at this point in the process, it might be wise to consider a different issue. Giving up on a topic after you have worked on it is bound to be frustrating, but if you have little interest in the issue and do not have any idea how you could address your readers, starting over may be the wisest course of action. The following collaborative activity may help you decide whether to go on with this issue or begin looking for an alternative.

Testing Your Choice: A Collaborative Activity	At this point in your invention work, you will find it helpful to get together with two or three other students to try out a bit of your argument. Their reactions will help you determine whether you will be able to construct a convincing argument for your position.

Arguers: Take turns briefly providing the context—the issue, purpose and readers, and your position—followed by one reason for your position. Choose a reason you think will carry weight with your readers and explain why you think so.

Listeners: Briefly tell each arguer how you think the intended readers are likely to respond to the reason. Also try to help the arguer by suggesting one way in which the reason could be made stronger—for example, by providing a clearer explanation of why readers should accept the position if they think the reason is plausible. Suggest an example, anecdote, or authority the writer could use to support the reason. If you think the reason is weak, explain the objections readers could raise.

Developing Your Argument

To construct a convincing argument, you need to list reasons for your position, choose the most plausible ones, and support them.

Listing Reasons.   *Write down every reason you can think of to convince readers of your position.* Try stating your reasons as part of a tentative thesis statement with *because* or *that* clauses, as in "My position is X because . . ." or "A reason I believe X is that. . . ."

Choosing the Most Plausible Reasons.   *Write several sentences on each reason to determine which reasons are most plausible; then identify your most plausible reasons.* To test the plausibility of your reasons, try to explain the logical *(if . . . then)* connection between each reason and your position. For each reason, draft a brief answer to this question: "Why do I think that *if* my readers accept this reason, *then* they also would accept my position?" If you decide that none of your reasons seems very plausible, you might need to reconsider your position, do some more research, or choose another issue.

Anticipating Readers' Objections and Questions

Listing Your Most Plausible Reasons.   *Review the choices you made at the end of the preceding activity.* List your two or three most plausible reasons, skipping a few lines between the reasons.

Listing Objections and Questions.   *Under each reason, list one or more objections or questions that readers could raise.* You may know how readers will respond to some of your reasons. For others, you may need to be inventive. Imagining yourself as a critical reader, look for places where your argument is vulnerable to criticism. For example, think of an assumption you are making that others might not accept or a value others might not share. Imagine how people in different situations—different neighborhoods, occupations, age groups, living arrangements—might react to your argument.

Accommodating a Legitimate Objection or Question.   *Choose one objection or question that makes sense to you and write for a few minutes on how you could accommodate it into your argument.* You may be able simply to acknowledge an objection or answer a question and explain why you think it does not negatively affect your argument. If the criticism is more serious, try not to let it shake your confidence. Instead, consider how you can accommodate it, perhaps by conceding the point and qualifying your position or changing the way you argue for it.

If the criticism is so damaging that you cannot accommodate it into your argument, however, you may need to rethink your position or even consider writing on a different issue. If you arrive at such an impasse, discuss the problem with your instructor; do not abandon your issue unless it is absolutely necessary.

Refuting an Illegitimate Objection or Question.   *Choose one objection or question that you do not accept to try to refute, and write for a few minutes planning your response.* Do not choose to refute only the weakest objection (sometimes called a *straw man*) while ignoring the strongest one. Consider whether you can show that an objection is based on a misunderstanding or that it does not really damage your argument.

Anticipating Opposing Positions

Now that you have planned your argument, you need to consider how you can respond to the arguments for other positions on the issue.

Considering Other Positions.   *Identify one or more widely held positions other than your own that people take on the issue.* If you can, identify the individuals or groups who support the positions you list.

Listing Reasons for the Opposing Position.   *Choose the opposing position you think is likely to be most attractive to your readers (there may only be one), and list the reasons people give for it.* Given what you now know, try to represent the argument accurately and fairly. Later, you may need to do some research to find out more about this opposing position.

Accommodating a Plausible Reason.   *Choose one reason that makes sense to you and write for a few minutes on how you could accommodate it into your argument.* Consider whether you can concede the point and put it aside as not really damaging to your central argument. You may also have to consider qualifying your position or changing the way you argue for it.

Refuting an Implausible Reason.   *Choose one reason that you do not accept and write for a few minutes on how you will plan your refutation.* Do not choose to refute a position no one really takes seriously. Also be careful not to misrepresent other people's positions or to criticize people personally (sometimes called an *ad hominem* attack). Do try to get at the heart of your disagreement.

You may want to argue that the values on which the opposing argument is based are not widely shared or are just plain wrong. Or perhaps you can point out that the reasoning is flawed (for instance, showing that an example applies only to certain people in certain situations and cannot be generalized). Or maybe you can show that the argument lacks convincing support (for instance, that the opposition's statistics can be interpreted differently or that quoted authorities do not qualify as experts). If you do not have all the information you need, make a note of what you need and where you might find it. Later, you can do more research to develop this part of your argument.

Considering Document Design

Think about whether including visual or audio elements—cartoons, photographs, tables, graphs, or snippets from films, television programs, or songs—would strengthen your argument. These are not a requirement of an effective essay arguing a position, but could be helpful. Consider also whether your readers might benefit from design features such as headings, bulleted or numbered lists, or other elements that would make your essay easier to follow. You could construct your own graphic elements, download materials from the Internet, copy images and sounds from television or other sources, or scan into your document visuals from books and magazines. When you reproduce visuals, make sure to acknowledge their sources.

Defining Your Purpose for Your Readers

Write a few sentences, defining your purpose in writing about your position on this issue for your particular readers. Remember that you already have analyzed your potential readers and developed your argument with these readers in mind. Given these readers, try now to define your purpose by considering the following possibilities and any others that might apply to your writing situation:

- If my readers are likely to be sympathetic to my point of view, what do I hope to achieve—give them reasons to commit to my position, arm them with ammunition to make their own arguments, or win their respect and admiration?

- If my readers are likely to be hostile to my point of view, what do I hope to accomplish—get them to concede that other points of view must be taken seriously, make them defend their reasons, show them how knowledgeable and committed I am to my position, or show them how well I can argue?

- If my readers are likely to take an opposing position but are not staunchly committed to it, what should I try to do—make them think critically about the reasons and the kinds of support they have for their position, give them reasons to change their minds, show them how my position serves their interests better, appeal to their values and sense of responsibility, or disabuse them of their preconceptions and prejudices against my position?

Formulating a Tentative Thesis Statement

Write several sentences that could serve as your tentative thesis statement. Assert your position carefully. You might also forecast your reasons, listing them in the order in which you will take them up in your argument. In other words, draft a thesis statement that tells your readers simply and directly what you want them to think about the issue and why. (For more on thesis and forecasting statements, see Chapter 8, pp. 273–75.) Leshner, for example, states his thesis and forecasts his argument in the second paragraph: "Addicts are frequently denied treatment that would not only improve their lives, but also would improve our own lives — by cutting crime, reducing disease and improving the productivity of employees and the economy."

Perhaps the most explicit and fully developed thesis statement in this chapter's readings is Jessica Statsky's. She asserts her thesis at the end of the first paragraph and then qualifies it and forecasts her reasons in the second paragraph:

> …When overzealous parents and coaches impose adult standards on children's sports, the result can be activities that are neither satisfying nor beneficial to children.
>
> I am concerned about all organized sports activities for children between the ages of six and twelve. The damage I see results from noncontact as well as contact sports, from sports organized locally as well as those organized nationally. Highly organized competitive sports such as Peewee Football and Little League Baseball are too often played to adult standards, which are developmentally inappropriate for children and can be both physically and psychologically harmful. Furthermore, because they eliminate many children from organized sports before they are ready to compete, they are actually counterproductive for developing either future players or fans. Finally, because they emphasize competition and winning, they unfortunately provide occasions for some parents and coaches to place their own fantasies and needs ahead of children's welfare.

As you formulate your own tentative thesis statement, pay attention to the language you use. It should be clear and unambiguous, emphatic but appropriately qualified, as well as arguable and based on plausible reasons. Although you will most probably refine this thesis statement as you work on your essay, trying now to articulate it will help give your planning and drafting direction and impetus. (For more on asserting a thesis, see Chapter 11, pp. 327–30.)

■ PLANNING AND DRAFTING

You should now review what you have learned about the issue, do further research if necessary, and plan your first draft by setting goals and making an outline.

Seeing What You Have

Pause now to reflect on your invention and research notes. Reread everything carefully in order to decide whether you have enough plausible reasons and convincing support to offer readers and whether you understand the debate well enough to anticipate and respond to your readers' likely objections.

If your invention notes are skimpy, you may not have given enough thought to the issue or know enough at this time to write a convincing argument about it. You can do further research at this stage or begin drafting and later do research to fill in the blanks.

If you fear that you are in over your head, consult your instructor to determine whether you should make a radical change. For example, your instructor might suggest that you tackle a smaller, more doable aspect of the issue, perhaps one with which you have firsthand experience. It is also possible that your instructor will advise you to give up on this topic for the time being and to try writing on a different issue.

Doing Further Research

If you think you lack crucial information you will need to plan and draft your essay, this is a good time to do some further research. Consider possible sources, including people you could interview as well as library materials and Internet sites. Then do your research, making sure to note down all the information you will need to cite your sources. (For help with research, see Chapters 12–14.)

Setting Goals

Before you begin writing your draft, consider some specific goals for your essay. The draft will not only be easier to write if you have some clear goals in mind, but also more focused. The following questions will help you set goals. You may find it useful to return to them while you are drafting, for they are designed to help you look at specific features and strategies of an essay arguing a position on a controversial issue.

Your Purpose and Readers

- Who are my readers and what can I realistically hope to accomplish by addressing them?

- Should I write primarily to change readers' minds, to get them to consider my arguments seriously, to confirm their opinions, to urge them to do something about the issue, or for some other purpose?

- How can I present myself so that my readers will consider me informed, knowledgeable, and fair?

The Beginning

- What opening would capture readers' attention? Should I begin as if I were telling a story, with phrases like "In the early 1990s" (Nelson) or "Over the past three decades" (Statsky)? Should I open with rhetorical questions, as Leshner does? Should I start with an arresting quotation or surprising statistic?

- Should I make clear at the outset exactly what my concerns are and how I see the issue, as Statsky does?

Presentation of the Issue

- Should I place the issue in a historical context, as Nelson does?
- Should I use examples—real or hypothetical—to make the issue concrete for readers, as Leshner does?
- Should I try to demonstrate that the issue is important by citing statistics, quoting authorities, or describing its negative effects, as Statsky does?

Your Argument and Counterargument

- How can I present my reasons so that readers will see them as plausible, leading logically to my position? Should I assume readers will see the connection, as Leshner does, or do I need to spell it out for them?
- If I have more than one reason, how should I sequence them?
- Should I forecast my reasons early in the essay, as Leshner and Statsky do?
- Which objections should I anticipate? Can I concede any objections without undermining my argument?
- Which opposing positions should I anticipate?
- How can I support my counterargument? Should I cite authorities and statistics, as Nelson does, or use anecdotes or examples?

The Ending

- How can I conclude my argument effectively? Should I reiterate my thesis?
- Should I try to unite readers with different allegiances by reminding them of values we share, as Leshner does?
- Could I conclude by looking to the future or by urging readers to take action or make changes, as Statsky does?

Outlining

An essay arguing a position on a controversial issue contains as many as four basic parts:

1. A presentation of the issue
2. A clear position
3. Reasons and support
4. Anticipating opposing positions and objections

These parts can be organized in various ways. If you expect some of your readers to oppose your argument, you might try to redefine the issue so that these readers can see the possibility that they may share some common values with you after all. To reinforce your connection to readers, you could go on to concede the wisdom of some aspect of their position before presenting the reasons and support for your position. You would conclude by reiterating the shared values upon which you hope to build agreement. In this case, an outline might look like this:

> Presentation of the issue
>
> Concession of some aspect of an opposing position
>
> Thesis statement
>
> First reason with support
>
> Second reason with support (etc.)
>
> Conclusion

If you have decided to write primarily for readers who agree rather than disagree with you, then you might choose to organize your argument as a refutation of opposing arguments in order to strengthen your readers' convictions. Begin by presenting the issue, stating your position, and reminding readers of your most plausible reasons. Then take up each opposing argument and try to refute it. You might conclude by calling your supporters to arms. Here's an outline showing what this kind of essay might look like:

> Presentation of the issue
>
> Thesis statement
>
> Your most plausible reasons
>
> First opposing argument with refutation
>
> Second opposing argument with refutation
>
> Conclusion

There are, of course, many other possible ways to organize an essay arguing for a position on a controversial issue, but these outlines should help you start planning your own essay. (For more on outlining, see Chapter 9, pp. 292–94.)

Drafting

Before you start drafting, you may want to review the general advice on drafting in Chapter 1, pp. 15–17. As you draft your essay, keep in mind your goals and the following tips for writing a position paper:

- Accept the burden of proof by offering specific and credible support for your argument and counterargument.
- Remember that the basis for disagreement about controversial issues often depends on values as much as on credible support. Try to think critically about

the values underlying your own as well as others' views so that your argument can take these values into account.

- Consider the tone of your argument and how you want to come across to readers.

- Remember that your outline is just a plan. Writers often make discoveries and reorganize as they draft. Be flexible.

- If you run into a problem as you draft, see whether any of your invention writing can help you solve it or whether it would help to return to one of the invention activities earlier in this chapter.

- If, as you draft, you find that you need more information, just make a note of what you have to find out and go on to the next point. When you are done drafting, you can go in search of the information you need.

CRITICAL READING GUIDE   Now is the time to get a good critical reading of your draft. Your instructor may arrange such a reading as part of your coursework; if not, you can ask a classmate, friend, or family member to read it over. If your campus has a writing center, you might ask a tutor there to read and comment on your draft using this guide to critical reading. (If you are unable to have someone else review your draft, turn ahead to the Revising section for help with reading your own draft critically.)

If You Are the Writer.   To provide focused, helpful comments, your critical reader must know your essay's intended audience, your purpose, and a problem in the draft that you need help solving. Briefly write out this information at the top of your draft.

- *Readers.* To whom are you directing your argument? What do you assume they think about this issue? Do you expect them to be receptive, skeptical, resistant, antagonistic?

- *Purpose.* What effect do you realistically expect your argument to have on these particular readers?

- *Problem.* Ask your reader to help you solve the single most important problem you see in your draft. Describe this problem briefly.

If You Are the Reader.   Use the following guidelines to help you give constructive, critical comments to others on their position papers.

1. *Read for a First Impression.* Tell the writer what you think the intended readers would find most and least convincing. If you personally think the argument is seriously flawed, share your thoughts. Then try to help the writer improve the argument for the designated readers.

Next, consider the problem the writer identified. If the problem will be covered by one of the other questions below, deal with it there. Otherwise, respond to the writer's concerns now.

2. *Analyze the Way the Issue Is Presented.* Look at the way the issue is presented and indicate if you think most readers would understand the issue differently. If you think that readers would need more information to grasp the issue and appreciate its importance, ask questions to help the writer fill in whatever is missing.

3. *Assess Whether the Position Is Stated Clearly.* Write a sentence or two summarizing the writer's position as you understand it from reading the draft. Then underline the sentence or sentences in the draft where the thesis is stated explicitly. (It may be restated in several places.) If you cannot find an explicit statement of the thesis, let the writer know. Given the writer's purpose and audience, consider whether the thesis statement is too strident or too timid and whether it needs to be better qualified, more sharply focused, or asserted more confidently. If you think that the thesis, as presented, is not really arguable—for example, if it asserts a fact no one questions or a matter of personal belief—let the writer know.

4. *Evaluate the Reasons and Support.* Underline the reasons. Tell the writer if you think any important reasons have been left out or any weak ones overemphasized. Indicate any contradictions or gaps in the argument. Point to any reasons that do not seem plausible to you, and briefly explain why. Then note any places where support is lacking or unconvincing. Help the writer think of additional support or suggest sources where more or better support might be found.

5. *Assess How Well Opposing Positions and Likely Objections Have Been Handled.* Find where opposing arguments or objections are mentioned and identify them in the margin. Consider whether the writer has ignored any important arguments or objections. Point to any places where the refutation could be strengthened or where shared assumptions or values offer the potential for concession.

6. *Consider Whether the Organization Is Effective.* Get an overview of the essay's organization and point out any places where more explicit cueing— transitions, summaries, or topic sentences—would clarify the relationship between parts of the essay.

- Reread the *beginning.* Let the writer know if you think readers will find it engaging. If not, see if you can recommend something from later in the essay that might work as a better opening.

- Study the *ending.* Does the essay conclude decisively and memorably? If not, suggest an alternative. Could something be moved to the end?

- Assess the *design features*. Comment on the contribution of any headings, tables, cartoons, or other design features that may have been included. Help the writer think of additional design features that could make a contribution to the essay.

7. *Give the Writer Your Final Thoughts.* What is this draft's strongest part? What part is most in need of further work?

■ REVISING

Now you are ready to revise your essay. Your instructor or other students may have given you advice on improving your draft. Nevertheless, you may have begun to realize that your draft requires not so much revising as rethinking. For example, you may recognize that your reasons do not lead readers to accept your position, that you cannot adequately support your reasons, or that you have been unable to refute damaging objections to your argument. Consequently, instead of working to improve parts of the draft, you may need to write a new draft that radically reenvisions your argument. It is not unusual for students—and professional writers—to find themselves in this situation. Learning to make radical revisions is a valuable lesson for all writers.

On the other hand, you may feel quite satisfied that your draft achieves most, if not all, of your goals. In that case, you can focus on refining specific parts of your draft. Very likely you have thought of ways of improving your draft, and you may even have begun improving it. This section will help you get an overview of your draft and revise it accordingly.

Getting an Overview

Consider your draft as a whole, following these two steps:

1. *Reread.* If at all possible, put the draft aside for a day or two before rereading it. When you return to it, start by reconsidering your purpose. Then read the draft straight through, trying to see it as your intended readers will.

2. *Outline.* Make a scratch outline, indicating the basic features as they appear in the draft. (For more on scratch outlines, see Chapter 9, pp. 292–93.)

Charting a Plan for Revision. Once you have an overview of your draft, you may want to make a two-column chart like the following one to keep track of the work you need to do as you revise. In the left-hand column, list the basic features of position papers. (Turn to pp. 161–63 to review the basic features.) As you analyze your draft and study any comments from other readers, use the right-hand column for noting problems you need to solve. (If making a chart on the computer is difficult, simply list the basic features and under each heading, list the problems to solve.)

Basic Features	*Problems to Solve*
The issue	
Position	
Reasons and support	
Opposing arguments or objections	

Analyzing the Basic Features of Your Own Draft.   Using the questions presented in the Critical Reading Guide on the preceding pages, reread your draft to identify specific problems you need to solve. Note the problems on your revision chart.

Studying Critical Comments.   Review all of the comments you have received from other readers, and add to the chart any suggestions you intend to act on. For each comment, look at the draft to see what might have led the reader to make that particular point. Try to be receptive to any criticism. By letting you see how other readers respond to your draft, these comments provide valuable information about how you might improve it.

Carrying Out Revisions

Having identified problems in your draft, you now need to come up with solutions and—most important—to carry them out. Basically, you have three ways of finding solutions:

1. Review your invention and planning notes for information and ideas to add to your draft.
2. Do additional invention and research to provide material you or your readers think is needed.
3. Look back at the readings in this chapter to see how other writers have solved similar problems.

The following suggestions, which are organized according to the basic features on your revision chart, will help you get started solving some common writing problems in position papers.

Presentation of the Issue

- ***Do readers have difficulty summarizing the issue or do they see it differently than you do?*** Try to anticipate possible misunderstandings or other ways of seeing the issue.
- ***Do readers need more information?*** Consider adding examples, quoting authorities, or simply explaining the issue further.
- ***Does the issue strike readers as unimportant?*** State explicitly why you think it is important and why you think your readers should think so, too. Try to provide

an anecdote, facts, or a quote from an authority that would demonstrate its importance.

A Clear Position

- *Do readers have difficulty summarizing your position or finding your thesis statement?* You may need to announce your thesis statement more explicitly or rewrite it to prevent misunderstanding.

- *Do any words seem unclear or ambiguous?* Use other words, explain what you mean, or add an example to make your position more concrete.

- *Do you appear to be taking a position that is not really arguable?* Consider whether your position is arguable. If you believe in your position as a matter of faith and cannot provide reasons and support, then your position probably is not arguable. Consult your instructor about changing your position or topic.

- *Could you qualify your thesis to account for exceptions or strong objections to your argument?* Add language that specifies when, where, under what conditions, or for whom your position applies.

Plausible Reasons and Convincing Support

- *Do readers have difficulty identifying your reasons?* Announce each reason explicitly, possibly with topic sentences. Consider adding a forecast early in the essay so readers know what reasons to expect. (For more on these cues for readers, see Chapter 8, pp. 273–88.)

- *Have you left out any reasons?* Consider whether adding particular reasons would strengthen your argument. To fit in new reasons, you may have to reorganize your whole argument.

- *Do any of your reasons seem implausible or contradictory?* Either delete implausible reasons or show how they relate logically to your position or to your other reasons.

- *Does your support seem unconvincing or scanty?* Where necessary, explain why you think the support should lead readers to accept your position. Review your invention notes or do some more research to gather additional examples, statistics, anecdotes, or quotations from authorities.

Anticipation of Opposing Arguments or Objections

- *Do readers have difficulty finding your response to opposing arguments or objections?* Add transitions that call readers' attention to each response.

- *Do you ignore any important objections or arguments?* Consider adding to your response. Determine whether you should replace a response to a relatively weak objection with a new response to a more important one.

- *Are there any concessions you could make?* Consider whether you should acknowledge the legitimacy of readers' concerns or concede particular objections. Show on what points you share readers' values, even though you may disagree on other points.

- *Does your attempt at refutation seem unconvincing?* Try to strengthen it. Avoid attacking your opponents. Instead, provide solid support—respected authorities, accepted facts, and statistics from reputable sources—to convince readers that your argument is credible.

The Organization

- *Do readers have trouble following your argument?* Consider adding a brief forecast of your main reasons at the beginning of your essay and adding explicit topic sentences and transitions to announce each reason as it is developed.

- *Does the beginning seem vague and uninteresting?* Consider adding a striking anecdote or surprising quotation to open the essay or find something in the essay you could move to the beginning.

- *Does the ending seem indecisive or abrupt?* Search your invention notes for a strong quotation, or add language that will reach out to readers. Try moving your strongest point to the ending.

- *Can you add illustrations or any other design features to make the essay more interesting to read and to strengthen your argument?* Consider incorporating a visual you came across in your research or one you can create on your own.

■ EDITING AND PROOFREADING

Now is the time to check your revised draft for connections between sentences and for errors in grammar, punctuation, and mechanics. As you reread, ask yourself whether the connection from one sentence to the next is logical and easy for readers to follow. If you sense a gap or disconnection that would cause a reader to stumble or become confused, try revising one or both sentences so that the gap is closed. Notice whether you shift from one word to another unnecessarily in one sentence to the next, and, if you do, consider repeating the same word instead. Look for sentences that might be combined to allow readers to follow your argument more easily and to discover more readily how you have anticipated their objections and questions. Look as well for long or garbled sentences that might be divided into two or three sentences.

As you work on your sentences, look for errors in spelling, capitalization, punctuation, usage, and grammar. Consult a writer's handbook for advice about how to correct any errors you cannot confidently correct on your own. Ask a friend or classmate to read over your draft, looking for errors.

Before you hand in your revised essay, proofread it carefully and run it through a spell-checker. Your goal is to hand in an error-free essay.

REFLECTING ON YOUR WRITING

Now that you have read and discussed several essays that argue a position on a controversial issue and written one of your own, take some time for reflection. Reflecting on your writing process will help you gain a greater understanding of what you learned about solving the problems you encountered.

Write a page or so telling your instructor about a problem you encountered in writing your essay and how you solved it. Before you begin, gather all of your invention and planning notes, drafts, critical comments, revision plan, and final revision. Review these materials as you complete this writing task.

1. *Identify one writing problem you needed to solve as you worked on the essay.* Do not be concerned with grammar and punctuation; concentrate instead on problems unique to developing an essay arguing for a position. For example: Did you puzzle over how to convince your readers that the issue is important? Did you have trouble asserting your position forcefully while acknowledging other points of view? Was it difficult to refute an important objection you knew readers would raise?

2. *Determine how you came to recognize the problem.* When did you first discover it? What called it to your attention? If you did not become aware of the problem until someone pointed it out to you, can you now see hints of it in your invention writings? If so, where specifically?

3. *Reflect on how you went about solving the problem.* Did you work on the wording of a passage, cut or add reasons or refutations, conduct further research, or move paragraphs or sentences around? Did you reread one of the essays in this chapter to see how another writer handled a similar problem, or did you look back at your invention writing? If you talked about the problem with another student, a tutor, or your instructor, did talking about it help? How useful was the advice you received?

4. *Write a brief explanation of how you identified the problem and tried to solve it.* Be as specific as possible in reconstructing your efforts. Quote from your invention notes and draft essay, others' critical comments, your revision plan, or your revised essay to show the various changes your writing—and thinking—underwent as you tried to solve the problem. If you are still uncertain about your solution, say so. Taking time to explain how you identified a particular problem, how you went about solving it, and what you learned from this experience can help you solve future writing problems more easily.

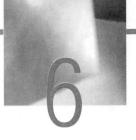

Proposing a Solution

Proposals are vital to a democracy. They inform citizens about problems affecting their well-being and suggest actions that could be taken to remedy these problems. People write proposals every day in business, government, education, and the professions. Proposals are a basic ingredient of the world's work.

As a special form of argument, proposals have much in common with position papers, described in Chapter 5. Both analyze a subject about which there is disagreement and take a definite stand on it. Both make an argument, giving reasons and support and acknowledging readers' likely objections or questions. Proposals, however, go further: They urge readers to take specific action. They argue for a proposed solution to a problem, and they succeed or fail by the strength of that argument.

Problem-solving is basic to most disciplines and professions. For example, scientists use the scientific method, a systematic form of problem-solving; political scientists and sociologists propose solutions to troubling political and social problems; engineers employ problem-solving techniques in building bridges, automobiles, and computers; teachers make decisions about how to help students with learning problems; counselors devote themselves to helping clients solve personal problems; business owners and managers daily solve problems large and small.

Problem-solving depends on a questioning attitude—wondering about alternative approaches to bringing about change, puzzling over how a goal might be achieved, questioning why a process unfolds in a particular way, posing challenges to the status quo. In addition, it demands imagination and creativity. To solve a problem, you need to see it anew, to look at it from new angles and in new contexts.

Because a proposal tries to convince readers that its way of defining and solving the problem makes sense, proposal writers must be sensitive to readers' needs and expectations. Readers need to know details of the solution and to be convinced that it will solve the problem and can be implemented. If readers initially favor a different solution, knowing why the writer rejects it will help them decide whether to support or reject the writer's proposed solution. Readers may be wary of costs, demands on their time, and grand schemes.

As you plan and draft a proposal, you will have to determine whether your readers are aware of the problem and whether they recognize its seriousness, and you will have to consider their views on any other solutions. Knowing what your readers know—their assumptions and biases, the kinds of arguments likely to appeal to them—is a central part of proposal writing.

The writing of proposals occurs in many different contexts, as the following examples suggest.

Writing in Your Other Courses

- For an economics class, a student writes an essay proposing a solution to the problem of inadequate housing for Mexican workers in the nearly three thousand maquiladora factories clustered along the Mexican side of the border with the United States. She briefly describes the binational arrangement that has produced over a million low-paying jobs for Mexican workers and increased profits for American manufacturers who own the assembly plants—along with job losses for thousands of American workers. She sketches the history of maquiladoras since the 1970s and then surveys some of the problems they have spawned. Focusing on inadequate housing, she argues that it, of all the problems, should be addressed first and is most amenable to modest, short-term solutions. The student argues that maquiladora owners must share with Mexican city and state governments the costs of planning and installing water delivery systems and minimal house plumbing installations, and provide low-interest loans to workers who want to buy indoor plumbing fixtures. Recognizing that this is only a first-stage solution to a major problem requiring long-term efforts, the student calls for an international competition to design entire maquiladora workers' communities, along with plans for adequate low-cost houses with plumbing and electricity. She rejects high-rise housing, arguing that it has failed to solve housing problems for the poor in U.S. cities and that land for housing developments in Mexico is relatively plentiful on the outskirts of border cities, if adequate bus service is provided for workers.

- For an education class, a student researches the history of educational television production and programming for two- to thirteen-year-old children, beginning with the 1969 production of Children's Television Workshop's *Sesame Street*. He also researches children's television in Australia, Great Britain, and Japan and learns that these countries provide much more support for children's television programming than the United States does. In an essay proposing a solution to this problem, he defines the problem as the absence of a plan to develop programming that might attract funding from the federal government and other sources. He presents the problem by reporting how far behind some other countries the United States has fallen in supporting children's television. Influenced by a book by the founder of Children's Television Workshop, the student proposes a solution that outlines conditions for developing new television programming for children. These conditions include demonstrating that television is the most efficient and effective way to teach particular skills or content, giving priority to the needs of children, making innovative educational television programming a national goal, aiming for calendar-year programming of at least one hour each weekday for children in three age groups, and planning to replace at least 25 percent of the content of every program each year. Arguing to support these conditions, the student concedes that attractive new programs continue to appear—for example, *Bill Nye, the Science Guy*—but argues that these are sporadic and cannot provide the amount or diversity of programming that is needed.

Writing in the Community

- A California high school junior enters an essay contest, "There Ought to Be a Law," sponsored by her state legislator. The goal of the contest is to encourage high school students to propose solutions to community problems. The student wins the contest with a proposal for a state law requiring school districts to replace textbooks every ten years. She presents the problem by describing her own battered, marked-up, dated textbooks, particularly a chemistry text older than she is. To gain a better understanding of the problems caused by outdated textbooks, she talks with several other students and with teachers. Recognizing that she lacks the expertise to outline a legislative solution, she speculates about the probable obstacles, chief among them the costs of implementing her solution. The legislator drafts a law based on the student's proposal, introduces the law at the opening of the next legislative session, and invites the student to attend the event.

- A social services administrator in a large northeastern city becomes increasingly concerned about the rise in numbers of adolescents in jail for minor and major crimes. From his observations and the research studies he reads, he becomes convinced that a partial solution to the problem would be to intervene at the first sign of delinquent behavior from eight- to twelve-year-olds. In developing a proposal to circulate among influential people in the local police department, juvenile justice system, school system, and business and religious communities, the administrator begins by describing the long-term consequences of jailing young criminals. Trying to make the problem seem significant and worth solving, he focuses mainly on the costs and the high rate of return to criminal activity after release from jail. He then lists and discusses at length the major components of his early-intervention program. These components include assigning mentors and companions to young people who are beginning to fail in school, placing social workers in troubled families to help out daily before and after school, hiring neighborhood residents to work full-time on the streets to counter the influence of gangs, and encouraging businesses to hire high school students as paid interns. The administrator acknowledges that early intervention to head off serious criminal activity will require the cooperation of many city agencies. He offers to take the lead in bringing about this cooperation and in launching the program.

Writing in the Workplace

- Frustrated by what they see as the failure of schools to prepare students for the workplace, managers of a pharmaceuticals manufacturer in the Midwest decide to develop a proposal to move vocational and technical training out of ill-equipped high school vocational programs and onto the plant's floor. Seven division managers meet weekly for four months to develop a proposal for schools in the region. They are joined by one of the firm's experienced technical writers, who takes notes of discussions, writes progress reports, and eventually drafts the proposal. Their discussions begin with the published research and arguments of an academic consultant to their project. They define the problem as schools being unable to offer the modern equipment, motivation, tutorial instruction, efficiency, or accountability of on-the-job training. They eventually propose a vocational track that would begin in grade 10, with all of the job training taking place in businesses and industries. Each year students would spend more time on the job, and by grade 12 they would work thirty-two hours a week and spend ten hours a week in school, mainly in courses in English (reading and writing) and advanced math. As the managers detail their solution, develop a timetable for implementing it, and speculate about how current school budgets could be reworked to support the program, they seek advice on early drafts of their proposal from business leaders, school board members, school administrators, representatives of teachers' unions, newspaper editorial boards, and key members of the state legislature. The near-final draft incorporates suggestions from these advisers and attempts to refute known arguments against the proposal. This draft is reviewed by a small group of the most well-informed and creative advisers. The published proposal is directed primarily to state legislators and school board members.

- A woman in her sixties who has been hauling asphalt and gravel in a double-bottom dump truck for sixteen years writes a proposal for trucking company owners and managers, who face a continual shortage of well-qualified drivers for heavy diesel tractor-and-trailer trucks, suggesting that the companies focus on recruiting more women. As she plans her proposal, she talks to the owner of the company she drives for and to the few women drivers she knows. She begins the proposal by describing her work briefly and explaining how she got a lucky break when her brother taught her how to drive his truck. She then points out the problem: that few women ever get the chance to learn this skill. She argues that the industry's starting salaries and equitable pay scales would appeal to many women, and that the seasonal nature of many trucking jobs would make them especially attractive to women who want to work only a few months a year. Then she proposes her solution to this problem: an in-house training program in which women recruits would be trained by company drivers on the job and after hours. Drivers would be paid for their after-hours training contributions, and the students would be paid a small stipend after agreeing to drive for the company for a certain number of months at a reduced salary. She argues that her proposal would succeed only if trucking companies sponsor a well-designed recruitment program relying on advertisements published on Web sites and in magazines read by working women, and she lists titles of several such publications. She attempts to refute the alternative solution of relying on already established truck-driving schools by arguing that many women cannot afford the tuition. Her proposal is first published in her company's internal newsletter and later, in slightly revised form, in a leading magazine read by trucking company owners and managers.

Practice Proposing a Solution to a Problem: A Collaborative Activity

The preceding scenarios suggest some occasions for writing proposals to solve problems. To get a sense of the complexities and possibilities involved in proposing solutions, think through a specific problem, and try to come up with a feasible proposal.

Part 1. Form a group with two or three other students, and select one person to take notes during your discussion.

- First, identify two or three problems within your college or community, and select one that you all recognize and agree needs to be solved.

- Next, consider possible solutions to this problem, and identify one solution that you can all support. You need not all be equally enthusiastic for this solution.

- Finally, determine which individual or group has the authority to take action on your proposed solution and how you would go about convincing this audience that the problem is serious and must be solved and that your proposed solution is feasible and should be supported. Make notes also about questions this audience might have about your proposal and what objections the audience might raise.

Part 2. As a group, discuss your efforts at proposing a solution to a problem. What surprised or pleased you most about this activity? What difficulties did you encounter in coming up with arguments that the problem must be solved and that your proposed solution would solve it? How did the objections you thought of influence your confidence in your proposed solution?

READINGS

The readings in this chapter illustrate the features of essays proposing solutions to problems and the strategies writers rely on to realize the features. No two essays in this genre are much alike, and yet they share defining features. The section Analyzing Writing Strategies and the Commentary following each reading touch on a few features best illustrated by that essay, capturing its special qualities and strengths. Together, the three essays cover many of the possibilities of proposals. Consequently, you will want to read as many of the essays and Commentaries as possible and, if time permits, complete the activities in Analyzing Writing Strategies. Following the last reading in the chapter, the Basic Features section offers a concise description of the features of proposals and provides examples from all of the readings.

Rob Ryder writes screenplays and directs movies. Because of his experience playing and coaching basketball, he has served as an adviser on several recent hoop-related movies.

Ryder's proposal to turn basketball into an eight-player game was published in 1998, in the sports section of the New York Times. *His style is informal, like that of a sports announcer at work. His sentences and paragraphs tend to be short, and his words are familiar ones, except for a few technical terms from basketball. Ryder mentions several professional basketball players and coaches, but you need not recognize them or know much about the game to follow his proposal. Your experience with any sport will help you understand Ryder's attempt to make basketball a more challenging and interesting game.*

Ten Is a Crowd, So Change the Game

Rob Ryder

Along with about a billion other people on this planet, I've had a lifelong love affair with basketball. I've known the game as a player (Princeton), as a coach (Hollywood Y.M.C.A. 5- to 8-year-olds), and as a basketball supervisor for the movies (*White Men Can't Jump, Blue Chips,* and *Eddie* among others). 1

So, it is with deep regret that I must finally go public with the truth: Basketball is a mess. A muddled, boring, chaotic, overcrowded, utterly predictable game of slapping, clawing, double- and triple-teaming, endless stoppages, timeouts, whistles, whining, and countless trips to the free-throw line where players continue to stupefy us with their ineptitude. 2

Yet the game is still punctuated by enough moments of pure poetry, grace, power and creativity to keep us coming back for more. 3

So, now that we can admit the game is flawed, let's fix it. 4

I'm not tinkering here—this is no "raise the rim," "widen the lane" Band-Aid I'm proposing. Rather, I'm going straight to the heart of the problem. It's just too crowded out there. Basketball is meant to be played four on four. 5

Too radical? You're forgetting your American heritage. It's our game. We invented it; we can change it if we want to. (I'm sure there was a lot of groaning when the forward pass was introduced to football.) 6

When I ran the concept of four-on-four basketball, or 8-Ball, by Doc Rivers during the filming of *Eddie,* his eyes lighted up. 7

"Guards would rule," he said. Not necessarily, but we'll get to that later. Working on another movie, *The Sixth Man,* I proposed the change to Jerry Tarkanian, who replied: "I've been saying that for years. I've been saying that for years." When I asked Marty Blake, the crusty old N.B.A. war horse, he responded, "What, are you nuts?" 8

Yeah. And so was James Naismith. The man almost got it right. But how many realize that in the old days, there was a jump ball after every basket scored? Or that teams were allowed to hold the ball indefinitely? Or that there wasn't always a 3-point shot? 9

The new game will be a lean, sleek, fluid game—dominated by high-flying superbly coordinated athletes, with no room for defensive ends. Charles Oakley, I love your work ethic, but you're going to have trouble keeping up. 10

Kobe Bryant, Tim Duncan, Keith Van Horn, Ray Allen, the future is yours. 11

Lisa Leslie, Teresa Edwards, Venus Lacey, you too will love 8-Ball. As will all the little 12 kids out there whose Saturday morning games often resemble two swarms of bees fighting over a Rollo.

Remember the pick-and-roll?—now it's more commonly known as the pick-and-collide-into-two-defenders-coming-from-the-weak-side. In 8-Ball, the pick-and-roll will rule. Help from the weak side leaves the defense much more vulnerable without the fifth defender there to rotate over the passing lane. 13

The old back-door play (which only Princeton seems to pull off regularly these days) will be back. Only now, there will be a cleaner path to the basket. Defenders, deny your man the ball at your own peril. 14

But what about Doc Rivers's comment that guards would rule playing four on four? Tell that to Hakeem Olajuwon, who cannot only run the floor but will now also have enough room for his dazzling array of post-up moves. 15

You see, everybody wins: The big men will finally have some space, the shooters will get plenty of open looks from the 3-point line, and the slashers, like Eddie Jones, should have a field day with one fewer defender out there to clog the lane. 16

So just what are we sacrificing by going to four on four? 17

Well, the lumbering big man will go the way of the dinosaur. Sorry, George Mhuresan, but no one's going to cover for you when your man releases and beats you downcourt. A four on three is infinitely tougher to defend than a five on four. 18

And for you little guys, if you can't shoot, you're a liability. 19

There'll be a lot less room for the role player out there because 8-Ball will demand that every player on the floor polish his or her overall skills. 20

So where's the downside? Nolan Richardson knows—as Arkansas' 94-feet-of-hell amoeba defense will be reduced to a quick detour through purgatory. It'll be a lot tougher to press full court with only four defenders. Any good ball-handler will be able to break the press, and this will definitely hurt the college and high school game. 21

For the pros, it's a moot point—full-court pressure disappeared years ago. Even Rick Pitino's on his way to discovering how tough it is to ask pro athletes to press full court over an 82-game season. 22

But will this mean a reduction of the 12-man roster, reduced playing time and howls from the N.B.A. Players' Association? 23

Not at all, for two reasons. One, 8-Ball will be a running game, and in some ways may adopt the more exciting characteristics of hockey (yes, hockey). Coaches may actually find themselves injecting four new players into a game simultaneously (a line change)—a nifty way to ratchet up the action while giving your starters a rest. 24

And secondly, in the world of 8-Ball, the time of game will expand; in the pros, from 48 to 60 minutes. But how do you keep these games from running over three hours? 25

In 8-Ball, the time wasted on stupor-inducing foul shooting will be reduced by two-thirds, allowing for extra minutes of real action. Whenever a player is fouled but not in the act of shooting, his team automatically gets the ball out of bounds. When fouled in the act of shooting, a player gets one free throw worth 2 points or 3 points, depending on the shot he was taking. But in both cases, the offensive team gets the option of skipping the foul line and taking the ball out of bounds. 26

This will eliminate the ugly strategy of intentional fouling, choke-induced shooting   27
and subhuman fan behavior all in one easy stroke.

A good basketball game is about rhythm, and 8-Ball will flow.   28

The substitutions will make for marvelous matchups. We'll see more fast breaks,   29
cleaner inside moves, purer shooting, more offensive rebounding, fewer turnovers, a lot
less standing around, more minutes of actual action, and more scoring.

Plus, 8-Ball would bring forth the elimination of what must be the stupidest addition   30
to N.B.A. rules: the illegal defense violation. Just try playing a four-man zone in 8-Ball. It'll
turn to a man-to-man real fast.

There it is, 8-Ball. Is there any realistic chance that the N.C.A.A. or the N.B.A. will   31
change over to four on four? "Never happen," Dick Vitale answered.

That's why a group of former Princeton players is launching a professional basket-   32
ball league—the "8BL." Look for it in '99 following a televised exhibition this fall. In the
meantime, all you rec league and intramural players out there—with your smaller courts
and running clocks and purists' love for the game—8-Ball's for you, too. Show us the way.

Connecting to Culture and Experience: Obsession with Watching Sports

Nearly all Americans of all ages have somewhere between a tepid to hot interest in watching and following competitive team sports. Few people have no interest in watching competitive sports. Even fewer will *admit* to having no interest. It is difficult to avoid sports news in America. Most newspapers devote an entire section to sports but only an occasional page to religion or education. Regional newspapers report results from the lowest-ranked high school leagues in surrounding counties. Entire television channels are devoted to sports events and news. National and local television news programs pay attention to sports.

With several other students, discuss this American—and worldwide—obsession with watching other people play competitive sports. Begin by telling each other which competitive sport, if any, you most enjoy watching and which team or athlete is your favorite. Then speculate about where your interest originated and what sustains it. Then, more generally, speculate about why so many Americans seem eager to go to stadiums or sit in front of a television set to watch other people play a sport. Why do you think they prefer to watch others play a sport instead of engaging in some sort of physical activity themselves?

Analyzing Writing Strategies

1. At the beginning of this chapter, we make several generalizations about essays that propose solutions to problems. Consider which of these assertions are true of Ryder's proposal:

- It defines the problem.
- It helps readers realize the seriousness of the problem.
- It describes the proposed solution.
- It attempts to convince readers that the solution will solve the problem and can be implemented.
- It anticipates readers' likely questions and objections.
- It evaluates alternative solutions that readers may initially favor.
- It urges readers to take specific action.

2. Ryder sets out to define the problem and describe a solution. Reread paragraphs 1–3, where Ryder defines the problem. How does he define it? How does he establish his authority to do so? Given his readers' likely knowledge of sports in general and of basketball in particular, how successfully do you think Ryder defines the problem?

    Next, reread paragraphs 4–16, where Ryder describes a solution to the problem he sees with five-on-five basketball. Underline the major features of his proposal for four-on-four basketball. Do these features add up to an adequate description of the solution, given Ryder's purpose and readers? If not, what more do you think he might have included? Why do you think he quotes three basketball experts in paragraph 8?

Commentary: Anticipating Readers' Objections and Questions

To have any hope of readers' taking his advice seriously, Ryder has to anticipate readers' questions and objections. Ryder takes an imaginative and direct approach to anticipating readers' questions: He tries to guess what their questions might be and then poses four of them (see paragraphs 17, 21, 23, and 25). Both the questions and his answers are part of his counterargument.

When you counterargue, you may merely acknowledge that you are aware of readers' objections and questions; or you may accommodate or concede their usefulness or refute them. By posing the questions—something few writers do—Ryder acknowledges that some readers may be thinking of them. Then he either accommodates or refutes them. He accommodates the first two questions, treating readers considerately at the beginning, and refutes the last two, challenging readers more directly after he draws them into his argument. For example, in accommodating, or conceding, the wisdom of the first question—"So just what are we sacrificing by going to four on four?" (paragraph 17)—Ryder admits that the game will change but only in ways readers would surely support: big, slow players have to go, along with little, fast players who cannot shoot. He seems to assume that nearly all readers would concede the wisdom and logic of these improvements to the game.

Consider the third question—"But will this mean a reduction of the 12-man roster . . . ?" (23)—which Ryder refutes. Here the question is more specific, and he firmly challenges the possibility that any intelligent reader would answer "Yes." He answers "Not at all" (24), giving two reasons to support his answer: A hard-running game like 8-Ball will require at least as many players as 10-Ball in order to give tired players a break, and the game will expand to sixty minutes, placing even further demands on players' stamina. Ryder seems to be saying to readers that there may be some worrisome questions raised about his proposal, but this is not one of them.

Ryder demonstrates that refutation need not be dismissive. As he refutes the third and fourth questions, he gives reasons and support (24–27). Ryder knows that readers who feel insulted or even misunderstood are not likely to want to take action on his proposed solution. In planning and developing your own essay, your goals should be to anticipate a wide range of readers' inevitable questions and objections as well as to attempt to concede or refute these questions and objections convincingly but sensitively.

Considering Topics for Your Own Essay

Following Ryder's lead, consider proposing a way to improve a popular sport. Your proposal need not seek to revolutionize the sport, though it might. Or it could offer only a small refinement such as changing a rule or adding a feature to the game. Your proposal could seek to improve the safety of the game for participants, the way records are kept, the way athletes are recruited into the sport, the way athletes are treated, or the entertainment value of the game to spectators. There are many other possibilities. You could focus on either a professional or amateur sport, a team sport or individual competition, high school or college teams, or the National Hockey League. You could address your proposal to players, officials, fans, or the general public.

Another idea for writing is to identify a problem that needs to be solved in some activity or enterprise that no one seems to be questioning or that people would strongly resist changing. Possible topics include having big, expensive weddings, taking honeymoons after weddings, commuting to work or school by car, the youth programs run by religious organizations, high school sports competitions (Italian secondary schools sponsor no sports teams), studying a different subject every period for a semester in high school rather than focusing on one or two subjects for two to four weeks, requiring 17- and 18-year-olds to attend high school, giving senior citizens discounts, nine-to-five work schedules, four-year college programs, buying or leasing a car, ATMs, or pumping your own gasoline.

Katherine S. Newman is the Ford Foundation professor of urban studies in the John F. Kennedy School of Government at Harvard University. She is also the director of Harvard's joint doctoral program in sociology and social policy. Formerly a professor at Columbia University, Newman has written several books on middle-class economic insecurity, including Falling from Grace *(1988) and* Declining Fortunes *(1993).*

Newman published this proposal in 1995 in the Brookings Review, *a journal concerned with public policy. Addressing fast-food corporate executives and managers, Newman tries to convince them to adopt policies that would help their employees find better jobs. Her proposal comes out of her two-year study of fast-food workers in Harlem in which she learned that workers experience great difficulty finding better jobs because they lack the kinds of "social networks" that middle-class workers depend on for job information and referrals. As you read Newman's proposal, notice why the social networks that inner-city fast-food workers do have fail to lead to better jobs and evaluate whether you think the proposed solution—an "employer consortium" (a group of cooperating employers)—will provide the type of networks that the workers need. For more on Newman's study of workers at fast-food restaurants in Harlem, see her 1999 book* No Shame in My Game: The Working Poor in the Inner City.

Dead-End Jobs: A Way Out

Katherine S. Newman

Millions of Americans work full-time, year-round in jobs that still leave them stranded in poverty. Though they pound the pavement looking for better jobs, they consistently come up empty-handed. Many of these workers are in our nation's inner cities.

Problem

I know, because I have spent two years finding out what working life is like for 200 employees—about half African-American, half Latino—at fast food restaurants in Harlem. Many work only part-time, though they would happily take longer hours if they could get them. Those who do work full-time earn about $8,840 (before taxes)—well below the poverty threshold for a family of four.

These fast food workers make persistent efforts to get better jobs, particularly in retail and higher-paid service sector occupations. They take civil service examinations and apply for jobs with the electric company or the phone company. Sometimes their efforts bear fruit. More often they don't.

A few workers make their way into the lower managerial ranks of the fast food industry, where wages are marginally better. An even smaller number graduate into higher management, a path made possible by the internal promotion patterns long practiced by these firms. As in any industry, however, senior management opportunities are limited. Hence most workers, even those with track records as reliable employees, are locked inside a low-wage environment. Contrary to those who preach the benefits of work and persistence, the human capital these workers build up—experience in food production, inventory management, cash register operation, customer relations, minor machinery repair, and cleaning—does not pay off. These workers are often unable to move upward out of poverty. And their experience is not unusual. Hundreds of thousands of low-wage workers in American cities run into the same brick wall. Why? And what can we do about it?

Stagnation in the Inner City

Harlem, like many inner-city communities, has lost the manufacturing job base that once sustained its neighborhoods. Service industries that cater to neighborhood consumers, coupled with now dwindling government jobs, largely make up the local economy. With official jobless rates hovering around 18 percent (14 people apply for every minimum-wage fast food job in Harlem), employers can select from the very top of the preference "queue." Once hired, even experienced workers have virtually nowhere to go.

One reason for their lack of mobility is that many employers in the primary labor mar-   6
ket outside Harlem consider "hamburger flipper" jobs worthless. At most, employers credit the fast food industry with training people to turn up for work on time and to fill out job applications. The real skills these workers have developed go unrecognized. However inaccurate the unflattering stereotypes, they help keep experienced workers from "gradu-ating" out of low-wage work to more remunerative employment. . . .

As Harry Holzer, an economist at Michigan State University, has shown, "central-city"   7
employers insist on specific work experience, references, and particular kinds of formal training in addition to literacy and numeracy skills, even for jobs that do not require a college degree. Demands of this kind, more stringent in the big-city labor markets than in the surrounding suburbs, clearly limit the upward mobility of the working poor in urban areas. If the only kind of job available does not provide the "right" work experience or for-mal training, many better jobs will be foreclosed.

Racial stereotypes also weaken mobility prospects. Employers view ghetto blacks,   8
especially men, as a bad risk or a troublesome element in the workplace. They prefer immigrants or nonblack minorities, of which there are many in the Harlem labor force, who appear to them more deferential and willing to work harder for low wages. As Joleen Kirshenman and Kathryn Neckerman found in their study of Chicago workplaces, stereo-types abound among employers who have become wary of the "underclass." Primary employers exercise these preferences by discriminating against black applicants, partic-ularly those who live in housing projects, on the grounds of perceived group characteris-tics. The "losers" are not given an opportunity to prove themselves. . . .

Social Networks

Social networks are crucial in finding work. Friends and acquaintances are far more useful   9
sources of information than are want ads. The literature on the urban underclass suggests that inner-city neighborhoods are bereft of these critical links to the work world. My work, however, suggests a different picture: the working poor in Harlem have access to two types of occupational social networks, but neither provides upward mobility. The first is a homoge-neous *lateral* network of age mates and acquaintances, employed and unemployed. It pro-vides contacts that allow workers to move sideways in the labor market—from Kentucky Fried Chicken to Burger King or McDonald's—but not to move to jobs of higher quality. Lat-eral networks are useful, particularly for poor people who have to move frequently, for they help ensure a certain amount of portability in the low-wage labor market. But they do not lift workers out of poverty; they merely facilitate "churning" laterally in the low-wage world.

Young workers in Harlem also participate in more heterogeneous *vertical* networks   10
with their older family members who long ago moved to suburban communities or better urban neighborhoods to become homeowners on the strength of jobs that were more

widely available 20 and 30 years ago. Successful grandparents, great-aunts and uncles, and distant cousins, relatives now in their 50s and 60s, often have (or have retired from) jobs in the post office, the public sector, the transportation system, public utilities, the military, hospitals, and factories that pay union wages. But these industries are now shedding workers, not hiring them. As a result, older generations are typically unable to help job-hunting young relatives.

Although little is known about the social and business networks of minority business 11 owners and managers in the inner city, it seems that Harlem's business community, particularly its small business sector, is also walled off from the wider economy of midtown. Fast food owners know the other people in their franchise system. They do business with banks and security firms inside the inner city. But they appear less likely to interact with firms outside the ghetto.

For that reason, a good recommendation from a McDonald's owner may represent a 12 calling card that extends no farther than the general reputation of the firm and a prospective employer's perception—poor, as I have noted—of the skills that such work represents. It can move someone from an entry-level job in one restaurant to the same kind of job in another, but not into a good job elsewhere in the city.

Lacking personal or business-based ties that facilitate upward mobility, workers in 13 Harlem's fast food market find themselves on the outside looking in when it comes to the world of "good jobs." They search diligently for them, they complete many job applications, but it is the rare individual who finds a job that pays a family wage. Those who do are either workers who have been selected for internal promotion or men and women who have had the luxury of devoting their earnings solely to improving their own educational or craft credentials. Since most low wage service workers are under pressure to support their families or contribute to the support of their parents' households, this kind of human capital investment is often difficult. As a result, the best most can do is to churn from one low-wage job to another.

The Employer Consortium

Some of the social ills that keep Harlem's fast food workers at the bottom of a short job 14 ladder—a poor urban job base, increasing downward mobility, discrimination, structural problems in the inner-city business sector—are too complex to solve quickly enough to help most of the workers I've followed. But the problem of poor social networks may be amenable to solution if formal organizations linking primary and secondary labor market employers can be developed. An "employer consortium" could help to move hard-working inner-city employees into richer job markets by providing the job information and precious referrals that "come naturally" to middle-class Americans.

How would an employer consortium function? It would include both inner-city 15 employers of the working poor and downtown businesses or nonprofit institutions with higher-paid employees. Employers in the inner city would periodically select employees they consider reliable, punctual, hard-working, and motivated. Workers who have successfully completed at least one year of work would be placed in a pool of workers eligible for hiring by a set of linked employers who have better jobs to offer. Entry-level employers would, in essence, put their own good name behind successful workers as they pass them on to their consortium partners in the primary sector.

Primary-sector employers, for their part, would agree to hire from the pool and meet   16
periodically with their partners in the low-wage industries to review applications and follow up on the performance of those hired through the consortium. Employers "up the line" would provide training or educational opportunities to enhance the employee's skills. These training investments would make it more likely that hirees would continue to move up the new job ladders.

As they move up, the new hirees would clear the way for others to follow. First, their   17
performance would reinforce the reputation of the employers who recommended them. Second, their achievements on the job might begin to lessen the stigma or fear their new employers may feel toward the inner-city workforce. On both counts, other consortium-based workers from the inner city would be more likely to get the same opportunities, following in a form of managed chain migration out of the inner-city labor market. Meanwhile, the attractiveness of fast food jobs, now no better reputed among inner-city residents than among the rest of society, would grow as they became, at least potentially, a gateway to something better.

Advantages for Employers

Fast food employers in Harlem run businesses in highly competitive markets. Constant   18
pressure on prices and profit discourage them from paying wages high enough to keep a steady workforce. In fact, most such employers regard the jobs they fill as temporary placements: they *expect* successful employees to leave. And despite the simple production processes used within the fast food industry to minimize the damage of turnover, sudden departures of knowledgeable workers still disrupt business and cause considerable frustration and exhaustion.

An employer consortium gives these employers—who *can't* raise wages if they   19
hope to stay in business—a way to compete for workers who will stay with them longer than usual. In lieu of higher pay, employers can offer access to the consortium hiring pool and the prospect of a more skilled and ultimately better-paying job upon graduation from this real world "boot camp." . . .

Consortiums would also appeal to the civic spirit of minority business owners, who   20
often choose to locate in places like Harlem rather than in less risky neighborhoods because they want to provide job opportunities for their own community. The big franchise operations mandate some attention to civic responsibility as well. Some fast food firms have licensing requirements for franchisees that require demonstrated community involvement.

At a time when much of the public is voicing opposition to heavy-handed govern-   21
ment efforts to prevent employment discrimination, employer consortiums have the advantage of encouraging minority hiring based on private-sector relationships. Institutional employers in particular—for example, universities and hospitals, often among the larger employers in East Coast cities—should find the consortiums especially valuable.

These employers typically retain a strong commitment to workforce diversity but are often put off by the reputation of secondary-sector workers as unskilled, unmotivated, and less worthy of consideration.

The practical advantages for primary-sector managers are clear. Hirees have been 22 vetted and tested. Skills have been assessed and certified in the most real world of settings. A valuable base of experience and skills stands ready for further training and advancement. The consortium assures that the employers making and receiving recommendations would come to know one another, thus reinforcing the value of recommendations — a cost-effective strategy for primary-sector managers who must make significant training investments in their workers.

Minimal Government Involvement

Despite the evident advantages for both primary and secondary labor market employers, 23 it may be necessary for governments to provide modest incentives to encourage wide participation. Secondary-sector business owners in the inner city, for example, might be deterred from participating by the prospect of losing some of their best employees at the end of a year. Guaranteeing these employers a lump sum or a tax break for every worker they promote into management internally or successfully place with a consortium participant could help break down such reluctance.

Primary-sector employers, who would have to provide support for training and possi- 24 bly for schooling of their consortium employees, may also require some kind of tax break to subsidize their efforts at skill enhancement. Demonstration projects could experiment with various sorts of financial incentives for both sets of employers by providing grants to underwrite the costs of training new workers.

Local governments could also help publicize the efforts of participating employers. 25 Most big-city mayors, for example, would be happy to shower credit on business people looking to boost the prospects of the deserving (read working) poor.

Government involvement, however, would be minimal. Employer consortiums could 26 probably be assembled out of the existing economic development offices of U.S. cities, or with the help of the Chamber of Commerce and other local institutions that encourage private-sector activity. Industry- or sector-specific consortiums could probably be put together with the aid of local industry councils.

Moreover, some of the negative effects of prior experiments with wage subsidies for 27 the "hard to employ" — efforts that foundered on the stigma assigned to these workers and the paperwork irritants to employers — would be reversed here. Consortium employees would be singled out for doing well, for being the cream of the crop. And the private-sector domination of employer consortiums would augur against extensive paperwork burdens.

Building Bridges

The inner-city fast food workers that I have been following in Harlem have proven them- 28 selves in difficult jobs. They have shown that they are reliable, they clearly relish their economic independence, and they are willing to work hard. Still, work offers them no escape from poverty. Trapped in a minimum-wage job market, they lack bridges to the kind of work that can enable them to support their families and begin to move out of poverty. For reasons I have discussed, those bridges have not evolved naturally in our inner cities. But where they are lacking, they must be created and fostered. And we can begin with employer consortiums, to the benefit of everyone, workers and employers alike.

Connecting to Culture and Experience: The Value of Routine, Repetitive Work

Newman explains that one reason fast-food workers cannot find better jobs is that employers believe such workers learn only routine, repetitive skills that do not prepare them for other types of jobs.

With several students, discuss this possible limitation of fast-food jobs and other kinds of routine jobs. You may hold such a job now, or you may have held one in the past. Maybe you parked cars, delivered pizzas, ran a cash register, wiped down cars in a car wash, bagged and carried groceries or other merchandise, wrapped holiday packages, or did cleanup work. Tell each other about the routine jobs you have held. Then consider many employers' criticism of these jobs: that they only teach workers how to show up on time and follow rudimentary directions. Is this a fair criticism, do you think? Have critics overlooked certain important kinds of learning on these jobs? If so, what might these kinds of learning be, and how do they prepare students for the jobs they hope to have after college? Or if you agree that these jobs are as limiting as the critics contend, what is limiting about them? What other kinds of low-paying work might teach students skills of importance to their education or future work?

Analyzing Writing Strategies

1. Reread paragraphs 1–8, where Newman defines the problem she believes needs to be solved. In a sentence or two, state what you understand the problem to be.

    At the end of paragraph 4, Newman asks why this problem continues. Underline the main reasons she gives in paragraphs 6–8. For her purpose and readers, does she present a well-defined problem? Can you think of questions readers might have about her presentation of the problem? Most important, does her proposed solution (employer consortiums) address all of the reasons the problem continues?

2. Readers are often aware of previous attempts to solve the problem, or they might think of solutions they believe are better than the one the writer is proposing. We call these alternative solutions: They are alternatives to the solution the writer is proposing. Writers who hope to win readers' support must evaluate the alternative solutions that their readers are most likely to be aware of. To evaluate an

alternative, writers may acknowledge that they are aware of it, but usually they go further and either concede that it has some merit or refute it as meritless and not worth further consideration.

Newman evaluates an alternative solution in paragraphs 9–13. How would you define this alternative to the employer consortium as a way for fast-food workers to find better jobs outside the inner city? What are the main reasons Newman gives for not taking it seriously and encouraging readers to do the same? Do you think she successfully refutes this alternative to her proposed solution?

Commentary: Describing the Proposed Solution

Newman describes her proposed solution relatively fully. In paragraphs 14–17, she provides many details about the employer consortium. She defines it at the end of paragraph 14 in terms of its purpose: to find better jobs for hardworking, ambitious fast-food workers. An employee consortium would provide information about jobs and referrals to specific available jobs, the two main resources inner-city fast-food employees lack.

Newman then describes how an employer consortium would function and points out some of its advantages for everyone involved (15–17). She outlines the responsibilities of the two key players in the consortium she envisions: the inner-city fast-food employers and the downtown employers with the better-paying jobs. Notice that she does not hesitate to specify criteria for eligible inner-city employees—they must be "reliable, punctual, hard-working, and motivated," and they must have completed one year of successful work (15). To make it clear that inner-city employers will not be doing all the work, she describes how downtown employers would meet with fast-food employers, review workers' job applications, and pay attention to workers once they are on the job. The downtown employers would also be required to offer on-the-job training for the new workers in order for them to be prepared to take better jobs (16).

As though anticipating inner-city employers' concern that they would be continually giving up their best workers, Newman speculates that employers' reputations would be enhanced and the image of fast-food work would change as the jobs came to be seen as a step to better jobs (17). Presumably, fast-food workers would be more committed to doing a good job if the quality of their work could lead to a better job downtown—and their employers would benefit as well.

Considering Topics for Your Own Essay

Think of barriers or obstacles you have met or expect to meet in realizing your goals and dreams. You might want to think specifically about obstacles to preparing for and entering the career of your choice, but you need not limit yourself to career goals. Perhaps you want to be a more effective speaker and writer but have been unable to find the instruction and support you think you need. Perhaps you are not able to get into an internship program that would give you some experience with the kind of work you hope to do. Perhaps your high school did not offer the courses you needed to prepare for the college major you are pursuing. Perhaps at some crucial point in your life you received inadequate medical care or counseling. Identify one of these obstacles and think of it as a general problem to be solved; that is, assume that other people have confronted the same obstacle. How would you define the problem? How might you propose to solve it? To be more than a personal complaint about bad luck or mistreatment, your proposal would need to appeal to readers who have experienced a similar obstacle or who would be able to remove the obstacle or give sound advice on getting around it.

Patrick O'Malley wrote the following proposal while he was a first-year college student. He proposes that college professors give students frequent brief examinations in addition to the usual midterm and final exams. After discussing with his instructor his unusual rhetorical situation—a student advising professors—he decided to revise the essay into the form of an open letter to professors at his college, a letter that might appear in the campus newspaper.

O'Malley's essay may strike you as unusually authoritative. This air of authority is due in large part to what O'Malley learned about the possibilities and problems of frequent exams as he interviewed two professors (his writing instructor and the writing program director) and talked with several students. As you read his essay, notice particularly how he anticipates professors' likely objections to his proposal and evaluates their preferred solutions to the problem he identifies.

More Testing, More Learning

Patrick O'Malley

It's late at night. The final's tomorrow. You got a C on the midterm, so this one will make or break you. Will it be like the midterm? Did you study enough? Did you study the right things? It's too late to drop the course. So what happens if you fail? No time to worry about that now—you've got a ton of notes to go over.

Although this last-minute anxiety about midterm and final exams is only too familiar to most college students, many professors may not realize how such major, infrequent, high-stakes exams work against the best interests of students both psychologically and intellectually. They cause unnecessary amounts of stress, placing too much importance on one or two days in the students' entire term, judging ability on a single or dual performance. They don't encourage frequent study, and they fail to inspire students' best performance. If professors gave additional brief exams at frequent intervals, students would be spurred to study more regularly, learn more, worry less, and perform better on midterms, finals, and other papers and projects.

Ideally, a professor would give an in-class test or quiz after each unit, chapter, or focus of study, depending on the type of class and course material. A physics class might require a test on concepts after every chapter covered, while a history class could necessitate quizzes covering certain time periods or major events. These exams should be given weekly, or at least twice monthly. Whenever possible, they should consist of two or three essay questions rather than many multiple-choice or short-answer questions. To preserve class time for lecture and discussion, exams should take no more than 15 or 20 minutes.

The main reason professors should give frequent exams is that when they do, and when they provide feedback to students on how well they are doing, students learn more in the course and perform better on major exams, projects, and papers. It makes sense that in a challenging course containing a great deal of material, students will learn more of it and put it to better use if they have to apply or "practice" it frequently on exams, which also helps them find out how much they are learning and what they need to go over again. A recent Harvard study notes students' "strong preference for frequent evaluation in a course." Harvard students feel they learn least in courses that have "only a midterm and a final exam, with no other personal evaluation." They believe they learn most in courses with "many opportunities to see how they are doing" (Light, 1990, p. 32). In a review of a number of studies of student learning, Frederiksen (1984) reports that students who take weekly quizzes achieve higher scores on final exams than students who take only a midterm exam and that testing increases retention of material tested.

Another, closely related argument in favor of multiple exams is that they encourage students to improve their study habits. Greater frequency in test taking means greater frequency in studying for tests. Students prone to cramming will be required—or at least strongly motivated—to open their textbooks and notebooks more often, making them less likely to resort to long, kamikaze nights of studying for major exams. Since there is so much to be learned in the typical course, it makes sense that frequent, careful study and review are highly beneficial. But students need motivation to study regularly, and nothing works like an exam. If students had frequent exams in all their courses, they would have to schedule study time each week and gradually would develop a habit of frequent study. It might be argued that students are adults who have to learn how to manage their own lives, but learning history or physics is more complicated than learning to drive a car or balance a checkbook. Students need coaching and practice in learning. The right way to learn new material needs to become a habit, and I believe that frequent exams are key to developing good habits of study and learning. The Harvard study concludes that "tying regular evaluation to good course organization enables students to plan their work more than a few days in advance. If quizzes and homework are scheduled on specific days, students plan their work to capitalize on them" (Light, 1990, p. 33).

By encouraging regular study habits, frequent exams would also decrease anxiety by reducing the procrastination that produces anxiety. Students would benefit psychologically if they were not subjected to the emotional ups and downs caused by major exams, when after being virtually worry-free for weeks they are suddenly ready to check into the psychiatric ward. Researchers at the University of Vermont found a strong relationship among procrastination, anxiety, and achievement. Students who regularly put off studying for exams had continuing high anxiety and lower grades than students who procrastinated less. The researchers found that even "low" procrastinators did not study regularly and recommended that professors give frequent assignments and exams to reduce procrastination and increase achievement (Rothblum, Solomon, & Murakami, 1986, pp. 393, 394).

Research supports my proposed solution to the problems I have described. Common sense as well as my experience and that of many of my friends support it. Why, then, do so few professors give frequent brief exams? Some believe that such exams take up too much of the limited class time available to cover the material in the course. Most courses meet 150 minutes a week — three times a week for 50 minutes each time. A 20-minute weekly exam might take 30 minutes to administer, and that is one-fifth of each week's class time. From the student's perspective, however, this time is well spent. Better learning and greater confidence about the course seem a good trade-off for another 30 minutes of lecture. Moreover, time lost to lecturing or discussion could easily be made up in students' learning on their own through careful regular study for the weekly exams. If weekly exams still seem too time-consuming to some professors, their frequency could be reduced to every other week or their length to 5 or 10 minutes. In courses where multiple-choice exams are appropriate, several questions could be designed to take only a few minutes to answer.   7

Another objection professors have to frequent exams is that they take too much time to read and grade. In a 20-minute essay exam, a well-prepared student can easily write two pages. A relatively small class of 30 students might then produce 60 pages, no small amount of material to read each week. A large class of 100 or more students would produce an insurmountable pile of material. There are a number of responses to this objection. Again, professors could give exams every other week or make them very short. Instead of reading them closely they could skim them quickly to see whether students understand an idea or can apply it to an unfamiliar problem; and instead of numerical or letter grades they could give a plus, check, or minus. Exams could be collected and responded to only every third or fourth week. Professors who have readers or teaching assistants could rely on them to grade or check exams. And the Scantron machine is always available for instant grading of multiple-choice exams. Finally, frequent exams could be given *in place of* a midterm exam or out-of-class essay assignment.   8

Since frequent exams seem to some professors to create too many problems, however, it is reasonable to consider alternative ways to achieve the same goals. One alternative solution is to implement a program that would improve study skills. While such a program might teach students how to study for exams, it cannot prevent procrastination or reduce "large test anxiety" by a substantial amount. One research team studying anxiety and test performance found that study skills training was "not effective in reducing anxiety or improving performance" (Dendato & Diener, 1986, p. 134). This team, which also reviewed other research that reached the same conclusion, did find that a combination of "cognitive/relaxation therapy" and study skills training was effective. This possible solution seems complicated, however, not to mention time-consuming and expensive. It seems much easier and more effective to change the cause of the bad habit rather than treat the habit itself. That is, it would make more sense to solve the problem at its root: the method of learning and evaluation.   9

Still another solution might be to provide frequent study questions for students to answer. These would no doubt be helpful in focusing students' time studying, but students would probably not actually write out the answers unless they were required to. To   10 get students to complete the questions in a timely way, professors would have to collect and check the answers. In that case, however, they might as well devote the time to grading an exam. Even if it asks the same questions, a scheduled exam is preferable to a set of study questions because it takes far less time to write in class, compared to the time students would devote to responding to questions at home. In-class exams also ensure that each student produces his or her own work.

Another possible solution would be to help students prepare for midterm and final   11
exams by providing sets of questions from which the exam questions will be selected or announcing possible exam topics at the beginning of the course. This solution would have the advantage of reducing students' anxiety about learning every fact in the textbook, and it would clarify the course goals, but it would not motivate students to study carefully each new unit, concept, or text chapter in the course. I see this as a way of complementing frequent exams, not as substituting for them.

From the evidence and from my talks with professors and students, I see frequent,   12
brief in-class exams as the only way to improve students' study habits and learning, reduce their anxiety and procrastination, and increase their satisfaction with college. These exams are not a panacea, but only more parking spaces and a winning football team would do as much to improve college life. Professors can't do much about parking or football, but they can give more frequent exams. Campus administrators should get behind this effort, and professors should get together to consider giving exams more frequently. It would make a difference.

References

Dondato, K. M., & Diener, D. (1986). Effectiveness of cognitive/relaxation therapy and study-skills training in reducing self-reported anxiety and improving the academic performance of test-anxious students. *Journal of Counseling Psychology, 33,* 131–135.

Frederiksen, N. (1984). The real test bias: Influences of testing on teaching and learning. *American Psychologist, 39,* 193–202.

Light, R. J. (1990). *Explorations with students and faculty about teaching, learning, and student life.* Cambridge, MA: Harvard University Graduate School of Education and Kennedy School of Government.

Rothblum, E. D., Solomon, L., & Murakami, J. (1986). Affective, cognitive, and behavioral differences between high and low procrastinators. *Journal of Counseling Psychology, 33,* 387–394.

Connecting to Culture and Experience: Experience with Frequent Exams

O'Malley advocates frequent brief exams as a solution to the problems of midterm- and final-exam anxiety, poor study habits, and disappointing exam performance.

With two or three other students, discuss O'Malley's proposal in light of your own experience in your courses. Which of your high school or college courses have included frequent exams? Describe these courses and the kinds of exams they offered. Did they offer the benefits O'Malley claims? Did you learn more because of them? Did courses without frequent exams produce the problems he identifies?

Analyzing Writing Strategies

1. O'Malley devotes almost a third of his essay to counterarguing readers' likely objections to his proposal that frequent exams will increase student learning and achievement. This section of the essay begins in the middle of paragraph 5 (with the sentence "It might be argued…") and then resumes in paragraphs 7 and 8. Begin by underlining the three objections, one each in paragraphs 5, 7, and 8. Then make notes about what strategies and resources O'Malley brings to counterarguing. Finally, evaluate how successful each counterargument seems to be for its intended readers—college professors who are going to resist changing their practices. Does O'Malley show respect for readers while challenging them? If so, how does he manage that? What seems most and least convincing in each counterargument?

2. Nearly always, readers of proposals are aware of solutions different from the one the writer is proposing, alternatives to the writer's solution. Readers may know of a solution someone has already proposed or one that has been tried with mixed results, or readers—as they have a tendency to do—may think of an alternative solution after learning about the writer's preferred one. Consequently, a proposal is rarely complete unless it evaluates one or more likely alternative solutions. O'Malley evaluates alternative solutions in paragraphs 9–10, a different one in each paragraph. Reread these counterarguments and notice two things: what strategies and resources O'Malley relies on and to what extent he concedes there may be some good ideas in each alternative or refutes it as unworkable. How do you think his intended readers will react to these paragraphs? What might they find most and least convincing?

Commentary: Supporting the Proposed Solution

The heart of an essay proposing a solution to a problem is the direct argument supporting the solution. Readers primarily want to know why they should take the proposed solution seriously. O'Malley's essay demonstrates the importance of addressing readers' concerns. Not only does he interview both those who would carry out his proposal (professors) and those who would benefit from it (students), but he also features in his essay what he has learned from these interviews. Paragraphs 7–11 directly acknowledge professors' objections, their questions, and the alternative solutions they would probably prefer. These counterarguments, which may be essential to convincing readers to support a proposal, are only part of the overall argument, which centers on the writer's direct support of the proposed solution. Most of O'Malley's direct argument can be found in paragraphs 4–6, in which O'Malley presents three reasons professors should give frequent exams: Students will (1) learn more and perform better on major exams, projects, and essays; (2) acquire better study habits; and (3) experience decreased anxiety and improved performance. He supports each reason with a combination of assertions based on his own experience and on references to reputable research studies carried out at three universities. He quotes and paraphrases these studies.

Argument and counterargument can be woven together in many different ways in an essay proposing a solution to a problem. Because O'Malley succeeds at balancing argument and counterargument, the organization of his proposal is worth noting. The following is a paragraph outline of his essay:

Opening: a scenario to introduce the problem (paragraph 1)

Presentation of the problem and introduction of the solution (2)

Details of the solution (3)

Reason 1: improved learning and performance (4)

Reason 2: improved study habits (5)

Refutation of objection 1: students as adults (5)

Reason 3: less procrastination and anxiety (6)

Accommodation of objection 2: limited class time (7)

Accommodation of objection 3: too much work (8)

Refutation of alternative solution 1: study-skills training (9)

Refutation of alternative solution 2: study questions (10)

Accommodation of alternative solution 3: sample exam questions (11)

Closing: reiteration of the proposed solution and advice on implementing it (12)

Except for a brief refutation in paragraph 5, O'Malley first presents the direct argument for frequent exams (4–6) and then counterargues (7–11). The outline reveals that counterargument takes up most of the space, a not unusual balance in proposals to solve problems. O'Malley might have counterargued first or counterargued as he presented his direct argument, as he does briefly in paragraph 5. The approach you take depends on what your readers know about the problem and their experience with other proposed solutions to it.

Considering Topics for Your Own Essay

Much of what happens in high school and college is predictable and conventional. Examples of conventional practices that have changed very little over the years are exams, group instruction, graduation ceremonies, required courses, and lowered admission requirements for athletes. Think of additional examples of established practices in high school or college; then select one that you believe needs to be improved or refined in some way. What changes would you propose? What individual or group might be convinced to take action on your proposal for improvement? What questions or objections should you anticipate? How could you discover whether others have previously proposed improvements in the practice you are concerned with? Whom might you interview to learn more about the practice and the likelihood of changing it?

■ PURPOSE AND AUDIENCE

Most proposals are calls to action. Because of this clear purpose, a writer must anticipate readers' needs and concerns more when writing a proposal than in any other kind of writing. The writer attempts not only to convince readers but also to inspire them, to persuade them to support or implement the proposed solution. What your particular readers know about the problem and what they are capable of doing to solve it determine how you address them.

Readers of proposals are often unaware of the problem. In this case, your task is clear: to present them with evidence that will convince them of its existence. This evidence may include statistics, testimony from witnesses or experts, and examples, including the personal experiences of people involved with the problem. You can also speculate about the cause of the problem and describe its ill effects.

Sometimes readers recognize the existence of a problem but fail to take it seriously. When readers are indifferent, you may need to connect the problem closely to their own concerns. For instance, you might show how much they have in common with the people directly affected by it or how it affects them indirectly. However you appeal to readers, you must do more than alert them to the problem; you must also make them care about it. You want to touch readers emotionally as well as intellectually.

At other times, readers concerned about the problem may assume that someone else is taking care of it and that they need not become personally involved. In this situation, you might want to demonstrate that the people they thought were taking care of the problem have failed. Another assumption readers might make is that a solution they supported in the past has already solved the problem. You might point out that the original solution has proved unworkable or that new solutions have become available through changed circumstances or improved technology. Your aim is to rekindle these readers' interest in the problem.

Perhaps the most satisfying proposals are addressed to parties who can take immediate action to remedy the problem. You may have the opportunity to write such a proposal if you choose a problem faced by a group to which you belong. Not only do you have a firsthand understanding of the problem but you also have a good idea what solution other members of the group will support. (You might informally survey some of them before you submit your proposal in order to test your definition of the problem and your proposed solution.) When you address readers who are in a position to take action, you obviously want to assure them that it is wise to do so. You must demonstrate that the solution is feasible — that it can be implemented and that it will work.

BASIC FEATURES: PROPOSING SOLUTIONS

A Well-Defined Problem

A proposal is written to offer a solution to a problem. Before presenting the solution, the writer must be sure that readers know and understand what the problem is. Patrick O'Malley, for example, devotes the first three paragraphs of his essay to defining the problem of infrequent course exams. It is wise to define the problem explicitly, as all the writers in this chapter do. Rob Ryder states precisely how he thinks basketball is limited, and Katherine S. Newman clearly identifies the problem of inner-city fast-food workers' lack of upward mobility.

Stating the problem is not enough, however; the writer also must establish the problem as serious enough to need solving. Sometimes a writer can assume that readers will recognize the problem and its seriousness. At other times, readers may not be aware of the problem and will need to be convinced that it deserves their attention. Newman, for instance, does not assume her readers will understand how difficult it is for inner-city fast-food workers to find better jobs.

In addition to defining the problem and establishing its seriousness for readers, a proposal writer may have to analyze the problem, exploring its causes, consequences, and history, including past efforts at dealing with it.

An Adequately Described Solution

Once the problem is defined and its existence established, the writer must describe the solution so that readers can readily imagine what it would be like. Because O'Malley assumes that his readers know what brief exams are like, he runs little risk in not describing them. He does, however, identify their approximate lengths and possible forms — brief essay, short answer, or multiple choice. In contrast, because Newman cannot assume her readers will know what she means by an "employer consortium," she describes it at length, focusing on who would be involved and the roles they would play.

A Convincing Argument in Support of the Proposed Solution

The main purpose of a proposal is to convince readers that the writer's solution is the best way of solving the problem. A writer must give reasons and support to show that the proposed solution will solve the problem. To this end, O'Malley gives three reasons why he proposes more brief exams and supports each reason with published research studies as well as his own experience.

Writers must also argue that the proposed solution is feasible — that it can actually be implemented and that it will work. The easier it is to implement, the more likely it is to win readers' support. Therefore, writers sometimes set out the steps required to put the proposed solution into practice, an especially important strategy when the solution might seem difficult, time-consuming, or expensive to enact. All the writers in this chapter offer specific suggestions for implementing their proposals, though none outlines all the steps required. For example, O'Malley offers professors several specific ways to give their students frequent, brief exams, and Newman offers many details about how an employer consortium would function.

An Anticipation of Readers' Objections and Questions

The writer arguing for a proposal must anticipate objections or reservations that readers may have about the proposed solution. Ryder, for example, addresses several questions that he knows his readers will likely ask about four-on-four basketball, such as "So just what are we sacrificing by going to four on four?" and "But how do you keep these games from running over three hours?" He accommodates or concedes some questions and refutes others.

An Evaluation of Alternative Solutions

The writer of a proposal wants to convince readers that the proposed solution is preferable to other possible solutions. To do so, the writer evaluates the alternative solutions and demonstrates what is wrong with each one. O'Malley considers study-skills training, study questions, and sample exam questions as alternatives to frequent exams. The best way to reject an alternative solution is simply to demonstrate that it does not work, as Newman does when she discusses the social networks available to job seekers who live in the inner-city neighborhood she studied. She identifies some connections that enable workers to make lateral job moves and others that might lead them into industries that were economically vital a generation ago but are now shrinking. She demonstrates that even though inner-city residents may seek better jobs via a social network, they remain cut off from "upward mobility." Another way to reject an alternative solution is to show that it solves only part of the problem. O'Malley uses this strategy in rejecting sample exam questions.

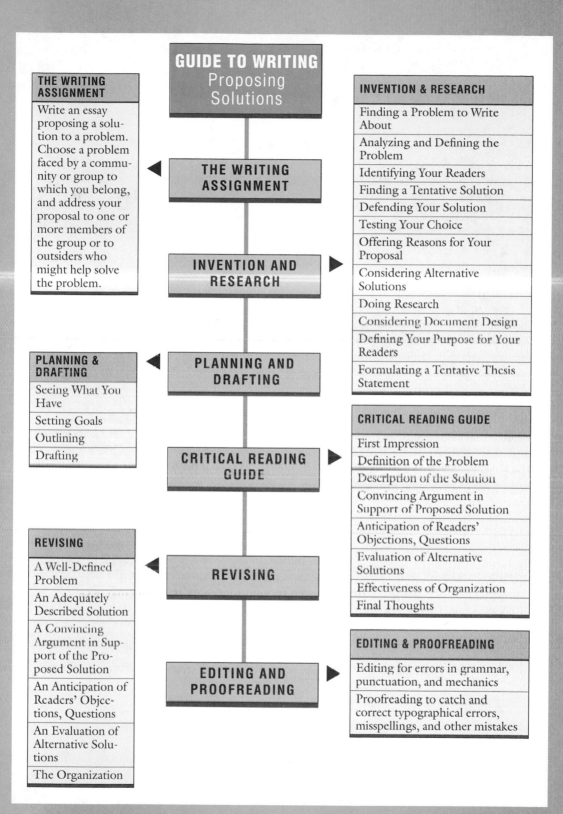

GUIDE TO WRITING
Proposing Solutions

THE WRITING ASSIGNMENT

Write an essay proposing a solution to a problem. Choose a problem faced by a community or group to which you belong, and address your proposal to one or more members of the group or to outsiders who might help solve the problem.

THE WRITING ASSIGNMENT

INVENTION & RESEARCH

Finding a Problem to Write About

Analyzing and Defining the Problem

Identifying Your Readers

Finding a Tentative Solution

Defending Your Solution

Testing Your Choice

Offering Reasons for Your Proposal

Considering Alternative Solutions

Doing Research

Considering Document Design

Defining Your Purpose for Your Readers

Formulating a Tentative Thesis Statement

INVENTION AND RESEARCH

PLANNING & DRAFTING

Seeing What You Have

Setting Goals

Outlining

Drafting

PLANNING AND DRAFTING

CRITICAL READING GUIDE

First Impression

Definition of the Problem

Description of the Solution

Convincing Argument in Support of Proposed Solution

Anticipation of Readers' Objections, Questions

Evaluation of Alternative Solutions

Effectiveness of Organization

Final Thoughts

CRITICAL READING GUIDE

REVISING

A Well-Defined Problem

An Adequately Described Solution

A Convincing Argument in Support of the Proposed Solution

An Anticipation of Readers' Objections, Questions

An Evaluation of Alternative Solutions

The Organization

REVISING

EDITING & PROOFREADING

Editing for errors in grammar, punctuation, and mechanics

Proofreading to catch and correct typographical errors, misspellings, and other mistakes

EDITING AND PROOFREADING

GUIDE TO WRITING

■ THE WRITING ASSIGNMENT

Write an essay proposing a solution to a problem. Choose a problem faced by a community or group to which you belong, and address your proposal to one or more members of the group or to outsiders who might help solve the problem.

■ INVENTION AND RESEARCH

The following activities will help you prepare to write a proposal. You will choose a problem you can write about, analyze and define the problem, identify your prospective readers, decide on and defend your proposed solution, test your choice, offer reasons and support for adopting your proposal, and consider readers' objections and alternative solutions, among other things. These activities are easy to complete. Doing them over several days will give your ideas time to ripen and grow. Be sure to keep a written record of your invention and research to use later when you draft and revise.

Finding a Problem to Write About

You may have already thought about a problem you could write about. Or you may have been drawn to one of the problems suggested by the Considering Topics for Your Own Essay activities following the readings in this chapter. Even so, you will want to consider several problems that need solving before making your final choice. The following activities will help you get started.

Listing Problems.   *Make a list of problems you could write about.* Divide a piece of paper into two columns. In the left-hand column, list communities, groups, or organizations to which you belong. Include as many communities as possible: college, neighborhood, hometown, and cultural or ethnic groups. Also include groups you participate in: sports, musical, work, religious, political, support, hobby, and so on. In the right-hand column, list any problems that exist within each group. Here is how such a chart might begin:

Community	*Problem*
My college	Poor advising or orientation
	Shortage of practice rooms in music building
	No financial aid for part-time students
	Lack of facilities for disabled students
	Lack of enough sections of required courses
	Class scheduling that does not accommodate working students or students with children

My neighborhood	Need for traffic light at dangerous intersection
	Unsupervised children getting into trouble
	Megastores driving away small businesses
	Lack of safe places for children to play

Listing Problems Related to Identity and Community.   Writing a proposal can give you special insight into issues of identity and community by helping you understand how members of a community negotiate their individual needs and concerns. You may already have made a chart of communities to which you belong and problems in those communities. The following categories may help you think of additional problems in those or other communities that you could add to your list:

- Disagreement over conforming to community standards
- Conflicting economic, cultural, or political interests within the community
- Problems with equity or fairness between men and women, rich and poor, different ethnic groups
- Lack of respect or trust among the members of the community
- Struggles for leadership of the community

Listing Problems Related to Work and Career.   Proposals are frequently written on the job and about the work people do. Based on your work experience, make a double-column chart like the following one. List the places you have worked in the left column and the problems you encountered on the job in the right column.

Workplace	*Problem*
Restaurant	Inadequate training
	Conflicts with supervisor
	Unfair shift assignments
Department store	Inadequate inventory
	Computer glitches
	Overcomplicated procedures
Office	Unfair workloads
	Changing requirements
	Inflexible work schedules
	Lack of information about procedures
	Difficulty in scheduling vacations
	Outdated technology

Choosing a Problem.   *Choose one problem from your list that seems especially impor-*
tant to you, that concerns others in the group or community, and that seems solvable. (You
need not know the exact solution now.) The problem should also be one that you can
explore in detail and are willing to discuss in writing.

Proposing to solve a problem in a group or community to which you belong gives
you an inestimably important advantage: You can write as an expert, an insider. You
know about the history of the problem, have felt the urgency to solve it, and perhaps
have already thought of possible solutions. Equally important, you will know precisely
to whom to address the proposal, and you can interview others in the group to get
their views of the problem and to understand how they might resist your solution.
From such a position of knowledge and authority comes confident, convincing writing.

Should you want to propose a solution for a social problem of national scope, concentrate on one with which you have direct experience and for which you can suggest a
detailed plan of action. Even better, focus on unique local aspects of the problem. For
example, if you would like to propose a solution to the lack of affordable child care for
children of college students or working parents, you have a great advantage if you are a
parent who has experienced the frustration of finding professional, affordable child care.
Moreover, it may well be that even though such a problem is national in scope, it can only
be solved campus by campus, business by business, or neighborhood by neighborhood.

Analyzing and Defining the Problem

Before you can begin to consider the best possible solution, you must analyze the
problem carefully and then try to define it. Keep in mind that you will have to demonstrate to readers that the problem exists, that it is serious, and that you have a more
than casual understanding of its causes and consequences. If you find that you cannot
do so, you will want to select some other problem to write about.

Analyzing.   *Start by writing a few sentences in response to these questions:*

- Does the problem really exist? How can I tell?
- What caused this problem? Can I identify any immediate causes? Any deeper
  causes? Is the problem caused by a flaw in the system, a lack of resources, individual misconduct or incompetence? How can I tell?
- What is the history of the problem?
- What are the bad effects of the problem? How does it harm members of the community or group? What goals of the group are endangered by the existence of this
  problem? Does it raise any moral or ethical questions?
- Who in the community or group is affected by the problem? Be as specific as possible: Who is seriously affected? Minimally affected? Unaffected? Does anyone
  benefit from its existence?
- What similar problems exist in this same community or group? How can I distinguish my problem from these?

Defining. *Write a definition of the problem, being as specific as possible.* Identify who or what seems responsible for it, and give one recent, telling example.

Identifying Your Readers

In a few sentences, describe your readers, stating your reason for directing your proposal to them. Then take a few minutes to write about these readers. Whom do you need to address—everyone in the community or group, a committee, an individual, an outsider? You want to address your proposal to the person or group who can help implement it. The following questions will help you develop a profile of your readers:

- How informed are my readers likely to be about the problem? Have they shown any awareness of it?
- Why would this problem be important to my readers? Why would they care about solving it?
- Have my readers supported any other proposals to solve this problem? If so, what do those proposals have in common with mine?
- Do my readers ally themselves with any group, and would that alliance cause them to favor or reject my proposal? Do we share any values or attitudes that could bring us together to solve the problem?
- How have my readers responded to other problems? Do their past reactions suggest anything about how they might respond to my proposal?

Finding a Tentative Solution

Solving problems takes time. Apparent solutions often turn out to be impossible. After all, a solution has to be both workable and acceptable to the community or group involved. Consequently, you should strive to come up with several possible solutions whose advantages and disadvantages you can weigh. You may notice that the most imaginative solutions sometimes occur to you only after you have struggled with a number of other possibilities.

    Look back at the way you defined the problem and described your readers. Then with these factors in mind, list as many possible solutions to the problem as you can think of. You might come up with only two or three possible solutions; but at this stage, the more the better. To come up with different solutions, use the following problem-solving questions:

- What solutions to this problem have already been tried?
- What solutions have been proposed for related problems? Might they solve this problem as well?
- Is a solution required that would disband or change the community or group in some way?
- What solution might eliminate some of the causes of the problem?

- What solution would eliminate any of the bad effects of the problem?
- Is the problem too big to be solved all at once? Can I divide it into several related problems? What solutions might solve one or more of these problems?
- If a series of solutions is required, which should come first? Second?
- What solution would ultimately solve the problem?
- What might be a daring solution, arousing the most resistance but perhaps holding out the most promise?
- What would be the most conservative solution, acceptable to nearly everyone in the community or group?

Give yourself enough time to let your ideas percolate as you continue to add to your list of possible solutions and to consider the advantages and disadvantages of each one in light of your prospective readers. If possible, discuss your solutions with those members of the community or group who can help you consider the advantages and disadvantages of each one.

Choosing the Most Promising Solution. *In a sentence or two, state what you consider the best possible way of solving the problem.*

Determining Specific Steps. *Write down the major stages or steps necessary to carry out your solution.* This list of steps will provide an early test of whether your solution can, in fact, be implemented.

Defending Your Solution

Proposals have to be feasible — that is, they must be both reasonable and practical. Imagine that one of your readers strongly opposes your proposed solution and confronts you with the following statements:

- It would not really solve the problem.
- I am comfortable with things as they are.
- We cannot afford it.
- It would take too long.
- People would not do it.
- Too few people would benefit.
- I do not even see how to get started on your solution.
- We already tried that, with unsatisfactory results.
- You support this proposal merely because it would benefit you personally.

Write a few sentences refuting each statement. Doing so will help you learn how to prepare responses to possible objections. If you feel that you need a better idea of how others are likely to feel about your proposal, talk with a few people who are directly involved with or affected by the problem. The more you know about your readers' concerns, the better you will be able to anticipate their reservations and preferred alternative solutions.

Testing Your Choice

Now examine the problem and your proposed solution to see whether you can write a strong proposal. Start by asking yourself the following questions:

- Is this a significant problem? Do other people in the community or group really care about it, or can they be persuaded to care?
- Will my solution really solve the problem? Can it be implemented?
- Can I answer objections from enough people in the community or group to win support for my solution?

As you plan and draft your proposal, you will probably want to consider these questions again. If at any point you decide that you cannot answer them with a confident "Yes," you may want to consider proposing a different, more feasible solution to the problem; if none exists, you may need to choose a different problem to write about.

Testing Your Choice, A Collaborative Activity

At this point, you will find it useful to get together with two or three other students and present your plans to one another. This collaborative activity will help you determine whether you can write this proposal in a way that will interest and convince others.

Presenters: Take turns briefly defining the problem you hope to solve, identifying your intended readers, and describing your proposed solution.

Listeners: Tell the presenter whether the proposed solution seems appropriate and feasible for the situation and intended readers. Suggest objections and reservations you believe readers may have.

Offering Reasons for Your Proposal

To make a convincing case for your proposed solution, you must offer your readers good reasons for adopting your proposal.

Listing Reasons. *Write down every plausible reason you could give that might persuade readers to accept your proposal.* These reasons should answer your readers' key question: "Why is this the best possible solution?"

Choosing the Strongest Reasons. *Put an asterisk next to the strongest reasons — the reasons most likely to be convincing to your intended readers.* If you do not consider at least two or three of your reasons strong, you will probably have difficulty developing a strong proposal and should reconsider your topic.

Evaluating Your Strongest Reasons. *Now look at your strongest reasons and explain briefly why you think each one will be effective with your particular readers, the members of the group or community you are addressing.*

Considering Alternative Solutions

List alternative solutions members of the group or community might offer when they learn about your solution, and consider the advantages and disadvantages of each one relative to your solution. Even if members are likely to consider your proposal reasonable, they will probably want to compare your proposed solution with other possible solutions. You might find it helpful to chart the information as follows:

Possible Solutions	Advantages	Disadvantages
My solution		
Alternative solution 1		
Alternative solution 2		
Etc.		

Doing Research

So far you have relied largely on your own knowledge and experience for ideas about solving the problem. You may now feel that you need to do some research to learn more about the causes of the problem and to find more technical information about implementing the solution. (For guidelines on library and Internet research, see Chapter 13.)

If you are proposing a solution to a problem about which others have written, you will want to find out how they have defined the problem and what solutions they have proposed. You may need to acknowledge these solutions in your essay, either accommodating or refuting them. Now is a good time — before you start drafting — to get any additional information you need. If you are proposing a solution to a local problem, you will want to conduct informal interviews with several people who are aware of or affected by the problem. Find out whether they know anything about its history and current ill effects. Try out your solution on them. Discover whether they have other solutions in mind. (For more on interviewing, see Chapter 12, pp. 346–49.)

Considering Document Design

Think about whether your readers might benefit from design features, such as headings, numbered lists, or other elements that would make your presentation of the problem easier to follow and your solution more convincing. In this chapter's readings, for instance, Katherine S. Newman uses headings to introduce the major sections of her proposal. Consider also whether visuals—drawings, photographs, tables, or graphs— would strengthen your argument. These are not at all a requirement of an essay proposing a solution, but they could be helpful. You may come across promising visuals in your research and either download them from the Internet or make photocopies from library materials. When you reproduce visuals, make sure to acknowledge their sources.

Defining Your Purpose for Your Readers

Write a few sentences, defining your purpose in proposing a solution to a problem of concern to the particular readers you have in mind. Remember that you have already identified your readers in the group or community you are addressing and developed your proposal with these readers in mind. Given these readers, try now to define your purpose by considering the following questions:

- Do I seek incremental, moderate, or radical change? Am I being realistic about what my readers are prepared to do? How can I overcome their natural aversion to change of any kind?

- How can I ensure that my readers will not remain indifferent to the problem?

- Who can I count on for support, and what can I do to consolidate that support? Who will oppose my solution? Shall I write them off or seek common ground with them?

- What exactly do I want my readers to do? To take my proposed solution as a starting point for further discussion about the problem? To take action immediately to implement my solution? To commit themselves to take certain preliminary steps, like seeking funding or testing the feasibility of the solution? To take some other action?

Formulating a Tentative Thesis Statement

Write one or more sentences that could serve as your tentative thesis statement. In most essays proposing solutions to problems, the thesis statement is a concise assertion or announcement of the solution. Think about how emphatic you should make the thesis and whether you should include in it a forecast of your reasons. (For more on thesis and forecasting statements, see Chapter 8, pp. 273–75.)

Review the readings in this chapter to see how other writers construct their thesis statements. For example, recall that Rob Ryder moves from describing the problem to announcing his solution ("It's just too crowded out there. Basketball is meant to be played four on four" [paragraph 5]) to supporting his argument for the feasibility of this solution. His thesis statement is clear. With its surprising challenge to five-on-five basketball, it certainly calls for argument. Similarly, Patrick O'Malley states his thesis early in his essay: "If professors gave additional brief exams at frequent intervals, students would be spurred to study more regularly, learn more, worry less, and perform better on midterms, finals, and other papers and projects" (paragraph 2). O'Malley's thesis announces his solution—brief, frequent exams—to the problems created for students in courses limited to anxiety-producing, high-stakes midterms and finals. The thesis lists the reasons students will benefit from the solution in the order in which the benefits appear in the essay. A forecast is not a requirement of a thesis statement, but it does enable readers to anticipate the stages of the argument, thereby increasing their understanding.

As you draft your own thesis statement, pay attention to the language you use. It should be clear and unambiguous, emphatic but appropriately qualified. Although you will probably refine your thesis statement as you draft and revise your essay, trying now to articulate it will help give your planning and drafting direction and impetus. (For more on asserting a thesis, see Chapter 11, pp. 327–30.)

■ PLANNING AND DRAFTING

This section will help you review your invention writing and research notes, determine specific goals for your essay, prepare a rough outline, and get started on your first draft.

Seeing What You Have

Reread your invention and research notes, asking yourself whether you have a good topic—an interesting problem with a feasible solution. If at this point you doubt the significance of the problem or question the success of your proposed solution, you might want to consider a new topic. If you are unsure about these basic points, you cannot expect to produce a persuasive draft.

However, if your invention material seems thin but promising, you may be able to strengthen it with additional invention writing. Ask yourself the following questions:

- Can I make a stronger case for the seriousness of the problem?
- Can I think of additional reasons for readers to support my solution?
- Are there any other ways of refuting alternative solutions to or troubling questions about my proposed solution?

Setting Goals

Before beginning to draft, think seriously about the overall goals of your proposal. Not only will the draft be easier to write once you have clear goals, but it will almost surely be more convincing as well.

Here are some questions that will help you set goals now. You may find it useful to return to them while drafting, for they are designed to help you focus on exactly what you want to accomplish with this proposal.

Your Purpose and Readers

- What do my readers already know about this problem?
- Are they likely to welcome my solution or resist it?
- Can I anticipate any specific reservations or objections they may have?
- How can I gain readers' enthusiastic support? How can I get them to want to implement the solution?
- How can I present myself so that I seem both reasonable and authoritative?

The Beginning

- How can I immediately engage my readers' interest? Should I open with a dramatic scenario, like O'Malley does? With statistics that highlight the seriousness of the problem (like Newman) or a reference to personal experience (like Ryder)? Should I open with a question?
- What information should I give first? Next? Last?

Defining the Problem

- How much do I need to tell about the problem's causes or history?
- How can I show the seriousness of the problem? Should I use statistics, as Newman does? Stress negative consequences, as O'Malley does?
- Is it an urgent problem? How can I emphasize its urgency? Should I redefine the problem?
- How much space should I devote to defining the problem? Only a little space (like O'Malley) or much space (like Newman)?

Describing the Proposed Solution

- How can I describe my solution so that it will look like the best way to proceed? Should I show how to implement it in stages, as Newman does? Or should I focus on my reasons to support it, as O'Malley does?
- How can I make the solution seem easy to implement? Or should I acknowledge that the solution may be difficult to implement and argue that it will be worth the effort?

Anticipating Readers' Objections

- Should I acknowledge every possible objection to my proposed solution? How might I choose among these objections?
- Has anyone already raised these objections? Should I name the person?
- Should I accommodate certain objections and refute others?

- What specific reasons can I give for refuting each objection? How can I support my refutations with reasons?
- How can I refute my readers' objections without seeming to attack anyone?

Evaluating Alternative Solutions

- How many alternative solutions do I need to mention? Which ones should I discuss at length? Should I indicate where each one comes from?
- What reasons should I give for rejecting the alternative solutions? Like O'Malley, can I offer any support for my reasons?
- How can I reject these other solutions without seeming to criticize their proponents? O'Malley, for example, succeeds at rejecting other solutions respectfully.

The Ending

- How should I conclude? Should I end by restating the problem and summarizing the solution? By arguing that some readers' preferred solution is sure to fail? Or simply by summarizing my solution and its advantages, as both O'Malley and Newman do in their conclusions?
- Is there something special about the problem that I should remind readers of at the end?
- Should I end with an inspiring call to action, like Ryder does, or with a scenario suggesting the consequences of a failure to solve the problem?
- Might a shift to humor or satire provide an effective way to end?

Outlining

After setting goals for your proposal, you are ready to make a working outline. The basic outline for a proposal is quite simple:

> The problem
>
> The solution
>
> The reasons for accepting the solution

This simple plan is nearly always complicated by other factors, however. In outlining your material, you must take into consideration many other details, such as whether readers already recognize the problem, how much agreement exists on the need to solve the problem, how many alternative solutions are available, how much attention must be given to these other solutions, and how many objections should be expected.

Here is a possible outline for a proposal where readers may not understand the problem fully and other solutions have been proposed:

Presentation of the problem

    Its existence

    Its seriousness

    Its causes

Consequences of failing to solve the problem

Description of the proposed solution

List of steps for implementing the solution

Reasons and support for the solution

    Acknowledgment of objections

    Accommodation or refutation of objections

Consideration of alternative solutions and their disadvantages

Restatement of the proposed solution and its advantages

(See p. 205 for another sample outline.)

Your outline will of course reflect your own writing situation. As you develop it, think about what your readers know and feel and about your own writing goals. Once you have a working outline, you should not hesitate to change it as necessary while drafting and revising. For instance, you might find it more effective to hold back on presenting your own solution until you have dismissed other possible solutions. Or you might find a better way to order the reasons for adopting your proposal. The purpose of an outline is to identify the basic features of your proposal and to help you organize them effectively, not to lock you into a particular structure.

Most of the information you will need to develop each feature of a proposal can be found in your invention writing and research notes. How much space you devote to each feature is determined by the topic, not the outline. Do not assume that each entry on your outline must be given one paragraph. For example, each reason for supporting the solution may require a paragraph, but you might instead present the reasons, objections, and refutations all in one paragraph. (For more on outlining, see Chapter 9, pp. 292–94.)

Drafting

Start drafting your proposal, keeping in mind the goals you set while you were planning. Also keep in mind the two main goals of proposals: (1) to establish that a problem exists and is serious enough to require a solution, and (2) to demonstrate that your proposed solution is both feasible and the best possible alternative. Use your outline to guide you as you write, but do not hesitate to stray from it whenever you find that drafting takes you in an unexpected direction.

If you get stuck while drafting, explore the problem by using some of the writing activities in the Invention and Research section of this chapter or reviewing the general advice on drafting in Chapter 1 (pp. 15–17). Perhaps the most important advice to remember about drafting is to write quickly without worrying about grammar and spelling. Later you can make corrections.

CRITICAL READING GUIDE

Now is the time to get a good critical reading of your draft. Writers usually find it helpful to have someone else read and comment on their drafts, and all writers know how much they learn when they read other writers' drafts. Your instructor may arrange such a reading as part of your coursework. If not, you can ask a classmate, friend, or family member to read your draft. You could also seek comments from a tutor at your campus writing center. (If you are unable to have someone else read your draft, turn ahead to the Revising section for help with reading your own draft critically.)

If You Are the Writer. In order to provide focused, helpful comments, your reader must know your essay's intended audience, your purpose, and a problem in the draft that you need help solving. Briefly write out this information at the top of your draft.

- *Readers.* Identify the intended readers of your essay. How much do they know about the problem?

- *Purpose.* What do you want your readers to do or think as a result of reading your proposal?

- *Problem.* Ask your reader to help you solve the single most important problem you see with your draft. Describe this problem briefly.

If You Are the Reader. Reading a draft critically means reading it more than once, first to get a general impression and then to analyze its basic features. (See pp. 207–8 to review the basic features.) Use the following questions to help you give critical comments to others on essays that propose solutions to problems.

1. *Read for a First Impression.* Read first to get a basic understanding of the problem and the proposed solution to it. Briefly write out your impressions. How convincing do you think the proposal will be for its particular readers? What do you notice about the way the problem is presented and the way the solution is argued for? Next, consider the problem the writer identified. If the problem will be covered by one of the other questions below, deal with it there. Otherwise, respond to the writer's concerns now.

2. *Evaluate How Well the Problem Is Defined.* Decide whether the problem is stated clearly. Does the writer give enough information about its causes and consequences? What more might be done to establish its seriousness? Is there more that readers might need or wish to know about it?

3. *Consider Whether the Solution Is Described Adequately.* Does the presentation of the solution seem immediately clear and readable? How could the presentation be strengthened? Has the writer laid out steps for implementation? If not, might readers expect or require them? Does the solution seem practical? If not, why?

4. *Assess Whether a Convincing Argument Is Advanced in Support of the Proposed Solution.* Look at the reasons offered for advocating this solution. Are they sufficient? Which are likely to be most and least convincing to the intended readers? What kind of support does the writer provide for each reason? How believable do you think readers will find it? Has the writer argued forcefully for the proposal without offending readers?

5. *Evaluate How Well the Writer Anticipates Readers' Objections and Questions.* Which accommodations and refutations seem most convincing? Which seem least convincing? Are there other objections or reservations that the writer should acknowledge?

6. *Assess the Writer's Evaluation of Alternative Solutions.* Are alternative solutions discussed and either accommodated or refuted? Which are the most convincing reasons given against other solutions? Which are least convincing, and why? Has the writer sought out common ground with readers who may advocate alternative solutions? Are such solutions accommodated or rejected without a personal attack on those who propose them? Try to think of other solutions that readers may prefer.

7. *Consider the Effectiveness of the Organization.* Evaluate the overall plan of the proposal, perhaps by outlining it briefly. Would any parts be more effectively placed earlier or later in the essay? Look closely at the way the writer orders the argument for the solution—the presentation of the reasons and the accommodation or refutation of objections and alternative solutions. How might the sequence be revised to strengthen the argument? Point out any gaps in the argument.

- Look at the *beginning*. Is it engaging? If not, how might it be revised to capture readers' attention? Does it adequately forecast the main ideas and the plan of the proposal? Suggest other ways the writer might begin.

- Look at the *ending*. Does it frame the proposal by echoing or referring to something at the beginning? If not, how might it do so? Does the ending convey a sense of urgency? Suggest a stronger way to conclude.

- Look at any *design elements and visuals* the writer has incorporated. Assess how well they are incorporated into the essay. Point to any items that do not strengthen either the presentation of the problem or the argument in support of the solution.

8. *Give the Writer Your Final Thoughts.* What is the draft's strongest part? What part is most in need of further work?

■ REVISING

Now you have the opportunity to revise your essay. Your instructor or other students may have given you advice on how to improve your draft. Or you may have begun to realize that your draft requires not so much revising as rethinking. For example, you may recognize that you are no longer convinced the problem is serious, that it is serious but cannot be solved now or anytime soon, that you cannot decide to whom to address the proposal, that you cannot come up with a set of convincing reasons why readers should support your solution, or that you have been unable to accommodate or refute readers' objections and questions or to evaluate alternative solutions. Consequently, instead of working to improve the various parts of your first draft, you may need to write a new draft that reshapes your argument. Many students—and professional writers— find themselves in this situation. Often a writer produces a draft or two and gets advice on them from others and only then begins to see what might be achieved.

If you feel satisfied that your draft achieves what you set out to do, you can focus on refining the various parts of it. This section will help you get an overview of your draft and revise it accordingly.

Getting an Overview

Consider your draft as a whole, following these two steps:

1. *Reread.* If at all possible, put the draft aside for a day or two before rereading it. When you do go back to it, start by reconsidering your audience and purpose. Then read the draft straight through, trying to see it as your intended readers will.

2. *Outline.* Make a quick scratch outline, indicating the basic features as they appear in the draft. (For more on scratch outlines, see Chapter 9, pp. 292–93.)

Charting a Plan for Revision.   You may want to make a double-column chart like the following one to help you keep track of any problems you need to solve. In the left-hand column, list the basic features of proposals. (Turn to pp. 207–8 to review the basic features.) As you analyze your draft and study any comments you have received from others, note the problems you want to solve in the right-hand column.

Basic Features	*Problems to Solve*
A well-defined problem	
An adequately described solution	
A convincing argument in support of the proposed solution	
An anticipation of readers' objections and questions	
An evaluation of alternative solutions	

Analyzing the Basic Features of Your Own Draft. Turn to the Critical Reading Guide on pp. 222–23. Using this guide, identify problems you now see in your draft. Note the problems on your chart.

Studying Critical Comments. Review all of the comments you have received from other readers. For each comment, look at the draft to determine what might have led the reader to make that particular point. Try to be receptive to constructive criticism. Ideally, these comments will help you see your draft as others see it. Add to your revision chart any problems readers have identified.

Carrying Out Revisions

Having identified problems in your draft, you now need to find solutions and—most important—to carry them out. You have three ways of finding solutions:

1. Review your invention and planning notes for additional information and ideas.
2. Do further invention writing or research to provide material you or your readers think is needed.
3. Look back at the readings in this chapter to see how other writers have solved similar problems.

The following suggestions, which are organized according to the basic features on your revision chart, will get you started solving some common writing problems in essays proposing solutions. For now, focus on solving the problems identified on your chart. Avoid tinkering with grammar and punctuation; those tasks will come later, when you edit and proofread.

A Well-Defined Problem

- **Is the definition of the problem unclear?** Consider sketching out its history, including past attempts to deal with it, discussing its causes and consequences more fully, dramatizing its seriousness more vividly, or comparing it to other problems that readers may be familiar with.

An Adequately Described Solution

- **Is the description of the solution inadequate?** Try outlining the steps or phases involved in its implementation. Help readers see how easy the first step will be, or acknowledge the difficulty of the first step.

A Convincing Argument in Support of the Proposed Solution

- **Does the argument seem weak?** Try to think of more reasons for readers to support your proposal.
- **Is the argument hard to follow?** Try to put your reasons in a more convincing order—leading up to the strongest one rather than putting it first, perhaps.

An Anticipation of Readers' Objections and Questions

- *Does your refutation of any objection or question seem unconvincing?* Consider accommodating it by modifying your proposal.

- *Have you left out any likely objections to the solution?* Acknowledge those objections and either accommodate or refute them.

An Evaluation of Alternative Solutions

- *Do you neglect to mention alternative solutions that some readers are likely to prefer?* Consider including one or more alternative solutions. For each one, try to acknowledge its good points but argue that it is not as effective a solution as your own. You may in fact want to strengthen your own solution by incorporating into it some of the features of alternatives.

The Organization

- *Is the beginning weak?* Think of a better way to start. Would an anecdote or an example of the problem engage readers more effectively?

- *Is the ending flat?* Consider framing your proposal by mentioning something from the beginning of your essay or ending with a call for action that expresses the urgency of implementing your solution.

- *Would design elements make the problem or proposed solution easier to understand?* Consider adding headings or visuals.

■ EDITING AND PROOFREADING

Now is the time to check your revised draft for connections between sentences and for errors in grammar, punctuation, and mechanics. As you reread, ask yourself whether the connection from one sentence to the next is logical and easy for readers to follow. If you sense a gap or disconnection that would cause a reader to stumble or become confused, try revising one or both sentences so that the gap is closed. Notice whether you shift from one word to another unnecessarily in one sentence to the next, and, if you do, consider repeating the same word instead. Look for sentences that might be combined to allow readers to follow the argument more easily and to discover more readily how you have anticipated their objections and questions. Look as well for long or garbled sentences that might be divided into two or three sentences.

As you work on your sentences, look for errors in spelling, capitalization, punctuation, usage, and grammar. Consult a writer's handbook for advice about how to correct any errors you cannot confidently correct on your own. Ask a friend or classmate to read over your draft, looking for errors.

Before you hand in your revised essay, proofread it carefully and run it through a spell-checker. Your goal is to hand in an error-free essay.

REFLECTING ON YOUR WRITING

Now that you have worked extensively with essays that propose solutions to problems—reading them, talking about them, writing one of your own—take some time for reflection. Reflecting on your writing process will help you gain a greater understanding of what you learned about solving the problems you encountered.

Write a page or so telling your instructor about a problem you encountered in writing your proposal essay and how you solved it. Before you begin, gather all of your writing—invention and planning notes, drafts, critical comments, revision notes and plans, and final revision. Review these materials as you complete this writing task.

1. *Identify one writing problem you had to solve as you worked on your proposal essay.* Do not be concerned with grammar and punctuation; concentrate instead on problems unique to developing a proposal. For example: Did you puzzle over how to convince readers that your proposed solution would actually solve the problem you identified? Did you find it difficult to support the reasons you gave for recommending the solution? Did you have trouble coming up with alternative solutions that your readers might favor?

2. *Determine how you came to recognize the writing problem.* When did you first discover it? What called it to your attention? If someone else pointed out the problem to you, can you now see hints of it in your invention writings? If so, where specifically? When you first recognized the problem, how did you respond?

3. *Reflect on how you went about solving the problem.* Did you reword a passage, cut or add details about the problem or solution, or move paragraphs or sentences around? Did you reread one of the essays in this chapter to see how another writer handled a similar problem, or did you look back at the invention suggestions? If you discussed the writing problem with another student, a tutor, or your instructor, did talking about it help? How useful was the advice you received?

4. *Write a brief explanation of the problem and your solution.* Be as specific as possible in reconstructing your efforts. Quote from your invention notes, draft essay, others' critical comments, your revision plan, and your revised essay to show the various changes your writing underwent as you tried to solve the problem. If you are still uncertain about your solution, say so. The point is not to prove that you have solved the problem perfectly but rather to show what you have learned about solving problems when writing proposals. Taking time to explain how you identified a particular problem, how you went about trying to solve it, and what you learned from this experience can help you solve future writing problems more easily.

7

Justifying an Evaluation

Evaluation involves making judgments. Many times each day, we make judgments about subjects as diverse as the weather, food, music, computer programs, sports events, politicians, and films. In everyday conversation, we often express judgments casually ("I like it" or "I don't like it"), seldom giving our reasons (for example, "I hate cafeteria food because it is bland and overcooked") or supporting them with specific examples ("Take last night's spaghetti. That must have been a tomato sauce because it was red, but it did not have the tang of tomatoes. And the noodles were so overdone, they were mushy").

When we write an evaluation, however, we know most readers expect that instead of merely asserting a judgment, we will provide reasons and support to back it up. We know that unless we argue convincingly, readers who disagree will simply dismiss our judgments as personal preferences.

Evaluators can argue convincingly in several ways. One way is by making the reasons for your judgment explicit and by providing specific examples to support your reasons. You can also demonstrate knowledge of the particular subject being evaluated as well as the general category to which the subject belongs. For example, in an evaluation of a new Arnold Schwarzenegger action film, you would want to reassure readers that you are judging the particular film against your experience of other action films by Schwarzenegger and comparable films like those by Jean-Claude Van Damme and Sylvester Stallone. Showing readers you understand how the particular subject relates to other subjects in the same general category demonstrates that your judgment is based on standards that readers recognize as appropriate for judging that kind of subject. For example, most people would agree that taste and consistency are appropriate standards for judging spaghetti served in the school cafeteria, but they would reject the high noise level and uncomfortable seating in a cafeteria as appropriate reasons for evaluating cafeteria food (although these reasons would be appropriate for judging the cafeteria itself).

As you can see, reading and writing evaluations contributes to your intellectual growth by teaching you to develop reasoned, well-supported arguments for your judgments. Evaluations also require you to look critically at the standards underlying your own judgments as well as those of other people. In the process, you learn to appreciate how fundamentally important values are in determining what we think and how crucial it is for us to examine with a critical eye our cherished, but often unexamined, values.

You will encounter evaluative writing in many different contexts, as the following examples suggest.

Writing in Your Other Courses

- For an essay evaluating two films (*Emma* and *Clueless*) based on the Jane Austen novel *Emma*, a student reads the novel, watches both films on videotape, and takes extensive notes. He also does an Internet search for reviews of the films. In his evaluation, the student argues that *Emma*, a period piece that faithfully follows the novel, is less successful than *Clueless*, a loose adaptation set in contemporary Beverly Hills, in capturing the spirit and romance of the novel. He supports his judgment with examples from the films and the novel as well as a few quotations from the movie reviews.

- For a political science course, a student writes a research paper evaluating the two major presidential candidates' performances during the first of their scheduled televised debates. Before watching the debate, she researches newspaper and newsmagazine reports on two previous presidential debates to see what kinds of standards others have used to evaluate televised debates. Then she watches the debate and records it so that she can review it later. As she views the debate, she makes notes evaluating each candidate's performance. Afterward, she copies the transcript of the debate from the newspaper and collects published, televised, and online reviews of the debate. She uses this material both to support her own judgment and to respond to possible objections and opposing judgments. Her final multimedia research paper includes downloaded Internet materials and videotaped excerpts from the debate.

Writing in the Community

- For the travel section of a local newspaper, a motorcycle enthusiast writes an article called "Hog Heaven" evaluating the tour at the Harley-Davidson factory and museum in York, Pennsylvania. He argues that Harley fans will enjoy the two dozen antique bikes on display and that people interested in business will be fascinated by the Harley plant because it includes both a classic assembly line (in which each worker performs an isolated operation on the motorcycles as they move along a conveyor belt) and a Japanese-inspired assembly team (in which three workers assemble an entire motorcycle from beginning to end in whatever way they think works best). He points out that, surprisingly, productivity is substantially higher for the assembly teams (forty-five minutes to assemble a motorcycle) than for the assembly-line workers (one hour and forty minutes). He concludes by emphasizing that the free tour offers something for everyone.

- For a campus publication, a college student writes an evaluation of a history course. She explains that the course includes three one-hour lectures per week by the professor plus a one-hour-per-week discussion led by a teaching assistant

(TA). She states her judgment that although the lectures are boring, hard to follow, and seemingly unrelated to the assigned reading, the discussions are stimulating and help students grasp important information in each week's lectures and readings. To support her judgment, she describes a typical lecture and contrasts it to a typical discussion. She praises the TA for his innovative "concept game," in which two teams of students compete to identify important concepts brought up in the week's lectures and reading, and for reviewing drafts via email. She concludes by recommending the course even though she wishes the TA could conduct the lectures as well as the discussions.

Writing in the Workplace

- In a written review of the work of a probationary employee, a supervisor judges the employee's performance as being adequate overall but still needing improvement in two key areas: completing projects on time and communicating effectively with others. The supervisor backs up his judgment with specific examples and anecdotes. He explains that in one instance the employee's lateness derailed a team of workers and tells how the employee's lack of tact and clarity in communicating with co-workers created a few serious misunderstandings during the six-month probation period.

- For a conference on innovations in education, an elementary school teacher evaluates *Schoolhouse Rock,* an animated educational television series developed in the 1970s and recently reinvented in several new formats: books, CD-ROM learning games, and music CDs. She praises the series as an entertaining and inventive way of presenting information, giving two reasons why the series is an effective teaching tool: Witty lyrics and catchy tunes make the information memorable, and cartoon-like visuals make the lessons painless. She supports each reason by showing and discussing videotaped examples of popular *Schoolhouse Rock* segments, such as "Conjunction Junction," "We the People," and "Three Is a Magic Number." She ends by expressing her hope that teachers and developers of multimedia educational software will learn from the example of *Schoolhouse Rock.*

Practice Evaluating a Subject: A Collaborative Activity

The preceding scenarios suggest some occasions for evaluating a subject. Think of several possible subjects that you know well enough to evaluate, and consider the reasons you would give for evaluating each one.

Part 1. Get together with two or three other students to discuss possible subjects. Then choose one subject that everyone in your group knows well enough to evaluate (such as music, action movies, computer games, football, or science-fiction novels). For example, if everyone in your group likes a particular style of music (such as country, blues, heavy metal, or rap), choose an artist or a recording with which you are all familiar. Note that for this activity you do not have to agree on a judgment. Instead, your aim is to see whether you can agree on appropriate reasons for evaluating the subject you choose.

Together, list all the reasons you can think of for evaluating the subject. For example, if your group decides to evaluate Me'shell Ndegéocello's second CD, *Peace beyond Passion* (1996), some possible reasons might include the following: the lyrics explore important social issues such as racism, religious intolerance, homophobia, and sexism; the bitter tone of the social commentary does not go with the slick, upbeat melodies of some of the songs; and some of the lyrics are hard to understand. Next, decide as a group which reasons are appropriate for evaluating the subject.

Part 2. As a group, spend ten to fifteen minutes discussing what happened when you tried to agree on appropriate standards for evaluating the subject:

- First focus on the reasons your group found *easiest* to agree on. Discuss how you explained (or defended) their appropriateness or inappropriateness. For example, if you agreed on the value of social commentary in a recording like Ndegéocello's, why did you consider social commentary an appropriate standard for evaluating her music?

- Then focus on the standards your group found *hardest* to agree on. Discuss why your group found these particular reasons so hard to agree on. For example, if you disagreed on the value of social commentary in a recording like Ndegéocello's, why did some group members consider it an appropriate standard while others considered it inappropriate? Where might your ideas about what was or was not an appropriate standard for evaluating the subject have come from?

READINGS

The readings in this chapter illustrate the features of essays that justify evaluations and the strategies writers rely on to realize the features. No two essays in this genre are much alike, and yet they share defining features. The section Analyzing Writing Strategies and the Commentary following each reading touch on a few features best illustrated by that essay, capturing its special qualities and strengths. Together, the three essays cover many of the possibilities of evaluative writing. Consequently, you will want to read as many of the essays and Commentaries as possible and, if time permits, complete the activities in Analyzing Writing Strategies. Following the last reading in the chapter, the Basic Features section offers a concise description of the features and strategies of evaluative essays and provides examples from all of the readings.

David Ansen, a senior editor and the chief film critic for Newsweek, *has also worked as a film critic for the Associated Press Radio and various television programs. He has been honored three times by the Newspaper Guild of New York and has won the National Headliner Award. In his weekly movie reviews, Ansen usually can assume that his reviews will have some influence on whether his readers decide to see a movie. But, as Ansen acknowledges, his review of the first new* Star Wars *film in sixteen years is unlikely to influence many readers. Nevertheless, he takes seriously the assignment to think critically about* Star Wars: The Phantom Menace *in this review, originally published in the May 17, 1999 issue of* Newsweek. *As you read, notice how Ansen gives readers specific examples from the film to support his judgment while also encouraging readers to think critically about their own judgment.*

Star Wars: The Phantom Movie

David Ansen

A new menace: Darth Maul (Ray Park).

Twenty-two years ago *Star Wars* came out of nowhere, and changed the world. *Star Wars: Episode I, The Phantom Menace* comes out amid a cacophony of media hype, carrying on its shoulders the wildest hopes of several generations of worshipful moviegoers. It's been 16 years since *Return of the Jedi,* the last installment of George Lucas's trilogy. In a country with a notoriously short attention span, it's nothing less than miraculous that the passage of time made no dent in our appetite for this intergalactic adventure. It's not hype to say that *Phantom Menace* is the most eagerly awaited movie ever made. (Pilgrims started camping out in front of theaters a month before its May 19 opening.) You'll be hard pressed to find anyone who doubts for a moment that it will recoup its $115 million budget. 1

I will beat around the bush no longer. The movie is a disappointment. A big one. Will you take my word for it? Of course not. This massively marketed movie is virtually critic-proof. Everyone feels he must find out for himself. 2

The oddest thing about *Episode I*—which takes us back to the childhood of Anakin Skywalker, who as we know will later become Darth Vader, father of Luke Skywalker—is that it's a tale that didn't need to be told. Or that should have been told in 20 minutes, so that we could get on to the good stuff. What we want to know is how Anakin Skywalker, Jedi knight, turned to the Dark Side. You won't find that out in *The Phantom Menace.* Lucas presents us with a cute, towheaded 9-year-old (Jake Lloyd), a slave on the outlaw planet Tatooine (everyone's favorite sci-fi funkytown), who is discovered by the Jedi warriors Qui-Gon Jinn (Liam Neeson) and his apprentice Obi-Wan Kenobi (Ewan McGregor). The two Jedi are trying, and failing, to prevent a war between the powerful Trade Federation and the peaceful planet of Naboo, and they have stopped off on Tatooine to find a hyperdrive generator for their battle-damaged spacecraft. The war seems to be about commerce, but Qui-Gon Jinn intuits a darker purpose behind it (just what *that* is also awaits in *Episode II*). 3

Traveling with our Jedi heroes is Naboo's young Queen Amidala (Natalie Portman), who apparently is destined to marry Anakin (also in the next movie).

This boy, the Jedi instantly see, is special. It's even heavily hinted that he's been immaculately conceived. Knowing what we know about his future, we want to see hints in this sweet child of his future monstrosity. Astonishingly, Lucas plants no seeds of evil. Instead, we are just told (by our old friend Yoda, in his pre-hermit days) that he senses a danger in him. What a rudimentary failure of storytelling. What was Lucas thinking when he turned Anakin into a banal youngster who, upon hearing he's going to leave home to train as a Jedi, proclaims, "Can I go, Mom? Yipee!" There is nothing strange, special or particularly interesting about the future Darth Vader here, and the casting of the conventionally adorable Lloyd, who looks like he should be hawking cereal on TV commercials, is no help. Neither is his good old-fashioned bad acting.

There's no shortage of action in *Phantom Menace*—lightsaber fights, attacking armies, exploding spacecraft—but there's a curious lack of urgency. Our emotions are rarely engaged. It's been 22 years since Lucas directed a movie, and he's gotten rusty. His rhythm is off. Many of the scenes feel shapeless and flat—they're not ended, but abandoned. He doesn't seem to care about building a character. Ewan McGregor, one of the most vital and versatile young actors around, is completely wasted: Obi-Wan is given nothing interesting to do or say. Liam Neeson brings a grave, slightly weary dignity to Qui-Gon, but he's a rather somber character to carry what is meant to be a slam-bang adventure fantasy. There is no equivalent here to the irreverent, wise-cracking Han Solo, and his light touch is missed. For comic relief, we get the computer-generated Jar Jar Binks, a goofy, floppy-eared, vest-wearing toy serpent with a clumsy two-legged lope and an incomprehensible Caribbean accent. (He's a kind of extraterrestrial Stepin Fetchit.) Funny not he is, as Yoda would say. A more successful debut is made by the devilish Darth Maul, a horned, painted Sith lord who works for shrouded Evil Genius Darth Sidious. There's fresh menace in his mien.

The genuine magic in *Episode I* is all in its design. Conceptual artist Doug Chiang and production designer Gavin Bocquet give us breathtaking vistas, fabulous imaginary cities that range from the Florentine splendor of Queen Amidala's domain to the teeming metropolis of Coruscan. The vaultlike Galactic Senate, whose box seats float through the air, is a triumph of baroque futurism. The sunset-drenched, open-air Jedi council chambers (shades of *Blade Runner*) glow like a remembered childhood picture book. (The art nouveau, glass-bubble undersea city, however, looks like a floating Lamps Plus showroom to me.) The massive, tree-crunching tanks of the droid armies have a brutal beauty; there's visual wit in the insectlike robot soldiers who do the Trade Federation's dirty work. Indeed, there's often so much to take in you wish Lucas would hold his shots longer, and let us feast on the details.

This is the impressive fruit of what Lucas calls his "digital backlot." *Phantom Menace* uses more computer-generated shots than any movie in history (95 percent of the frames employ some digital work). The technical significance can't be denied—Lucas is blurring the line between live action and animation. When it works—in the spectacular pod-racing sequence on Tatooine, in which Anakin and his repulsive rival Sebulba fly like the wind through jagged desert canyons—the movie re-creates the buoyant adrenaline rush the original *Star Wars* so lightheartedly and consistently generated.

Lucas even uses digital techniques to tinker with the performances—seamlessly merging, for example, an actor's frown in take three upon his face in take six. This may be the first step toward a cinematic future in which virtual actors replace flesh-and-blood ones—and unfortunately it sometimes seems as if he's drained the flesh and blood from his own cast. The usually vibrant Portman is decked out in wonderful Kabuki-like makeup and dressed in beautifully bejeweled costumes, but most of the time she looks lost in space, stranded without a character to play. All the state-of-the-art technology in the world is no help to an actor saddled with Lucas's tinny dialogue. The original had its share of cheesy, B-movie performances: it was part of its retro "Buck Rogers" charm. But in these more extravagant settings, the lapses seem puzzling. 8

The arc of Anakin's story—a boy leaving home to become a Jedi and a hero, saving the day in battle—recapitulates Luke's story in *Star Wars.* You can understand why Lucas would want to carbon-copy his golden oldies—why tamper with the most success-ful formula in movie history? But you can't go home again. Lucas's sensibility, which was never particularly sophisticated to begin with, hasn't evolved in two decades. The *Phantom Menace* is more of the same, without the innocence and without the juice. And in the year of *The Matrix,* which offers a new style of special effects and a dystopian fantasy that hits closer to home, Lucas's childlike vision is beginning to look merely childish. 9

Connecting to Culture and Experience: Stereotypes

Some viewers of *The Phantom Menace* have complained about the ethnic stereotyping of certain characters. Lucas's "noseless leaders of the Galactic Trade Federation," reviewer Andrew Gumbel wrote online, "are clearly a throwback to the Yellow Peril characters popular in *Flash Gordon* and other series, but risk being interpreted as a racial slur" ("*Star Wars* Battles Charges of Racism" <http://www.freep.com/fun/starwars/nstar4.htm>). Ansen himself compares the digitized character Jar Jar Binks to a "kind of extraterrestrial Stepin Fetchit," referring to a 1930s actor who portrayed an African American stereotype now considered insulting, even racist (paragraph 5). Negative reaction to this character has been so strong that numerous Web sites have been created with titles like *The Jar Jar Hate Page* and *Die Jar Jar Binks, Die!*

With two or three other students, explore your views on ethnic, gender, or other stereotyping in films. Take turns trying to name movie characters that you think fit an ethnic stereotype. Then discuss as a group whether stereotyping should be taken into account when evaluating a film.

Analyzing Writing Strategies

1. At the beginning of this chapter, we make several generalizations about evaluative essays. Consider which of these statements is true of Ansen's evaluation:

- It asserts a judgment.
- It makes explicit the reasons for the judgment.
- It provides specific support for the judgment.
- It tries to demonstrate knowledge of the particular subject as well as the general category to which the subject belongs.

2. Reread paragraphs 3–5, where Ansen presents his reasons for judging *The Phantom Menace* as "disappointing," and underline each reason. To get started, underline the last part of sentence 1 in paragraph 3: "it's a tale that didn't need to be told."

Commentary: Subject and Judgment

Ansen identifies the subject by name in the title and twice in the first paragraph. Because the film is so widely anticipated, he can assume readers already know something about it. Nevertheless, he reminds them of its history as the latest installment in the *Star Wars* series by George Lucas. In subsequent paragraphs, Ansen identifies the actors, describes the main characters, and presents the story.

All of this information is necessary to give readers a context for the judgment. From the way Ansen addresses readers ("Anakin Skywalker, who as we know . . ." and "What we want to know is . . ." [paragraph 3]), he obviously expects them to know a great deal about the *Star Wars* films and even a little about *The Phantom Menace* from all the advance publicity. What readers cannot know, however, until they read his review, is his assessment of the film, which he announces in a clear, definitive thesis statement: "The movie is a disappointment" (paragraph 2). Ansen's thesis statement has two of the three qualities of a good thesis—that it be clear and arguable. The key word "disappointment" is clear in that everyone understands that it asserts an overall negative evaluation. Moreover, Ansen helps readers grasp what he means by showing them exactly what about the film he finds disappointing. The thesis is also obviously arguable since others disagree with his judgment. Ansen's thesis statement does not have the third quality—that the thesis be appropriately qualified. Instead of modifying his judgment, he makes it even more extreme by following the word "disappointment" with the phrase "A big one." Nevertheless, Ansen's essay is not all negative. In fact, he spends nearly as much space praising the film's "design" and "state-of-the-art technology" (6–8), as he does criticizing its "failure of storytelling" (3–5).

Considering Topics for Your Own Essay

List several movies that you would enjoy reviewing, and choose one from your list that you recall especially well. Of course, if you were actually to write about this movie, you would need to see it several times (in the theater or on video) in order to develop your reasons and find supporting examples. For this activity, however, you do not have to view the film again. Just be sure it is one about which you have a strong judgment. Then consider how you would argue for your judgment. Specifically, what reasons do you think you would give your readers? Why do you assume that your readers would recognize the standards these reasons reflect as appropriate for evaluating this particular film?

Kristine Potter was a college student when she wrote this essay evaluating a Web site related to her son's medical condition. As you read, notice what she looks for in evaluating medical information on the Web. Then consider whether the standards Potter applies to the Web differ from those you would apply to research sources found in the library or through interviews and observations.

Asthma on the Web

Kristine Potter

The World Wide Web (or WWW) has served as a convenient starting point for much of my college research, but I was still not sure whether it would also be useful for researching questions concerning my personal life. Since my nine-year-old son, Jeremy, suffers from asthma, I am particularly interested in using the Web to learn about the most current treatments for the disease. The Web's up-to-date information and easy accessibility from my home make it an especially attractive research tool. However, I am also aware that Web-based material must be evaluated carefully because anyone with technological know-how can publish on the Web. I have found that when I research medical information on the Web, I need to consider the same basic questions I use when researching for my college courses: (1) Is the information easily accessible? (2) Is it helpful? and (3) Is it reliable? My evaluation of the Canadian Lung Association's *Asthma* Web site, located at <http://www.lung.ca/asthma>, led me to the conclusion that this site successfully meets my criteria for accessible, helpful, and reliable information.

I accessed the *Asthma* home page from a list of search results produced by Yahoo!, <http://www.yahoo.com>, a popular Internet search engine, and was happy to learn that one important criterion for Web site usefulness—speedy access to information—was immediately satisfied. Unlike my earlier visit to another asthma-related Web site where I spent an average of thirty seconds waiting for each new page to load, the Canadian Lung Association's *Asthma* home page loaded instantaneously, and I could see at a glance that it might be useful for my needs. The page downloaded quickly because it does not use a lot of graphics to attract visitors. Although the information at the other site may have been useful in my research, graphic downloads took so long that I left in search of other sites that might more efficiently satisfy my research purposes. While the speed at which a Web page loads will vary from one computer to the next, according to Yale's *Web Style Guide,* "research has shown that for most computing tasks the threshold of frustration is around 10 seconds" (Lynch and Horton). Researchers, like myself, who access the Internet from home at less-than-ethernet speeds appreciate quick downloading of information more than fancy graphics. Therefore, the speed at which the Canadian Lung Association's home page appeared in my browser contributed largely to my decision to explore the Web site further.

The Canadian Lung Association's *Asthma* Web site seems well designed, incorporating a variety of links and other features that make it easy to navigate the site and find information quickly. As shown in Figure 1, for example, the *Asthma* home page includes several different links to additional pages of information at the site. At the top of the home page are three clickable buttons: "Home," for accessing the Canadian Lung Association's home

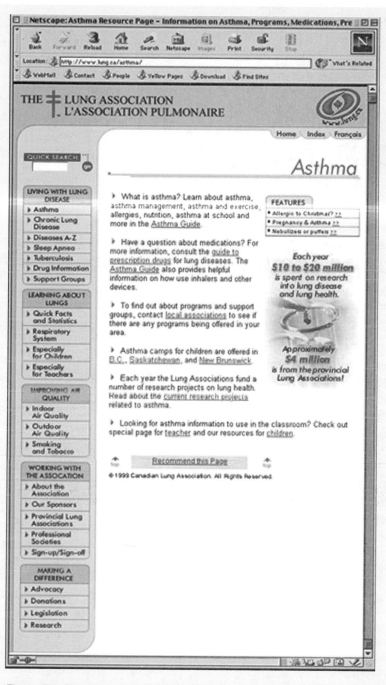

Fig. 1. The Canadian Lung Association's Asthma home page.

page; "Index," for accessing a list of the site's contents; and "Français," for giving users a choice between the French and English language versions of the Web site. On the left side of the screen are a "Quick Search" option and a lengthy menu of topics. The "Quick Search" option gives users an opportunity to search for information by keywords, while the menu organizes information under various topic headings with hyperlinks to available information at the site. In the center of the *Asthma* home page are two additional sets of hyperlinks for accessing specific information about asthma: first, keywords, underlined and printed in red, within the easy-to-read bulleted text (such as "<u>Asthma Guide</u>") and, second, underlined double arrows in a "Features" box (for example, "Pregnancy & Asthma <u>>></u>").

Other pages at the *Asthma* site also feature useful ways of accessing information. 4 The most important of these is a site map, which displays large buttons as hyperlinks to important topics on asthma. As shown in Figure 2, the *Asthma Resource Guide* maps out the site's contents. It can be accessed by clicking on the underlined keywords "<u>Asthma Guide</u>" on the *Asthma* home page (Figure 1). The site map reappears at the bottom of every page within the Canadian Lung Association's *Asthma* Web site. Look, for example, at Figure 3, the *Asthma Management* page accessed by clicking on the "Management" button in Figure 2. As you can see, the *Asthma Management* page includes the site map at the bottom of the screen as well as the search and menu options at the top and left side of the screen. It also introduces yet another way of maneuvering within the Web site: "Go back" and "Go to" clickable arrows.

By giving users a variety of options, the designers of this Web site have made it very 5 easy for users to access information. The site map, in particular, enables users to return to pages they visited earlier by clicking on the corresponding links, rather than having to retype the URL or rely on the "Back" button in their browsers to retrace their steps. I found only one problem in the site's system of hyperlinks: Two buttons, both labeled "Asthma," one in the site map and the other in the left-frame menu, lead to different pages. The site map "Asthma" button correctly links to the *Asthma* home page (Figure 1), whereas the menu "Asthma" button incorrectly links to a general information page on asthma adapted from a 1997 article by a Canadian doctor (see Figure 4). Apart from this one hyperlink problem, the Web site provides easy access to information about the Canadian Lung Association in general and asthma in particular.

Furthermore, the hyperlinks at the *Asthma* Web site offer quality information that 6 helped in my research. For example, the "Medications" link on the site map leads to information on various drug treatments and their possible side effects. I was grateful to learn that Jeremy's doctor is not treating him with drugs that produce serious side effects. I also learned about the different causes of asthma and clarified a confusion I had gotten from visiting a different Web site, *Adult/Pediatric Allergy Asthma Center,* <http://www.allergies-asthma.com>, which had led me to misunderstand the importance of symptoms that asthma and allergies have in common (Dantzler). However, according to Jeremy's doctor, my son's asthmatic attacks are responses to viral infections, not allergic reactions to things like dust and pollen. The Canadian Lung Association's site confirmed what the doctor had told me. Now I know which symptoms indicate that Jeremy is having an asthmatic attack and which indicate he is having a harmless allergic reaction to high pollen counts.

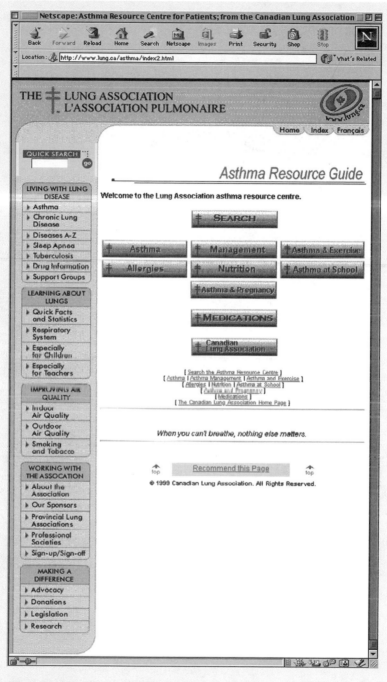

Fig. 2. The Canadian Lung Association's Asthma Resource Guide *page.*

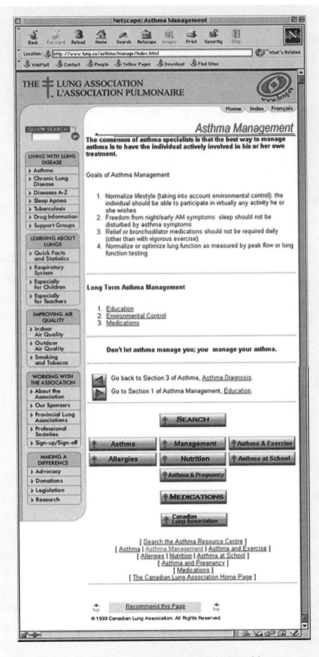

Fig. 3. The Canadian Lung Association's Asthma Management page, accessed via the "Management" button shown in Fig. 2.

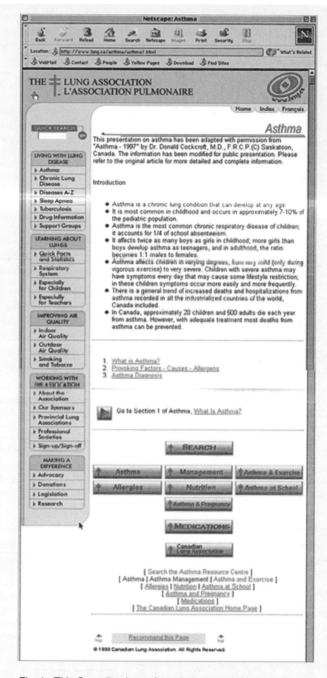

Fig. 4. This Canadian Lung Association general information page was accessed via the left-frame menu "Asthma" button shown in Fig. 1, indicating a hyperlink problem.

In addition to confirming information that Jeremy's doctor had already given me, the 7
Canadian *Asthma* site offers useful new information, including the suggestion that I collab-
orate with the doctor on a "Written 'Rescue' Action Plan." The plan gives instructions on
what to do at each stage of an asthmatic attack so as to avoid a "full-blown episode" (Canadian Lung Association). I also learned about the Peak Flow Meter, a device that can detect
each stage in an asthmatic attack and that can help implement the action plan appropriately. Because I felt this new information might benefit Jeremy, I downloaded the pages to
my hard drive and printed them out to bring to Jeremy's next doctor's appointment.

Not only is the Canadian Lung Association's *Asthma* Web site easy to access and 8
full of helpful information, but it is also reliable. For a Web site to be reliable, it must have
authoritative, up-to-date information and not profit from distributing that information.
Although it can be difficult for a layperson to judge the quality and currency of information, most Web sites indicate who has sponsored and authored the site, as well as when
it was last revised. The *Asthma* home page, for example, identifies itself as an official site
of the Canadian Lung Association, <http://www.lung.ca>, which links to the American
Lung Association, <http://www.lungusa.org> (and vice versa), completing a circle that
shows that each organization considers the other to be a trustworthy source of information. Although both the Canadian and American Lung Association Web sites solicit dona-
tions to help fund research, the information available at the sites is free and meant to
promote healthy lungs, not empty pocketbooks.

Because new research in medicine and health care constantly changes, it is impor- 9
tant to seek out information that is up-to-date. Of course, currency is supposed to be one
of the advantages of researching on the Web. Many Web designers indicate on a general
information page when the information at a Web site was created or last updated. A copyright notice at the bottom of the pages at the *Asthma* site indicates it was created in 1999
by the Canadian Lung Association. The general information page shown in Figure 4 has
the 1999 copyright but includes a headnote indicating that it is adapted from a 1997 article.
The headnote also identifies the author's name, academic credentials, and professional
affiliations.

The time I have spent at the Canadian Lung Association's *Asthma* Web site has 10
been worthwhile. I consider the information there useful to my research because it provides answers to my questions concerning accessibility, helpfulness, and reliability.
Despite the problem with the left-frame menu "Asthma" hyperlink, I find the site to be well
organized and efficient (I can move quickly among pages). I also find the material helpful
because it substantiates information I already knew about asthma and gives me new and
practical ways to monitor Jeremy's health. Finally, the fact that the *Asthma* site is sponsored by the Canadian Lung Association convinces me that it is a reliable source of up-
to-date information on successful treatments for asthma.

Works Cited

American Lung Association. 1998. 8 Nov. 1999 <http://www.lungusa.org>.
Canadian Lung Association. *Asthma*. 1999. 18 Nov. 1999 <http://www.lung.ca/asthma>.

Dantzler, Brian S. *Adult/Pediatric Allergy Asthma Center.* 5 July 1999 <http://www.allergies-asthma.com>.

Lynch, Patrick J., and Sarah Horton. *Web Style Guide.* 1997. Yale University. 5 July 1999 <http://info.med.yale.edu/caim/manual/interface/basic_interface2.html>.

Connecting to Culture and Experience: Responsibility

Access to medical information on the Web has increased at the same time that confidence in the quality of health care in the United States has declined. Like Potter, many people want to verify that their doctor is up-to-date and offering all of the available treatment options, not just those that the insurance company or HMO (health maintenance organization) wants to pay for. In the past, patients seemed to rely more on doctors not only for information, but for decision making as well. When doctors made diagnoses or prescribed particular treatments, patients usually would simply accept their doctors' decisions. Only in special cases would patients ask for a consultation with another doctor and seldom would patients try to do research themselves to learn about other possible diagnoses or treatment options. Now, however, more and more people are trying to inform themselves and take an active role in their own and their family's health care. Instead of granting all the authority to their doctors, they are taking on more responsibility for their own health care decisions.

With two or three other students, discuss how this change was brought about or accelerated by the widespread accessibility of medical information on the Web. Take turns telling about your own experience. Have you, your family, or your friends attempted to research a medical condition or treatment option? Do you normally rely on your doctor's expertise and authority, or do you try to take some responsibility for health care decisions?

In what other areas, besides health care, are individuals without special training informing themselves and trying to share responsibility with (or perhaps wrest authority from) the experts? Home schooling? Stock trading? Computer programming?

Analyzing Writing Strategies

1. Potter supports her argument with examples: figures displaying screen shots of Web pages she refers to in her essay. To see how they contribute to her argument, skim paragraphs 3–5, where the figures are referred to and discussed. Then choose *one* reference to examine closely. Look both at the sentences explaining what the figure is supposed to illustrate and at the figure itself. Consider whether the figure is really needed and whether the explanation is sufficient.

   Finally, notice that in paragraphs 6–8, Potter refers to particular Web sites but does not illustrate them with figures. In some cases, readers could look at a figure referred to earlier to see what she is referring to. But in a couple of cases,

Potter would have to add new figures. If you were the author of this essay, how do you think you would decide which figures to include and which to leave out?

2. Reread paragraph 1 and underline Potter's thesis statement, the place where she asserts her overall judgment of the Canadian Lung Association's *Asthma* Web site. Then skim the essay, marking other places where she restates her judgment. Determine whether her thesis statement meets the three standards of a good thesis: Is it clear, arguable, and appropriately qualified? If you think it could be improved, indicate how you would revise it. (For more on asserting a thesis, see Chapter 11, 327–30.)

Commentary: Reasons

Potter gives three reasons in support of her judgment of the Canadian Lung Association's *Asthma* Web site: It is a useful site because the information it contains is accessible, helpful, and reliable. Although these standards seem to be commonsensical, Potter assumes her readers need explanations in order to understand what she means by the key terms *accessible, helpful,* and *reliable* as well as why she thinks these reasons are appropriate for her evaluation. For example, in paragraph 2, she explains what she means by *accessible:* "speedy access to information" and "quick downloading" of pages. To support her reason, Potter relates her own experience with slow-loading pages, cites an expert, and describes in paragraphs 3–5 the features that make the *Asthma* Web site easy to navigate. Readers with frustrating experiences like hers will readily agree that accessibility is a plausible reason for judging a Web site being used for research. Similarly, to explain what she considers *helpful* information, Potter identifies and then discusses several categories of "quality information that helped in my research": Information that confirms (or presumably does not contradict) what her son's doctor has told her, information that clarifies confusion, and information that offers new and practical suggestions for monitoring an asthmatic attack (paragraphs 6 and 7).

Because Potter wants her readers to understand her reasons, she tries to make her writing direct and clear. She forecasts her reasons in a series of questions at the end of the opening paragraph, and then takes up each reason in that order in her essay, as this scratch outline shows:

Paragraph 1 introduces the subject, states the thesis, and forecasts three reasons.

Paragraphs 2–5 develop and support the first reason ("accessible").

Paragraphs 6–7 develop and support the second reason ("helpful").

Paragraphs 8–9 develop and support the third reason ("reliable").

Paragraph 10 concludes by summarizing the main points.

Potter also tends to begin her paragraphs with a topic sentence announcing what she will discuss next; for example, "Furthermore, the hyperlinks at the *Asthma* Web site offer quality information that helped in my research" (paragraph 6). In some cases, the topic sentence serves as well to remind readers of the topic they just read about in the preceding paragraph, as in these examples: "In addition to confirming information that Jeremy's doctor had already given me, the Canadian *Asthma* site offers useful new information" (7), and "Not only is the Canadian Lung Association's *Asthma* Web site easy to access and full of helpful information, but it is also reliable" (8). The topic sentences help keep readers oriented; without these cues, readers might get lost in the details and examples Potter gives to support her reasons. (For more on forecasting and topic sentences, see Chapter 8, pp. 275–79.)

Considering Topics for Your Own Essay

Potter uses the Web for medical and academic research, but it has many other uses as well. Some people use the Web to keep up with information through Usenet groups or other specialized sites. Others like to shop online for certain kinds of products— computer equipment, music, books, and stocks—or play online games with other users. List some of the Web sites you use regularly; then note which *one* site you might want to evaluate. Look at the site itself and consider what makes a visit to it worthwhile. If you were to write an essay evaluating what you like and do not like about this Web site, which features of the site would you focus on in your evaluation?

Christine Romano wrote the following essay when she was a first-year college student. In it she evaluates an argument essay written by another student, Jessica Statsky's "Children Need to Play, Not Compete," which appears in Chapter 5 of this book (pp. 155–59). Romano focuses not on the writing strategies or basic features of this essay arguing a position but rather on its logic—on whether the argument is likely to convince its intended readers. She evaluates the logic of the argument according to the standards presented in Chapter 10. You might want to review these standards on pp. 321–23 before you read Romano's evaluation. Also, if you have not already read Statsky's essay, you might want to do so now, thinking about what seems most and least convincing to you about her argument that competitive sports can be harmful to young children.

"Children Need to Play, Not Compete," by Jessica Statsky: An Evaluation

Christine Romano

Parents of young children have a lot to worry about and to hope for. In "Children Need to Play, Not Compete," Jessica Statsky appeals to their worries and hopes in order to convince them that organized competitive sports may harm their children physically and psychologically. Statsky states her thesis clearly and fully forecasts the reasons she will offer to justify her position: Besides causing physical and psychological harm, competitive sports discourage young people from becoming players and fans when they are older and inevitably put parents' needs and fantasies ahead of children's welfare. Statsky also carefully defines her key terms. By *sports*, for example, she means to include both contact and noncontact sports that emphasize competition. The sports may be organized locally at schools or summer sports camps or nationally, as in the examples of Peewee Football and Little League Baseball. She is concerned only with children six to twelve years of age.

In this essay, I will evaluate the logic of Statsky's argument, considering whether the support for her thesis is appropriate, believable, consistent, and complete. While her logic *is* appropriate, believable, and consistent, her argument also has weaknesses. I will focus on two: Her argument seems incomplete because she neglects to anticipate parents' predictable questions and objections, and because she fails to support certain parts of it fully.

Statsky provides appropriate support for her thesis. Throughout her essay, she relies for support on different kinds of information (she cites eleven separate sources, including books, newspapers, and Web sites). Her quotations, examples, and statistics all support the reasons she believes competitive sports are bad for children. For example, in paragraph 3, Statsky offers the reason that "overly competitive sports" may damage children's growing bodies and that contact sports, in particular, may be especially hazardous. She supports this reason by paraphrasing Koppett that muscle strain or even lifelong injury may result when a twelve-year-old throws curve balls. She then quotes Tutko on the dangers of tackle football. The opinions of both experts are obviously appropriate. They are relevant to her reason, and we can easily imagine that they would worry many parents.

Not only is Statsky's support appropriate, but it is also believable. Statsky quotes or summarizes authorities to support her argument in paragraphs 3–6, 8, 9, and 11. The question is whether readers would find these authorities credible. Since Statsky relies almost entirely on authorities to support her argument, readers must believe these authorities for her argument to succeed. I have not read Statsky's sources, but I think there are good reasons to consider them authoritative. First of all, the newspaper authors she quotes write for two of America's most respected newspapers, the *New York Times* and the *Los Angeles Times.* These newspapers are read across the country by political leaders and financial experts and by people interested in the arts and popular culture. Both have sports reporters who not only report on sports events but also take a critical look at sports issues. In addition, both newspapers have reporters who specialize in children's health and education. Second, Statsky gives background information about the authorities she quotes, which is intended to increase the person's believability in the eyes of parents of young children. In paragraph 3, she tells readers that Thomas Tutko is "a psychology professor at San Jose State University and co-author of the book *Winning Is Everything and Other American Myths.*" In paragraph 5, she announces that Martin Rablovsky is "a former sports editor for the *New York Times,*" and she notes that he has watched children play organized sports for many years. Third, she quotes from two Web sites—the official *Little League Online* site and an AOL message board. Parents are likely to accept the authority of the *Little League Online* site and be interested in what other parents and coaches (most of whom are also parents) have to say.

In addition to quoting authorities, Statsky relies on examples and anecdotes to support the reasons for her position. If examples and anecdotes are to be believable, they must seem representative to readers, not bizarre or highly unusual or completely unpre-

2

3

4

5

dictable. Readers can imagine a similar event happening elsewhere. For anecdotes to be believable, they should, in addition, be specific and true to life. All of Statsky's examples and anecdotes fulfill these requirements, and her readers would find them believable. For example, early in her argument, in paragraph 4, Statsky reasons that fear of being hurt greatly reduces children's enjoyment of contact sports. The anecdote comes from Tosches's investigative report on Peewee Football, as does the quotation by the mother of an eight-year-old player who says that the children become frightened and pretend to be injured in order to stay out of the game. In the anecdote, a seven-year-old makes himself vomit to avoid playing. Because these examples echo the familiar "I feel bad" or "I'm sick" excuse children give when they do not want to go somewhere (especially school) or do something, most parents would find them believable. They could easily imagine their own children pretending to be hurt or ill if they were fearful or depressed. The anecdote is also specific. Tosches reports what the boy said and did and what the coach said and did.

Other examples provide support for all the major reasons Statsky gives for her position:

- That competitive sports pose psychological dangers—children becoming serious and unplayful when the game starts (paragraph 5)
- That adults' desire to win puts children at risk—parents fighting each other at a Peewee Football game and a coach setting fire to an opposing team's jersey (8)
- That organized sports should emphasize cooperation and individual performance instead of winning—a coach banning scoring but finding that parents would not support him and a New York City basketball league in which all children play an equal amount of time and scoring is easier (11)

All of these examples are appropriate to the reasons they support. They are also believable. Together, they help Statsky achieve her purpose of convincing parents that organized, competitive sports may be bad for their children and that there are alternatives.

If readers are to find an argument logical and convincing, it must be consistent and complete. While there are no inconsistencies or contradictions in Statsky's argument, it is seriously incomplete because it neglects to support fully one of its reasons, it fails to anticipate many predictable questions parents would have, and it pays too little attention to noncontact competitive team sports. The most obvious example of thin support comes in paragraph 11, where Statsky asserts that many parents are ready for children's team sports that emphasize cooperation and individual performance. Yet the example of a Little League official who failed to win parents' approval to ban scores raises serious questions about just how many parents are ready to embrace noncompetitive sports teams. The other support, a brief description of City Sports for Kids in New York City, is very convincing but will only be logically compelling to those parents who are already inclined to agree with Statsky's position. Parents inclined to disagree with Statsky would need additional evidence. Most parents know that big cities receive special federal funding for evening, weekend, and summer recreation. Brief descriptions of six or eight noncompetitive teams in a variety of sports in cities, rural areas, suburban neighborhoods—some funded publicly, some funded privately—would be more likely to convince skeptics. Statsky here neglects to accept the burden of proof, a logical fallacy.

Statsky's argument is also incomplete in that it fails to anticipate certain objections and questions that some parents, especially those she most wants to convince, are almost sure to raise. In the first sentences of paragraphs 6, 9, and 10, Statsky does show that she is thinking about her readers' questions. She does not go nearly far enough, however, to have a chance of influencing two types of readers: those who themselves are or were fans of and participants in competitive sports and those who want their six- to twelve-year-old children involved in mainstream sports programs despite the risks, especially the national programs that have a certain prestige. Such parents might feel that competitive team sports for young children create a sense of community with a shared purpose, build character through self-sacrifice and commitment to the group, teach children to face their fears early and learn how to deal with them through the support of coaches and team members, and introduce children to the principles of social cooperation and collaboration. Some parents are likely to believe and to know from personal experience that coaches who burn opposing teams' jerseys on the pitching mound before the game starts are the exception, not the rule. Some young children idolize teachers and coaches, and team practice and games are the brightest moments in their lives. Statsky seems not to have considered these reasonable possibilities, and as a result her argument lacks a compelling logic it might have had. By acknowledging that she was aware of many of these objections—and perhaps even accommodating more of them in her own argument, as she does in paragraph 10, while refuting other objections—she would have strengthened her argument.

Finally, Statsky's argument is incomplete because she overlooks examples of non-contact team sports. Track, swimming, and tennis are good examples that some readers would certainly think of. Some elementary schools compete in track meets. Public and private clubs and recreational programs organize competitive swimming and tennis competitions. In these sports, individual performance is the focus. No one gets trampled. Children exert themselves only as much as they are able to. Yet individual performances are scored, and a team score is derived. Because Statsky fails to mention any of these obvious possibilities, her argument is weakened.

The logic of Statsky's argument, then, has both strengths and weaknesses. The support she offers is appropriate, believable, and consistent. The major weakness is incompleteness—she fails to anticipate more fully the likely objections of a wide range of readers. Her logic would prevent parents who enjoy and advocate competitive sports from taking her argument seriously. Such parents and their children have probably had positive experiences with team sports, and these experiences would lead them to believe that the gains are worth whatever risks may be involved. Many probably think that the risks Statsky points out can be avoided by careful monitoring. For those parents inclined to agree with her, Statsky's logic is likely to seem sound and complete. An argument that successfully confirms readers' beliefs is certainly valid, and Statsky succeeds admirably at this kind of argument. Because she does not offer compelling counterarguments to the legitimate objections of those inclined not to agree with her, however, her success is limited.

Connecting to Culture and Experience: Team Sports and Community

Romano reasons in paragraph 8 that some parents "feel that competitive team sports for young children create a sense of community with a shared purpose, build character through self-sacrifice and commitment to the group, teach children to face their fears early and learn how to deal with them through the support of coaches and team members, and introduce children to the principles of social cooperation and collaboration."

With other students, discuss this view of the role of sports in developing a child's sense of community. Begin by telling one another about your own, your siblings', or your children's experiences with team sports between the ages of six and twelve. Explain how participating in sports at this young age did or did not help create a sense of community. If you think team sports failed to create community or had some other effect, explain the effect it did have. Then, discuss how each of you is defining the term *community*, and consider whether you are using it in the same way that Romano uses it in her essay.

Analyzing Writing Strategies

1. Reread Romano's essay to identify the reasons she gives for her judgment of Statsky's essay. As you read, put brackets around the sentences where she states each reason. Then make a paragraph-by-paragraph scratch outline like the one shown on p. 244 for Kristine Potter's essay. (For more on scratch outlines, see Chapter 10, pp. 311–12.)

   Finally, reflect on what you can learn from the way Romano presents her reasons. Are they clear and easy to follow? Do you think her intended readers—her instructor and parents of young children (the same audience Statsky is trying to convince)—are likely to consider her reasons plausible? In other words, are these reasons appropriate for evaluating an essay that argues a position?

2. Romano applies to Statsky's essay the ABC test for evaluating the logic of an argument, which is presented in Chapter 10 of this book on pp. 321–23. Choose *one* quality of a good argument—appropriateness, believability, or consistency and completeness—and use it to evaluate Romano's argument. Support your evaluation with one or two examples from her essay.

Commentary: Support and Counterargument

Because she is evaluating a written text, Romano uses textual evidence to support her argument. To provide textual evidence, writers can quote, paraphrase, or summarize passages from the text. Romano quotes selectively, usually brief phrases. In paragraph 4, for example, Romano supports her argument about the believability of Statsky's sources with a quote showing how Statsky presents authorities:

> In paragraph 3, she tells readers that Thomas Tutko is "a psychology professor at San Jose State University and coauthor of the book *Winning Is Everything and Other*

American Myths." In paragraph 5, she announces that Martin Rablovsky is "a former sports editor for the *New York Times.*"

In addition to quoting, Romano paraphrases and summarizes passages from Statsky's essay. Summarizing, a distillation of the main ideas, tends to be briefer than paraphrasing. Paraphrasing, in contrast, tries to capture the rich detail of the original. A good example of paraphrasing appears in the opening paragraph, where Romano represents Statsky's argument. Compare Romano's paraphrase to the original passage from Statsky's essay:

Statsky's Original Version

Highly organized competitive sports such as Peewee Football and Little League Base-ball are too often played to adult standards, which are developmentally inappropriate for children and can be both physically and psychologically harmful. Furthermore, because they eliminate many children from organized sports before they are ready to compete, they are actually counterproductive for developing either future players or fans. (paragraph 2)

Romano's Paraphrase

Besides causing physical and psychological harm, competitive sports discourage young people from becoming players and fans when they are older and inevitably put parents' needs and fantasies ahead of children's welfare. (paragraph 1)

Notice that in the paraphrase, Romano mostly uses her own words, with a few significant exceptions for key terms like *physical* and *psychological, players* and *fans.*

Romano uses summarizing primarily to describe parts of Statsky's argument, as in the following excerpt:

Romano's Summary

...in paragraph 3, Statsky offers the reason that "overly competitive sports" may damage children's growing bodies and that contact sports, in particular, may be especially hazardous. She supports this reason by paraphrasing Koppett that muscle strain or even lifelong injury may result when a twelve-year-old throws curve balls. She then quotes Tutko on the dangers of tackle football. (paragraph 3)

If you compare this summary with Romano's paraphrase, you will notice another important distinction between summarizing and paraphrasing. When summarizing, writers usually describe what the author is doing in the passage. In the summarized passage, for instance, Romano uses Statsky's name and the pronoun *she* to relate the different strategic moves Statsky makes in the paragraph being summarized. When paraphrasing, however, writers typically leave out references to the author and his or her moves. Like Romano does in the preceding sample paraphrase, writers simply restate what the author has written.

Especially when you write an evaluation of a written document, a Web site (like Potter does), or a film (like Ansen does), these are the strategies you need to employ for citing textual evidence. (For additional examples of paraphrasing and summarizing, see Chapter 10, pp. 312–15. For guidance on integrating quotations into your writing, see Chapter 14, pp. 390–92.)

Finally, Romano's essay demonstrates the way writers of evaluation typically counterargue: by pointing out weaknesses as well as strengths in their subject. In paragraph 8, for example, Romano observes that Statsky "fails to anticipate certain objections and questions" her readers "are almost sure to raise." Romano herself has analyzed Statsky's readers and tried to anticipate their likely questions and objections as well as the judgments they may be inclined to take on the subject. Romano argues that Statsky's argument is "weakened" by her failure to anticipate and respond to her readers' likely criticism. By acknowledging the shortcomings in Statsky's essay, Romano has anticipated possible criticisms of her own highly favorable evaluation. As you write your own evaluation, think carefully about other points of view before you praise your subject as perfect or damn it as a complete failure.

Considering Topics for Your Own Essay

List several written texts you would consider evaluating. For example, you might include in your list an essay from one of the chapters in this book. If you choose an argument from Chapters 5–7, you could evaluate its logic, its use of emotional appeals, or its credibility. You might prefer to evaluate a children's book you read when you were younger or one you now read to your own children, a magazine for people interested in a particular topic like computers or cars, a scholarly article you read for a research paper, or a short story you like. You need not limit yourself to texts written on paper; also consider texts available online such as the Internet webzine *Slate*. Choose one possibility from your list, and come up with two or three reasons why it is a good or bad text.

■ PURPOSE AND AUDIENCE

When you evaluate something, you seek to influence readers' judgments and possibly their actions. Your primary aim is to convince readers that your judgment is well informed and reasonable and, therefore, that they can feel confident in making decisions based on it. Good readers do not simply accept reviewers' judgments, however, especially on important subjects. More likely they read reviews to learn more about a subject so that they can make an informed decision themselves. Consequently, most readers care less about the forcefulness with which you assert your judgment than about the reasons and support you give for it.

Effective writers develop an argumentative strategy designed for their particular readers. Your argumentative strategy determines every writing decision you make, from what you reveal about the subject to the way you construct your argument—which reasons you use, how you explain your reasoning, how much and what kind of support you give.

You may want to acknowledge directly your readers' knowledge of the subject, perhaps revealing that you understand how they might judge it differently. You might even let readers know that you have anticipated their objections to your argument. In responding to objections, reservations, or different judgments, you could agree to disagree on certain points but try to convince readers that on other points you do share the same or at least similar standards.

BASIC FEATURES: EVALUATIONS

A Well-Presented Subject

The subject must be clearly identified if readers are to know what is being evaluated. Most writers name it explicitly. When the subject is a film, essay, or Web site, naming is easy. When it is something more general, naming may be difficult.

Evaluations should provide only enough information to give readers a context for the judgment. However, certain kinds of evaluations—such as book, television, and movie reviews—usually require more information than other kinds of evaluations because reviewers have to assume that readers will be unfamiliar with the subject and are reading, in part, to learn more about it. Ansen tells readers who the actors and director of *The Phantom Menace* are, where and when the film's story takes place, and generally what happens in it. For a recently released film, the writer must decide how much of the plot to reveal—trying not to spoil the suspense while explaining how well or how poorly the suspense is managed. For a classic film, reviewers may be released from this constraint.

A Clear, Authoritative Judgment

Evaluation essays are built around a judgment—an assertion that the subject is good or bad or that it is better or worse than something else of the same kind. This judgment is the thesis of the essay. The thesis statement may appear in the first sentence or elsewhere in the essay. Potter asserts her thesis at the end of the first paragraph, whereas Ansen and Romano put theirs in the second paragraph. Writers also may restate the thesis at the end of the essay, summarizing their main points. Wherever the thesis appears, it must satisfy three requirements: that it be arguable, clear and unambiguous, and appropriately qualified.

Although readers expect a definitive judgment, they also appreciate a balanced one. All of the writers in this chapter acknowledge both good and bad qualities of the subject they are evaluating. Romano praises the strengths and criticizes the weaknesses of Statsky's logic. Ansen criticizes the storytelling but praises the design of *The Phantom Menace*. Potter is enthusiastic about the Canadian Lung Association's *Asthma* Web site, but points out a problem with a hyperlink.

Appropriate Reasons and Convincing Support

Writers assert the reasons for their judgment, often explain their reasons in some detail, and provide support for their reasons. For example, Potter states that accessibility is one of the reasons for her judgment that the Canadian Lung Association's *Asthma* Web site is useful. She then goes on to explain specifically what she means by *accessible,* and she includes figures displaying screen shots of Web pages to support her explanations.

For an argument to be convincing, readers have to accept the reasons as appropriate for evaluating the subject. Romano applies at here a uses the ABC test suggested in this book for evaluating the logic of Statsky's argument: appropriateness, believability, consistency and completeness. Potter chooses reasons for evaluating the usefulness of a Web site on asthma because they seem commonsensical to her and, she hopes, to most of her readers.

Evaluators not only give reasons but must also support their reasons. They may use various kinds of support. Romano and Ansen, for example, rely primarily on textual evidence to support their reasons, presenting it in quotations, paraphrases, and summaries. In evaluating a Web site, Potter supports her argument with examples (figures showing screen shots from the Web site).

Many writers also use comparisons to support an evaluative argument. For example, Ansen's references to other science-fiction films (such as *Blade Runner* and *The Matrix*) are designed to convince readers that he is an expert who knows what kinds of standards knowledgeable people normally apply when evaluating this kind of film. Potter briefly compares the Canadian Lung Association's *Asthma* Web site to another site on asthma.

Effective Counterargument

Writers often try to anticipate readers' possible alternative judgments as well as likely questions and objections to the argument. Writers may counterargue by acknowledging, conceding, or trying to refute judgments and objections with which they disagree. Ansen, for example, begins his essay by anticipating readers' alternative judgment of *The Phantom Menace.* He then tries to refute this judgment by counterarguing that it is based more on the film's skillful advertising together with viewers' enthusiasm for the earlier *Star Wars* films than on a direct evaluation of the film itself. Romano, in her evaluation of Statsky's essay, accommodates various criticisms she thinks Statsky's readers would have. Thus, her evaluation turns out to be mixed—praising the strengths, but also acknowledging the weaknesses of the argument she is evaluating. Evaluation essays often counterargue in just this way.

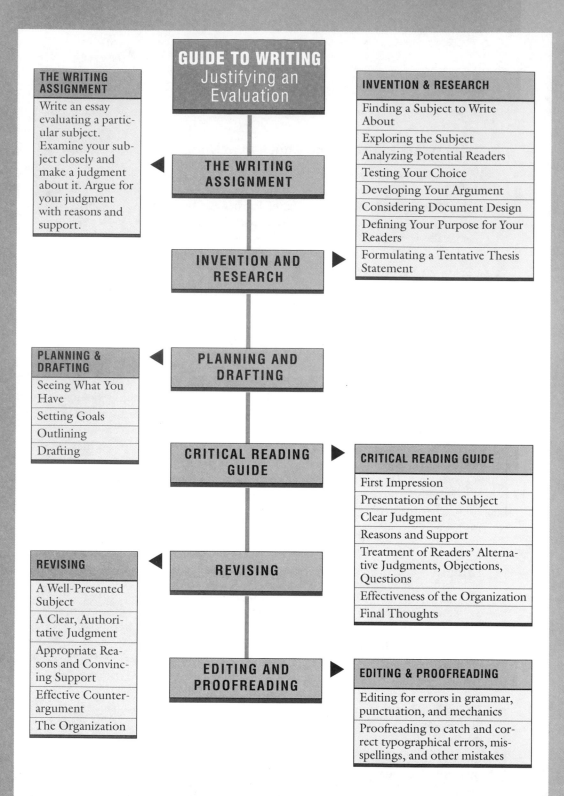

GUIDE TO WRITING
Justifying an Evaluation

THE WRITING ASSIGNMENT

Write an essay evaluating a particular subject. Examine your subject closely and make a judgment about it. Argue for your judgment with reasons and support.

THE WRITING ASSIGNMENT

INVENTION AND RESEARCH

INVENTION & RESEARCH

Finding a Subject to Write About

Exploring the Subject

Analyzing Potential Readers

Testing Your Choice

Developing Your Argument

Considering Document Design

Defining Your Purpose for Your Readers

Formulating a Tentative Thesis Statement

PLANNING & DRAFTING

Seeing What You Have

Setting Goals

Outlining

Drafting

PLANNING AND DRAFTING

CRITICAL READING GUIDE

CRITICAL READING GUIDE

First Impression

Presentation of the Subject

Clear Judgment

Reasons and Support

Treatment of Readers' Alternative Judgments, Objections, Questions

Effectiveness of the Organization

Final Thoughts

REVISING

A Well-Presented Subject

A Clear, Authoritative Judgment

Appropriate Reasons and Convincing Support

Effective Counterargument

The Organization

REVISING

EDITING AND PROOFREADING

EDITING & PROOFREADING

Editing for errors in grammar, punctuation, and mechanics

Proofreading to catch and correct typographical errors, misspellings, and other mistakes

GUIDE TO WRITING

◾ THE WRITING ASSIGNMENT

Write an essay evaluating a particular subject. Examine your subject closely and make a judgment about it. Argue for your judgment with reasons and support.

◾ INVENTION AND RESEARCH

The following activities will help you choose and explore a subject, consider your judgment, and develop your argument. These activities are easy to complete. Doing them over several days will give your ideas time to ripen and grow. Keep a written record of your invention and research to use later when you draft and revise.

Finding a Subject to Write About

You may already have a subject in mind and some ideas on how you will evaluate it. Even so, it is wise to take a few minutes to consider some other possible subjects. That way you can feel confident not only about having made the best possible choice but also about having one or two alternative subjects in case your first choice does not work. The following activities will help you make a good choice.

Listing Subjects.   *Make a list of subjects you might be interested in evaluating.* Make your list as complete as you can, including, for example, the subjects suggested by the Considering Topics for Your Own Essay activity following each reading in this chapter. The following categories may give you some ideas.

- *Culture:* Television program, magazine or newspaper, computer game, band, songwriter, recording, film, actor, performance, dance club, coffeehouse, artist, museum exhibit, individual work of art
- *Written work:* Poem, short story, novel, magazine article, newspaper column, letter to the editor, textbook, autobiography, essay from this book
- *Education:* School, program, teacher, major department, library, academic or psychological counseling service, writing center, campus publication, sports team
- *Government:* Government department or official, proposed or existing law, agency or program, candidate for public office
- *Leisure:* Amusement park, museum, restaurant, resort, sports team, sports equipment, national or state park

Listing Subjects Related to Identity and Community.   The following are ideas for an evaluative essay on issues of identity and community.

- Evaluate your performance as a student, athlete, musician, parent, sibling, or spouse.
- Evaluate how well one of the following meets the needs of residents of your town or city: a community center, public library, health clinic, college, athletic team, festival, neighborhood watch or block parent program, meals-on-wheels program, theater or symphony, school or school program.
- Evaluate how well one of the following serves the members of your religious community: a religious school, youth or senior group, religious leader, particular sermon, bingo, revival meeting, choir, building and grounds.
- Evaluate how well one of the following aspects of local government serves the needs of the community: a mayor, city council, police, courts, department of motor vehicles, social services, park system, zoning commission.

Listing Subjects Related to Work and Career.   Following are some suggestions for an evaluative essay on issues involving work and career.

- Evaluate a job you have had or currently have, evaluate yourself as a worker, or evaluate someone else you have observed closely, such as a co-worker or supervisor.
- Evaluate a local job training program, either one in which you have participated or one where you can observe and interview other students.
- Evaluate how well suited you may be for some career in which you are interested.
- Evaluate the work done by city or campus employees—the police, trash collectors, road repair workers, emergency service providers, class schedulers, advisers, cafeteria workers, dorm counselors.

Choosing a Subject.   *Review your list and choose the one subject that seems most promising.* Your subject should be one that you can evaluate with some authority, either one that you already know quite well or one that you could study. Although your judgment of this subject need not be fully formed at this point, you should have some sense of how you will evaluate it.

Exploring the Subject

To explore the subject, you need to reflect on what you know about it, determine whether you need to do research, and consider how you will evaluate the subject.

Reflecting on the Subject.   *To begin reflecting on the subject and how you will evaluate it, write for a few minutes to collect your thoughts.* Focus your thinking by considering questions like these:

- What do I like and/or dislike about the subject I am evaluating?
- What category of subject is this? What do I usually look for in evaluating a subject of this kind? What do other people look for? In other words, what standards of judgment are considered appropriate for evaluating this kind of subject?

- What details do I know about the subject that I could use in my essay? What details do I need to find out about the subject? (For example, if I were to evaluate the storytelling of a film, what details would I need to point out about the film?)

Planning Research. *If you do not know very much about the subject or the standards people typically use when evaluating this kind of subject, make some notes about how you will go about doing research.* If you are writing about a film, for example, you may need to rent the film and view it, taking notes about the storytelling, special effects, acting, direction, or any other aspect of the film you think is important. If you do not know the standards usually used to evaluate this kind of film, you may want to read some reviews.

If you need to do more research than time permits or you cannot review your subject to find the details needed to support an evaluation of it, then you may need to consider choosing a different, more accessible subject.

Considering Your Judgment. *Reread what you have written; then write a few sentences stating your best current judgment of the subject.* Your judgment may only be tentative at this stage, or you may feel quite confident in it. Or your judgment may be mixed: You may have a high regard for certain aspects of the subject and, at the same time, a rather low assessment of other aspects. As you consider your judgment, keep in mind that readers of evaluative essays not only expect writers to balance their evaluation of a subject by pointing out things they like as well as things they dislike; readers also expect writers to state a definitive judgment about the subject, not a vague, wishy-washy, or undecided judgment.

Analyzing Potential Readers

Write several sentences analyzing your readers, with the following questions in mind:

- What are my readers likely to know about my subject? Will I be introducing the subject to them (as in a film or book review), or will they already be familiar with it, and if so, how expert on the subject are they likely to be?

- How are my readers likely to judge my subject? What about it will they like, and what will they dislike?

- What reasons might they give for their judgment?

- On what standards is their judgment likely to be based? Do I share these standards, or at least recognize their appropriateness?

Testing Your Choice

Pause now to decide whether you have chosen a subject about which you can make a convincing evaluative argument. Reread your invention notes to see whether you know enough about your subject or can get the information you need by researching the subject. Also consider whether you feel confident in your judgment.

As you develop your argument, you should become even more confident. If, however, you begin to doubt your choice, consider doing further research or beginning again with a different subject selected from your list of possibilities. Before changing your subject, however, discuss your ideas with another student or your instructor to see whether they make sense to someone else.

Testing Your Choice: A Collaborative Activity

At this point in your invention work, you will find it helpful to get together with two or three other students to discuss your subjects and test out ways of evaluating them.

Presenters: Take turns briefly describing your subject without revealing your judgment. Take notes on your group's response.

Evaluators: Take turns explaining to the presenters how you would evaluate a subject of this kind. For example, would you judge a science-fiction film by the story, acting, ideas, special effects, or some other aspect of the film? Would you judge a lecture course by how interesting or entertaining the lectures are, how hard the tests are, how well the lectures are organized, or on some other basis? In other words, tell the presenter what standards you would apply to his or her particular subject.

Developing Your Argument

Listing Reasons.   *Write down every reason you can think of to convince readers of your judgment.* Try stating your reasons as part of a tentative thesis statement with *because* or *that* clauses, like this: "My judgment is X because..." or "A reason I like (or dislike) X is that...." Then look over your list to consider which reasons you regard as most important and which would be most convincing to your readers, given the standards on which they ordinarily base their evaluations of subjects of this kind. *Put an asterisk by the reasons likely to be convincing for your readers.*

Finding Support.   *Make notes about how to support your most promising reasons.* To evaluate a text such as an essay, Web site, recording, or film, you will need to find textual evidence—quotation, summary, or paraphrase—from your own close analysis of the subject. For other kinds of subjects, you may need to do research in the library or on the Internet for supporting authorities, statistics, or anecdotes.

Drawing Comparisons.   *Write for several minutes, trying to support one or more of your reasons with an argument based on comparisons and contrasts to related subjects.* Remember that comparisons and contrasts are often used to establish a writer's credibility by demonstrating not only that the writer is knowledgeable but also that the argument is based on standards that readers would agree are appropriate for judging that kind of subject.

Anticipating Readers' Alternative Judgments and Objections.   *Assuming your readers might evaluate the subject differently or that they might have objections or questions about your argument, identify one likely objection or question and write for a few minutes trying out a counterargument.* To help you anticipate readers' concerns, look back at the notes you took for Testing Your Choice: A Collaborative Activity to see what your fellow students said about your reasons. Remember that a counterargument could involve simply acknowledging disagreement, accommodating readers' views by conceding certain points, or trying to refute readers' arguments by challenging the standards on which they are based or their reasons and support.

Considering Document Design

Think about whether visual or audio elements — cartoons, photographs, tables, graphs, or snippets from films, television programs, or songs — would strengthen your argument. These are not at all a requirement of an effective evaluation essay, but they could be helpful. Consider also whether your readers might benefit by such design features as headings, bulleted or numbered lists, or other elements that would make your essay easier to follow. You could construct your own graphic elements, download materials from the Internet, videotape images and sounds from television or other sources, or scan into your document visuals from books and magazines. When you reproduce visuals, make sure to acknowledge their sources.

Defining Your Purpose for Your Readers

Write a few sentences, defining your purpose in writing this evaluation for your readers. Remember that you already have analyzed your potential readers and developed your argument with these readers in mind. Given these readers, try now to define your purpose by considering the following possibilities and any others that might apply to your writing situation:

- If my readers are likely to agree with my judgment, should I try to give them confidence in their own judgment? How can I help them refute others' judgments or suggest how they might respond to questions and objections?

- If my readers and I share certain standards for evaluating a subject of this kind, but we disagree on how to judge this particular subject, how can I build a convincing argument based on these shared standards or, at least, get readers to acknowledge the legitimacy of my judgment?

- If my readers use different standards of judgment, what should I try to do — urge them to think critically about their own judgment, to consider seriously other ways of judging the subject, or to see certain aspects of the subject they might have overlooked?

Formulating a Tentative Thesis Statement

Write several sentences that could serve as your tentative thesis statement. Think about how you should state your judgment—how emphatic you should make it, whether you should qualify it, and whether you should include in the thesis a forecast of your reasons and support. (For more on thesis and forecasting statements, see Chapter 8, pp. 273–75.)

Review the readings in this chapter to see how other writers construct thesis statements. For example, recall that Ansen boldly asserts a judgment he knows will not be expected by his readers. His thesis statement is simple and direct: "The movie is a disappointment" (paragraph 2).

Potter and Romano use the thesis statement to forecast their reasons as well as to express their judgment. Both these writers begin by indicating the standards they think are appropriate for evaluating their subjects. Their thesis statements show that they base their reasons on these standards. Potter, for example, writes: "My evaluation of the Canadian Lung Association's *Asthma* Web site, located at < http://www.lung.ca /asthma >, led me to the conclusion that this site successfully meets my criteria for accessible, helpful, and reliable information" (paragraph 1). Romano's thesis statement lets readers know in advance what she likes about the subject she is evaluating as well as what she does not like: "While [Statsky's] logic *is* appropriate, believable, and consistent, her argument also has weaknesses" (paragraph 2). In contrast to Ansen, who states his thesis rather forcefully, Romano makes her thesis statement seem thoughtful and balanced. There is no ambivalence or confusion, however, about Romano's judgment. She is clear and emphatic, not vague or wishy-washy.

As you draft your own tentative thesis statement, pay attention to the language you use. It should be clear and unambiguous, emphatic but appropriately qualified. Although you will probably refine your thesis statement as you draft and revise your essay, trying now to articulate it will help give your planning and drafting direction and impetus. (For more on asserting a thesis, see Chapter 11, pp. 327–30.)

■ PLANNING AND DRAFTING

This section will help you review what you have learned about evaluating your subject, determine specific goals for your essay, make a tentative outline, and get started on your first draft.

Seeing What You Have

Pause now to reread your invention and research notes. Consider whether you have enough reasons and support to offer readers and whether you understand—even if you do not share—your readers' standards for judging a subject of this kind. Highlight anything you think you will be able to use in your draft and note connections between ideas.

If your invention notes seem skimpy, you may need to do further research at this stage or you could begin drafting now and later do research to fill in the blanks.

If your confidence in your judgment has been shaken or if you are concerned that you will not be able to write an argument to support your judgment, consult your instructor to determine whether you should try evaluating a different subject.

Setting Goals

Before you begin drafting, set some specific goals to guide the decisions you will make as you draft and revise your essay. The draft will not only be easier to write, but also more focused if you start with clear goals in mind. The following questions will help you set goals. You may find it useful to return to them while you are drafting, for they are designed to help you focus on specific features and strategies of evaluative essays.

Your Purpose and Readers

- What do I want my readers to think about the subject after reading my essay? Do I want to show them how the subject I am evaluating fails (as Ansen does), or how it succeeds (as Potter does)? Or do I want to demonstrate its strengths and weaknesses (as Romano does)?

- Should I assume that my readers are likely to have read other evaluations of the subject (perhaps like Ansen) or to have developed their own evaluation of it (like Romano)? Or should I assume that I am introducing readers to the subject (like Potter)?

- How should I present myself to my readers — as knowledgeable, balanced, impassioned, or in some other way?

The Beginning

- What opening would capture readers' attention? Should I open by abruptly stating my judgment? Or should I begin by giving readers a context for my evaluation, as Ansen and Potter do?

- Should I try to make clear to readers at the outset the standards I will apply, as Romano and Potter do? Should I begin by comparing my subject with a subject more familiar to readers, as Ansen does? Should I begin by describing the subject?

The Presentation of the Subject

- What should I name the subject? Should I name it after something readers will be familiar with? Should I name it after a recognized category or genre, as Ansen does in referring to science-fiction films?

- What about the subject should I describe? Can I use visuals to illustrate it, as Potter does?

- Should I place the subject historically, as Ansen does when he discusses the earlier *Star Wars* films?

- If the subject has a story, how much of it should I tell? Can I simply set the scene and identify the characters, as Ansen does, without giving away the story?

Your Evaluative Argument

- How should I state my thesis? Should I forecast my reasons early in the essay, as Potter and Romano do? Should I place my thesis at the beginning or wait until after I have provided a context?

- How can I convince readers to consider my judgment seriously even if they disagree with it? Should I defend my standards (like Potter and Romano)? Should I build my argument on shared standards or try to present a balanced judgment by praising some things and criticizing others?

- How can I present my reasons? Should I explain the standards on which I base my reasons, as Romano and Potter do?

- If I have two or more reasons, how should I sequence them?

- How can I support my reasons? Can I find examples from a text to quote, paraphrase, or summarize, as Ansen and Romano do? Can I call on authorities? What examples, statistics, or other support could I use?

- What objections or questions should I counterargue? How should I respond—by merely acknowledging them, by conceding legitimate objections and qualifying my judgment, or by trying to refute objections I consider illegitimate or weak?

The Ending

- How should I conclude? Should I try to frame the essay by echoing something from the opening or from another part of the essay?

- Should I conclude by restating my judgment, as Romano and Potter do, or by comparing my subject to others, as Ansen does?

- Should I end by making a recommendation?

Outlining

An evaluative essay contains as many as four basic parts:

1. A presentation of the subject
2. A judgment of the subject
3. A presentation of reasons and support
4. A consideration of readers' objections and alternative judgments

These parts can be organized in various ways. If, for example, you expect readers to disagree with your judgment, you could try to show them what about the subject you think they have overlooked or misjudged. You could begin by presenting the subject; then you could assert your thesis, present your reasons and support, and anticipate readers' likely objections.

Presentation of the subject

Thesis statement (judgment)

First reason and support

Anticipation and refutation of objection

Second reason and support

Counterargument

Conclusion

If you expect some of your readers to disagree with your negative judgment even though they base their judgment on the same standard on which you base yours, you could try to show them that the subject really does not satisfy the standard. You could begin by reinforcing the standard you share and then demonstrate how the subject fails to meet it.

Establish shared standard

Acknowledge alternative judgment

State thesis (judgment) that subject fails to meet shared standard

First reason and support showing how the subject fails standard

Second reason and support (etc.)

Conclusion

There are, of course, many other possible ways to organize an evaluative essay, but these outlines should help you start planning your own essay. (For more on outlining, see Chapter 9, pp. 292–94.)

Drafting

Before you start drafting, you may want to review the general advice on drafting in Chapter 1, pp. 15–17. As you draft your essay, keep in mind the goals you set while you were planning and these tips on writing an evaluative argument:

- Accept the burden of proof by offering reasons and support for your judgment.
- Remember that the basis for judgment often depends on standards as much as reasons and support. Try to think critically about the standards on which you base your judgment as well as the standards others apply to subjects of the kind you are evaluating.
- Remember that your outline is just a plan. Writers often make discoveries and reorganize as they draft. Be flexible.

- If you run into a problem as you draft, see whether any of your invention writing can help you solve it or whether returning to one of the invention activities earlier in this chapter would help.

- If, as you draft, you discover that you need more information, just make a note of what you have to find out and go on to the next point. When you are done drafting, you can go in search of the information you need.

Perhaps the most important advice to remember about drafting is to write quickly without worrying about grammar and spelling. Later you can make corrections.

CRITICAL READING GUIDE

Now is the time to get a good critical reading of your draft. Writers usually find it helpful to have someone else read and comment on their drafts, and all writers know how much they learn about writing when they read other writers' drafts. Your instructor may arrange such a reading as part of your coursework. If not, you can ask a classmate, friend, or family member to read your draft. You could also seek comments from a tutor at your campus writing center. (If you are unable to have someone else read your draft, turn ahead to the Revising section for help with reading your own draft critically.)

If You Are the Writer.   In order to provide focused, helpful comments, your reader must know your essay's intended audience, your purpose, and a problem in the draft that you need help solving. Briefly write out this information at the top of your draft.

- *Readers.* Identify the intended readers of your essay. What do you assume they think about your subject? Do you expect them to be receptive, skeptical, resistant, antagonistic?

- *Purpose.* What effect do you realistically expect your argument to have on these particular readers?

- *Problem.* Ask your reader to help you solve the single most important problem you see in your draft. Describe this problem briefly.

If You Are the Reader.   Reading a draft critically means reading it more than once, first to get a general impression and then to analyze its basic features. (See pp. 252–53 to review the basic features.) Use the following guidelines to help you give constructive, critical comments to others on evaluation essays.

1. *Read for a First Impression.* Tell the writer what you think the intended readers would find most and least convincing. If you personally think the argument is seriously flawed, share your thoughts.

Next, consider the problem the writer identified. If the problem will be covered by one of the other questions below, deal with it there. Otherwise, respond to the writer's concerns now.

2. *Analyze How Well the Subject Is Presented.* Locate where in the draft the subject is presented and ask questions that will help the writer fill in whatever is missing. If you are surprised by the way the writer has presented the subject, briefly explain how you usually think of this particular subject or subjects of this kind. Also indicate if any of the information about the subject seems unnecessary. Finally, and most important, let the writer know if any of the information about the subject seems inaccurate or only partly true.

3. *Assess Whether the Judgment Is Stated Clearly.* Write a sentence or two summarizing the writer's judgment as you understand it from reading the draft. Then underline the sentence or sentences in the draft where the thesis is stated explicitly. (It may be restated in several places.) If you cannot find an explicit statement of the thesis, let the writer know. Given the writer's purpose and audience, consider whether the thesis is arguable, clear, and appropriately qualified. If the judgment seems indecisive or too extreme, suggest how it might be made clearer or qualified to account for the subject's strengths and weaknesses.

4. *Evaluate the Reasons and Support.* Underline the reasons. Look closely at the reasons and support that seem most problematic, and briefly explain what bothers you — for example, that the reason does not seem appropriate for judging this kind of subject, that you do not fully understand the reason or how it applies to this particular subject, that the connection between a particular reason and its support is not clear or convincing to you, or that the support is too weak or there is not enough of it to hold up the argument. Be as specific and constructive as you can, not only pointing out what does not work but also suggesting what the writer might do to solve the problem. For example, if the reason seems inappropriate, explain why you think so, and indicate what kinds of reasons you expect the intended readers to recognize as acceptable for judging this kind of subject. If the support is lacking, suggest how it could be strengthened. Indicate whether any visual or audio elements that have been included fail to support the evaluation and offer suggestions for improvement.

5. *Assess How Well Readers' Alternative Judgments and Objections or Questions Have Been Handled.* Mark where the writer acknowledges, accommodates, or tries to refute readers' opposing judgments, objections, or questions. Point to any places where these counterarguments seem superficial or dismissive and suggest how they could be strengthened. Help the writer anticipate any important objections or questions that have been overlooked, providing advice on how to respond to them. Keep in mind that the writer may choose to acknowledge, accommodate, or refute opposing arguments.

6. *Consider the Effectiveness of the Organization.* Get an overview of the essay's organization and point out any places where more explicit cueing—transitions, summaries, or topic sentences—would clarify the relationship between parts of the essay.

- Look at the *beginning*. Let the writer know if you think readers will find it engaging. If not, suggest moving something from later in the essay that might work as a better opening.

- Look at the *ending*. Does the essay conclude decisively and memorably? If not, suggest an alternative. Could something be moved to the end?

- Look at the *design features*. Comment on the contribution of figures, headings, tables, and other design features. Help the writer think of additional visual or audio elements that could make a contribution to the essay.

7. *Give the Writer Your Final Thoughts.* What is the draft's strongest part? What part is most in need of further work?

■ REVISING

Now you are ready to revise your essay. Your instructor or other students may have given you advice on improving your draft. Nevertheless, you may have begun to realize that your draft requires not so much revising as rethinking. For example, you may recognize that your reasons do not lead readers to accept your evaluation, that you cannot adequately support your reasons, or that you are unable to refute damaging objections to your argument. Consequently, instead of working to improve parts of the draft, you may need to write a new draft that radically reenvisions your argument. It is not unusual for students—and professional writers—to find themselves in this situation. Learning to make radical revisions is a valuable lesson for any writer.

If you feel satisfied that your draft achieves most, if not all, of your goals, you can focus on refining specific parts of your draft. Very likely you have thought of ways of improving your draft, and you may even have begun improving it. This section will help you get an overview of your draft and revise it accordingly.

Getting an Overview

Consider your draft as a whole, following these two steps:

1. *Reread.* If at all possible, put the draft aside for a day or two before rereading it. When you return to it, start by reconsidering your purpose. Then read the draft straight through, trying to see it as your intended readers will.

2. *Outline.* Make a quick scratch outline, indicating the basic features as they appear in the draft. (For more on scratch outlines, see Chapter 9, pp. 292–93.)

Charting a Plan for Revision.   Once you have an overview of your draft, you may want to make a two-column chart like the following one to keep track of any problems you need to solve. In the left-hand column, list the basic features of evaluation essays. (Turn to pp. 252–53 to review the basic features.) As you analyze your draft and study any comments you have received from other readers, note the problems you need to solve in the right-hand column.

Basic Features	*Problems to Solve*
A well-presented subject	
A clear, authoritative judgment	
Appropriate reasons and convincing support	
Effective counterargument	

Analyzing the Basic Features of Your Own Draft.   Using the Critical Reading Guide on the preceding pages, identify problems you now see in your draft. Note them on your revision chart.

Studying Critical Comments.   Review all of the comments you have received from other readers and add to your chart any that you intend to act on. For each comment, look at the draft to determine what might have led the reader to make that particular point. Try to be objective about any criticism. Ideally, these comments will help you see your draft as others see it, providing valuable information about how you can improve it.

Carrying Out Revisions

Having identified problems in your draft, you now need to come up with solutions and—most important—to carry them out. Basically, you have three ways of finding solutions:

1. Review your invention and planning notes for information and ideas to add to your draft.
2. Do additional invention and research to provide additional material you or your readers think is needed.
3. Look back at the readings in this chapter to see how other writers have solved similar problems.

The following suggestions, which are organized according to the basic features on your revision chart, will help you solve some common writing problems in evaluation essays.

A Well-Presented Subject

- *Is the subject hard to find or unclear?* Try to give it a name or to identify the general category to which it belongs. If you need more information about the subject, review your invention writing to see if you have left out any details you could now add. You may also need to do further invention writing or research to answer questions your readers have raised or your intended readers might have.

- *Is the subject presented in too much detail?* Cut extraneous and repetitive details. If your subject is a film or book, try not to give away too much.

- *Is any of the information inaccurate or only partly true?* Reconsider the accuracy and completeness of the information you present. If any of the information will be surprising to readers, consider how you might reassure them that the information is accurate, perhaps by citing your sources.

A Clear, Authoritative Judgment

- *Is your overall judgment hard to find?* Announce your thesis explicitly. If your judgment is mixed—pointing out what you like and do not like about the subject—let readers know that from the beginning.

- *Does your judgment seem indecisive or too extreme?* If your readers do not know what your judgment is or if they think you are either too adulatory or too harsh, you may need to clarify your thesis statement or qualify it more carefully.

Appropriate Reasons and Convincing Support

- *Do any of the reasons or support seem inappropriate to readers?* Explain why you think the reason or support is appropriate. Consider using comparison or authorities to show that your argument employs a standard commonly used for evaluating subjects of this kind.

- *Are any of your reasons and support unclear?* To clarify them, you may need to explain your reasoning in more detail or use examples and comparisons to make your ideas understandable. You may need to do some additional exploratory writing or research to figure out how to explain your reasoning. Consider also whether any of the reasons should be combined, separated, or cut.

- *Are any of the reasons and support thin or unconvincing?* To find additional support, review your invention writing or reexamine the subject. You may also need to do library research to find information—examples, statistics, expert testimony—to support your argument.

Effective Counterargument

- *Do readers fail to recognize your counterargument?* Make your disagreement with readers or other evaluators explicit.

- *Are any important objections or questions overlooked?* Review your invention writing to see if you have left out something or do some more invention or research to develop a response to these objections and questions.

The Organization

- *Does the essay seem disorganized or confusing?* You may need to add a forecasting statement, transitions, summaries, or topic sentences. You may also need to do some major restructuring, such as moving your presentation of the subject or reordering your reasons.

- *Is the beginning weak?* See if there is a better place to start. Review your notes for an interesting quotation, comparison, or example to open with.

- *Is the ending weak?* See if you can frame the essay by echoing a point made earlier, restating your thesis, or summarizing your argument.

- *Can you add any design features to make the essay more interesting to read and to strengthen your argument?* Consider adding features you came across in your research or creating visual or audio elements of your own.

■ EDITING AND PROOFREADING

Now is the time to check your revised draft for connections between sentences and for errors in grammar, punctuation, and mechanics. As you reread, ask yourself whether the connection from one sentence to the next is logical and easy for readers to follow. If you sense a gap or disconnection that would cause a reader to stumble or become confused, try revising one or both sentences so that the gap is closed. Notice whether you shift from one word to another unnecessarily in one sentence to the next, and, if you do, consider repeating the same word instead. Look for sentences that might be combined to allow readers to follow the argument more easily and to discover more readily how you have anticipated their objections and questions. Look as well for long or garbled sentences that might be divided into two or three sentences.

As you work on your sentences, look for errors in spelling, capitalization, punctuation, usage, and grammar. Consult a writer's handbook for advice about how to correct any errors you cannot confidently correct on your own. Ask a friend or classmate to read over your draft, looking for errors.

Before you hand in your revised essay, proofread it carefully and run it through a spell-checker. Your goal is to hand in an error-free essay.

REFLECTING ON YOUR WRITING

Now that you have read and discussed several evaluation essays and written one of your own, take some time for reflection. Reflecting on your writing process will help you gain a greater understanding of what you learned about solving the problems you encountered in writing an evaluation.

Write a page or so telling your instructor about a problem you encountered in writing your evaluation essay and how you solved it. Before you begin, gather all of your writing—invention and planning notes, drafts, critical comments, revision plan, and final revisions. Review these materials as you complete this writing task.

1. *Identify one writing problem you needed to solve as you worked on the essay.* Do not be concerned with grammar and punctuation; concentrate instead on problems unique to developing an evaluation essay. For example: Did you puzzle over how to present your subject? Did you have trouble asserting an overall judgment while acknowledging what you liked as well as disliked? Was it difficult to refute an important objection you knew readers would raise?

2. *Determine how you came to recognize the problem.* When did you first discover it? What called it to your attention? If you did not become aware of the problem until someone else pointed it out to you, can you now see hints of it in your invention writings? If so, where specifically? When you first recognized the problem, how did you respond?

3. *Reflect on how you went about solving the problem.* Did you work on the wording of a passage, cut or add reasons or refutations, conduct further research, move paragraphs or sentences around? Did you reread one of the essays in this chapter to see how another writer handled a similar problem, or did you look back at your invention writing? If you talked about the problem with another student, a tutor, or your instructor, did talking about it help? How useful was the advice you received?

4. *Write a brief explanation of the problem and your solution.* Be as specific as possible in reconstructing your efforts. Quote from your invention notes or draft essay, others' critical comments, your revision plan, or your revised essay to show the various changes your writing—and thinking—underwent as you tried to solve the problem. If you are still uncertain about your solution, say so. Taking time to explain how you identified a particular problem, how you went about trying to solve it, and what you learned from this experience can help you solve future writing problems more easily.

Part Two

STRATEGIES
FOR WRITING
AND RESEARCH

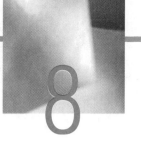

Strategies for Cueing Readers

Readers need guidance. To guide readers through a piece of writing, a writer can provide five basic kinds of cues or signals:

1. *Thesis and forecasting statements,* to orient readers to ideas and organization
2. *Paragraphing,* to group related ideas and details
3. *Cohesive devices,* to connect ideas to one another and bring about coherence and clarity
4. *Connectives,* to signal relationships or shifts in meaning
5. *Headings and subheadings,* to group related paragraphs and help readers locate specific information quickly

This chapter illustrates how each of these cueing strategies works.

■ ORIENTING STATEMENTS

To help readers find their way, especially in difficult and lengthy texts, you can provide two kinds of orienting information: a thesis statement, which declares the main point, and a forecasting statement, which previews subordinate points, showing the order in which they will be discussed in the essay.

Thesis Statements

To help readers understand what is being said about a subject, writers often provide a thesis statement early in the essay. The *thesis statement* operates as a cue by letting readers know which is the most important general idea among the writer's many ideas and observations. Here are three thesis statements from essays in Part One:

> O.K., let's cut out all this nonsense about romantic love. Let's bring some scientific precision to the party. Let's put love under a microscope.
> When rigorous people with Ph.D.s after their names do that, what they see is not some silly, senseless thing. No, their probe reveals that love rests firmly on the foundations of evolution, biology and chemistry.
>
> —ANASTASIA TOUFEXIS, Chapter 4

But for as many as five million Americans, experts say, the Internet has become a destructive force, its remarkable benefits overshadowed by its potential to disrupt the lives of those who can't resist the lure of round-the-clock social opportunities, entertainment, and information. For such people, work, friends, family, and sleep are replaced by a virtual world of chat rooms and games.

– CAROL POTERA, Chapter 4

She did not say, but I understood at once, that they had their pursuits (coffee?) and I had mine. She did not say, but I began to understand then, that you do what you do out of your private passion for the thing itself.

– ANNIE DILLARD, Chapter 2

Most thesis statements, like Toufexis's, can be expressed in a single sentence; others may require two or more sentences. Dillard's thesis explicitly states the point of a remembered event, but many autobiographical essays imply the thesis rather than state it directly.

Readers naturally look for something that will tell them the point of an essay, a focus for the many diverse details and ideas they encounter as they read. The lack of an explicit thesis statement can make this task more difficult. Therefore, careful writers keep readers' needs and expectations in mind when deciding how to state the thesis as clearly and directly as possible.

Another important decision is where to place the thesis statement. Most readers expect to find some information early on that will give them a context for reading the essay, particularly if they are reading about a new and difficult subject. Therefore, a thesis statement, like that of Toufexis, placed at the beginning of an essay enables readers to anticipate the content of the essay and more easily understand the relationships among its various ideas and details.

Occasionally, however, particularly in fairly short, informal essays and in some autobiographical and argumentative essays, a writer may save a direct statement of the thesis until the conclusion, which is where Dillard puts hers. Ending with the thesis has the effect of bringing together the various strands of information or supporting details introduced over the course of the essay and making clear the essay's main idea.

■ Exercise 8.1

In the essay by Jessica Statsky in Chapter 5, underline the thesis statement, the last sentence in paragraph 1. Notice the key terms in this thesis, the words that seem to be essential to presenting Statsky's ideas: "overzealous parents and coaches," "impose adult standards," "children's sports," "activities...neither satisfying nor beneficial." Then skim the essay, stopping to read the sentence at the beginning of each paragraph. Also read the last paragraph.

Consider whether the idea in every paragraph's first sentence is anticipated by the key terms in the thesis. Consider also the connection between the ideas in the last paragraph and the key terms in the thesis. What can you conclude about how a thesis might assert the point of an essay, anticipate the ideas that follow, and help readers relate the ideas to each other?

Forecasting Statements

Some thesis statements, like Jessica Statsky's in Chapter 5, include a *forecast,* which overviews the way a thesis will be developed. For example, note the role of the forecasting statement in this opening paragraph from an essay by William Langer on the bubonic plague:

> In the three years from 1348 through 1350 the pandemic of plague known as the Black Death, or, as the Germans called it, the Great Dying, killed at least a fourth of the population of Europe. It was undoubtedly the worst disaster that has ever befallen mankind. Today we can have no real conception of the terror under which people lived in the shadow of the plague. For more than two centuries plague has not been a serious threat to mankind in the large, although it is still a grisly presence in parts of the Far East and Africa. Scholars continue to study the Great Dying, however, as a historical example of human behavior under the stress of universal catastrophe. In these days when the threat of plague has been replaced by the threat of mass human extermination by even more rapid means, there has been a sharp renewal of interest in the history of the 14th-century calamity. With new perspective, students are investigating its manifold effects: demographic, economic, psychological, moral and religious.
>
> —WILLIAM LANGER, "The Black Death"

This introductory paragraph informs us that Langer's article is about the effects of the Black Death. His thesis (underlined) states that there is renewed interest in studying the social effects of the bubonic plague and that these new studies focus on five particular categories of effects. As a reader would expect, Langer then goes on to divide his essay into explanations of the research into these five effects, taking them up in the order in which they appear in the forecasting statement.

■ **Exercise 8.2**

Turn to Christine Romano's essay in Chapter 7, and underline the forecasting statement in paragraph 2. (After the first sentence, which states Romano's thesis, the remaining sentences offer a forecast of Romano's main points and the order in which she will take them up.) Then skim the essay, pausing to read the first sentence in each paragraph. Notice whether Romano takes up every point she mentions in the forecasting statement and whether she sticks to the order she promises readers. What can you conclude about how a forecasting statement assists readers?

■ PARAGRAPHING

Paragraph cues as obvious as indentation keep readers on track. You can also arrange material in a paragraph to help readers see what is important or significant. For example, you can begin with a topic sentence, help readers see the relationship between the previous paragraph and the present one with an explicit transition, and place the most important information toward the end. This section illustrates these cues and others.

Paragraph Cues

The indentation that signals the beginning of a new paragraph is a relatively modern printing convention. Old manuscripts show that paragraph divisions were not always marked. To make reading easier, scribes and printers began to use the symbol ¶ to mark paragraph breaks. Later, indenting became common practice, but even that relatively modern custom has changed in some forms of writing today. Instead of indenting, most business writers now distinguish one paragraph from another by leaving a line of space above and below each paragraph. Writing on the Internet is also usually paragraphed in this way.

Paragraphing helps readers by signaling when a sequence of related sentences begins and ends. Such paragraph signals tell them when they can stop holding meaning-making in suspension. Writers must constantly consider the need for this kind of closure so that readers can more easily follow the development of ideas.

Paragraphing also helps readers judge what is most important in what they are reading. Writers typically emphasize important information by placing it at the two points where readers are most attentive — the beginning and the end of a paragraph. Many writers put information to orient readers at the beginning of a paragraph and save the most important information for last.

You can give special emphasis to information by placing it in a paragraph of its own.

■ Exercise 8.3

Turn to Patrick O'Malley's essay in Chapter 6, and read paragraphs 4–6 with the following questions in mind: Does all the material in each paragraph seem to be related? Do you feel a sense of closure at the end of each paragraph? Does the last sentence offer the most important or significant or weighty information in the paragraph?

Topic Sentence Strategies

A *topic sentence* lets readers know the focus of a paragraph in simple and direct terms. It is a cueing strategy for the paragraph, much as a thesis or forecasting statement is for the whole essay. Because paragraphing usually signals a shift in focus, readers expect some kind of reorientation in the opening sentence. They need to know whether the new paragraph will introduce another aspect of the topic or develop one already introduced.

Announcing the Topic. Some topic sentences simply announce the topic. Here are some examples taken from Barry Lopez's book *Arctic Dreams:*

A polar bear walks in a way all its own.

What is so consistently striking about the way Eskimos used parts of an animal is the breadth of their understanding about what would work.

The Mediterranean view of the Arctic, down to the time of the Elizabethan mariners, was shaped by two somewhat contradictory thoughts.

These topic sentences do more than merely identify the topic; they also indicate how the topic will be developed in subsequent sentences — by describing how bears walk, giving examples of animal parts Eskimos used and explaining what they understood about how each part could be useful, or contrasting two preconceptions about the Arctic.

The following paragraph shows how one of Lopez's topic sentences (underlined) is developed:

> What is so consistently striking about the way Eskimos used parts of an animal is the breadth of their understanding about what would work. Knowing that muskox horn is more flexible than caribou antler, they preferred it for making the side prongs of a fish spear. For a waterproof bag in which to carry sinews for clothing repair, they chose salmon skin. They selected the strong, translucent intestine of a bearded seal to make a window for a snowhouse — it would fold up for easy traveling and it would not frost over in cold weather. To make small snares for sea ducks, they needed a springy material that would not rot in salt water — baleen fibers. The down feather of a common eider, tethered at the end of a stick in the snow at an angle, would reveal the exhalation of a quietly surfacing seal. Polar bear bone was used anywhere a stout, sharp point was required, because it is the hardest bone.
>
> — BARRY LOPEZ, *Arctic Dreams*

■ **Exercise 8.4**

Turn to David Ansen's Essay in Chapter 7. Underline the topic sentence (the first sentence) in paragraphs 4–9. Consider how these sentences help you anticipate the paragraph's topic and method of development.

Making a Transition.   Not all topic sentences simply point to what will follow. Some also refer to earlier sentences. Such sentences work both as topic sentences, stating the main point of the paragraph, and as transitions, linking that paragraph to the previous one. Here are a few topic sentences from "Quilts and Women's Culture," by Elaine Hedges, that use specific transitions (underlined) to tie the sentence to a previous statement:

Within its broad traditionalism and anonymity, however, variations and distinctions developed.

Regionally, too, distinctions were introduced into quilt making through the interesting process of renaming.

With equal inventiveness women renamed traditional patterns to accommodate to the local landscape.

Finally, out of such regional and other variations come individual, signed achievements.

Quilts, then, were an outlet for creative energy, a source and emblem of sisterhood and solidarity, and a graphic response to historical and political change.

Sometimes the first sentence of a paragraph serves as a transition, and a later sentence states the topic. The underlined sentences in the following example illustrate this strategy:

> . . . What a convenience, what a relief it will be, they say, never to worry about how to dress for a job interview, a romantic tryst, or a funeral!
> Convenient, perhaps, but not exactly a relief. Such a utopia would give most of us the same kind of chill we feel when a stadium full of Communist-bloc athletes in identical sports outfits, shouting slogans in unison, appears on TV. Most people do not want to be told what to wear any more than they want to be told what to say. In Belfast recently four hundred Irish Republican prisoners "refused to wear any clothes at all, draping themselves day and night in blankets," rather than put on prison uniforms. Even the offer of civilian-style dress did not satisfy them; they insisted on wearing their own clothes brought from home, or nothing. Fashion is free speech, and one of the privileges, if not always one of the pleasures, of a free world.
>
> — ALISON LURIE, *The Language of Clothes*

Occasionally, whole paragraphs serve as transitions, linking one sequence of paragraphs with those that follow. This transition paragraph summarizes what went before (evidence of contrast) and sets up what will follow (evidence of similarity):

> Yet it was not all contrast, after all. Different as they were—in background, in personality, in underlying aspiration—these two great soldiers had much in common. Under everything else, they were marvelous fighters. Furthermore, their fighting qualities were really very much alike.
>
> — BRUCE CATTON, "Grant and Lee: A Study in Contrasts"

■ **Exercise 8.5**

Turn to Anastasia Toufexis's essay in Chapter 4, and read paragraphs 9–15. As you read, underline the part of the first sentence in paragraphs 10–15 that refers to the previous paragraph, creating a transition from one to the next. Notice the different ways Toufexis creates these transitions. Consider whether they are all equally effective.

Positioning the Topic Sentence.   Although topic sentences may occur anywhere in a paragraph, stating the topic in the first sentence has the advantage of giving readers a sense of how the paragraph is likely to be developed. The beginning of the paragraph is therefore the most common position for a topic sentence.

A topic sentence that does not open a paragraph is most likely to appear at the end. When a topic sentence concludes a paragraph, it usually summarizes or generalizes preceding information. In the following example, the topic is not stated explicitly until the last sentence.

> Even black Americans sometimes need to be reminded about the deceptiveness of television. Blacks retain their fascination with black characters on TV: Many of us buy *Jet* magazine primarily to read its weekly television feature, which lists every black character (major or minor) to be seen on the screen that week. Yet our fixation with the presence of black characters on TV has blinded us to an important fact that *Cosby*, which began in 1984, and its offshoots over the years demonstrate convincingly: There is very

little connection between the social status of black Americans and the fabricated images of black people that Americans consume each day. The representation of blacks on TV is a very poor index to our social advancement or political progress.

            — HENRY LOUIS GATES JR., "TV's Black World Turns — But Stays Unreal"

When a topic sentence is used in a narrative, it often appears as the last sentence as a way to evaluate or reflect on events:

I hadn't known she could play the piano. She wasn't playing very well, I guess, because she stopped occasionally and had to start over again. She concentrated intensely on the music, and the others in the room sat absolutely silently. My mother was facing me but didn't seem to see me. She seemed to be staring beyond me toward something that wasn't there. All the happy excitement died in me at that moment. Looking at my mother, so isolated from us all, I saw her for the first time as a person utterly alone.

            — RUSSELL BAKER, *Growing Up*

It is possible for a single topic sentence to introduce two or more paragraphs. Subsequent paragraphs in such a sequence have no separate topic sentences of their own. Here is a two-paragraph sequence in which the topic sentence opens the first paragraph:

Anthropologists Daniel Maltz and Ruth Borker point out that boys and girls socialize differently. Little girls tend to play in small groups or, even more common, in pairs. Their social life usually centers around a best friend, and friendships are made, maintained, and broken by talk — especially "secrets." If a little girl tells her friend's secret to another little girl, she may find herself with a new best friend. The secrets themselves may or may not be important, but the fact of telling them is all important. It's hard for newcomers to get into these tight groups, but anyone who is admitted is treated as an equal. Girls like to play cooperatively; if they can't cooperate, the group breaks up.

    Little boys tend to play in larger groups, often outdoors, and they spend more time doing things than talking. It's easy for boys to get into the group, but not everyone is accepted as an equal. Once in the group, boys must jockey for their status in it. One of the most important ways they do this is through talk: verbal display such as telling stories and jokes, challenging and sidetracking the verbal displays of other boys, and withstanding other boys' challenges in order to maintain their own story — and status. Their talk is often competitive talk about who is best at what.

            — DEBORAH TANNEN, *That's Not What I Meant!*

◼ Exercise 8.6

Consider the variety and effectiveness of the topic sentences in your most recent essay. Begin by underlining the topic sentence in each paragraph after the first one. The topic sentence may not be the first sentence in a paragraph, though often it will be.

    Then double-underline the part of the topic sentence that provides an explicit transition from one paragraph to the next. You may find a transition that is separate from the topic sentence. You may not always find a topic sentence.

    Reflect on your topic sentences, and evaluate how well they serve to orient your readers to the sequence of topics or ideas in your essay.

■ COHESIVE DEVICES

Cohesive devices guide readers, helping them follow your train of thought by connecting key words and phrases throughout a passage. Among such devices are pronoun reference, word repetition, synonyms, repetition of sentence structure, and collocation.

Pronoun Reference

One common cohesive device is pronoun reference. As noun substitutes, pronouns refer to nouns that either precede or follow them and thus serve to connect phrases or sentences. The nouns that come before the pronouns are called *antecedents*. In the following paragraph, the pronouns *(it* and *its)* form a chain of connection with their antecedent, *George Washington Bridge.*

> In New York from dawn to dusk to dawn, day after day, you can hear the steady rumble of tires against the concrete span of the George Washington Bridge. The bridge is never completely still. It trembles with traffic. It moves in the wind. Its great veins of steel swell when hot and contract when cold; its span often is ten feet closer to the Hudson River in summer than in winter.
>
> — GAY TALESE, "New York"

This example has only one pronoun-antecedent chain, and the antecedent comes first, so all the pronouns refer back to it. When there are multiple pronoun-antecedent chains with references forward as well as back, writers have to make sure that readers will not mistake one pronoun's antecedent for another's.

Word Repetition

To avoid confusion, writers often repeat words and phrases. This device is especially helpful if a pronoun might confuse readers:

> The first step is to realize that in our society we have permitted the kinds of vulnerability that characterize the victims of violent crime and have ignored, where we could, the hostility and alienation that enter into the making of violent criminals. No rational person condones violent crime, and I have no patience with sentimental attitudes toward violent criminals. But it is time that we open our eyes to the conditions that foster violence and that ensure the existence of easily recognizable victims.
>
> — MARGARET MEAD, "A Life for a Life: What That Means Today"

In the next example, several overlapping chains of *word repetition* prevent confusion and help the reader follow the ideas:

> Natural selection is the central concept of Darwinian theory — the fittest survive and spread their favored traits through populations. Natural selection is defined by Spencer's phrase "survival of the fittest," but what does this famous bit of jargon really mean? Who are the fittest? And how is "fitness" defined? We often read that fitness involves no more than "differential reproductive success" — the production of more surviving offspring than other competing members of the population. Whoa! cries

Bethell, as many others have before him. This formulation defines fitness in terms of survival only. The crucial phrase of natural selection means no more than "the survival of those who survive"—a vacuous tautology. (A tautology is a phrase—like "my father is a man"—containing no information in the predicate ["a man"] not inherent in the subject ["my father"]. Tautologies are fine as definitions, but not as testable scientific statements—there can be nothing to test in a statement true by definition.)
                                                      —STEPHEN JAY GOULD, *Ever Since Darwin*

Notice that Gould uses repetition to keep readers focused on the key concepts of "natural selection," "survival of the fittest," and "tautology." These key terms may vary in form—*fittest* becomes *fitness,* and *survival* changes to *surviving* and *survive*—but they serve as links in the chain of meaning.

Synonyms

In addition to word repetition, you can use *synonyms,* words with identical or very similar meanings, to connect important ideas. In the following example, the author develops a careful chain of synonyms and word repetitions:

Over time, small bits of knowledge about a region accumulate among local residents in the form of stories. These are remembered in the community; even what is unusual does not become lost and therefore irrelevant. These narratives comprise for a native an intricate, long-term view of a particular landscape. . . . Outside the region this complex but easily shared "reality" is hard to get across without reducing it to generalities, to misleading or imprecise abstraction.
                                                      —BARRY LOPEZ, *Arctic Dreams*

Note the variety of synonym sequences:

"particular landscape," "region"

"local residents," "community," "native"

"stories," "narratives"

"accumulate," "remembered," "does not become lost," "comprise"

"intricate, long-term view," "complex . . . 'reality'," "without reducing it to generalities"

The result is a coherent paragraph that constantly reinforces the author's point.

Sentence Structure Repetition

Writers occasionally *repeat the same sentence structure* to emphasize the connections among their ideas, as in this example:

But the life forms are as much part of the structure of the Earth as any inanimate portion is. It is all an inseparable part of a whole. If any animal is isolated totally from other forms of life, then death by starvation will surely follow. If isolated from water, death by dehydration will follow even faster. If isolated from air, whether free or dissolved in

water, death by asphyxiation will follow still faster. If isolated from the Sun, animals will survive for a time, but plants would die, and if all plants died, all animals would starve.
— Isaac Asimov, "The Case against Man"

From the third sentence to the last, Asimov repeats the "If this . . . then that" sentence structure to show that the sentences or clauses are logically related; every one expresses a consequence of isolation.

Collocation

Words *collocate* when they occur together in expected ways around a particular topic. For example, in a paragraph on a high school graduation, a reader might expect to encounter such words as *valedictorian, diploma, commencement, honors, cap and gown,* and *senior class.* Collocations occur quite naturally to a writer, and they usually form a recognizable network of meaning for readers. The paragraph that follows uses five collocation chains:

housewife, cooking, neighbor, home

clocks, calculated cooking times, progression, precise

obstinacy, vagaries, problem

sun, clear days, cloudy ones, sundial, cast its light, angle, seasons, sun, weather

cooking, fire, matches, hot coals, smoldering, ashes, go out, bed-warming pan

The seventeenth-century housewife not only had to make do without thermometers, she also had to make do without clocks, which were scarce and dear throughout the sixteen hundreds. She calculated cooking times by the progression of the sun; her cooking must have been more precise on clear days than on cloudy ones. Marks were sometimes painted on the floor, providing her with a rough sundial, but she still had to make allowance for the obstinacy of the sun in refusing to cast its light at the same angle as the seasons changed; but she was used to allowing for the vagaries of sun and weather. She also had a problem starting her fire in the morning; there were no matches. If she had allowed the hot coals smoldering under the ashes to go out, she had to borrow some from a neighbor, carrying them home with care, perhaps in a bed-warming pan.
— Waverly Root and Richard de Rouchement, *Eating in America*

■ **Exercise 8.7**

Now that you know more about pronoun reference, word repetition, synonyms, sentence structure repetition, and collocation, turn to Alan I. Leshner's essay in Chapter 5 and identify the cohesive devices you find in paragraphs 1–5. Underline each cohesive device you can find; there will be many devices. You might also want to try to connect with lines the various pronoun, related-word, and synonym chains you find. You could also try listing the separate collocation chains. Consider how these cohesive devices help you read and make sense of the passage.

■ **Exercise 8.8**

Choose one of your recent essays, and select any three contiguous paragraphs. Identify the cohesive devices you find in these three paragraphs. Underline every cohesive device you can find; there will be many devices. Try to connect with lines the various pronoun, related-word, and synonym chains you find. Also try listing the separate collocation chains.

You will be surprised and pleased at how extensively you rely on cohesive ties. Indeed, you could not produce readable text without cohesive ties. Consider these questions relevant to your development as a writer: Are all of your pronoun references clear? Are you straining for synonyms when repeated words would do? Do you ever repeat sentence structures to emphasize connections? Do you trust yourself to put collocation to work?

■ CONNECTIVES

A *connective*—often called a transition—serves as a bridge, connecting one paragraph, sentence, clause, or word with another. It not only signals a connection but also identifies the kind of connection by indicating to readers how the item preceding the connective relates to the one that follows it. Connectives help readers anticipate how the next paragraph or sentence will affect the meaning of what they have just read. There are three basic groups of connectives, based on the relationships they indicate: *logical, temporal,* and *spatial.*

Logical Relationships

Connectives help readers follow the logic of an argument. How such connectives work is illustrated in this tightly and passionately reasoned paragraph by James Baldwin:

> The black man insists, by whatever means he finds at his disposal, that the white man cease to regard him as an exotic rarity and recognize him as a human being. This is a very charged and difficult moment, for there is a great deal of will power involved in the white man's naïveté. Most people are not naturally malicious, and the white man prefers to keep the black man at a certain human remove because it is easier for him thus to preserve his simplicity and to avoid being called to account for crimes committed by his forefathers, or his neighbors. He is inescapably aware, nevertheless, that he is in a better position in the world than black men are, nor can he quite put to death the suspicion that he is hated by black men therefore. He does not wish to be hated, neither does he wish to change places, and at this point in his uneasiness he can scarcely avoid having recourse to those legends which white men have created about black men, the most unusual effect of which is that the white man finds himself enmeshed, so to speak, in his own language which describes hell, as well as the attributes which lead one to hell, as being black as night.
>
> —JAMES BALDWIN, "Stranger in the Village"

Connectives Showing Logical Relationships

- *To introduce another item in a series:* first, second; in the second place; for one thing . . . , for another; next; then; furthermore; moreover; in addition; finally; last; also; similarly; besides; and; as well as

- *To introduce an illustration or other specification:* in particular; specifically; for instance; for example; that is; namely

- *To introduce a result or a cause:* consequently; as a result; hence; accordingly; thus; so; therefore; then; because; since; for

- *To introduce a restatement:* that is; in other words; in simpler terms; to put it differently

- *To introduce a conclusion or summary:* in conclusion; finally; all in all; evidently; clearly; actually; to sum up; altogether; of course

- *To introduce an opposing point:* but; however; yet; nevertheless; on the contrary; on the other hand; in contrast; still; neither; nor

- *To introduce a concession to an opposing view:* certainly; naturally; of course; it is true; to be sure; granted

- *To resume the original line of reasoning after a concession:* nonetheless; all the same; even though; still; nevertheless

Temporal Relationships

In addition to showing logical connections, connectives may indicate temporal relationships—a sequence or progression in time—as this example illustrates:

> That night, we drank tea and then vodka with lemon peel steeped in it. The four of us talked in Russian and English about mutual friends and American railroads and the Rolling Stones. Seryozha loves the Stones, and his face grew wistful as we spoke about their recent album, "Some Girls." He played a tape of "Let It Bleed" over and over, until we could translate some difficult phrases for him; after that, he came out with the phrases at intervals during the evening, in a pretty decent imitation of Jagger's Cockney snarl. He was an adroit and oddly formal host, inconspicuously filling our teacups and politely urging us to eat bread and cheese and chocolate. While he talked to us, he teased Anya, calling her "Piglet," and she shook back her bangs and glowered at him. It was clear that theirs was a fiery relationship. After a while, we talked about ourselves. Anya told us about painting and printmaking and about how hard it was to buy supplies in Moscow. There had been something angry in her dark face since the beginning of the evening; I thought at first that it meant she didn't like Americans; but now I realized that it was a constant, barely suppressed rage at her own situation.
>
> —ANDREA LEE, *Russian Journal*

Connectives Showing Temporal Relationships

- *To indicate frequency:* frequently; hourly; often; occasionally; now and then; day after day; every so often; again and again

- *To indicate duration:* during; briefly; for a long time; minute by minute; while
- *To indicate a particular time:* now; then; at that time; in those days; last Sunday; next Christmas; in 1999; at the beginning of August; at six o'clock; first thing in the morning; two months ago; when
- *To indicate the beginning:* at first; in the beginning; since; before then
- *To indicate the middle:* in the meantime; meanwhile; as it was happening; at that moment; at the same time; simultaneously; next; then
- *To indicate the end and beyond:* eventually; finally; at last; in the end; subsequently; later; afterward

Spatial Relationships

Spatial connectives orient readers to the objects in a scene, as illustrated in these paragraphs:

> On Georgia 155, I crossed Troublesome Creek, then went through groves of pecan trees aligned one with the next like fenceposts. The pastures grew a green almost blue, and syrupy water the color of a dusty sunset filled the ponds. Around the farmhouses, from wires strung high above the ground, swayed gourds hollowed out for purple martins.
>
> The land rose again on the other side of the Chattahoochee River, and Highway 34 went to the ridgetops where long views over the hills opened in all directions. Here was the tail of the Appalachian backbone, its gradual descent to the Gulf. Near the Alabama stateline stood a couple of LAST CHANCE! bars. . . .
>
> —WILLIAM LEAST HEAT MOON, *Blue Highways*

Connectives Showing Spatial Relationships

- *To indicate closeness:* close to; near; next to; alongside; adjacent to; facing
- *To indicate distance:* in the distance; far; beyond; away; there
- *To indicate direction:* up/down; sideways; along; across; to the right/left; in front of/behind; above/below; inside/outside; toward/away from

■ **Exercise 8.9**

Turn to Peggy Orenstein's essay in Chapter 3. Relying on the lists of connectives just given, underline the logical, temporal, and spatial connectives in paragraphs 9 and 10. Consider how the connectives relate the ideas and events from sentence to sentence. Do you see the need for further connectives to make the relationships clear?

■ **Exercise 8.10**

Select a recent essay of your own. Choose at least three paragraphs and, relying on the lists of connectives given in the text, underline the logical, temporal, and spatial connectives. Depending on the kind of writing you were doing, you may find few, if any, connectives in one category or another. For example, an essay speculating about causes may not include any spatial connectives; writing about a remembered event might not contain connectives showing logical relationships.

Consider how your connectives relate the ideas from sentence to sentence. Comparing your connectives to those in the lists, do you find that you are making full use of the repertoire of connectives? Do you find gaps between any of your sentences that a well-chosen connective would close?

■ HEADINGS AND SUBHEADINGS

Headings, brief phrases set off from the text in various ways, can provide visible cues to readers about the content and organization of a text. Headings can be distinguished from text in numerous ways, including the selective use of capital letters, bold or italic type, or different sizes of type. To be most helpful to readers, headings should be phrased similarly and follow a predictable system. In this chapter, the headings in the section "Paragraphing," beginning on p. 275, provide a good example of a system of headings that can readily be outlined:

PARAGRAPHING

Paragraph Cues

Topic Sentence Strategies

    Announcing the Topic.

    Making a Transition.

    Positioning the Topic Sentence.

Notice that in this example the system has three levels. In the first level, all the letters are capitalized, and the heading stands out most visibly among the others. (It is one of five such capitalized headings in this chapter.) In the second level, the first letter in each word (except for articles and prepositions) is capitalized and the others are lowercased; like the heading in the first level, this second-level heading is aligned with the left margin. The first of these second-level headings has no subheadings beneath it, while the second has three. These subheadings make up the third level in the system. They are run in as part of the paragraph they introduce, as you can see if you pause now to turn the pages of this section.

All of these headings are set apart from the surrounding text by the special use of capital letters or spacing or both. At each level, they follow a parallel grammatical structure: nouns at the first level, which you can confirm by skimming the chapter in order to look at the other four first-level heads; nouns at the second level ("cues" and "strategies"); and "-ing" nouns at the third level. For papers written in MLA style, note the particular requirement that sentences immediately following headings be able to stand alone grammatically. (For more on MLA style, see Chapter 14.)

Headings may not be necessary in the short essays you will be writing for your first-year composition course. Short essays offer readers thesis statements, forecasting statements, well-positioned topic sentences, and transition sentences so that they have all the cues they may need. Headings are rare in some genres, such as autobiography and essays profiling people and places (Chapters 2 and 3). Headings appear more frequently in concept explanations, position papers, proposals, and evaluations (Chapters 4–7).

Frequency and Placement of Headings

Before dividing their essays into sections with headings and subheadings, writers need to make sure their discussion is detailed enough to support at least one heading at each level. The frequency and placement of headings depend entirely on the content and how it is divided and organized. Keep in mind that headings do not reduce the need for other cues to keep readers on track.

Katherine S. Newman's essay, "Dead-End Jobs: A Way Out," in Chapter 6, uses six headings to cue readers. Notice that they are grammatically parallel (noun phrases or gerunds):

Stagnation in the Inner City

Social Networks

The Employer Consortium

Advantages for Employers

Minimal Government Involvement

Building Bridges

If you take the time now to read or skim her essay (pp. 192–98), you will recognize that the first heading covers material concerned with defining and providing reasons for a problem—the lack of job mobility in inner-city communities. The noun phrase "stagnation in the inner city" captures the problem, which is then illustrated and explained in the paragraphs that follow. The last heading covers a much briefer section arguing that bridges need to be built to give inner-city, fast-food workers access to the kinds of jobs that will enable them to support their families and move out of poverty. Although the headings do not cover equal amounts of material, they divide the content logically and allow the reader to anticipate the main point of each section.

Exercise 8.11

Turn to Carol Potera's essay in Chapter 4, and survey the system of headings. (If you have not read the essay, read or skim it now. If you have not already worked on the Chapter 4 assignment, read Basic Features: Explaining Concepts at the end of the Readings section to familiarize yourself with the genre.) Consider how the headings help readers anticipate what is coming and how the argument is organized. Analyze whether the headings substitute for or complement a strong system of other cues for keeping readers on track. Decide whether the headings guide readers through particular stages of the genre. Then, try to answer these questions: Do any of the headings suggest subheadings? Might fewer or more headings be helpful to readers? Are the headings grammatically parallel? Finally, revise any headings that aren't grammatically parallel. Keep in mind that any headings you come up with need to maintain the same relationship to the content, despite any grammatical changes you make.

■ **Exercise 8.12**

Select one of your essays that might benefit from headings. Develop a system of headings, and insert the headings where appropriate. Be prepared to justify your headings in light of the discussion about headings in this section.

Strategies for All-Purpose Invention

Writers are like scientists: They ask questions, systematically inquiring about how things work, what they are, where they occur, and how more information can be learned about them. Writers are also like artists in that they use what they know and learn to create something new and imaginative.

The invention and inquiry strategies—also known as *heuristics*—described in this chapter are not mysterious or magical. They are available to all writers, and one or more of them may appeal to your common sense and experience. These techniques represent ways creative writers, engineers, scientists, composers—in fact, all of us— solve problems.

Once you have mastered these strategies, you can use them to tackle many of the writing situations you will encounter in college, on the job, and in the community. The best way to learn them is to use them as you write an actual essay. Chapters 2–7 show you when these strategies can be most helpful and how to make the most efficient use of them. The Guides to Writing in those chapters offer easy-to-use adaptations of these general strategies, adaptations designed to satisfy the special requirements of each kind of writing. You will learn how and when to use these strategies and see how to combine them to achieve your goals.

The strategies for invention and inquiry in this chapter are grouped into two categories:

Mapping: A brief visual representation of your thinking or planning

Writing: The composition of phrases or sentences to discover information and ideas and to make connections among them

These invention and inquiry strategies can be powerful tools for thinking about your topic and planning your writing. They will help you explore and research a topic fully before you begin drafting and then help you creatively solve problems as you draft and revise your draft. In this chapter, strategies are arranged alphabetically within each of the two categories.

■ MAPPING

Mapping strategies involve making a visual record of invention and inquiry. Many writers find that mapping helps them think about a topic. In making maps, they usually use key words and phrases to record material they want to remember, questions they need to answer, and new sources of information they want to check. The maps show the ideas, details, and facts they are examining. They also show possible ways whereby materials can be connected and focused. Maps might be informal graphic displays with words and phrases circled and connected by lines to show relationships, or they might be formal sentence outlines. Mapping can be especially useful for collaborative writing situations, to prepare oral presentations, and create visual aids for written or oral reports. Mapping strategies include clustering, listing, and outlining.

Clustering

Clustering is a strategy for revealing possible relationships among facts and ideas. Unlike listing (the next mapping strategy), clustering requires a brief period of initial preparation. You must first come up with a tentative division of the topic into subparts or main ideas. Clustering works as follows:

1. In a word or phrase, write your topic in the center of a piece of paper. Circle it.

2. Also in words or phrases, write down the main parts or central ideas of your topic. Circle these, and connect them with lines to the topic in the center.

3. Next, think of facts, details, examples, or ideas related in any way to these main parts. Cluster these around the main parts.

Clustering can be useful for any kind of writing. You can use it in the early stages of planning an essay to find subtopics and organize information. You may try out and discard several clusters before finding one that is promising. Many writers use clustering to plan brief sections of an essay as they are drafting or revising. (A model of clustering is on the next page.)

Listing

Listing is a familiar activity. We make shopping lists and lists of errands to do or people to call. Listing can also be a great help in planning an essay. It enables you to recall what you already know about a topic and suggests what else you may need to find out. It is an easy way to get started with your invention writing, instead of just worrying about what you will write. A list rides along on its own momentum, the first item leading naturally to the next.

A basic activity for all writers, listing is especially useful to those who have little time for planning—for example, reporters facing deadlines and college students taking essay exams. Listing lets you order your ideas quickly. It can also serve as a first step in discovering possible writing topics.

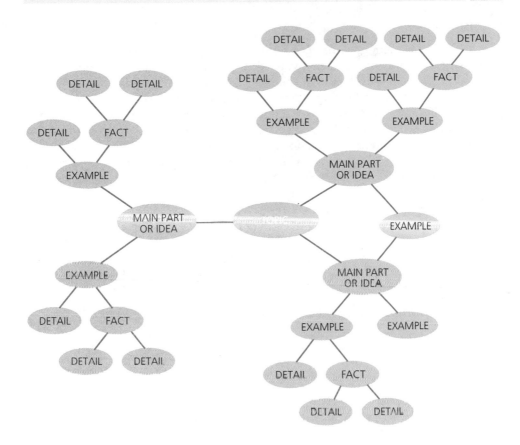

Listing is a solitary form of brainstorming, a popular technique of problem-solving in groups. When you work with a group to generate ideas for a collaborative writing project, you are engaged in true brainstorming. Here is how listing works best for invention work:

1. Give your list a title that indicates your main idea or topic.

2. Write as fast as you can, relying on short phrases.

3. Include anything that seems at all useful. Try not to be judgmental at this point.

4. After you have finished, or even as you write, reflect on the list and organize it in the following way. This step is very important, for it may lead you to further discoveries about your topic.

   Put an asterisk next to the most promising items.
   Number key items in order of importance.
   Put items in related groups.
   Cross out items that do not seem promising.
   Add new items.

Outlining

Like listing and clustering, *outlining* is both a means of inventing what you want to say in an essay and a way of organizing your ideas and information. As you outline, you nearly always see new possibilities in your subject, discovering new ways of dividing or grouping information and seeing where you need additional information to develop your ideas. Because outlining lets you see at a glance where your essay's strengths and weaknesses lie, outlining can also help you read and revise your essay with a critical eye.

There are two main forms of outlining: informal scratch outlining and formal topic or sentence outlining. (Keep in mind that clustering is also a type of informal outlining.)

A *scratch outline* is considered an informal outline because it is little more than a list of the essay's main points. You have no doubt made scratch outlines many times—to plan essays or essay exams, to revise your own writing, and to analyze a difficult reading passage. The Planning and Drafting sections of the Guides to Writing in Chapters 2–7 illustrate many different scratch outlines. Here are sample scratch outlines for two different kinds of essays. The first outlines Annie Dillard's essay in Chapter 2 (see pp. 26–28), and the second shows one way to organize a position paper (Chapter 5).

Scratch Outline: Essay about a Remembered Event

1. Gives history of her desire to have a microscope and tells when she got one
2. Describes workplace and supplies
3. Tells of failed efforts to see one-celled animals in hay infusion
4. Tells of failed efforts to see diatoms—one-celled creatures—in diatomaceous earth
5. Summarizes what she saw or failed to see in microscope during the winter
6. Explains that what she wanted to see but failed repeatedly to find was the amoeba (the one-celled animal that lives in the hay infusion and elsewhere)
7. Announces that in late spring she saw the amoeba; tells what led up to her seeing the amoeba; describes the amoeba
8. Tells that as soon as she found the amoeba, she ran upstairs to tell her parents
9. Describes father and mother lounging after dinner
10. Summarizes what her mother said
11. Explains what she understood her mother to mean
12. Reflects on the significance of what she had learned from her mother by telling what happened in the years that followed this event
13. Returns to the time of the event to tell what she did that night—studied the amoeba and gave it pond water
14. Recalls looking forward to seeing many other creatures through the microscope

Scratch Outline: Essay Arguing a Position

Presentation of the issue

Concession of some aspect of an opposing position

Thesis statement

First reason with support

Second reason with support (etc.)

Conclusion

Remember that the items in a scratch outline do not necessarily coincide with paragraphs. Sometimes two or more items may be developed in the same paragraph or one item may be covered in two or more paragraphs.

Topic and *sentence outlines* are considered more formal than scratch outlines because they follow a conventional format of numbered and lettered headings and subheadings:

I. (Main topic)
    A. (Subtopic of I)
    B.
        1. (Subtopic of I.B)
        2.
            a. (Subtopic of I.B.2)
            b.
                (1) (Subtopic of I.B.2.b)
                (2)
    C.
        1. (Subtopic of I.C)
        2.

The difference between a topic and sentence outline is obvious: Topic outlines simply name the topics and subtopics, whereas sentence outlines use complete or abbreviated sentences. To illustrate, here are two partial formal outlines of an essay arguing a position, Jessica Statsky's "Children Need to Play, Not Compete," from Chapter 5 (pp. 156–59).

Formal Topic Outline

I. Organized sports harmful to children
    A. Harmful physically
        1. Curve ball (Koppett)
        2. Tackle football (Tutko)

B. Harmful psychologically
   1. Fear of being hurt
      a. *Little League Online*
      b. Mother
      c. Reporter
   2. Competition
      a. Rablovsky
      b. Studies

Formal Sentence Outline

I. Highly organized competitive sports such as Peewee Football and Little League Baseball can be physically and psychologically harmful to children, as well as counterproductive for developing future players.

  A. Physically harmful because sports entice children into physical actions that are bad for growing bodies.
    1. Koppett claims throwing a curve ball may put abnormal strain on developing arm and shoulder muscles.
    2. Tutko argues that tackle football is too traumatic for young kids.

  B. Psychologically harmful to children for a number of reasons.
    1. Fear of being hurt detracts from their enjoyment of the sport.
      a. *Little League Online* ranks fear of injury seventh among the seven top reasons children quit.
      b. One mother says "kids get so scared. . . . They'll sit on the bench and pretend their leg hurts."
      c. A reporter tells about a child who made himself vomit to get out of playing Peewee Football.
    2. Too much competition poses psychological dangers for children.
      a. Rablovsky reports: "The spirit of play suddenly disappears, and sport becomes joblike."
      b. Studies show that children prefer playing on a losing team to "warming the bench on a winning team."

In contrast to an informal outline in which anything goes, a formal outline must follow many conventions. The roman numerals and capital letters are followed by periods. In topic and sentence outlines, the first word of each item is capitalized, but items in topic outlines do not end with a period as items in sentence outlines do. Every level of a formal outline except the top level (identified by the roman numeral *I*) must include at least two items. Items at the same level of indentation in a topic outline should be grammatically parallel—all beginning with the same part of speech. For example, *I.A.* and *I.B.* are parallel when they both begin with an adverb (*Physically harmful* and *Psychologically harmful*) or with a noun (*Harmful physically* and *Harmful psychologically*); they would not be parallel if one began with an adverb (*Physically harmful*) and the other with a noun (*Harmful psychologically*).

WRITING

Writing is itself a powerful tool for thinking. As you write, you can recall details, remember facts, develop your ideas, find connections in new information you have collected, examine assumptions, and critically question what you know.

Unlike most mapping strategies, *writing strategies* of invention invite you to produce complete sentences. Sentences provide considerable generative power. Because they are complete statements, they take you further than listing or clustering. They enable you to explore ideas and define relationships, bring ideas together or show how they differ, and identify causes and effects. Sentences can also help you develop a logical chain of thought.

Some of these invention and inquiry strategies are systematic, while others are more flexible. Even though they call for complete sentences that are related to one another, they do not require preparation or revision. You can use them to develop oral as well as written presentations.

These writing strategies include cubing, dialoguing, dramatizing, keeping journals, looping, questioning, and quick drafting.

Cubing

Cubing is useful for quickly exploring a writing topic, probing it from six different perspectives. It is known as *cubing* because a cube has six sides. These are the six perspectives in cubing:

Describing. What does your subject look like? What size is it? What is its color? Its shape? Its texture? Name its parts.

Comparing. What is your subject similar to? Different from?

Associating. What does your subject make you think of? What connections does it have to anything else in your experience?

Analyzing. What are the origins of your subject? What are its parts or features? How are its parts related?

Applying. What can you do with your subject? What uses does it have?

Arguing. What arguments can you make for your subject? Against it?

Here are some guidelines to help you use cubing productively.

1. Select a topic, subject, or part of a subject. This can be a person, a scene, an event, an object, a problem, an idea, or an issue. Hold it in focus.

2. Limit your writing to three to five minutes for each perspective. The whole activity should take no more than half an hour.

3. Keep going until you have written about your subject from all six perspectives. Remember that cubing offers the special advantage of enabling you to generate multiple perspectives quickly.

4. As you write from each perspective, begin with what you know about your subject. However, do not limit yourself to your present knowledge. Indicate what else you would like to know about your subject, and suggest where you might find that information.

5. Reread what you have written. Look for bright spots, surprises. Recall the part that was easiest for you to write. Recall the part where you felt a special momentum and pleasure in the writing. Look for an angle or an unexpected insight. These special parts may suggest a focus or topic within a larger subject, or they may provide specific details to include in a draft.

Dialoguing

A dialogue is a conversation between two or more people. You can use *dialoguing* to search for topics, find a focus, explore ideas, or consider opposing viewpoints. When you write a dialogue as an invention strategy, you need to make up all parts of the conversation (unless, of course, you are writing collaboratively—on a network, for example). To construct a dialogue by yourself, imagine two particular people talking, hold a conversation yourself with some imagined person, or simply talk out loud to yourself. To construct a dialogue independently or collaboratively, follow these steps:

1. Write a conversation between two speakers. Label the participants *Speaker A* and *Speaker B*, or make up names for them.

2. If you get stuck, you might have one of the speakers ask the other a question.

3. Write brief responses in order to keep the conversation moving fast. Do not spend much time planning or rehearsing responses. Write what first occurs to you, just as in a real conversation, where people take quick turns to prevent any awkward silences.

Dialogues can be especially useful with personal experience and persuasive essays because they help you remember conversations and anticipate objections.

Dramatizing

Dramatizing is an invention activity developed by the philosopher Kenneth Burke as a way of thinking about how people interact and as a way of analyzing stories and films.

Thinking about human behavior in dramatic terms can be very productive for writers. Drama has action, actors, setting, motives, and methods. Since stars and acting go together, you can use a five-pointed star to remember these five points of dramatizing: Each point on the star provides a different perspective on human behavior. We can think of each point independently and in combination. Let us begin by looking at each point to see how it helps us analyze people and their interactions.

Action.   An action is anything that happens, has happened, will happen, or could happen. Action includes events that are physical (running a marathon), mental (think-

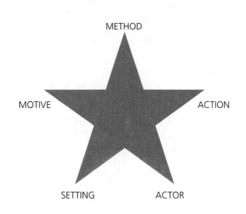

ing about a book you have read), and emotional (falling in love). This category also refers to the results of activity (an essay).

Actor. The actor is involved in the action—either responsible for it or simply affected by it. (The actor does not have to be a person. It can be a force, something that causes an action. For example, if the action is a rise in the price of gasoline, the actor could be increased demand or short supply.) Dramatizing may also include a number of coactors working together or at odds.

Setting. The setting is the situation or background of the action. We usually think of setting as the place and time of an event, but it may also be the historical background of an event or the childhood of a person.

Motive. The motive is the purpose or reason for an action—the actor's intention. Actions may have multiple, even conflicting, motives.

Method. The method explains how an action occurs, including the techniques an actor uses. It refers to whatever makes things happen.

Each of these points suggests a simple invention question:

Action: What?
Actor: Who?
Setting: When and where?
Motive: Why?
Method: How?

This list looks like the questions reporters typically ask. But dramatizing goes further: It enables us to ask a much fuller set of invention questions that we generate by considering relations between and among these five elements. We can think about actors' motives, the effect of the setting on the actors, the relations between actors, and so on.

You can use this invention strategy to learn more about yourself or about other significant people in your life. You can use it, as well, to explore, analyze, or evaluate characters in stories or movies. Moreover, dramatizing is especially useful in analyzing the readers you want to inform or convince.

To use dramatizing, imagine the person you want to understand better in a particular situation. Holding this image in mind, write answers to any questions in the following list that apply. You may draw a blank on some questions, have little to say to some, and find a lot to say to others. Be exploratory and playful with the questions. Write responses quickly, relying on words and phrases, even drawings.

- What is the actor doing?
- How did the actor come to be involved in this situation?
- Why does the actor do what he or she does?
- What else might the actor do?
- What is the actor trying to accomplish?
- How do other actors influence — help or hinder — the main actor?
- What do the actor's actions reveal about him or her?
- What does the actor's language reveal about him or her?
- How does the event's setting influence the actor's actions?
- How does the time of the event influence what the actor does?
- Where does this actor come from?
- How is this actor different now from what he or she used to be?
- What might this actor become?
- How is this actor like or unlike the other actors?

Keeping a Journal

Professional writers often use *journals* to keep notes, and so might you. Starting a writer's journal is quite easy. Buy a special notebook, or open a new file on your computer, and start writing. Here are some possibilities:

- Keep a list of new words and concepts you learn in your courses. You could also write about the progress and direction of your learning in particular courses — the experience of being in the course, your feelings about what is happening and what you are learning.
- Respond to your reading, both assigned and personal. Write about your personal associations as you read, your reflections, reactions, evaluations. Summarize or copy memorable or especially important passages and comment on them. (Copying and commenting have been practiced by students and writers for centuries in special journals called *commonplace books*.)

- Write to prepare for particular class meetings. Write about the main ideas you have learned from assigned readings and about the relationship of these new ideas to other ideas in the course. After class, write to summarize what you have learned. List questions you have about the ideas or information discussed in class. Journal writing of this kind involves reflecting, evaluating, interpreting, synthesizing, summarizing, and questioning.
- Record observations and overheard conversations.
- Write for ten or fifteen minutes every day about whatever is on your mind. Focus these meditations on your new experiences as you try to understand, interpret, and reflect on them.
- Write sketches of people who catch your attention.
- Organize your time. Write about your goals and priorities, or list specific things to accomplish and what you plan to do.
- Keep a log over several days or weeks about a particular event unfolding in the news — a sensational trial, an environmental disaster, a political campaign, a campus controversy, the fortunes of a sports team.

You can use a journal in many ways. All of the writing in your journal has value for learning. You may also be able to use parts of your journal for writing in your other courses.

Looping

Looping is especially useful for the first stages of exploring a topic. As its name suggests, *looping* involves writing quickly to explore some aspect of a topic and then looping back to your original starting point or to a new starting point to explore another aspect. Beginning with almost any starting point, looping enables you to find a center of interest and eventually a thesis for your essay. The steps are simple:

1. Write down your area of interest. You may know only that you have to write about another person or a movie or a cultural trend that has caught your attention. Or you may want to search for a topic in a broad historical period or for one related to a major political event. Although you may wander from this topic as you write, you will want to keep coming back to it. Your purpose is to find a focus for writing.

2. Write nonstop for ten minutes. Start with the first thing that comes to mind. Write rapidly, without looking back to reread or to correct anything. *Do not stop writing. Keep your pencil moving.* Continuous writing is the key to looping. If you get stuck for a moment, rewrite the last sentence. Trust the act of writing to lead you to new insights. Follow diversions and digressions, but keep returning to your topic.

3. After ten minutes, pause to reread what you have written. Decide what is most important — a single insight, a pattern of ideas, an emerging theme, a visual detail,

anything at all that stands out. Some writers call this a "center of gravity" or a "hot spot." To complete the first loop, restate this center in a single sentence.

4. Beginning with this sentence, write nonstop for another ten minutes.

5. Summarize in one sentence again to complete the second loop.

6. Keep looping until one of your summary sentences produces a focus or thesis. You may need only two or three loops; you may need more.

Questioning

Asking *questions* about a subject is a way to learn about it and decide what to write. When you first encounter a subject, however, your questions may be scattered. Also, you are not likely to think right away of all the important questions you ought to ask. The advantage of having a basic list of questions for invention, like the ones for cubing and for dramatizing discussed earlier in this chapter, is that it provides a systematic approach to exploring a subject.

The questions that follow come from classical rhetoric (what the Greek philosopher Aristotle called *topics*) and a modern approach to invention called *tagmemics*. Based on the work of linguist Kenneth Pike, tagmemics provides questions about different ways we make sense of the world, the ways we sort and classify experience in order to understand it.

Here are the steps in using questions for invention:

1. In a sentence or two, identify your subject. A subject could be any event, person, problem, project, idea, or issue — in other words, anything you might write about.

2. Start by writing a response to the first question in the following list, and move right through the list. Try to answer each question at least briefly with a word or a phrase. Some questions may invite several sentences or even a page or more of writing. You may draw a blank on a few questions. Skip them. Later, when you have more experience with questions for invention, you can start anywhere in the list.

3. Write your responses quickly, without much planning. Follow digressions or associations. Do not screen anything out. Be playful.

What Is Your Subject?

- What is your subject's name? What other names does it have? What names did it have in the past?

- What aspects of the subject do these different names emphasize?

- Imagine a still photograph or a moving picture of your subject. What would it look like?

- What would you put into a time capsule to stand for your subject?

- What are its causes and results?

- How would it look from different vantage points or perspectives?
- What particular experiences have you had with the subject? What have you learned?

What Parts or Features Does Your Subject Have and How Are They Related?

- Name the parts or features of your subject.
- Describe each one, using the questions in the preceding subject list.
- How is each part or feature related to the others?

How Is Your Subject Similar to and Different from Other Subjects?

- What is your subject similar to? In what ways are these subjects alike?
- What is your subject different from? In what ways are the subjects different?
- What seems to you most unlike your subject? In what ways are the two things unlike each other? Now, just for fun, note how they are alike.

How Much Can Your Subject Change and Still Remain the Same?

- How has your subject changed from what it once was?
- How is it changing now—moment to moment, day to day, year to year?
- How does each change alter your way of thinking about your subject?
- What are some different forms your subject takes?
- What does it become when it is no longer itself?

Where Does Your Subject Fit in the World?

- When and where did your subject originate?
- What would happen if at some future time your subject ceased to exist?
- When and where do you usually experience the subject?
- What is this subject a part of, and what are the other parts?
- What do other people think of your subject?

Quick Drafting

Sometimes you know what you want to say or have little time for invention. In these situations, *quick drafting* may be a good strategy. There are no special rules for quick drafting, but you should rely on it only if you know your subject well, have had experience with the kind of writing you are doing, and will have a chance to revise your draft. Quick drafting can help you discover what you already know about the subject and what you need to find out. It can also help you develop and organize your thoughts.

10

Strategies for
Reading Critically

To become a thoughtful, effective writer, you must also become a critical reader. This chapter presents strategies to help you *read with a critical eye*. Reading critically means not just comprehending passively and remembering what you read but also scrutinizing actively and making thoughtful judgments about your reading. When you read a text critically, you need to alternate between understanding and questioning—on the one hand, striving to understand the text on its own terms; on the other hand, taking care to question its ideas and authority. You will benefit greatly from reading what others have written—and reading your own writing—in this way.

The strategies here complement and supplement reading strategies presented in Part One, Chapters 2–7. Critical reading is central to your success with the writing assignments in those chapters. The Connecting to Culture and Experience activity following each reading in Part One helps you think about the selection in light of your own experience and awareness of social issues, while the Analyzing Writing Strategies questions help you understand how the text works and evaluate how well it achieves its purpose with its readers. The Critical Reading Guide in each Part One chapter helps you read other students' drafts as well as your own to find out what is working and what needs improvement.

Reading is, after all, inextricably linked to writing, and the reading strategies in this chapter can help you not only enrich your thinking as a reader but also participate in conversations as a writer. These strategies include the following:

- *Annotating.* Recording your reactions to, interpretations of, and questions about a text as you read it
- *Taking inventory.* Listing and grouping your annotations and other notes to find meaningful patterns
- *Outlining.* Listing the text's main ideas to reveal how it is organized
- *Paraphrasing.* Restating what you have read to clarify or refer to it
- *Summarizing.* Distilling the main ideas or gist of a text
- *Synthesizing.* Integrating into your own writing ideas and information gleaned from different sources
- *Contextualizing.* Placing a text in its historical and cultural contexts

- *Exploring the significance of figurative language.* Examining how metaphors, similes, and symbols are used in a text to convey meaning and evoke feelings
- *Looking for patterns of opposition.* Analyzing the values and assumptions embodied in the language of a text
- ✓ *Reflecting on challenges to your beliefs and values.* Critically examining the bases of your personal responses to a text
- *Evaluating the logic of an argument.* Determining whether a thesis is well reasoned and adequately supported
- *Recognizing emotional manipulation.* Identifying texts that unfairly and inappropriately use emotional appeals based on false or exaggerated claims
- *Judging the writer's credibility.* Considering whether writers represent different points of view fairly and know what they are writing about

Critical reading strategies can help you connect information from different sources and relate it to what you already know; distinguish fact from opinion; uncover and question assumptions; and subject other people's ideas as well as your own to reasoned argument. You can readily learn these strategies and apply them not only to a critical reading of the selections in Part One but also to your other college reading. Although mastering the strategies will not make critical reading easy, it can make your reading much more satisfying and productive and thus help you handle even difficult material with confidence. Critical reading strategies will, in addition, often be useful in your reading outside of school — for instance, these strategies can help you understand, evaluate, and comment on what political figures, advertisers, and other writers are saying.

■ ANNOTATING

Annotations are the marks — underlines, highlights, and comments — you make directly on the page as you read. *Annotating* can be used to record immediate reactions and questions, outline and summarize main points, and evaluate and relate the reading to other ideas and points of view. Especially useful for studying and preparing to write, annotating is also an essential element of many other critical reading strategies. Your annotations can take many forms, such as the following:

Writing comments, questions, or definitions in the margins

Underlining or circling words, phrases, or sentences

Connecting ideas with lines or arrows

Numbering related points

Bracketing sections of the text

Noting anything that strikes you as interesting, important, or questionable

Most readers annotate in layers, adding further annotations on second and third readings. Annotations can be light or heavy, depending on the reader's purpose and the difficulty of the material. Your purpose for reading also determines how you use your annotations.

The following selection, excerpted from Martin Luther King Jr.'s "Letter from Birmingham Jail," is annotated to illustrate some of the ways you can annotate as you read. Add your own annotations, if you like.

Martin Luther King Jr. (1929–1968) first came to national notice in 1955, when he led a successful boycott against the policy of restricting African American passengers to rear seats on city buses in Montgomery, Alabama, where he was minister of a Baptist church. He subsequently formed a national organization, the Southern Christian Leadership Conference, that brought people of all races from all over the country to the South to fight nonviolently for racial integration. In 1963, King led demonstrations in Birmingham, Alabama, that were met with violence; a bomb was detonated in a black church, killing four young girls. King was arrested for his role in organizing the protests, and while in prison, he wrote the famous "Letter from Birmingham Jail" to answer the criticism of local clergy and to justify to the nation his strategy of civil disobedience, which he called "nonviolent direct action."

King begins his letter by discussing his disappointment with the lack of support he has received from white moderates, such as the group of clergy who published criticism in the local newspaper. As you read this excerpt from his letter, try to infer from King's written response what the clergy's specific criticisms might have been. Also, notice the tone King uses to answer his critics. Would you characterize the writing as apologetic, conciliatory, or accusatory, or would you characterize it in some other way?

An Annotated Sample from "Letter from Birmingham Jail"
Martin Luther King Jr.

I must confess that over the past few years I have been gravely disappointed with the white moderate. I have almost reached the regrettable conclusion that the Negro's [great stumbling block in his stride toward freedom] is not the White Citizen's Counciler or the Ku Klux Klanner, but the white moderate, who is more devoted to "order" than to justice; who prefers a negative peace which is the absence of tension to a positive peace which is the presence of justice; who constantly says: "I agree with you in the goal you seek, but I cannot agree with your methods of direct action"; who (paternalistically) believes he can set the timetable for another man's freedom; who lives by a mythical concept of time and who constantly advises the Negro to wait for a "more convenient season." Shallow understanding from people of good will is more frustrating than absolute misunderstanding from people of ill will. Lukewarm acceptance is much more bewildering than outright rejection.

1

¶1. White moderates block progress

order vs. justice
negative vs. positive

ends vs. means
treating others like children

I had hoped that the white moderate would understand that 2
law and order exist for the purpose of establishing justice and that
when they fail in this purpose they become the [dangerously
structured dams that block the flow of social progress.] I had
hoped that the white moderate would understand that the present
tension in the South is a necessary phase of the transition from an
[obnoxious negative peace,] in which the Negro passively accepted
his unjust plight, to a [substantive and positive peace,] in which
all men will respect the dignity and worth of human personality.
Actually, we who engage in nonviolent direct action are not the cre-
ators of tension. We merely bring to the surface the hidden tension
that is already alive. We bring it out in the open, where it can be
seen and dealt with. [Like a boil that can never be cured so long
as it is covered up but must be opened with all its ugliness to the
natural medicines of air and light, injustice must be exposed, with
all the tension its exposure creates, to the light of human conscience and the air of national opinion before it can be cured.]

¶2. Tension
necessary for
progress.

Tension already
exists anyway.

True?

Simile: hidden
tension is "like a
boil"

In your statement you assert that our actions, even though 3
peaceful, must be condemned because they precipitate violence.
But is this a logical assertion? Isn't this like condemning (a robbed
man) because his possession of money precipitated the evil act of
robbery? Isn't this like condemning (Socrates) because his unswerving commitment to truth and his philosophical inquiries precipitated the act by the misguided populace in which they made him
drink hemlock? Isn't this like condemning (Jesus) because his
unique God-consciousness and never-ceasing devotion to God's
will precipitated the evil act of crucifixion? We must come to see
that, as the federal courts have consistently affirmed, it is wrong to
urge an individual to cease his efforts to gain his basic constitu-
tional rights because the question may precipitate violence. [Soci-
ety must protect the robbed and punish the robber.]

¶3. Questions
clergymen's logic:
condemning his
actions =
condemning victims,
Socrates, Jesus.

Yes!

I had also hoped that the white moderate would reject the 4
myth concerning time in relation to the struggle for freedom. I
have just received a letter from a white brother in Texas. He writes:
"All Christians know that the colored people will receive equal
rights eventually, but it is possible that you are in too great a religious hurry. It has taken Christianity almost two thousand years to
accomplish what it has. The teachings of Christ take time to come
to earth." Such an attitude stems from a tragic misconception of
time, from the strangely irrational notion that there is something in
the very flow of time that will inevitably cure all ills. [Actually, time
itself is neutral; it can be used either destructively or constructively.]
More and more I feel that the people of ill will have used time much
more effectively than have the people of good will. We will have to

example of a white
moderate

repent in this generation not merely for the [hateful words and actions of the bad people] but for the [appalling silence of the good people.] Human progress never rolls in on [wheels of inevitability;] it comes through the tireless efforts of men willing to be co-workers with God, and without this hard work, time itself becomes an ally of the forces of social (stagnation.) [We must use time creatively, in the knowledge that the time is always ripe to do right.] Now is the time to make real the promise of democracy and transform our pending [national elegy] into a creative [psalm of brotherhood.] Now is the time to lift our national policy from the [quicksand of racial injustice] to the [solid rock of human dignity.]

Silence is as bad as hateful words and actions.

metaphor

not moving

¶14. Time must be used to do right.
metaphors

You speak of our activity in Birmingham as extreme. At first I was rather disappointed that fellow clergymen would see my nonviolent efforts as those of an extremist. I began thinking about the fact that I stand in the middle of two opposing forces in the Negro community. One is a [force of complacency,] made up in part of Negroes who, as a result of long years of oppression, are so drained of self-respect and a sense of "somebodiness" that they have adjusted to segregation; and in part of a few middle-class Negroes, who because of a degree of academic and economic security and because in some ways they profit by segregation, have become insensitive to the problems of the masses. The other [force is one of bitterness and hatred,] and it comes perilously close to advocating violence. It is expressed in the various black nationalist [groups that are springing up] across the nation, the largest and best-known being Elijah Muhammad's Muslim movement. Nourished by the Negro's frustration over the continued existence of racial discrimination, this movement is made up of people who have lost faith in America, who have absolutely repudiated Christianity, and who have concluded that the white man is an incorrigible "devil."

5   King accused of being an extremist

¶15. King in middle of two extremes: complacent & angry

Malcolm X?

I have tried to stand between these two forces, saying that we need emulate neither the "do-nothingism" of the complacent nor the hatred and despair of the black nationalist. For there is the more excellent way of love and nonviolent protest. I am grateful to God that, through the influence of the Negro church, the way of nonviolence became an integral part of our struggle.

6   ¶16. King offers better choice.

How did nonviolence become part of King's movement?

If this philosophy had not emerged, by now many streets of the South would, I am convinced, be flowing with blood. And I am further convinced that if our white brothers dismiss as "rabble-rousers" and "outside agitators" those of us who employ nonviolent direct action, and if they refuse to support our nonviolent efforts, millions of Negroes will, out of frustration and despair, seek (solace) and security in black-nationalist ideologies—a development that would inevitably lead to a frightening racial nightmare.

7   ¶17. King's movement prevented racial violence. Threat?

Gandhi?

The church?

If . . . then . . . comfort

(Oppressed people cannot remain oppressed forever.) The 8
yearning for freedom eventually manifests itself, and that is what
has happened to the American Negro. Something within has
reminded him of his birthright of freedom, and something without
has reminded him that it can be gained. Consciously or uncon-
sciously, he has been caught up by the (Zeitgeist,) and with his
black brothers of Africa and his brown and yellow brothers of
Asia, South America and the Caribbean, the United States Negro
is moving with a sense of great urgency toward the [promised
land of racial justice.] If one recognizes this [vital urge that has
engulfed the Negro community,] one should readily understand
why public demonstrations are taking place. The Negro has many
[pent-up resentments] and latent frustrations, and he must release
them. So let him march; let him make prayer pilgrimages to the
city hall; let him go on freedom rides—and try to understand why
he must do so. If his repressed emotions are not released in nonviolent ways, they will seek expression through violence; this is
not a threat but a fact of history. So I have not said to my people:
"Get rid of your discontent." Rather, I have tried to say that this
normal and healthy discontent can be [channeled into the creative outlet of nonviolent direct action.] And now this approach is
being termed extremist.

spirit of the times
worldwide uprising
against injustice

not a threat?

¶8. Discontent is
normal & healthy
but must be
channeled.

But though I was initially disappointed at being categorized 9
as an extremist, as I continued to think about the matter I gradually gained a measure of satisfaction from the label. Was not
Jesus an extremist for love: "Love your enemies, bless them that
curse you, do good to them that hate you, and pray for them which
despitefully use you, and persecute you." Was not (Amos) an
extremist for justice: "Let justice roll down like waters and righ-
teousness like an ever-flowing stream." Was not (Paul) an extremist
for the Christian gospel: "I bear in my body the marks of the Lord
Jesus." Was not (Martin Luther) an extremist: "Here I stand; I cannot
do otherwise, so help me God." And (John Bunyan): "I will stay in jail
to the end of my days before I make a butchery of my conscience."
And (Abraham Lincoln:) "This nation cannot survive half slave and
half free." And (Thomas Jefferson:) "We hold these truths to be self-
evident, that all men are created equal. . . ." So the question is not
whether we will be extremists, but what kind of extremists we will be.
Will we be extremists for hate or for love? Will we be extremists for
the preservation of injustice or for the extension of justice? In that
dramatic scene on Calvary's hill three men were crucified. We
must never forget that all three were crucified for the same crime—
the crime of extremism. Two were extremists for immorality, and
thus fell below their environment. The other, (Jesus Christ,) was an

Hebrew prophet

Christ's disciple

Founded
Protestantism.

English preacher

No choice but to be
extremists. But
what kind?

extremist for love, truth and goodness, and thereby rose above his environment. Perhaps the South, the nation and the world are in dire need of creative extremists.

¶9. Creative extremists are needed.

I had hoped that the white moderate would see this need. Perhaps I was too optimistic; perhaps I expected too much. I suppose I should have realized that few members of the oppressor race can understand the deep groans and passionate yearnings of the oppressed race, and still fewer have the vision to see that injustice must be rooted out by strong, persistent and determined action. I am thankful, however, that some of our white brothers in the South have grasped the meaning of this social revolution and committed themselves to it. They are still all too few in quantity, but they are big in quality. Some—such as Ralph McGill, Lillian Smith, Harry Golden, James McBride Dabbs, Ann Braden and Sarah Patton Boyle—have written about our struggle in eloquent and prophetic terms. Others have marched with us down nameless streets of the South. They have languished in filthy, roach-infested jails, suffering the abuse and brutality of policemen who view them as "dirty nigger-lovers." Unlike so many of their moderate brothers and sisters, they have recognized the urgency of the moment and sensed the need for powerful "action" antidotes to combat the disease of segregation.

10

Disappointed in the white moderate

¶10. Some whites have supported King.

Who are they?

what they did

been left unaided

■ **Checklist: Annotating**

1. Mark the text using notations like these:
- Circle words to be defined in the margin.
- Underline key words and phrases.
- Bracket important sentences and passages.
- Use lines or arrows to connect ideas or words.

2. Write marginal comments like these:
- Number and summarize each paragraph.
- Define unfamiliar words.
- Note responses and questions.
- Identify interesting writing strategies.
- Point out patterns.

3. Layer additional markings on the text and comments in the margins as you reread for different purposes.

TAKING INVENTORY

An inventory is simply a list or grouping of items. *Taking inventory* helps you analyze your annotations for different purposes. When you take inventory, you make various kinds of lists to explore patterns of meaning you find in the text. For instance, in reading the annotated passage by Martin Luther King Jr., you might have noticed that many famous people are named or that certain similes and metaphors are used. By listing the names (Socrates, Jesus, Luther, Lincoln, etc.) and then grouping them into categories (people who died for their beliefs, leaders, teachers, and religious figures) you could better understand why the writer refers to these particular people. Obviously, taking inventory of your annotations can be very helpful in writing about a text you are reading.

Checklist: Taking Inventory

1. Examine your annotations for patterns or repetitions such as recurring images, stylistic features, repeated words and phrases, repeated examples or illustrations, and reliance on particular writing strategies.

2. List and group the items in the pattern.

3. Decide what the pattern indicates about the reading.

OUTLINING

Outlining is an especially helpful critical reading strategy for understanding the content and structure of a reading. *Outlining*, which identifies the text's main ideas, may be part of the annotating process, or it may be done separately. Writing an outline in the margins of the text as you read and annotate makes it easier to find information later. Writing an outline on a separate piece of paper gives you more space to work with; therefore, such an outline usually includes more detail.

The key to outlining is distinguishing between the main ideas and the supporting material such as examples, quotations, statistics, anecdotes, and reasons. The main ideas form the backbone, which holds the various parts and pieces of the text together. Outlining the main ideas helps you uncover this structure.

Making an outline, however, is not simple. The reader must exercise judgment in deciding which are the most important ideas. Because importance is relative, different readers can make different — and equally reasonable — decisions based on what interests them in the reading. Readers also must decide whether to use the writer's words, their own words, or a combination of the two. The words used in an outline reflect the reader's interpretation and emphasis. Reading is never a passive or neutral act; the process of outlining shows how constructive reading can be.

You may make either a formal, multileveled outline with roman (I, II) and arabic (1, 2) numerals together with capital and lowercase letters or an informal scratch outline that lists the main idea of each paragraph. A *formal outline* is harder to make and much more time consuming than a scratch outline. You might choose to make a formal outline of a reading about which you are writing an in-depth analysis or evaluation. For example, here is a formal outline a student wrote for a paper evaluating the logic of the King excerpt. Notice that the student uses roman numerals for the main ideas or claims, capital letters for the reasons, and arabic numerals for supporting evidence and explanation.

Formal Outline

I. The Negro's great stumbling block in his stride toward freedom is . . . the white moderate.
   A. Because the white moderate is more devoted to "order" than to justice (paragraph 2).
      1. Law and order should exist to establish justice.
      2. Law and order compare to dangerously structured dams that block the flow of social progress.
   B. Because the white moderate prefers a negative peace (absence of tension) to a positive peace (justice) (paragraph 2).
      1. The tension already exists.
      2. It is not created by nonviolent direct action.
      3. Society that does not eliminate injustice compares to a boil that hides its infections. Both can be cured only by exposure (boil simile).
   C. Because even though the white moderate agrees with the goals, he does not support the means to achieve them (paragraph 3).
      1. The argument that the means--nonviolent direct action--are wrong because they precipitate violence is flawed.
      2. Analogy of the robbed man condemned because he had money.
      3. Comparison with Socrates and Jesus.
   D. Because the white moderate paternalistically believes he can set a timetable for another man's freedom (paragraph 4).
      1. Rebuts the white moderate's argument that Christianity will cure man's ills and man must wait patiently for that to happen.
      2. Argues that time is neutral and that man must use time creatively for constructive rather than destructive ends.
II. Creative extremism is preferable to moderation.
   A. Classifies himself as a moderate (paragraphs 5-8).

1. I stand between two forces: the complacency of some Negroes and the Black Muslims' rage.
2. If nonviolent direct action were stopped, more violence, not less, would result.
3. "[M]illions of Negroes will, out of frustration and despair, seek solace and security in black-nationalist ideologies" (paragraph 7).
4. Repressed emotions will be expressed--if not in non-violent ways, then through violence (paragraph 8).

B. Redefines himself as a "creative extremist" (para-graph 9).
1. Extremism for love, truth, and goodness is creative extremism.
2. Identifies himself with the creative extremists Jesus, Amos, Paul, Martin Luther, John Bunyan, Abra-ham Lincoln, and Thomas Jefferson.

C. Not all white people are moderates, many are creative extremists (paragraph 10).
1. Lists names of white writers.
2. Refers to white activists.

Making a scratch outline takes less time than making a formal outline, but it still requires careful reading. A *scratch outline* will not record as much information as a formal outline, but it is sufficient for most critical reading purposes. To make a scratch outline, you first need to locate the topic of each paragraph in the reading. The topic is usually stated in a word or phrase, and it may be repeated or referred to throughout the paragraph. For example, the opening paragraph of the King excerpt (p. 304) makes clear that its topic is the white moderate.

After you have found the topic of the paragraph, figure out what is being said about it. To return to our example: King immediately establishes the white moderate as the topic of the opening paragraph, and at the beginning of the second sentence announces the conclusion he has come to — namely, that the white moderate is "the Negro's great stumbling block in his stride toward freedom." The rest of the para-graph specifies the ways the white moderate blocks progress.

The annotations of the King excerpt include a paragraph-by-paragraph outline (look again at the annotated letter). Here is the same outline as it might appear on a separate piece of paper, slightly expanded and reworded:

Paragraph Scratch Outline

¶1. White moderates block progress in the struggle for racial justice.

¶2. Tension is necessary for progress.

¶3. The clergymen's criticism is not logical.

¶4. King justifies urgent use of time.

¶5. Clergymen accuse King of being extreme, but he claims to stand between two extreme forces in the black community.

¶6. King offers a better choice.

¶7. King's movement has prevented racial violence by blacks.

¶8. Discontent is normal and healthy but must be channeled creatively rather than destructively.

¶9. Creative extremists are needed.

¶10. Some whites have supported King.

■ **Checklist: Outlining**

1. Reread each paragraph systematically, identifying the topic and what is being said about it. Do not include examples, specific details, quotations, or other explanatory and supporting material.

2. List the author's main ideas in the margin of the text or on a separate piece of paper.

■ PARAPHRASING

Paraphrasing is restating something you have read using mostly your own words. As a critical reading strategy, paraphrasing can help to clarify the meaning of an obscure or ambiguous passage. It is one of the three ways of integrating other people's ideas and information into your own writing, along with *quoting* (reproducing exactly the language of the source text) and *summarizing* (distilling the main ideas or gist of the source text). You might choose to paraphrase rather than quote when the source's language is not especially arresting or memorable. You might paraphrase short passages but summarize longer ones.

Following are two passages. The first is from paragraph 2 of the excerpt from King's "Letter." The second passage is a paraphrase of the first:

Original

I had hoped that the white moderate would understand that law and order exist for the purpose of establishing justice and that when they fail in this purpose they become the dangerously structured dams that block the flow of social progress. I had hoped that the white moderate would understand that the present tension in the South is a necessary phase of the transition from an obnoxious negative peace, in which the Negro passively accepted his unjust plight, to a substantive and positive peace, in which all men will respect the dignity and worth of human personality.

Paraphrase

> King writes that he had hoped for more understanding from white moderates--specifically that they would recognize that law and order are not ends in themselves but means to the greater end of establishing justice. When law and order do not serve this greater end, they stand in the way of progress. King expected the white moderate to recognize that the current tense situation in the South is part of a transition process that is necessary for progress. The current situation is bad because although there is peace, it is an "obnoxious" and "negative" kind of peace based on blacks passively accepting the injustice of the status quo. A better kind of peace, one that is "substantive," real and not imaginary, as well as "positive," requires that all people, regardless of race, be valued.

When you compare the paraphrase to the original, you can see that the paraphrase contains all the important information and ideas of the original. Notice also that the paraphrase is somewhat longer than the original, refers to the writer by name, and encloses King's original words in quotation marks. Although the paraphrase tries to be neutral, to avoid inserting the reader's opinions or distorting the original writer's ideas, it does inevitably express the reader's interpretation of the original text's meaning. Another reader might paraphrase the same passage differently.

■ Checklist: Paraphrasing

1. Reread the passage to be paraphrased, looking up unfamiliar words in a college dictionary.
2. Translate the passage into your own words, putting quotation marks around any words or phrases you quote from the original.
3. Revise to ensure coherence.

■ SUMMARIZING

Summarizing is one of the most widely used strategies for critical reading because it helps the reader understand and remember what is most important in the reading. Another advantage of summarizing is that it creates a condensed version of the reading's ideas and information, which can be referred to later or inserted into the reader's own writing. Along with quoting and paraphrasing, summarizing enables you to refer to and integrate other writers' ideas into your own writing.

A summary is a relatively brief restatement, primarily in the reader's own words, of the reading's main ideas. Summaries vary in length, depending on the reader's purpose. Some summaries are very brief—a sentence or even a subordinate clause. For example, if you were referring to the excerpt from "Letter from Birmingham Jail" and simply needed to indicate how it relates to your other sources, your summary might focus on only one aspect of the reading. It might look something like this: "There have always been advocates of extremism in politics. Martin Luther King Jr., in 'Letter from Birmingham Jail,' for instance, defends nonviolent civil disobedience as an extreme but necessary means of bringing about racial justice." If, on the other hand, you were surveying the important texts of the civil rights movement, you might write a longer, more detailed summary that not only identifies the reading's main ideas but also shows how the ideas relate to one another.

Many writers find it useful to outline the reading as a preliminary to writing a summary. A paragraph scratch outline (like the one on pp. 311–12) lists the reading's main ideas in the sequence in which they appear in the original. But summarizing requires more than merely stringing together the entries in an outline. It fills in the logical connections between the author's ideas. Notice in the following example that the reader repeats selected words and phrases and refers to the author by name, indicating, with verbs like *expresses, acknowledges,* and *explains,* the writer's purpose and strategy at each point in the argument.

Summary

King expresses his disappointment with white moderates who, by opposing his program of nonviolent direct action, have become a barrier to progress toward racial justice. He acknowledges that his program has raised tension in the South, but he explains that tension is necessary to bring about change. Furthermore, he argues that tension already exists. But because it has been unexpressed, it is unhealthy and potentially dangerous.

He defends his actions against the clergy's criticisms, particularly their argument that he is in too much of a hurry. Responding to charges of extremism, King claims that he has actually prevented racial violence by channeling the natural frustrations of oppressed blacks into nonviolent protest. He asserts that extremism is precisely what is needed now--but it must be creative, rather than destructive, extremism. He concludes by again expressing disappointment with white moderates for not joining his effort as some other whites have.

■ **Checklist: Summarizing**

1. Make a paragraph scratch outline of the reading.

2. Write a paragraph or more that presents the author's main ideas largely in your own words. Use the outline as a guide, but reread parts of the original text as necessary.

3. To make the summary coherent, fill in connections between ideas.

■ SYNTHESIZING

Synthesizing involves presenting ideas and information gleaned from different sources. As a critical reading strategy, synthesizing can help you see how different sources relate to one another—for example, offering supporting details or opposing arguments.

When you synthesize material from different sources, you construct a conversation among your sources, a conversation in which you also participate. Synthesizing contributes most to critical thinking when writers use sources not only to support their ideas, but to challenge and extend them as well.

In the following example, the reader uses a variety of sources related to the King passage (pp. 304–8). The synthesis brings the sources together around a central idea. Notice how quotation, paraphrase, and summary are all used to present King's and the other sources' ideas.

Synthesis

When King defends his campaign of nonviolent direct action against the clergymen's criticism that "our actions, even though peaceful, must be condemned because they precipitate violence" (King excerpt, paragraph 3), he is using what Vinit Haksar calls Mohandas Gandhi's "safety-valve argument" ("Civil Disobedience and Non-Cooperation" 117). According to Haksar, Gandhi gave a "non-threatening warning of worse things to come" if his demands were not met. King similarly makes clear that advocates of actions more extreme than those he advocates are waiting in the wings: "The other force is one of bitterness and hatred, and it comes perilously close to advocating violence" (King excerpt, paragraph 5). King identifies this force with Elijah Muhammad, and although he does not name him, King's contemporary readers would have known that he was referring also to Malcolm X who, according to Herbert J. Storing, "urged that Negroes take seriously the idea of revolution" ("The Case against Civil Disobedience" 90). In fact, Malcolm X accused King of

```
being a modern-day Uncle Tom, trying "to keep us under con-
trol, to keep us passive and peaceful and nonviolent" (Mal-
colm X Speaks 12).
```

■ **Checklist: Synthesizing**

1. Find and read a variety of sources on your topic, annotating the passages that give you ideas about the topic.

2. Look for patterns among your sources, possibly supporting or refuting your ideas or those of other sources.

3. Write a paragraph or more synthesizing your sources, using quotation, paraphrase, and summary to present what they say on the topic.

■ CONTEXTUALIZING

All texts were written sometime in the past and therefore may embody historical and cultural assumptions, values, and attitudes different from your own. To read critically, you need to become aware of these differences. *Contextualizing* is a critical reading strategy that enables you to make inferences about a reading's historical and cultural context and to examine the differences between its context and your own.

The excerpt from King's "Letter from Birmingham Jail" is a good example of a text that benefits from being read contextually. If you knew little about the history of slavery and segregation in the United States, Martin Luther King Jr., or the civil rights movement, it would be very difficult to understand the passion for justice and impatience with delay expressed in this passage from King's writings. To understand the historical and cultural context in which King organized his demonstrations and wrote his "Letter from Birmingham Jail," you could do some library or Internet research. A little research would enable you to appreciate the intense emotions that swept the nation at the time. You would see that the threat of violence was all too real. Comparing the situation at the time King wrote the "Letter" in 1963 to situations with which you are familiar would help you understand some of your own attitudes toward King and the civil rights movement.

Here is what one reader wrote to contextualize King's writing:

Notes from a Contextualized Reading

```
1. I am not old enough to remember what it was like in the
   early 1960s when Dr. King was leading marches and sit-ins,
   but I have seen television documentaries showing demonstra-
   tors being attacked by dogs, doused by fire hoses, beaten and
   dragged by helmeted police. Such images give me a sense of
   the violence, fear, and hatred that King was responding to.
```

The tension King writes about comes across in his writing. He uses his anger and frustration creatively to inspire his critics. He also threatens them, although he denies it. I saw a film on Malcolm X, so I could see that King was giving white people a choice between his own nonviolent way and Malcolm's more confrontational way.

2. Things have certainly changed since the sixties. Legal segregation has ended, but there are still racists like the detective in the O. J. Simpson trial. African Americans like General Colin Powell are highly respected and powerful. The civil rights movement is over. So when I'm reading King today, I feel like I'm reading history. But then again, every once in a while there are reports of police brutality because of race (think of Rodney King) and of what we now call hate crimes.

■ Checklist: Contextualizing

1. Describe the historical and cultural situation as it is represented in the reading and in other sources with which you are familiar. Your knowledge may come from other reading, television or film, school, or elsewhere. (If you know nothing about the historical and cultural context, you could do some library or Internet research.)

2. Compare the historical and cultural situation in which the text was written to your own historical and cultural situation. Consider how your understanding and judgment of the reading is affected by your own context.

■ EXPLORING THE SIGNIFICANCE OF FIGURATIVE LANGUAGE

Figurative language—metaphor, simile, and symbolism—enhances literal meaning by embodying abstract ideas in vivid images and by evoking feelings and associations.

Metaphor implicitly compares two different things by identifying them with each other. For instance, when King calls the white moderate "the Negro's great stumbling block in his stride toward freedom" (paragraph 1), he does not mean that the white moderate literally trips the Negro who is attempting to walk toward freedom. The sentence makes sense only if understood figuratively: The white moderate trips up the Negro by frustrating every effort to achieve justice.

Simile, a more explicit form of comparison, uses the word *like* or *as* to signal the relationship of two seemingly unrelated things. King uses simile when he says that injustice is "like a boil that can never be cured so long as it is covered up" (paragraph 2). This simile makes several points of comparison between injustice and a boil. It suggests that injustice is a disease of society as a boil is a disease of the body and that injustice, like a boil, must be exposed or it will fester and infect the entire body.

Symbolism compares two things by making one stand for the other. King uses the white moderate as a symbol for supposed liberals and would-be supporters of civil rights who are actually frustrating the cause.

How these figures of speech are used in a text reveals something of the writer's feelings about the subject. Exploring possible meanings in a text's figurative language involves (1) annotating and then listing the metaphors, similes, and symbols you find in a reading; (2) grouping the figures of speech that appear to express related feelings or attitudes, and labeling each group; and (3) writing to explore the meaning of the patterns you have found.

The following example shows the process of exploring figures of speech in the King excerpt.

Listing Figures of Speech

```
order is a dangerously structured dam

social progress should flow

stumbling block in the stride toward freedom

injustice is like a boil that can never be cured

the light of human conscience and air of national opinion

quicksand of racial injustice
```

Grouping Figures of Speech

<u>Sickness:</u> Segregation is a disease; action is healthy, the only antidote; injustice is like a boil . . .

<u>Underground:</u> Tension is hidden; resentments are pent up, repressed; injustice must be rooted out . . .

<u>Blockage:</u> The dam, stumbling block; human progress never rolls in on wheels of inevitability; social progress should flow . . .

Writing to Explore Meaning

The patterns labeled <u>underground</u> and <u>blockage</u> suggest a feeling of frustration. Inertia is a problem; movement forward toward progress or upward toward the promised land is stalled. The strong need to break through the resistance may represent King's feelings both about his attempt to lead purposeful, effective demonstrations and his effort to write a convincing argument.

The simile of injustice being "like a boil" links the two patterns of underground and sickness, suggesting something bad, a disease, is inside the people or the society. The cure is to expose or to root out the blocked hatred and injustice as well as to release the tension or emotion that has long been repressed. This implies that repression itself is the evil, not simply what is repressed. Therefore, writing and speaking out through political action may have curative power for individuals and society alike.

■ Checklist: Exploring the Significance of Figurative Language

1. Annotate and then list all the figures of speech you find in the reading — metaphors, similes, and symbols.

2. Group the figures of speech that appear to express related feelings and attitudes, and label each group.

3. Write one or two paragraphs exploring the meaning of these patterns. What do they tell you about the text?

■ LOOKING FOR PATTERNS OF OPPOSITION

All texts carry within themselves voices of opposition. These voices may echo the views and values of critical readers the writer anticipates or predecessors to whom the writer is responding in some way; they may even reflect the writer's own conflicting values. Careful readers look closely for such a dialogue of opposing voices within the text.

When we think of oppositions, we ordinarily think of polarities: *yes* and *no, up* and *down, black* and *white, new* and *old*. Some oppositions, however, may be more subtle. The excerpt from King's "Letter from Birmingham Jail" is rich in such oppositions: *moderate* versus *extremist, order* versus *justice, direct action* versus *passive acceptance, expression* versus *repression*. These oppositions are not accidental; they form a significant pattern that gives a critical reader important information about the essay.

A careful reading will show that King always values one of the two terms in an opposition over the other. In the passage, for example, *extremist* is valued over *moderate* (paragraph 9). This preference for extremism is surprising. The critical reader should ask why, when white extremists like the Ku Klux Klan have committed so many outrages against African Americans, King would prefer extremism. If King is trying to convince his readers to accept his point of view, why would he represent himself as an extremist? Moreover, why would a clergyman advocate extremism instead of moderation?

Studying the *patterns of opposition* enables you to answer these questions. You will see that King sets up this opposition to force his readers to examine their own values and realize that they are in fact misplaced. Instead of working toward justice, he says, those who support law and order maintain the unjust status quo. By getting his readers to think of white moderates as blocking rather than facilitating peaceful change, King brings them to align themselves with him and perhaps even embrace his strategy of nonviolent resistance.

Looking for patterns of opposition involves annotating words or phrases in the reading that indicate oppositions, listing the opposing terms in pairs, deciding which term in each pair is preferred by the writer, and reflecting on the meaning of the patterns. Here is a partial list of oppositions from the King excerpt, with the preferred terms marked by an asterisk:

Listing Patterns of Opposition

moderate	*extremist
order	*justice
negative peace	*positive peace
absence of justice	*presence of justice
goals	*methods
*direct action	passive acceptance
*exposed tension	hidden tension

■ **Checklist: Looking for Patterns of Opposition**

1. Annotate the selection for words or phrases indicating oppositions.

2. List the pairs of oppositions. (You may have to paraphrase or even supply the opposite word or phrase if it is not stated directly in the text.)

3. For each pair of oppositions, put an asterisk next to the term that the writer seems to value or prefer over the other.

4. Study the patterns of opposition. How do they contribute to your understanding of the essay? What do they tell you about what the author wants you to believe?

■ REFLECTING ON CHALLENGES TO YOUR BELIEFS AND VALUES

To read critically, you need to scrutinize your own assumptions and attitudes as well as those expressed in the text you are reading. If you are like most readers, however, you will find that your assumptions and attitudes are so ingrained that you are not fully aware of them. A good strategy for getting at these underlying beliefs and values is to identify and reflect on the ways the text challenges you, how it makes you feel—disturbed, threatened, ashamed, combative, or some other way.

For example, here is what one student wrote about the King passage:

Reflections

In paragraph 1, Dr. King criticizes people who are "more devoted to 'order' than to justice." This criticism upsets me because today I think I would choose order over justice. When I analyze my feelings and try to figure out where they come from, I realize that what I feel most is fear. I am terrified by the violence in society today. I'm afraid of sociopaths who don't respect the rule of law, much less the value of human life.

I know Dr. King was writing in a time when the law itself was unjust, when order was apparently used to keep people from protesting and changing the law. But things are different now. Today, justice seems to serve criminals more than it serves law-abiding citizens. That's why I'm for order over justice.

■ Checklist: Reflecting on Challenges to Your Beliefs and Values

1. Identify challenges by marking the text where you feel your beliefs and values are being opposed, criticized, or unfairly characterized.

2. Write a few paragraphs reflecting on why you feel challenged. Do not defend your feelings; instead, analyze them to see where they come from.

■ EVALUATING THE LOGIC OF AN ARGUMENT

An argument includes a thesis backed by reasons and support. The *thesis* asserts an idea, a position on a controversial issue, or a solution to a problem that the writer wants readers to accept. The *reasons* tell readers why they should accept the thesis and the *support* (such as examples, statistics, authorities, and textual evidence) gives readers grounds for accepting it. For an argument to be considered logically acceptable, it must meet the three conditions of what we call the ABC test:

The ABC Test

A. The reasons and support must be *appropriate* to the thesis.

B. The reasons and support must be *believable*.

C. The reasons and support must be *consistent* with one another as well as *complete*.

(For more on argument, see Chapter 11. For an example of the ABC test, see Christine Romano's essay in Chapter 7, pp. 245–48.)

Testing for Appropriateness

As a critical reader, you must decide whether the argument's reasons and support are appropriate and clearly related to the thesis. To test for appropriateness, ask these questions: How does each reason or piece of support relate to the thesis? Is the connection between reasons and support and the thesis clear and compelling? Or is the argument irrelevant or only vaguely related to the thesis?

Readers most often question the appropriateness of reasons and support when the writer argues by analogy or by invoking authority. For example, in paragraph 2, King argues that when law and order fail to establish justice, "they become the dangerously structured dams that block the flow of social progress." The analogy asserts the following logical relationship: Law and order are to progress toward justice what a dam is to water. If you do not accept this analogy, the argument fails the test of appropriateness.

King uses both analogy and authority in the following passage: "Isn't this like condemning Socrates because his unswerving commitment to truth and his philosophical inquiries precipitated the act by the misguided populace in which they made him drink hemlock?" (paragraph 3). Not only must you judge the appropriateness of the analogy comparing the Greek populace's condemnation of Socrates to the white moderates' condemnation of King, but you must also judge whether it is appropriate to accept Socrates as an authority on this subject. Since Socrates is generally respected for his teaching on justice, his words and actions are likely to be considered appropriate to King's situation in Birmingham. (For more on invoking authorities, see Chapter 11, pp. 333–34.)

Testing for Believability

Believability is a measure of your willingness to accept as true the reasons and support the writer gives in defense of a thesis.

To test for believability, ask: On what basis am I being asked to believe this reason or support is true? If it cannot be proved true or false, how much weight does it carry?

In judging facts, examples, statistics, and authorities, consider the following points.

Facts are statements that can be proved objectively to be true. The believability of facts depends on their *accuracy* (they should not distort or misrepresent reality), their *completeness* (they should not omit important details), and the *trustworthiness* of their sources (sources should be qualified and unbiased). King, for instance, asserts as fact that the African American will not wait much longer for racial justice (paragraph 8). His critics might question the factuality of this assertion by asking, is it true of all African Americans? How much longer will they wait? How does King know what African Americans will and will not do?

Examples and *anecdotes* are particular instances that may or may not make you believe a general statement. The believability of examples depends on their *representativeness* (whether they are truly typical and thus generalizable) and their *specificity* (whether particular details make them seem true to life). Even if a vivid example or gripping anecdote does not convince readers, it usually strengthens argumentative writing by clarifying the meaning and dramatizing the point. In paragraph 5 of the King excerpt, for example, King supports his generalization that some African American nationalist extremists are motivated by bitterness and hatred by citing the specific example of Elijah Muhammad's Black Muslim movement. Conversely, in paragraph 9, he refers to Jesus, Paul, Luther, and others as examples of extremists motivated by love and Christianity. These examples support his assertion that extremism is not in itself wrong and that any judgment of extremism must be based on its motivation and cause.

Statistics are numerical data, including correlations. The believability of statistics depends on the *comparability* of the data (the price of apples in 1985 cannot be compared to the price of apples in 2002 unless the figures are adjusted to account for inflation), the *precision* of the methods employed to gather and analyze data (representative samples should be used and variables accounted for), and the *trustworthiness* of the sources (sources should be qualified, unbiased, and—except in historical contexts—as recent as possible).

Authorities are people to whom the writer attributes expertise on a given subject. Not only must such authorities be appropriate, as mentioned earlier, but they must be believable as well. The believability of authorities depends on their *credibility,* on whether the reader accepts them as experts on the topic at hand. King cites authorities repeatedly throughout his essay. He refers to religious leaders (Jesus and Luther) as well as to American political leaders (Lincoln and Jefferson). These figures are certain to have a high degree of credibility among King's readers.

Testing for Consistency and Completeness

In looking for consistency, you should be concerned that all the parts of the argument work together and that none of the reasons or support contradict any of the other reasons or support. In addition, the reasons and support, taken together, should be sufficient to convince readers to accept the thesis or at least take it seriously. To test for consistency and completeness, ask: Are any of the reasons and support contradictory? Do they provide sufficient grounds for accepting the thesis? Does the writer fail to counterargue—to acknowledge, accommodate, or refute any opposing arguments or important objections? (For more on counterarguing, see Chapter 11, pp. 337–41.)

A critical reader might regard as contradictory King's characterizing himself first as a moderate between the forces of complacency and violence and later as an extremist opposed to the forces of violence. King attempts to reconcile this apparent contradiction by explicitly redefining extremism in paragraph 9. Similarly, the fact that King fails to examine and refute every legal recourse available to his cause might allow a critical reader to question the sufficiency of his argument.

■ **Checklist: Evaluating the Logic of an Argument**

Use the ABC test:

A. *Test for appropriateness* by checking that the reasons and support are clearly and directly related to the thesis.

B. *Test for believability* by deciding whether you can accept the reasons and support as true.

C. *Test for consistency and completeness* by ascertaining whether there are any contradictions in the argument and whether any important objections or opposing arguments have been ignored.

■ RECOGNIZING EMOTIONAL MANIPULATION

Many different kinds of essays appeal to readers' emotions. Rick Bragg's remembered event essay (in Chapter 2) may be sobering for some readers, Brian Cable's profile (in Chapter 3) may be disturbing, and Mariah Burton Nelson's position paper (in Chapter 5) may be annoying to some readers because of her strong tone.

Writers often try to arouse emotions in readers to excite their interest, make them care, or move them to take action. There is nothing wrong with appealing to readers' emotions. What is wrong is manipulating readers with false or exaggerated appeals. As a critical reader, you should be suspicious of writing that is overly or falsely sentimental, that cites alarming statistics and frightening anecdotes, that demonizes others and identifies itself with revered authorities, or that uses symbols (flag-waving) or emotionally loaded words (such as *racist*).

King, for example, uses the emotionally loaded word *paternalistically* to refer to the white moderate's belief that "he can set the timetable for another man's freedom" (paragraph 1). In the same paragraph, King uses symbolism to get an emotional reaction from readers when he compares the white moderate to the "Ku Klux Klanner." To get readers to accept his ideas, he also relies on authorities whose names evoke the greatest respect, such as Jesus and Lincoln. But some readers might object that comparing King's crusade to that of Jesus and other leaders of religious and political groups is pretentious and manipulative. A critical reader might also consider King's discussion of African American extremists in paragraph 7 to be a veiled threat designed to frighten readers into agreement.

■ **Checklist: Recognizing Emotional Manipulation**

1. Annotate places in the text where you sense emotional appeals are being used.
2. Assess whether any of the emotional appeals are unfairly manipulative.

■ JUDGING THE WRITER'S CREDIBILITY

Writers often try to persuade readers to respect and believe them. Because readers may not know them personally or even by reputation, writers must present an image of themselves in their writing that will gain their readers' confidence. This image cannot be made directly but must be made indirectly, through the arguments, language, and system of values and beliefs expressed or implied in the writing. Writers establish credibility in their writing in three ways:

By showing their knowledge of the subject

By building common ground with readers

By responding fairly to objections and opposing arguments

Testing for Knowledge

Writers demonstrate their knowledge through the facts and statistics they marshal, the sources they rely on for information, and the scope and depth of their understanding. As a critical reader, you may not be sufficiently expert on the subject yourself to know whether the facts are accurate, the sources are reliable, and the understanding is sufficient. You may need to do some research to see what others say about the subject. You can also check credentials—the writer's educational and professional qualifications, the respectability of the publication in which the selection first appeared, and reviews of the writer's work—to determine whether the writer is a respected authority in the field. For example, King brings with him the authority that comes from being a member of the clergy and a respected leader of the Southern Christian Leadership Conference.

Testing for Common Ground

One way writers can establish common ground with their readers is by basing their reasoning on shared values, beliefs, and attitudes. They use language that includes their readers *(we)* rather than excludes them *(they)*. They qualify their assertions to keep them from being too extreme. Above all, they acknowledge differences of opinion and try to make room in their argument to accommodate reasonable differences. As a critical reader, you want to notice such appeals.

King creates common ground with readers by using the inclusive pronoun *we*, suggesting shared concerns between himself and his audience. Notice, however, his use of masculine pronouns and other references ("the Negro . . . he," "our brothers"). Although King addressed his letter to male clergy, he intended it to be published in the local newspaper, where it would be read by an audience of both men and women. By using language that excludes women, a common practice at the time the selection was written, King misses the opportunity to build common ground with half of his readers.

Testing for Fairness

Writers reveal their character by how they handle opposing arguments and objections to their argument. As a critical reader, you want to pay particular attention to how writers treat possible differences of opinion. Be suspicious of those who ignore differences and pretend that everyone agrees with their viewpoints. When objections or opposing views are represented, consider whether they have been distorted in any way; if they are refuted, be sure they are challenged fairly—with sound reasoning and solid support.

One way to gauge the author's credibility is to identify the tone of the argument, for it conveys the writer's attitude toward the subject and toward the reader. Examine the text carefully for indications of tone: Is the text angry? Sarcastic? Evenhanded? Shrill? Condescending? Bullying? Do you feel as if the writer is treating the subject— and you, as a reader—with fairness? King's tone might be characterized in different passages as patient (he doesn't lose his temper), respectful (he refers to white moderates as "people of good will"), or pompous (comparing himself to Jesus and Socrates).

■ **Checklist: Judging the Writer's Credibility**

1. Make annotations about credibility—whether the writer demonstrates knowledge of the subject, establishes common ground, and deals fairly with objections and opposing arguments.

2. Decide what in the essay you find credible and what you question.

Strategies for Arguing

Arguing involves reasoning as well as making assertions. When you write an essay in which you assert a point of view, you are obliged to come up with reasons for your point of view and to find ways to support your reasons. In addition to arguing for your point of view, you must think carefully about what your readers know and believe in order to argue against—to *counterargue*—opposing points of view. If you ignore what your readers may be thinking, you will be unlikely to convince them to take your argument seriously.

This chapter presents the basic strategies for making assertions and reasoning about a writing situation. We focus on asserting a thesis, backing it up with reasons and support, and anticipating readers' questions and objections.

■ ASSERTING A THESIS

Central to any argument is the thesis—the point of view the writer wants readers to consider. The *thesis statement* may appear at the beginning of the essay or at the end, but wherever it is placed, its job is simple: to announce as clearly and straightforwardly as possible the main point the writer is trying to make in the essay. (For more on thesis statements, see p. 273–74.)

There are three different kinds of argumentative essays in Part One of this book. Each of these essays requires a special kind of assertion and reasoning. Here we first define each type of assertion and suggest a question it is designed to answer. Then we illustrate each assertion and question with a thesis from a reading in Chapters 5–7:

- *Assertion of opinion.* What is your position on a controversial issue? (Chapter 5, "Arguing a Position")

  When overzealous parents and coaches impose adult standards on children's sports, the result can be activities that are neither satisfying nor beneficial to children.
  —JESSICA STATSKY, "Children Need to Play, Not Compete"

- *Assertion of policy.* What is your understanding of a problem, and what do you think should be done to solve it? (Chapter 6, "Proposing a Solution")

Although this last-minute anxiety about midterm and final exams is only too familiar to most college students, many professors may not realize how such major, infrequent, high-stakes exams work against the best interests of students both psychologically and intellectually. . . . If professors gave additional brief exams at frequent intervals, students would be spurred to study more regularly, learn more, worry less, and perform better.

— PATRICK O'MALLEY, "More Testing, More Learning"

- *Assertion of evaluation.* What is your judgment of a subject? (Chapter 7, "Justifying an Evaluation")

The movie is a disappointment. A big one.

— DAVID ANSEN, "*Star Wars:* The Phantom Movie"

As these different thesis statements indicate, the kind of thesis you assert depends on the occasion for which you are writing and the question you are trying to answer for your readers. Whatever the writing situation, to be effective, every thesis must satisfy the same three standards: it must be *arguable, clear,* and *appropriately qualified.*

Arguable Assertions

Reasoned argument seems called for when informed people disagree over an issue or remain divided over how best to solve a problem, as is so often the case in social and political life. Hence the thesis statement in a reasoned argument asserts possibilities or probabilities, not certainties. Argument becomes useful in situations in which there are uncertainties, situations in which established knowledge and facts cannot provide the answers.

Therefore, a statement of fact could not be an arguable thesis statement because facts are easy to verify—whether by checking an authoritative reference book, asking an authority, or observing the fact with your own eyes. For example, these statements assert facts:

Jem will be thirty-six years old on May 6, 2008.
I am less than five feet tall.
Eucalyptus trees were originally imported into California from Australia.

Each of these assertions can be easily verified. To find out Jem's age, you can ask him or look at his driver's license, among other things. To determine a person's height, you can use a tape measure. To discover where California got its eucalyptus trees, you can refer to a source in the library. There is no point in arguing over such statements (though you might question the authority of a particular source or the accuracy of someone's measurement). If a writer were to assert something as fact and attempt to support the assertion with authorities or statistics, the essay would be considered not an argument but a report of information.

Like facts, expressions of personal feelings are not arguable assertions. Whereas facts are unarguable because they can be definitively proved true or false, feelings are unarguable because they are purely subjective. Personal feelings can be explained, but it would be unreasonable to attempt to convince others to change their views or take action solely on the basis of your personal feelings.

You can declare, for example, that you love Ben & Jerry's Chunky Monkey ice cream or that you detest eight o'clock classes, but you cannot offer an argument to support such assertions. All you can do is explain why you feel as you do. Even though many people agree with you about eight o'clock classes, it would be pointless to try to convince others to share your feelings. If, however, you were to restate the assertion as "Eight o'clock classes are counterproductive," you could then construct an argument that does not depend solely on your subjective feelings, memories, or preferences. Your argument could be based on reasons and support that apply to others as well as to yourself. For example, you might argue that students' ability to learn is at an especially low ebb immediately after breakfast and provide scientific support, in addition, perhaps, to personal experience and interviews with your friends.

Clear and Precise Wording

The way a thesis is worded is as important as its arguability. The wording of a thesis, especially its key terms, must be clear and precise.

Consider the following assertion: "Democracy is a way of life." The meaning of this claim is uncertain, partly because the word *democracy* is abstract and partly because the phrase *way of life* is inexact. Abstract ideas like democracy, freedom, and patriotism are by their very nature hard to grasp, and they become even less clear with overuse. Too often, such words take on connotations that may obscure the meaning you want to emphasize. *Way of life* is fuzzy: What does it mean? Moreover, can a form of government be a way of life? It depends on what is meant by *way of life*. Does it refer to daily life, to a general philosophy or attitude toward life, or to something else?

Thus a thesis is vague if its meaning is unclear; it is ambiguous if it has more than one possible meaning. For example, the statement "My English instructor is mad" can be understood in two ways: The teacher is either angry or insane. Obviously, these are two very different assertions. You would not want readers to think you mean one when you actually mean the other.

Whenever you write argument, you should pay special attention to the way you phrase your thesis and take care to avoid vague and ambiguous language.

Appropriate Qualification

In addition to being arguable and clear, an argument thesis must suit your writing situation. If you are confident that your case is so strong that readers will accept your argument without question, state your thesis emphatically and unconditionally. If, however, you expect readers to challenge your assumptions or conclusions, you must qualify your statement. Qualifying a thesis makes it more likely that readers will take it seriously. Expressions like *probably, very likely, apparently,* and *it seems* all serve to qualify a thesis.

■ **Exercise 11.1**

Write an assertion of opinion that states your position on one of the following contro-versial issues:

Should English be the official language of the United States and the only language used in local, state, and federal government agencies in oral and written communica-tions?

Should women serve in combat positions in the military?

Should fathers have an equal chance of gaining custody after a divorce?

Should girls and boys be treated differently by their families or schools?

Should schools attempt to teach spiritual and moral values?

These issues are complicated and have been debated for a long time. Constructing a persuasive argument would obviously require careful deliberation and research. For this exercise, however, all you need to do is construct a thesis on the issue you have chosen, a thesis that is arguable, clear, and appropriately qualified.

■ **Exercise 11.2**

Find the thesis in one of the argument essays in Chapters 5–7. Then decide whether the thesis meets the three requirements: that it be arguable, clear, and appropriately qualified.

■ **Exercise 11.3**

If you have written or are currently working on one of the argument assignments in Chapters 5–7, consider whether your essay's thesis meets the three requirements: that it be arguable, clear, and appropriately qualified. If you believe it does not meet the requirements, revise it appropriately.

■ GIVING REASONS AND SUPPORT

Whether you are arguing a position, proposing a solution, or justifying an evaluation, you need to give reasons and support for your thesis.

Reasons can be thought of as the main points arguing for a thesis. Often they answer the question "Why do you think so?" For example, if you assert among friends that you value a certain movie highly, one of your friends might ask, "Why do you like it so much?" And you might answer, "*Because* it has challenging ideas, unusual camera work, and memorable acting." Similarly, you might oppose restrictions on students' use of offensive language at your college *because* the restrictions would make students reluctant to enter into frank debates on important issues, offensive speech is hard to define, and such restrictions violate the free-speech clause of the First Amendment. These *because* phrases are your reasons. You may have one or many reasons, depend-ing on your subject and your writing situation.

For your argument to succeed with your readers, you must not only give reasons but also provide support. The main kinds of *support* writers use are examples, statistics, authorities, anecdotes, and textual evidence. Following is a discussion and illustration of each kind, along with standards for judging the reliability of that particular type of support.

Examples

Examples may be used as support in all types of arguments. They are an effective way to demonstrate that your reasons should be taken seriously. For examples to be believable and convincing, they must be representative (typical of all the relevant examples you might have chosen), consistent with the experience of your readers (familiar and not extreme), and adequate in number (numerous enough to be convincing and yet selective and not likely to overwhelm readers).

The following passage comes from a book on illiteracy in America by Jonathan Kozol, a prominent educator and writer. In these paragraphs, Kozol presents several examples to support a part of his argument that the human costs of illiteracy are high.

> Illiterates cannot read the menu in a restaurant.
>
> They cannot read the cost of items on the menu in the *window* of the restaurant before they enter.
>
> Illiterates cannot read the letters that their children bring home from their teachers. They cannot study school department circulars that tell them of the courses that their children must be taking if they hope to pass the SAT exams. They cannot help with homework. They cannot write a letter to the teacher. They are afraid to visit in the classroom. They do not want to humiliate their child or themselves.
>
> Illiterates cannot read instructions on a bottle of prescription medicine. They cannot find out when a medicine is past the year of safe consumption; nor can they read of allergenic risks, warnings to diabetics, or the potential sedative effect of certain kinds of nonprescription pills. They cannot observe preventive health care admonitions. They cannot read about "the seven warnings signs of cancer" or the indications of blood-sugar fluctuations or the risks of eating certain foods that aggravate the likelihood of cardiac arrest.
>
> —JONATHAN KOZOL, *Illiterate America*

These examples probably seem to most readers to be representative of all the examples Kozol collected in his many interviews with people who could neither read nor write. Though all of his readers are literate and have never experienced the frustrations of adult illiterates, Kozol assumes they can recognize that the experiences are a familiar part of illiterates' lives. Most readers will believe the experiences to be neither atypical nor extreme.

■ Exercise 11.4

Turn to the Readings section in Chapter 5, and underline the examples in paragraphs 9 and 11 of Jessica Statsky's essay and paragraphs 9–12 of Mariah Burton Nelson's. (If you have not read the essays, pause to skim them so that you can evaluate each writer's use of examples within the context of the entire essay.) How well do the examples—individually and as a set—meet the standards of representativeness, consistency with experience of readers, and adequacy in number? You will not have all the information you need to evaluate the examples—you rarely do unless you are an expert on the subject—but make the best judgment you can based on the information available to you in the headnotes and the essays.

Statistics

In many kinds of arguments about economic, educational, or social issues, statistics may be essential. When you use *statistics* in your own arguments, you will want to ensure that they are up to date (they should be current, the best presently available facts on the subject), relevant (they should be appropriate for your argument), and accurate (they should not distort or misrepresent the subject). In addition, take care to select statistics from reliable sources and to use statistics from the sources in which they originally appeared if at all possible. For example, you would want to get medical statistics from a reputable and authoritative professional periodical like the *New England Journal of Medicine* rather than from a supermarket tabloid or an unaffiliated Web site. If you are uncertain about the most authoritative sources, ask a reference librarian or a professor who knows about your topic.

The following selection comes from an argument speculating about the decline of civic life in the United States. Civic life includes all of the clubs, organizations, and activities people choose to participate in. The author, a Harvard University professor, believes that since the early 1960s, Americans have participated less and less in civic life because they have been spending more and more time watching television. In these paragraphs, he uses statistics to support this possible causal relationship.

The culprit is television.

First, the timing fits. The long civic generation was the last cohort of Americans to grow up without television, for television flashed into American society like lightning in the 1950s. In 1950 barely 10 percent of American homes had television sets, but by 1959, 90 percent did, probably the fastest diffusion of a major technological innovation ever recorded. The reverberations from this lightning bolt continued for decades, as viewing hours grew by 17–20 percent during the 1960s and by an additional 7–8 percent during the 1970s. In the early years, TV watching was concentrated among the less educated sectors of the population, but during the 1970s the viewing time of the more educated sectors of the population began to converge upward. Television viewing increases with age, particularly upon retirement, but each generation since the introduction of television has begun its life cycle at a higher starting point. By 1995 viewing per TV household was more than 50 percent higher than it had been in the 1950s.

Most studies estimate that the average American now watches roughly four hours per day (excluding periods in which television is merely playing in the background). Even a more conservative estimate of three hours means that television absorbs 40 percent of the average American's free time, an increase of about one-third since 1965. Moreover, multiple sets have proliferated: By the late 1980s three-quarters of all U.S.

homes had more than one set, and these numbers too are rising steadily, allowing ever more private viewing. . . . This massive change in the way Americans spend their days and nights occurred precisely during the years of generational civic disengagement.
— ROBERT D. PUTNAM, "The Strange Disappearance of Civic America"

These statistics come primarily from the U.S. Bureau of the Census, a nationwide count of the number of Americans and a survey, in part, of their buying habits, levels of education, and leisure activities. The Census reports are widely considered to be accurate and trustworthy. They qualify as original sources of statistics.

■ Exercise 11.5

Turn to the Readings section in Chapter 5, and underline the statistics in paragraphs 7–9 of Alan I. Leshner's essay and paragraphs 5 and 6 of Jessica Statsky's. (If you have not read the essays, pause to skim them so that you can evaluate each writer's use of statistics within the context of the whole essay.) How well do the statistics meet the standards of up-to-dateness, relevance, accuracy, and reliance on the original source? (If you find that you do not have all the information you need, base your judgments on whatever information is available to you.) Does the writer indicate where the statistics come from? What do the statistics contribute to the argument?

Authorities

To support an argument, writers often cite *authorities* or experts on the subject who agree with their point of view. Quoting, paraphrasing, or even just referring to a respected authority can add to a writer's credibility. Authorities must be selected as carefully as facts and statistics. One qualification for authorities to support arguments is suggested by the way we refer to them: They must be authoritative — that is, trustworthy and reputable. They must also be specially qualified to contribute to the subject you are writing about. For example, a well-known expert on the American presidency might be a poor choice to support an argument on whether adolescents who commit serious crimes should be tried in the courts as adults. Finally, qualified authorities must have training at respected institutions or have unique real-world experiences, and they must have a record of research and publications recognized by other authorities.

The following example comes from a *New York Times* article about the increasing intolerance by teachers, parents, and experts of boys' behavior. The author believes that their concern with "boyish behavior" is exaggerated and potentially dangerous to boys, and she wants to understand why it is increasing. In the full argument, she is particularly concerned about the number of boys who are being given Ritalin, a popular drug for treating attention-deficit disorder.

Today, the world is no longer safe for boys. A boy being a shade too boyish risks finding himself under the scrutiny of parents, teachers, guidance counselors, child therapists — all of them on watch for the early glimmerings of a medical syndrome, a bona fide behavioral disorder. Does the boy disregard authority, make snide comments in class, push other kids around and play hooky? Maybe he has a conduct disorder. Is he fidgety, impulsive, disruptive, easily bored? Perhaps he is suffering from attention-deficit hyperactivity disorder, or ADHD, the disease of the hour and the most frequently diagnosed behavioral disorder of childhood. Does he prefer computer games and goofing off to homework? He might have dyslexia or another learning disorder.

"There is now an attempt to pathologize what was once considered the normal range of behavior of boys," said Melvin Konner of the departments of anthropology and psychiatry at Emory University in Atlanta. "Today, Tom Sawyer and Huckleberry Finn surely would have been diagnosed with both conduct disorder and ADHD." And both, perhaps, would have been put on Ritalin, the drug of choice for treating attention-deficit disorder.

– NATALIE ANGIER, "Intolerance of Boyish Behavior"

Notice the way the writer establishes the professional qualifications of the authority she quotes. She places him at a major research university (Emory University) and indicates by his department affiliations (anthropology and psychiatry) that he has special training to comment on how a culture treats its young men. Readers can infer from these two facts that he has almost certainly earned a doctorate in anthropology or psychiatry and that he has probably published research studies. This carefully selected quotation supports the writer's argument that there is a problem and that readers should care about it.

In this example, the writer relies on *informal* citation within her essay to introduce the authority she quotes. In newspapers, magazines, and some books, writers rely on informal citation, mentioning the title or author in the essay itself. In other books and in research reports, writers rely on a *formal* style of citation that allows them to refer briefly in an essay to a detailed list of works cited appearing at the end of the essay. This list provides the author, title, date, and publisher of every source of information referred to in the essay. To evaluate the qualifications of an authority in an argument relying on a list of works cited, you may have to rely solely on the information provided in the list. (For examples of two formal citation styles often used in college essays, see Chapter 14.)

■ **Exercise 11.6**

Analyze the way authorities are used in paragraphs 4 and 12 of Carol Potera's essay in Chapter 4 and in paragraphs 4 and 5 of Patrick O'Malley's essay in Chapter 6. Underline the authorities and their contributions to these paragraphs, whether through quotation, summary, or paraphrase. (If you have not read the essays, take time to skim them so that you can evaluate each writer's use of authorities within the context of the whole essay.) On the basis of the evidence you have available, decide to what extent each source is authoritative on the subject: qualified to contribute to the subject, trained appropriately, and recognized widely. How does the writer establish each authority's credentials? What does each authority contribute to the argument as a whole?

Anecdotes

Anecdotes are brief stories about events or experiences, recounted in an engaging way. If they are relevant to the argument, well told, and true to life, they can provide very convincing support. To be relevant, an anecdote must strike readers as more than an entertaining diversion; it must seem to make an irreplaceable contribution to an argument. If it is well told, the narrative or story is easy to follow and the people and scenes are described memorably, even vividly. There are many concrete details that help readers imagine what happened. A true-to-life anecdote is one that seems to represent a possible life experience of a real person. It has to be believable, even if the experience is foreign to readers' experiences.

The following anecdote appeared in an argument taking a position on a familiar issue: gun ownership and control. The writer, an essayist, poet, and environmental writer who is also a rancher in South Dakota, always carries a pistol and believes that other people may have an urgent personal need to carry one and should have the right to do so. To support her argument, she tells several anecdotes, including this one:

> I was driving the half-mile to the highway mailbox one day when I saw a vehicle parked about midway down the road. Several men were standing in the ditch, relieving themselves. I have no objection to emergency urination, but I noticed they'd dumped several dozen beer cans in the road. Besides being ugly, cans can slash a cow's feet or stomach.
>
> The men noticed me before they finished and made quite a performance out of zipping their trousers while walking toward me. All four of them gathered around my small foreign car, and one of them demanded what the hell I wanted.
>
> "This is private land. I'd appreciate it if you'd pick up the beer cans."
>
> "What beer cans?" said the belligerent one, putting both hands on the car door and leaning in my window. His face was inches from mine, and the beer fumes were strong. The others laughed. One tried the passenger door, locked; another put his foot on the hood and rocked the car. They circled, lightly thumping the roof, discussing my good fortune in meeting them and the benefits they were likely to bestow upon me. I felt very small and very trapped and they knew it.
>
> "The ones you just threw out," I said politely.
>
> "I don't see no beer cans. Why don't you get out here and show them to me, honey?" said the belligerent one, reaching for the handle inside my door.
>
> "Right over there," I said, still being polite, "—there, and over there." I pointed with the pistol, which I'd slipped under my thigh. Within one minute the cans and the men were back in the car and headed down the road.
>
> I believe this incident illustrates several important principles. The men were trespassing and knew it; their judgment may have been impaired by alcohol. Their response to the polite request of a woman alone was to use their size, numbers, and sex to inspire fear. The pistol was a response in the same language. Politeness didn't work; I couldn't match them in size or number. Out of the car, I'd have been more vulnerable. The pistol just changed the balance of power.
>
> —Linda M. Hasselstrom, "Why One Peaceful Woman Carries a Pistol"

Most readers would readily agree that this anecdote is well told. It has many concrete, memorable details. As in any good story, something happens—there is action, suspense, climax, resolution. There is even dialogue. It is about a believable, possible experience. Most important, as support for an argument, it is relevant to the writer's point, as she makes clear in the final paragraph.

■ Exercise 11.7

Analyze the way an anecdote is used in paragraph 4 of Jessica Statsky's essay in Chapter 5. (If you have not read her essay, pause to skim it so that you can evaluate the anecdote in the context of the entire essay.) Consider whether the story is well told and true to life. Decide whether it seems to be relevant to the whole argument. Does the writer make the relevance clear? Do you find the anecdote convincing?

Textual Evidence

When you argue claims of value (Chapter 7), *textual evidence* will be very important. In your other college courses, if you are asked to evaluate a controversial book, you must quote, paraphrase, or summarize passages so that readers can understand why you think the author's argument is or is not credible. Textual evidence will also be important if you are interpreting a novel for one of your classes; you must include numerous excerpts to show just how you arrived at your conclusion. In both situations, you are integrating bits of the text you are evaluating or interpreting into your own text and building your argument on these bits.

For these bits of textual evidence to be considered effective support for an argument, they must be carefully selected to be relevant to the argument's thesis and reasons. You must help readers see the connection between each piece of evidence and the reason it supports. Textual evidence must also be highly selective; that is, chosen from among all the available evidence to provide the support needed without overwhelming the reader with too much evidence or weakening the argument with marginally relevant evidence. Textual evidence usually has more impact if it is balanced between quotation and paraphrase from the text. For these selective, balanced choices of evidence to be comprehensible and convincing to readers, the evidence must be smoothly integrated into the sentences of the argument. Finally, the relevance of textual evidence is rarely obvious: The writer must ordinarily explain the link between the evidence and the writer's intended point.

The following example comes from a student essay in which the writer argues that the main character (referred to as "the boy") in the short story "Araby" by James Joyce is so self-absorbed that he learns nothing about himself or other people. These paragraphs offer reasons why the writer believes readers should take her argument seriously. She attempts to support her reasons with textual evidence from the story.

> The story opens and closes with images of blindness. The street is "blind" with an "uninhabited house [. . .] at the blind end." As he spies on Mangan's sister, from his own house, the boy intentionally limits what he is able to see by lowering the "blind" until it is only an inch from the window sash. At the bazaar in the closing scene, the "light was out," and the upper part of the hall was "completely dark." The boy is left "gazing up into the darkness," seeing nothing but an inner torment that burns his eyes.
>
> This pattern of imagery includes images of reading, and reading stands for the boy's inability to understand what is before his eyes. When he tries to read at night,

for example, the girl's "image [comes] between [him] and the page," in effect blinding him. In fact, he seems blind to everything except this "image" of the "brown-clad figure cast by [his] imagination." The girl's "brown-clad figure" is also associated with the houses on "blind" North Richmond Street, with their "brown imperturbable faces." The houses stare back at the boy, unaffected by his presence and gaze.

—SALLY CRANE, "Gazing into Darkness"

Notice first how the writer quotes selected words and phrases about blindness to support her reasoning that the boy learns nothing because he is blinded. There are ten quotations in these two paragraphs, all of them relevant and perhaps not so many as to overwhelm the reader. The writer relies not only on quotes but also on paraphrases of information in the story. The second and third sentences in paragraph 1 are largely paraphrases. (For more information on paraphrasing, see pp. 312–13 in Chapter 10.) The quotations in particular are integrated smoothly into the sentences so that readers' momentum is not blocked. Most important, the writer does not assume that the evidence speaks for itself; she comments and interprets throughout. For example, in the first paragraph, all the sentences except the fourth one offer some comment or explanation.

■ **Exercise 11.8**

Analyze the use of evidence in paragraphs 3–5 of Christine Romano's essay in Chapter 7. (If you have not read this essay, pause to skim it so that you can evaluate the evidence in the context of Romano's full argument.) The quotes are easy to identify. The paraphrases you could identify with confidence only by reading Statsky's essay in Chapter 5, but you can probably identify some of them without doing so. Then try to identify the phrases or sentences that comment on or explain the evidence. Finally, consider whether Romano's evidence in these three paragraphs seems relevant to her thesis and reasons, appropriately selective, well balanced between quotes and paraphrases, integrated smoothly into her sentences, and explained helpfully.

■ COUNTERARGUING

Asserting a thesis and backing it with reasons and support are essential to a successful argument. Thoughtful writers go further, however, by *counterarguing*—anticipating and responding to their readers' objections, challenges, and questions. To anticipate readers' concerns, try to imagine other people's points of view, what they might know about the subject, and how they might feel about it. Try also to imagine how readers would respond to your argument as it unfolds step by step. What will they be thinking and feeling? What objections would they raise? What questions would they ask?

To counterargue, writers rely on three basic strategies: acknowledging, accommodating or conceding, and refuting. Writers show they are aware of readers' objections and questions (acknowledge), modify their position to accept readers' concerns they think are legitimate (accommodate), or explicitly show why readers' objections are invalid or why their concerns are irrelevant (refute). Writers may use one or more of these three strategies in the same essay. According to research by rhetoricians and communications specialists, readers find arguments more convincing when writers have anticipated their concerns in these ways. Acknowledging readers' concerns and either accommodating or refuting them wins readers' respect, attention, and some-times even agreement.

Acknowledging Readers' Concerns

When you *acknowledge* readers' questions or objections, you show that you take their point of view seriously even if you do not agree with it. In the following example, Peter Marin directly acknowledges his readers' possible concerns. These are the open-ing paragraphs of an article arguing that some of America's homeless have chosen that way of life. Marin knows that readers may immediately doubt this surprising assertion. It seems inconceivable that people would choose to sleep on sidewalks and eat out of garbage cans. He acknowledges three different doubts his readers may have.

> The homeless, it seems, can be roughly divided into two groups: those who have had marginality and homelessness forced upon them and want nothing more than to escape them, and a smaller number who have at least in part chosen marginality, and now accept, or, in a few cases, embrace it.
>
> I understand how dangerous it can be to introduce the idea of choice into a dis-cussion of homelessness. It can all too easily be used for all the wrong reasons by all the wrong people to justify indifference or brutality toward the homeless, or to argue that they are getting only what they deserve.
>
> And I understand, too, how complicated the notion can become: Many of the veterans on the street, or battered women, or abused and runaway children, have cho-sen this life only as the lesser of evils, and because, in this society, there is often no place else to go.
>
> And finally, I understand how much that happens on the street can combine to create an apparent acceptance of homelessness that is nothing more than the absolute absence of hope.
>
> Nonetheless we must learn to accept that there may indeed be people on the street who have seen so much of our world, or have seen it so clearly, that to live in it becomes impossible.
>
> – Peter Marin, "Go Ask Alice"

You might think that acknowledging readers' objections in this way—addressing readers directly, listing their possible objections, and discussing each one—would weaken an argument. It might even seem reckless to suggest objections that not all readers would think of. However, readers who expect writers to explore an issue thor-oughly respond positively to this strategy because it makes the writer seem thoughtful and reasonable, more concerned with seeking the truth than winning an argument. By researching your subject and your readers, you will be able to use this strategy con-fidently in your own argumentative essays. And you will learn to look for it in argu-ments you read and use it to make judgments about the writer's credibility.

■ Exercise 11.9

Katherine S. Newman acknowledges readers' concerns in paragraph 14 of her essay in Chapter 6, and David Ansen does so in paragraphs 2–5 of his essay in Chapter 7. (If you have not read the essays, pause to skim them so that you can evaluate each writer's counterargument in the context of the whole essay.) How, specifically, do these authors attempt to acknowledge their readers' concerns? What do you find most and least successful in the two acknowledgments? How do the acknowledgments affect your judgment of the writers' credibility?

Accommodating Readers' Concerns

To argue effectively, you must often take special care to acknowledge your readers' objections, questions, and alternative positions, causes, or solutions. Occasionally, however, you may have to go even further. Instead of merely acknowledging your readers' concerns, you may decide to *accommodate* or accept some of them and incorporate them into your own argument. This strategy can be very disarming to readers. It is sometimes referred to as *concession,* for it seems to concede that opposing views have merit.

The following example comes from an essay enthusiastically endorsing email. After supporting his own reasons for this positive endorsement, the writer accommodates his readers' likely reservations by conceding that email poses certain problems.

> To be sure, egalitarianism has its limits. The ease and economy of sending email, especially to multiple recipients, makes us all vulnerable to any bore, loony, or commercial or political salesman who can get our email address. It's still a lot less intrusive than the telephone, since you can read and answer or ignore email at your own convenience. But as normal people's email starts mounting into the hundreds daily, which is bound to happen, filtering mechanisms and conventions of etiquette that are still in their primitive stage will be desperately needed.
>
> Another supposed disadvantage of email is that it discourages face-to-face communication. At Microsoft, where people routinely send email back and forth all day to the person in the next office, this is certainly true. Some people believe this tendency has more to do with the underdeveloped social skills of computer geeks than with Microsoft's role in developing the technology email relies on. I wouldn't presume to comment on that. Whether you think email replacing live conversation is a good or bad thing depends, I guess, on how much of a misanthrope you are. I like it.
>
> —MICHAEL KINSLEY, "Email Culture"

Notice that Kinsley's accommodation or concession is not grudging. He readily concedes that email brings users a lot of unwanted messages and may discourage conversation in the workplace.

■ Exercise 11.10

How does Patrick O'Malley attempt to accommodate readers in paragraphs 7 and 8 of his essay arguing for more frequent exams (in Chapter 6)? (If you have not read his essay, pause to skim it so that you can evaluate his counterargument in the context of the whole essay.) What seems successful or unsuccessful in his argument? What do his efforts at accommodation contribute to the essay?

Refuting Readers' Objections

Your readers' objections and views cannot always be accommodated. Sometimes they must be refuted. When you *refute* likely objections, you assert that they are wrong and argue against them. Refutation does not have to be delivered arrogantly or dismissively, however. Writers can refute their readers' objections in a spirit of shared inquiry in solving problems, establishing probable causes, deciding the value of something, or understanding different points of view in a controversy. Differences are inevitable. Reasoned argument provides a peaceful and constructive way for informed, well-intentioned people who disagree strongly to air their differences.

In the following example, an economist refutes one explanation for the increasing numbers of women in the workforce. First, he acknowledges a "frequently mentioned" explanation. Then he concedes a point ("there is little doubt") before beginning his refutation of the causal connection ("but it is not clear"):

> One frequently mentioned but inadequately evaluated explanation for the surge of women into paid employment is the spread of time-saving household innovations such as clothes washers and dryers, frozen foods, and dishwashers. There is little doubt that it is easier to combine paid employment with home responsibilities now than it was fifty years ago, but it is not clear whether these time-saving innovations were the cause of the rise in female labor force participation or whether they were largely a response to meet a demand created by working women. Confusion about this point is most evident in comments that suggest that the rapid growth of supermarkets and fast-food outlets is a cause of women going to work. Similar time-saving organizations were tried at least sixty years ago, but with less success because the value of time was much lower then. The absence of supermarkets and fast-food eating places in low-income countries today also shows that their rapid growth in the United States is primarily a result of the rising value of time and the growth of women in the work force, not the reverse.
>
> —VICTOR FUCHS, "Why Married Mothers Work"

As this example illustrates, writers cannot simply dismiss readers' concerns with a wave of the hand. Fuchs refutes one proposed cause by arguing that it is actually an effect or result of the trend. The last two sentences support his refutation. Effective refutation requires a restrained tone and careful argument. Although, reading this, you may not accept the refutation, you can agree that it is well reasoned and supported. You do not feel attacked personally because the writer disagrees with you.

■ **Exercise 11.11**

Analyze and evaluate the use of refutation in paragraphs 6–11 of Alan I. Leshner's essay in Chapter 5. (If you have not read his essay, pause to skim it so that you can evaluate his counterargument in the context of the whole essay.) How does he signal or announce the refutation? How does he support the refutation? What is the tone of the refutation, and how effective do you think the tone would be in convincing readers to take the argument seriously?

■ LOGICAL FALLACIES

Fallacies are errors or flaws in reasoning. Although essentially unsound, fallacious arguments seem superficially plausible and often have great persuasive power. Fallacies are not necessarily deliberate efforts to deceive readers. Writers may introduce a fallacy accidentally by not examining their own reasons or underlying assumptions critically, by failing to establish solid support, or by using unclear or ambiguous words. Here is a summary of the most common logical fallacies (listed alphabetically):

- *Begging the question.* Arguing that a claim is true by repeating the claim in different words. Sometimes called *circular reasoning.*
- *Confusing chronology with causality.* Assuming that because one thing preceded another, the former caused the latter. Also called *post hoc, ergo propter hoc* (Latin for "after this, therefore because of this").
- *Either-or reasoning.* Assuming that there are only two sides to a question and representing yours as the only correct one.
- *Equivocating.* Misleading or hedging with ambiguous word choices.
- *Failing to accept the burden of proof.* Asserting a claim without presenting a reasoned argument to support it.
- *False analogy.* Assuming that because one thing resembles another, conclusions drawn from one also apply to the other.
- *Hasty generalization.* Offering only weak or limited evidence to support a conclusion.
- *Overreliance on authority.* Assuming that something is true simply because an expert says so and ignoring evidence to the contrary.
- *Oversimplifying.* Giving easy answers to complicated questions, often by appealing to emotions rather than logic.
- *Personal attack.* Demeaning the proponents of a claim instead of refuting their argument. Also called *ad hominem* (Latin for "against the man") *attack.*
- *Red herring.* Attempting to misdirect the discussion by raising an essentially unrelated point.
- *Slanting.* Selecting or emphasizing the evidence that supports your claim and suppressing or playing down other evidence.
- *Slippery slope.* Pretending that one thing inevitably leads to another.
- *Sob story.* Manipulating readers' emotions in order to lead them to draw unjustified conclusions.
- *Straw man.* Directing the argument against a claim that nobody actually holds or that everyone agrees is very weak.

Strategies for Field Research

In universities, government agencies, and the business world, field research can be as important as library research or experimental research. If you major in education, communication, or one of the social sciences, you will probably be asked to do writing based on your own observations and interviews. You will also read large amounts of information based on these methods of learning about individuals, groups, and institutions. You also might use observations or interviews to help you select or gain background for a service-learning project (a project that combines classroom education with community experience).

Observations and interviews are essential for writing profiles (Chapter 3). In proposing a solution to a problem (Chapter 6), you might want to interview people involved. In writing to explain an academic concept (Chapter 4), you might want to interview a faculty member who is a specialist on the subject. As you consider how you might use such research most appropriately, ask your instructor whether your institution will require you to obtain approval for your field research.

■ OBSERVATIONS

This section offers guidelines for planning an observational visit, taking notes on your observations, writing them up, and preparing for follow-up visits. Some kinds of writing are based on observations from single visits—travel writing, social workers' case reports, insurance investigators' accident reports—but most observational writing is based on several visits. An anthropologist or a sociologist studying an unfamiliar group or activity might observe it for months, filling several notebooks with notes. If you are profiling a place (Chapter 3), you almost certainly will want to make more than one observational visit, some of them perhaps combined with interviews.

Second and third visits to observe further are important because as you learn more about a place from initial observations, interviews, or reading, you will discover new ways to look at it. Gradually, you will have more and more questions that can be answered only by follow-up visits. You also may want to combine observations with other field research, especially if you are preparing an ethnographic study of the culture of a group or organization.

Planning the Visit

To ensure that your observational visits are productive, you must plan them carefully.

Getting Access.   If the place you propose to visit is public, you will probably have easy access to it. If everything you need to see is within view of anyone passing by or using the place, you can make your observations without any special arrangements. Indeed, you may not even be noticed. However, most observational visits require special access. Hence, you will need to arrange your visit, calling ahead or stopping by to introduce yourself, state your purpose, and get acquainted. Find out the times you may visit, and be certain you can gain access easily.

Announcing Your Intentions.   State your intentions directly and fully. Say who you are, where you are from, and what you hope to do. You may be surprised at how receptive people can be to a college student on assignment for a class or a service-learning project. Not every place you wish to visit will welcome you, however. In addition, private businesses as well as public institutions place a variety of constraints on outside visitors. But generally, if people know your intentions, they may be able to tell you about aspects of a place or an activity you would not have thought to observe.

Taking Your Tools.   Take a notebook with a firm back so that you will have a steady writing surface. Remember also to take a pen. Some observers dictate their observations into a tape recorder and transcribe their notes later. You might want to experiment with this method. We recommend, though, that you record your first observations in writing. Your instructor or other students in your class may want to see your notes, and transcribing a recording can take a lot of time.

Observing and Taking Notes

Here are some basic guidelines for observing and taking notes.

Observing.   Some activities invite the observer to watch from multiple vantage points, whereas others may limit the observer to a single perspective. Take advantage of every perspective available to you. Come in close, take a middle position, and stand back. Study the scene from a stationary position, and then try to move around it. The more varied your perspectives, the more details you are likely to observe.

Your purposes in observing are twofold: to describe the activity or place and to analyze it. You will want to look closely at the activity or place itself, but you will also want to think about what makes it special, what seems to you to be significant about it.

Try initially to be an innocent observer: Pretend that you have never seen anything like this activity or place before. Then consider your own and your readers' likely preconceptions. Ask yourself what details are surprising and what reinforces expectations.

Taking Notes.   You will undoubtedly find your own style of notetaking, but here are a few pointers:

- Write on only one side of the page. Later, when you organize your notes, you may want to cut up the pages and file notes under different headings.

- Take notes in words, phrases, or sentences. Draw diagrams or sketches, if they will help you see and understand the place or activity or recall details of it later on.

- Use abbreviations as much as you like, but use them consistently and clearly.

- Note any ideas or questions that occur to you.

- If you are expecting to see a certain behavior, try not to let this expectation influence what you actually do see.

- Use quotation marks around any overheard remarks or conversations you record.

Perhaps the most important advice about notetaking during an observational visit is to record as many details as possible about the place or activity and to write down your impressions as they come to mind. Do not focus on taking notes in a systematic way. Be flexible. Later you will have the chance to reorganize your notes and fill in gaps. At the same time, however, you want to be sure to include details about the setting, the people, and your reactions.

The Setting.   Describe the setting: Name or list objects you see there, and then record details of some of them—their color, shape, size, texture, function, relation to similar or dissimilar objects. Although your notes will probably contain mainly visual details, you might also want to record details about sounds and smells. Be sure to include some notes about the shape, dimensions, and layout of the place as a whole. How big is it? How is it organized?

The People.   Note the number of people you observe, their activities, their movements and behavior. Describe their appearance or dress. Record parts of overheard conversations. Indicate whether you see more men than women, more members of one nationality or ethnic group than of another, more older than younger people. Most important, note anything surprising, interesting, or unusual about the people and how they interact with each other.

Your Personal Reactions.   Write down your impressions, questions, ideas, or insights as they occur to you.

Reflecting on Your Observations

Immediately after your observational visit (within a few minutes, if possible), find a quiet place to reflect on what you saw, review your notes, and fill in any gaps with additional details or ideas. Give yourself at least a half-hour to add to your notes and to write a few sentences about the significance of the place or activity. Ask yourself the following questions:

- What did I learn from my observational visit?
- How did what I observed fit my own or my readers' likely preconceptions of the place or activity?
- What dominant impression do my notes seem to convey?
- What, if anything, seemed contradictory or out of place?

Writing Up Your Notes

Your instructor may ask you to write up your notes on the observational visit, as Brian Cable did after visiting the Goodbody mortuary for his profile essay (see pp. 70–73). If so, review your notes, looking for a meaningful pattern in the details you have noted down. You might find clustering (p. 290) or taking inventory (p. 309) useful for discovering patterns in your notes.

Assume that your readers have never been to the place, and decide on the dominant impression of the place you want your readers to get from reading your writing. Choose details that will convey this impression. Then draft a brief description of the place. Your purpose is to select details from your notes that will convey to readers a vivid impression of the place.

■ Exercise 12.1

Arrange to meet with a small group (three or four students) for an observational visit somewhere on campus, such as the student center, campus gym, cafeteria or restaurant, or any other place where some activity is going on. Take notes by assigning each person in your group a specific task: One person can take notes on the appearance of the people, for example; another can take notes on their activities; another on their conversations; and another on what the place looks and smells like. Take about twenty to thirty minutes, and then report to each other on your observations. This will give you some good practice on what you will need to do when you observe on your own, and you will get to see some of the difficulties associated with observing people and places.

Preparing for Follow-Up Visits

Rather than repeat yourself in follow-up visits, try to build on what you have already discovered. You should probably do some interviewing and reading before another observational visit so that you will have a greater understanding of the subject when you observe it again. You might want to present your notes from your first visit to your instructor or to a small group from your class so that you can use their responses as well, especially if you are working on a specific assignment such as a profile. It is also important to develop a plan for your follow-up visits: questions to be answered, hypotheses to be tested, types of information you would like to discover.

■ INTERVIEWS

Like making observations, interviewing tends to involve four basic steps: (1) planning and setting up the interview, (2) taking interview notes, (3) reflecting on the interview, and (4) writing up your notes.

Planning and Setting Up the Interview

The initial steps in interviewing involve choosing an interview subject and then arranging and planning for the interview.

Choosing an Interview Subject.   First, decide whom to interview. If you are writing about some activity in which several people are involved, choose subjects representing a variety of perspectives—a range of roles, for example. For a profile of a single person, most or all of your interviews would be with that person. But for a service-learning project, for instance, you might interview several members of an organization in order to gain a more complete picture of its mission or activities. You should be flexible because you may be unable to speak with the person you initially targeted and may wind up interviewing someone else—the person's assistant, perhaps. Do not assume that this interview subject will be of little use to you. With the right questions, you might even learn more from the assistant than you would from the person you had originally expected to see.

Arranging an Interview.   You may be nervous about calling up a busy person and asking for some of his or her time. Indeed, you may get turned down. But if so, it is possible that you will be referred to someone who will see you, someone whose job it is to communicate with the public.

Do not feel that just because you are a student, you do not have the right to ask for people's time. You will be surprised at how delighted people are to be asked about themselves, particularly if you reach them when they are not feeling harried. Most people love to talk—about anything! And since you are a student on assignment, some people may feel that they are performing a public service by talking with you.

When introducing yourself to arrange the interview, give a short and simple description of your project. If you talk too much, you could prejudice or limit the interviewee's response. At the same time, it is a good idea to exhibit some sincere enthusiasm for your project. If you lack enthusiasm, the person may see little reason to talk with you.

Keep in mind that the person you want to interview will be donating valuable time to you. Be certain that you call ahead to arrange a specific time for the interview. Arrive on time. Dress appropriately. Bring all the materials you need. Express your thanks when the interview is over. Finally, try to represent your institution well, whether your interview is for a single course assignment or part of a larger service-learning project.

Planning for the Interview. The best interview is generally the well-planned interview. It will help if you have made an observational visit and done some background reading beforehand. In preparation for the interview, you should do two things in particular: Consider your objectives and prepare some questions.

Think about your main objectives:

- Do you want an orientation to the place or your topic (the "big picture") from this interview?
- Do you want this interview to lead you to interviews with other key people?
- Do you want mainly facts or opinions?
- Do you need to clarify something you have heard in another interview, observed, or read?
- Do you want to learn more about the person, the place, or the activity through the interview — or all of these?

The key to good interviewing is flexibility. You may be looking for facts, but your interview subject may not have any to offer. In that case, you should be able to shift gears and go after whatever your subject is in a position to discuss. Be aware that the person you are interviewing represents only one point of view. You may need to speak with several people to get a more complete picture. Talking with more than one person may also help you discover contradictions or problems that could contribute to the significance you decide to emphasize.

Composing Questions. Take care in composing the questions you prepare in advance; they can be the key to a successful interview. Any question that places unfair limits on respondents is a bad question. Avoid forced-choice questions and leading questions.

Forced-choice questions impose your terms on respondents. Let us assume you are interviewing a counselor at a campus rape crisis center and want to know what he or she thinks is the motivation for rape. You could ask this question: "Do you think rape is an expression of sexual passion or of aggression?" But the counselor might think neither sexual passion nor aggression satisfactorily explains the motivation for rape. A better way to phrase the question would be as follows: "People often fall into two camps on the issue of rape. Some think it is an expression of sexual passion, while others argue it is really not sexual but aggressive. Do you think it is either of these? If not, what is your opinion?" Phrasing the question in this way allows you to get a reaction to what others have said at the same time that it gives the interviewee freedom to set the terms for his or her response.

Leading questions assume too much. An example of this kind of question is this: "Do you think the number of rapes has increased because women are perceived as competitors in a highly competitive economy?" This question assumes that there is an increase in the occurrence of rape, that women are perceived (apparently by rapists) as economic competitors, and that the state of the economy is somehow related to acts of rape. A better way of asking the question might be to make the assumptions more explicit by dividing the question into its parts: "Do you think the number of rapes has increased? What could have caused this increase? I've heard some people argue that the economy has something to do with it. Do you think so? Do you think rapists perceive women as competitors for jobs? Could the current economic situation have made this competition more severe?"

Good questions come in many different forms. One way of considering them is to divide them into two basic types: open and closed. *Open questions* give the respondent range and flexibility. They also generate anecdotes, personal revelations, and expressions of attitudes. *Closed questions* usually request specific information.

Suppose you are interviewing a small-business owner, for example. You might begin with a specific (closed) question about when the business was established and then follow up with an open-ended question such as, "Could you take a few minutes to tell me something about your early days in the business? I'd be interested to hear how it got started, what your hopes were, and what problems you had to face." Consider asking directly for an anecdote ("What happened when your employees threatened to strike?"), encouraging reflection ("What do you think has helped you most? What has hampered you?"), or soliciting advice ("What advice would you give to someone trying to start a new business today?"). Here are some examples of open and closed questions:

Open Questions

- What do you think about *(name a person or an event)*?
- Describe your reaction when *(name an event)* happened.
- Tell me about a time you were *(name an emotion)*.

Closed Questions

- How do you *(name a process)*?
- What does *(name a word or phrase)* mean?
- What does *(name a person, object, or place)* look like?
- How was it made?

The best questions encourage the subject to talk freely but to the point. If an answer strays too far from the point, you may need to ask a follow-up question to re-focus the talk. Another tack you might want to try is to rephrase the subject's answer, to say something like "Let me see if I have this right" or "Am I correct in saying that you feel . . . ?" Often, a person will take the opportunity to amplify the original response by adding just the anecdote or quotable comment you have been looking for.

Bringing Your Tools.   As for an observational visit, when you interview someone, you will need a notebook with a firm back so you can write in it easily without the benefit of a table or desk. You might find it useful to divide several pages into two columns by drawing a line about one-third of the width of the page from the left margin. Use the left-hand column to note details about the scene, the person, the mood of the interview, and other impressions. Head this column *Details and Impressions*. At the top of the right-hand column, write several questions. You may not use them, but they will jog your memory. This column should be titled *Information*. In it, you will record what you learn from answers to your questions.

Taking Notes during the Interview

Because you are not taking a verbatim transcript of the interview (if you want a literal account, use a tape recorder or shorthand), your goals are to gather information and to record a few quotable bits of information, comments, and anecdotes. In addition, because the people you interview may be unused to giving interviews and so will need to know you are paying attention, it is probably a good idea to do more listening than notetaking. You may not have much confidence in your memory, but if you pay close attention, you are likely to recall a good deal of the conversation afterward. Take some notes during the interview: a few quotations; key words and phrases, details of the scene, the person, and the mood of the interview. Remember that how something is said is as important as what is said. Look for material that will give texture to your writing—gesture, verbal inflection, facial expression, body language, physical appearance, dress, hair, or anything else that makes the person an individual.

Reflecting on the Interview

As soon as you finish the interview, find a quiet place to reflect on it and review your notes. This reflection is essential because so much happens in an interview that you cannot record at the time. Spend at least a half-hour adding to your notes and thinking about what you learned.

At the end of this time, write a few sentences about your main impressions from the interview. Ask yourself these questions:

- What did I learn?
- What seemed contradictory or surprising about the interview?
- How did what was said fit my own or my readers' likely expectations about the person, activity, or place?
- How can I summarize my impressions?

Writing Up Your Notes

Your instructor may ask you to write up your interview notes. If so, review them for useful details and ideas. Decide what main impression you want to give of this person. Choose details that will contribute to this impression. Select quotations and paraphrases of information you learned from the person.

You might also review notes from any related observations or other interviews, especially if you plan to combine these materials in a profile, an ethnographic study, or other project.

13

Strategies for Library and Internet Research

Research requires patience, careful planning, good advice, and even luck. The rewards are many, however. Each new research project leads you to unexplored regions of the library or of cyberspace. You may find yourself in a rare book room reading a manuscript written hundreds of years ago or involved in a lively discussion on the Internet with people hundreds of miles away. One moment you may be keyboarding commands, and the next, you may be threading a microfilm reader, viewing a videodisk, or squinting at the fine print in an index. You may breeze through an encyclopedia entry introducing you to a new subject or struggle with a just-published report of a highly technical research study on the same subject.

This chapter is designed to help you learn how to use the resources available in your college library and on the Internet. It gives advice on how to learn about the library and the Internet, develop efficient search strategies, keep track of your research, locate appropriate sources, and read them with a critical eye. Chapter 14 provides guidelines for using and acknowledging these sources in an essay.

■ ORIENTING YOURSELF TO THE LIBRARY

To conduct research in most college libraries, you will need to become familiar with a wide variety of resources. Online public access catalogs (often called *OPACs*) provide information on books. Periodical indexes and abstracts, used to locate magazine and journal articles, are available in databases, in print volumes, on CD-ROMs, through the library catalog, or through the World Wide Web. The materials you look up may be in print, on microfilm (reels) or microfiche (cards), or in electronic text files accessible through an electronic periodical index or library Web site.

Taking a Tour

Make a point of getting acquainted with your campus library. Your instructor may arrange a library orientation tour for your composition class. If not, you can join one of the regular orientation tours scheduled by the librarians or design your own tour (for suggestions, see Table 13.1). Because nearly all college libraries are more complex and offer more services than typical high school or public libraries, you will need to learn how your campus library's catalog and reference room are organized, how you can access computer catalogs and databases, whom to ask for help if you are confused, and where you can find books, periodicals, and other materials.

Pick up copies of any available pamphlets and guidelines. Nearly every college library offers a Web page and handouts describing its resources and services. Also look

Table 13.1 Designing Your Self-Guided Library Tour

Here is a list of important locations or departments to look for in your college library.

Library Location	Services Provided
Loan Desk	Obtain library cards, check out materials, place holds and recalls, and pay fees or fines.
Reference Desk	Obtain help from reference librarians to locate and use library resources.
Information Desk	Ask general and directional questions.
Reserves Desk	Gain access to books and journal articles that are on reserve for specific classes.
Interlibrary Loan Department	Request materials not available on site.
Public Access Computers	Gain access to the library catalog, electronic periodical indexes and abstracts, the campus network, and the Internet.
Current Periodicals	Locate unbound current issues of newspapers, journals, and magazines.
Directories of Books and Journals	Use directories to find the location of books and journals shelved by call numbers.
Reference Collection	Find reference materials such as encyclopedias, dictionaries, handbooks, atlases, bibliographies, statistics, and periodical indexes and abstracts.
Government Publications Department	Locate publications from federal, state, and local government agencies.
Multimedia Resources	Locate nonprint materials such as videos, CD-ROMs, and audiotapes.
Microforms	Locate materials on microfilm (reels) and microfiche (cards).
Special Collections	Refer to rare and valuable materials not readily available in most library collections; in larger libraries only.
Archives	Find archival materials, collections of papers from important individuals and organizations that provide source material for original research; in larger libraries only.
Maps and Atlases	Locate maps and atlases in a special location because of their size and format.
Copy Service	Use self-service and special-function copiers.
Reading Rooms	Read in quiet, comfortable areas.
Study Rooms	Study in rooms reserved for individuals or small groups.

for a floor map of materials and facilities. See whether your library offers any research guidelines, special workshops, or presentations on strategies for locating resources.

Consulting a Librarian

Think of college librarians as instructors whose job is to help you understand the library and get your hands on sources you need to complete your research projects. Librarians at the information or reference desk are there to provide reference services, and most have years of experience answering the very questions you are likely to ask. You should not hesitate to approach them with any questions you have about locating sources. Remember, however, that they can be most helpful when you can explain your research assignment clearly.

Knowing Your Research Task

Before you go to the library to start an assigned research project, learn as much as you can about the assignment. Should you need to ask a librarian for advice, it is best to have the assignment in writing. Ask your instructor to clarify any confusing terms and to define the purpose and scope of the project. Find out how you can narrow or focus the project once you begin the research. Asking a question or two in advance can prevent hours—or even days—of misdirected work. You should try to get to the library as soon as you understand the assignment. If many of your classmates will be working on similar projects, there may be competition for a limited number of books and other resources.

Using Self-Help Options

Library resources and the research environment are constantly changing, and all researchers, including students, need to learn to be self-sufficient in their information quest. Look for and use online help, tutorials, and other self-help guides when using information resources, particularly electronic resources.

■ A LIBRARY SEARCH STRATEGY

For your library research to be manageable and productive, you will want to work carefully and systematically. Although specific search strategies may vary to fit the needs of individual research tasks, the general process presented in Figure 13.1 should help you get started, keep track of all your research, use library materials to get an overview of your subject, locate the sources you need, and read those sources with a critical eye. It is important to remember that research is a recursive, repetitive process, not a linear one. You will be constantly refining and revising your research strategy as you find out more about your topic.

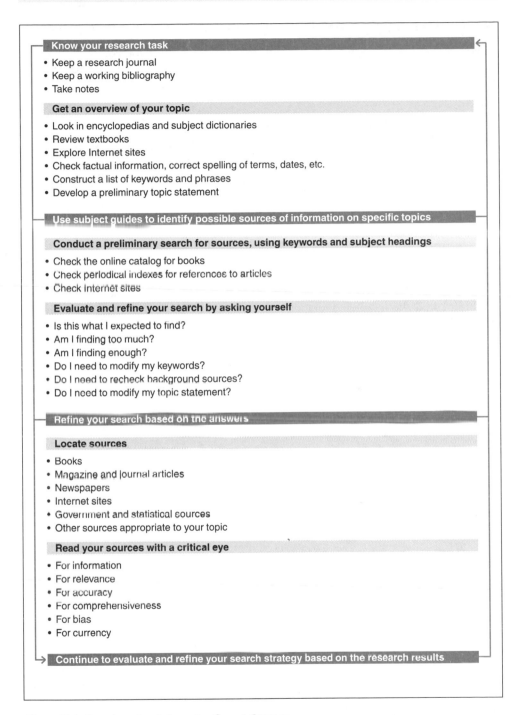

Know your research task

• Keep a research journal
• Keep a working bibliography
• Take notes

Get an overview of your topic

• Look in encyclopedias and subject dictionaries
• Review textbooks
• Explore Internet sites
• Check factual information, correct spelling of terms, dates, etc.
• Construct a list of keywords and phrases
• Develop a preliminary topic statement

Use subject guides to identify possible sources of information on specific topics

Conduct a preliminary search for sources, using keywords and subject headings

• Check the online catalog for books
• Check periodical indexes for references to articles
• Check Internet sites

Evaluate and refine your search by asking yourself

• Is this what I expected to find?
• Am I finding too much?
• Am I finding enough?
• Do I need to modify my keywords?
• Do I need to recheck background sources?
• Do I need to modify my topic statement?

Refine your search based on the answers

Locate sources

• Books
• Magazine and journal articles
• Newspapers
• Internet sites
• Government and statistical sources
• Other sources appropriate to your topic

Read your sources with a critical eye

• For information
• For relevance
• For accuracy
• For comprehensiveness
• For bias
• For currency

Continue to evaluate and refine your search strategy based on the research results

Figure 13.1 Overview of an Information Search Strategy

■ KEEPING TRACK OF YOUR RESEARCH

As you research your topic, you will want to keep a careful record of all the sources you locate by setting up a working bibliography. You will also want to take notes on your sources in some systematic way.

Keeping a Working Bibliography

A *working bibliography* is a preliminary, ongoing record of books, articles, Web sites—all the sources of information you discover as you research your subject. In addition, you can use your working bibliography to keep track of any encyclopedias, bibliographies, and indexes you consult, even though you do not identify these general sources in an essay.

Each entry in a working bibliography is called a *bibliographic citation*. The information you record in each bibliographic citation will help you locate the material you need in the source and refer to it, or *cite* it, in the bibliography—the list of references or works cited you provide at the end of an essay. Recording this information for each source as you locate it, rather than reconstructing it later, will save you hours of work. In addition to the bibliographic information, note the library location where you will be able to find the material and the source where you located the reference, just in case you have to track it down again. (See Figures 13.2 and 13.3 for examples of how to organize bibliographic and other information for a working bibliography.)

As you locate books in the library, record this information in your working bibliography for each book you look up.

Author: _____

Title: _____

Place of publication: _____

Publisher: _____

Date of publication: _____

Library where book is located: _____

Call number: _____

Special location (such as in reference or government publications dept.): _____

Is the book available or checked out?: _____

Figure 13.2 Information for Working Bibliography—Books

As you locate articles in the library, record this information in your working bibliography for each article you look up.

Author of article: _____

Title of article: _____

Title of journal: _____

Volume number: _____   Issue number: _____

Date of issue: _____   Inclusive page numbers: _____

Library and special location: _____   _____

Figure 13.3 Information for Working Bibliography—Periodical Articles

Confirm with your instructor which documentation style is required for your assignment so that you can make all the sources listed in your working bibliography conform to that style of documentation. Chapter 14 presents two common documentation styles, one adopted by the Modern Language Association (MLA) and widely used in the humanities, and the other advocated by the American Psychological Association (APA) and used in the social sciences. Individual disciplines often have their own preferred styles of documentation.

Practiced researchers keep their working bibliography on index cards, in a notebook, or in a computer file. They may keep bibliographic information separate from notes they take on the sources. Many researchers find index cards most convenient because the cards are easy to arrange in the alphabetical order required for the list of works cited or references. Others find cards too easy to lose and prefer instead to keep everything—working bibliography, notes, and drafts—in one notebook. Researchers who use computers set up working bibliographies in word processing programs or bibliographic management programs that can format information according to one of the preset documentation styles (such as MLA or APA) or a customized style created by the user. These programs can also create in-text citations and insert them into the essay text, as well as format the final list of works cited. Some of these documentation programs can interact with electronic indexes and other databases, downloading source information from the database into a bibliographic file and then correctly formatting the information.

Whether you use index cards, a notebook, or a computer file for your working bibliography, the important thing is to make your entries accurate and complete. If the call number for a book is incomplete or inaccurate, for example, you will not be able to find the book in the stacks. If the volume number for a periodical is incorrect, you may not be able to locate the article. If the author's name is misspelled, you may have trouble finding the book in the library catalog.

Taking Notes

After you have located some possible sources, you will want to begin taking notes. If you can obtain a photocopy of the relevant parts, you may want to annotate right on the page. Otherwise, you should paraphrase, summarize, and outline useful information as separate notes. In addition, you will want to write down quotations you might want to use in your essay. (Outlining, paraphrasing, and summarizing are discussed in Chapter 10, and quoting is discussed in Chapter 14.)

You may already have a method of notetaking you prefer. Some researchers like to use index cards for notes as well as for their working bibliography. They use 3- by 5-inch cards for their bibliography and larger ones (4- by 6-inch or 5- by 7-inch) for notes. Some use cards of different colors to organize their notes, whereas other people prefer to keep their notes in a notebook, and still others enter their notes into a computer file. Whatever method you use, be sure to keep accurate notes.

Care in notetaking is of paramount importance to minimize the risks of copying facts incorrectly and of misquoting. Another common error in notetaking is copying an author's words without enclosing them in quotation marks. This error could lead easily to plagiarism, the unacknowledged and therefore improper use of another's words or ideas. Double-check all your notes, and be as accurate as you can. (For tips on avoiding plagiarism, see Chapter 14, p. 396.)

You might consider photocopying materials from sources that look especially promising. All libraries house photocopy machines or offer a copying service. However, because photocopying can be costly, you will want to be selective. Photocopying can facilitate your work, allowing you to reread and analyze important sources as well as to highlight material you may wish to quote, summarize, or paraphrase. Be sure to photocopy title pages or other publication information for each source you copy, or write this information on the photocopied text, especially if you are copying excerpts from several sources. Bring paper clips or a stapler with you to the library to help keep your photocopies organized.

■ GETTING STARTED

"But where do I start?" That common question is easily answered. You first need an overview of your topic. If you are researching a concept or an issue in a course you are taking, a bibliography in your textbook or your course materials provides the obvious starting point. Your instructor can advise you about other sources that provide overviews of your topic. If your topic is just breaking in the news, you will want to consult current newspapers, magazines, or Internet sites. For all other topics—and for background information—encyclopedias and disciplinary (subject) guides are often the place to start. They introduce you to diverse aspects of a subject, from which you might find a focus for your research.

Consulting Encyclopedias

General encyclopedias, such as the *Encyclopaedia Britannica* and the *Encyclopedia Americana,* give basic information about many topics; however, general encyclopedias alone are not adequate resources for college research. Specialized encyclopedias cover topics in the depth appropriate for college writing. In addition to providing an overview of a topic, a specialized encyclopedia often includes an explanation of issues related to the topic, definitions of specialized terminology, and selective bibliographies of additional sources.

As starting points, specialized encyclopedias have two distinct advantages: (1) They provide a comprehensive introduction to key terms related to your topic, terms that are especially useful in identifying the subject headings used to locate material in catalogs and indexes, and (2) they provide a comprehensive presentation of a subject, enabling you to see many possibilities for focusing your research on one aspect of it.

The following list identifies some specialized encyclopedias in the major academic disciplines:

ART	*Dictionary of Art.* 34 vols. 1996.
BIOLOGY	*Concise Encyclopedia Biology.* 1995.
CHEMISTRY	*Concise Encyclopedia Chemistry.* 1993.
COMPUTERS	*Encyclopedia of Computer Science and Technology.* 15 vols. 1975–.
ECONOMICS	*Fortune Encyclopedia of Economics.* 1993.
EDUCATION	*Encyclopedia of Educational Research.* 1992.
ENVIRONMENT	*Encyclopedia of the Environment.* 1994.
FOREIGN RELATIONS	*Encyclopedia of U.S. Foreign Relations.* 1997. *Encyclopedia of the Third World.* 1992.
HISTORY	*Encyclopedia USA.* 20 vols. 1983–. *New Cambridge Modern History.* 14 vols. 1957–1980, 1990–.
LAW	*The American Law Dictionary.* 1991.
LITERATURE	*Encyclopedia of World Literature in the 20th Century.* 5 vols. 1981–1993. *Encyclopedia of Literature and Criticism.* 1990.
MUSIC	*New Grove Dictionary of Music and Musicians.* 20 vols. 1980.
PHILOSOPHY	*Encyclopedia of Philosophy.* 4 vols. 1973.
PSYCHOLOGY	*Encyclopedia of Psychology.* 2nd edition. 1994.
RELIGION	*Encyclopedia of Religion.* 16 vols. 1987.
SCIENCE	*McGraw-Hill Encyclopedia of Science and Technology.* 20 vols. 1992.
SOCIAL SCIENCES	*International Encyclopedia of the Social Sciences.* 19 vols. 1968–.
WOMEN'S STUDIES	*Women's Studies Encyclopedia.* 3 vols. 1989–1991.

You can locate any of these in the library by doing a title search in the online cata-log and looking for the encyclopedia's call number. Find other specialized encyclope-dias by looking in the catalog under the subject heading for the discipline, such as "psychology," and adding the subheading "encyclopedia" or "dictionary."

Three particular reference sources can help you identify other specialized encyclo-pedias covering your topic:

ARBA Guide to Subject Encyclopedias and Dictionaries (1997). Lists special-ized encyclopedias by broad subject categories, with descriptions of coverage, focus, and any special features.

First Stop: The Master Index to Subject Encyclopedias (1989). Lists specialized encyclopedias by broad subject categories and provides information about articles within them. By looking under the key terms that describe a topic, you can search for related articles in any of over four hundred specialized encyclopedias.

Kister's Best Encyclopedias (1994). Surveys and evaluates more than a thousand encyclopedias, both print and electronic. It includes a title and topic index that you can use to find references to encyclopedias on special topics.

Consulting Disciplinary Guides

Once you have a general overview of your topic, you can consult one of the research guides within the discipline. The following guides can help you identify the major handbooks, encyclopedias, bibliographies, journals, periodical indexes, and computer databases in the various disciplines. You need not read any of these extensive works straight through, but you will find them to be valuable references. The *Guide to Ref-erence Books,* edited by Robert Balay, will help you find disciplinary guides for subjects not listed here.

ANTHROPOLOGY	*Introduction to Library Research in Anthropology,* 2nd edition. 1998. By John M. Weeks.
ART	*Visual Arts Research: A Handbook.* 1986. By Elizabeth B. Pollard.
EDUCATION	*Education: A Guide to Reference and Information Sources.* 1989. By Lois Buttlar.
FILM	*On the Screen: A Film, Television, and Video Research Guide.* 1986. By Kim N. Fisher.
GENERAL	*Guide to Reference Books,* 11th edition. 1996. Edited by Robert Balay.
HISTORY	*A Student's Guide to History,* 6th edition. 1994. By Jules R. Benjamin.
HUMANITIES	*The Humanities: A Selective Guide to Information Sources,* 4th edition. 1994. By Ron Blazek and Elizabeth S. Aversa.

LITERATURE	*Reference Works in British and American Literature*. 2 vols. 1998. By James K. Bracken. *Literary Research Guide: An Annotated Listing of Reference Sources in English Literary Studies*. 1998. By James L. Harner.
MUSIC	*Music: A Guide to the Reference Literature*. 1987. By William S. Brockman.
PHILOSOPHY	*Philosophy: A Guide to the Reference Literature*, 2nd edition. 1997. By Hans E. Bynagle.
POLITICAL SCIENCE	*Information Sources of Political Science*, 4th edition. 1986. By Frederick L. Holler.
PSYCHOLOGY	*Library Use: A Handbook for Psychology*, 2nd edition. 1992.
SCIENCE AND TECHNOLOGY	*Scientific and Technical Information Sources*, 2nd edition. 1987. By Ching-chih Chen.
SOCIAL SCIENCES	*The Social Sciences: A Cross-Disciplinary Guide to Selected Sources*. 1996. By Nancy L. Herron.
SOCIOLOGY	*Sociology: A Guide to Reference and Information Sources*, 2nd edition. 1997. By Stephen H. Aby.
WOMEN'S STUDIES	*Introduction to Library Research in Women's Studies*. 1985. By Susan E. Searing.

Consulting Bibliographies

Like encyclopedias and disciplinary guides, bibliographies give an overview of what has been published on the subject. A bibliography is simply a list of publications on a given subject. Its scope may be broad or narrow. Some bibliographers try to be exhaustive, including every title they can find, but most are selective. To discover how selections were made, check the bibliography's preface or introduction. Occasionally, bibliographies are annotated with brief summaries and evaluations of the entries. Bibliographies may be found in a variety of places: in encyclopedias, in the library catalog, and in research guides. All specialized encyclopedias and disciplinary guides have bibliographies. Research articles include bibliographies to document their sources of information.

Even if you attend a large research university, your library is unlikely to hold every book or journal article a bibliography might direct you to. The library catalog and serial record (a list of periodicals the library holds) will tell you whether the book or journal is available on-site or whether you will have to get it through interlibrary loan.

◼ IDENTIFYING KEYWORDS AND SUBJECT HEADINGS

To extend your research beyond encyclopedias, you need to find appropriate keywords and subject headings. *Subject headings* are specific words and phrases used in libraries to categorize the contents of books and periodicals. As you read about your subject in an encyclopedia or other reference book, you should keep a list of *keywords* or phrases that describe your topic. Make sure you spell your keywords correctly. Computers are very unforgiving of spelling errors.

A good way to begin your search for subject headings is to consult the *Library of Congress Subject Headings* (LCSH), which can usually be found near the library catalog. This reference book lists the standard subject headings used in library catalogs. Here is an example from the LCSH:

Home schooling *(May Subd Geog)* ◄─────────── Additional information may follow heading
    Here are entered works on the provision of compulsory education in the home by parents as an alternative to traditional public or private schooling. General works on the provision of education in the home by educational personnel are entered under Domestic Education.

Used for ──────────►	UF	Education, Home	
		Home-based education	
		Home education	NT = Narrower term
		Home instruction	SA = See also
		Home teaching by parents	
		Homeschooling	
		Instruction, Home	
		Schooling, Home	
Broader Term ──────►	BT	Education	
Related Term ──────►	RT	Education—United States	
		Education—Parent participation	

Subject headings provide you with keywords to use as you look through catalogs and indexes. Notice that the LCSH entry begins by explaining the type of books that would be found under the subject heading (in this instance, "Home schooling"), and those that would be found elsewhere. An LCSH entry like the sample above could be useful even if, for example, you searched your school's library catalog using the keyword "Home schooling" and didn't find anything. You could refer to the "Related Term" section of the LCSH entry, which in this case includes "Education—United States" and "Education—Parent participation," for additional keywords to try.

Another way to locate subject headings when you are using the library's computer catalog is to select the keyword search option and type in the words or phrases that you think describe your topic. As you review the results of your search, look for the titles that most closely match the topics that you are looking for. When you call up the detailed displays for these titles, look for the section labeled SUBJECT or SUBJECT HEADING. (In the example that follows, this section is abbreviated as "Subj-lcsh.") In many computerized catalogs and indexes, these subject headings are links. You can click on them to look for other materials on the same subject. Make a note of all the subject headings that describe your topic in your working bibliography. Then you can use them the next time you start looking for information on your topic. Here is an example of an online catalog reference to a book on home schooling:

| Title: | Pathways to privatization in education / by Joseph Murphy . . . [et al.] |
| Imprint: | Greenwich, Conn.: Ablex Pub. Corp., c1998 |

LOCATION	CALL NO	STATUS
MAIN	LB2806.36 .P38 1998	NOT CHCKD OUT

Description:	xiii, 244 p.; 24 cm
Series:	Contemporary studies in social and policy issues in education
Subj-lcsh	**Privatization in education—United States**
	Educational vouchers—United States
	Home schooling—United States
Add author:	Murphy, Joseph, 1949–
Note(s):	Includes bibliographical references (p. 209–236) and index
ISBN:	1567503632 (cloth)
	1567503640 (pbk.)

Determining the Most Promising Sources

As you follow a subject heading into the library catalog and indexes, you will discover many seemingly relevant books and articles. How do you decide which ones to track down and examine? With little to go on but author, title, date, and publisher or periodical name, you may feel at a loss, but these details actually provide useful clues. Look again, for example, at the online catalog reference to a book on home schooling (see above). The title, *Pathways to Privatization in Education,* is the first clue to the subject coverage of the book. Note that the publication date, 1998, is somewhat recent. The subject headings show that this book focuses on various aspects of the privatization of education, which includes home schooling, and that the geographic focus of the book is the United States. The "Note(s)" section indicates that the book includes an extensive bibliography of other sources.

Now look at the following entry from *Education Index,* a periodical index:

> **Home schooling**
> Do children have to go to school? [Great Britain]
> C. Henson. *Child Educ (Engl)* v73 p68 Mr '96
> Homegrown learning [Twin Ridges Elementary School
> District combines homeschooling with regular
> classroom instruction] D. Hill. il *Teach Mag* v7 p40-5
> Ap '96
> Should we open extracurriculars to home-schoolers?
> J. Watford; B. Dickinson. il *Am Teach* v80 p4 Mr '96

This entry lists articles that address different aspects of home schooling, briefly describing some of the articles. The first article deals with the issue from a British point of view, which might provide an interesting cross-cultural perspective. The title of the third article seems to indicate an argument on the issue; that it appears in a magazine for teachers suggests it gives that profession's attitudes toward home schooling.

In addition, each entry contains the information needed to locate the source in a library. Going back to the first article, here is what each piece of information means:

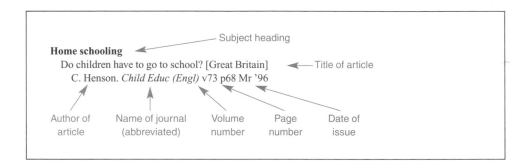

When you look in catalogs and indexes, consider the following points to help you to decide whether you should track down a particular source:

- *Relevance to your topic.* Do the title, subtitle, description, subject headings, and abstract help you determine just how directly the particular source addresses your topic?

- *Publication date.* How recent is the source? For current controversies, emerging trends, and continuing technical or medical developments, you must consult the most recent material. For historical or biographical topics, you will want to start with present-day perspectives but keep in mind that older sources also offer authoritative perspectives.

- *Description.* Does the length indicate a brief or an extended treatment of the topic? Does the work include illustrations that may elaborate on concepts discussed in the text? Does the work include a bibliography that could lead you to other works or an index that could give you an overview of what is discussed in the text? Does the abstract indicate the focus of the work?

From among the sources that look promising, select publications that seem by their titles to address different aspects of your topic or to approach it from different perspectives. Try to avoid selecting sources by the same author, from the same publisher, or in the same journal. Common sense will lead you to an appropriate decision about diversity in source materials.

■ SEARCHING LIBRARY ONLINE CATALOGS AND DATABASES

Through public access computers, most college libraries now offer access to their online catalog and databases. The library catalog is a database listing of books available on-site. Separate databases list the library's other holdings (such as periodicals, government documents, and some specialized CD-ROM products), provide access to periodical and newspaper indexes, and allow you to search the holdings of other libraries. Check your campus library's home page on one of the computers for a list of the resources that are available through its computer system.

Using Different Search Techniques

Many of the tools that are used to locate library sources are electronic, and you will be able to use these tools effectively if you have some idea how they work. Computerized library catalogs and databases consist of hundreds or thousands of records, each representing an individual item. The record is made up of different fields describing the item and allowing users to retrieve it from the database. Here is a record for a book from a library's online catalog with the searchable fields in bold:

Author:	Gordon, William MacGuire, 1935–
Title:	The law of home schooling / William M. Gordon, Charles J. Russo, Albert S. Milon. Topeka, Kan : National Organization on Legal Problems of Education, c1994.
Location:	Main
Call No:	JLL 74-383 no. 52
Description:	74 p.; 23 cm.
Series:	NOLPE monograph series no. 52.
Notes:	Includes bibliographical references and index.
Subjects:	Home schooling—Law and legislation—United States. Educational law and legislation—United States. Education—Parent participation—United States.
Other entries:	Russo, Charles J.

Basic search strategies include author, title, and subject searches. When you request an *author search,* the computer looks for a match between the name you type and the names listed in the author field of all the records in the online catalog or other database. When you request a *title search,* the computer looks for a match in the title field. Computers are very literal. They only try to match the *exact* terms you enter, and most do not recognize variant or incorrect spellings. That is an incentive to become a good speller and a good typist. In addition, you can be flexible where the computer cannot; for instance, if you were researching the topic of home schooling, you could do a *subject search* not only for "home schooling" but also for "homeschooling." Table 13.2 describes some search capabilities commonly offered by library catalogs and databases.

Table 13.2 Common Search Capabilities Offered by Library Catalogs and Databases

Type of Search	*How the Computer Conducts the Search*	*Things to Know*
Author Search (exact) • Individual (*Guterson, David*) • Organization (*U.S. Dept. of Education*)	Looks in the author field for the words entered	• Author searches generally are exact-match searches, so authors' names are entered *last name, first name* (for example, "Shakespeare, William"). If you enter "William Shakespeare," the computer will generate a list of authors whose last names are William. • Organizations can be considered authors. Enter the name of the organization in natural word order. • An exact-match author search is useful for finding books and articles by a particular author.
Title Search (exact) • Book title • Magazine or journal title • Article title	Looks in the title field for words in the exact order you enter them	An exact-match title search is useful for identifying the location of known items, such as when you are looking for a particular journal or book.
Subject Search (exact)	Looks in the subject heading or descriptor field for words in the exact order you enter them	An exact-match subject search is useful when you are sure about the subject heading.
Keyword Search	Looks in the title, note, subject, abstract, and text fields for the words entered	A keyword search is the broadest kind you can use. It is useful during early exploration of a subject.
Title Word Search • Book title • Magazine or journal title • Article title	Looks in the title field of the record for the words entered and ignores word order	Since this is not an exact-match search, entering "home and schooling" will retrieve the same records as entering "schooling and home."
Subject Word Search	Looks in the subject heading or descriptor field of the record for the words entered and ignores word order	Since this is not an exact-match search, entering "education privatization" will retrieve the same records as "privatization education."

Using Boolean Operators

The real power of using an online catalog or other database is demonstrated when you need to look up books or articles using more than one keyword or phrase. For example, suppose you want information about home schooling, but you are only interested in articles about home schooling in California. Rather than looking through an index that lists all the articles on home schooling and picking out those that mention California, you can ask the computer to do the work for you by linking your two keywords with the Boolean operator AND. Online searching operates according to *Boolean logic* (developed by and named after George Boole, a nineteenth-century mathematician). To understand Boolean logic, picture two sets of articles: the first contains all the articles in the database about home schooling, and the second contains all the articles in the database about California. A third set is formed by all the articles that belong in both sets because they are about both home schooling AND California. There are three Boolean operators: AND, OR, and NOT. Figure 13.4 on p. 366 provides an illustration of how each Boolean operator works.

Using Truncation

Another useful search strategy employs what is called *truncation*. With this technique, you can drop the ending of a word and replace it with a truncation symbol. For example, by entering the term "home school#" you would retrieve all the records that had terms such as "home school, home schooling, home schools, home schooled, or home schoolers." Truncation is useful when you want to retrieve both the plural and singular forms of a word or any word for which you are not sure of the ending. Truncation symbols vary with the catalog or database. The question mark (?), asterisk (*), and pound sign (#) are frequently used.

Table 13.3 offers some suggestions for expanding or narrowing your electronic search.

Table 13.3   Electronic Search Tips

If You Find Too Many Sources on Your Topic	If You Find Insufficient Information on Your Topic
• Use a subject heading search instead of a keyword search.	• Use a keyword or title search instead of a subject heading search.
• Add a concept word to your search.	• Eliminate unimportant words or secondary concepts from your search terms.
• Use a more precise vocabulary to describe your topic.	• Try truncated forms of your keyword.
	• Use different words to describe your topic.
	• Check the spelling of each term you type.

AND

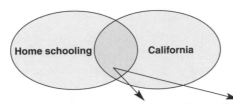

Returns references that contain both the terms **home schooling** AND **California**

- Narrows the search
- Combines unrelated terms
- Is the default used by most online catalogs and databases

OR

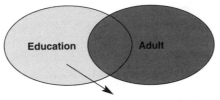

Returns all references that contain either the term **school** OR the term **education,** but not both

- Broadens the search **("OR is more")**
- Is useful with synonyms and variant spellings: ("home schooling" and "homeschooling")

NOT

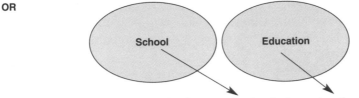

Returns references that include the term **education** but NOT the term **adult**

- Narrows the search
- May eliminate relevant material

Figure 13.4 The Boolean Operators: AND, OR, and NOT

■ LOCATING SOURCES

The following are guidelines for finding books, periodical articles, newspaper articles, government documents and statistical information, and other types of sources. To review the basic steps for finding books and periodicals, see Table 13.4.

Finding Books

The primary source for books is the library's computerized or online catalog. Besides flexibly searching keywords and subject headings, the catalog may tell you whether a

Table 13.4 Finding Books and Periodical Articles

Finding Books	Finding Periodical Articles
• Determine keywords or subject headings.	• Select an appropriate periodical index or database.
• Enter terms in the online catalog.	
• Evaluate results.	• Select a search option.
• Refine results if necessary.	• Display and evaluate the results of the search.
• Locate the books.	• Refine your search strategy if necessary.
	• Interpret results in order to locate the articles.
	• Print, email, or download results for later use.

book is currently available or checked out. It also allows you to print out source information rather than having to copy it by hand. However, it will require correct spelling and may contain only material received and cataloged after a certain date.

Whether you search a library catalog by author, title, subject, or keyword, each record you find will provide the following standard information. (See examples of records in online catalogs on pp. 361 and 363.) You will need this information to cite the book in your working bibliography and to locate it in the library.

1. *Call number:* This number, which usually appears on a separate line in the online catalog record, is your key to finding the book in the library. Most college libraries use the Library of Congress call-number system, whereas the Dewey system is used by most public libraries and some small college libraries. It is important to note the Library of Congress system uses both letters and numbers in the call number, and both are needed to locate a book. Call numbers serve two purposes: They provide an exact location for every book in the library and, because they are assigned according to subject classifications, they group books on the same topic together so that you know where browsing the stacks might be useful. Call numbers also give information about special collections of books kept in other library locations such as the reference room or government publications department. If the online catalog covers more than one library, the name of the library that has the book will also be included.

2. *Author:* The author's name appears last name first, followed by birth and death dates. For books with multiple authors, the record includes an author entry under each author's name.

3. *Title:* The title appears exactly as it does on the title page of the book, except that only the first word and proper nouns and adjectives are capitalized.

4. *Publication information:* The place of publication (usually just the city), the publisher, and the year of publication are listed. If the book was published simultaneously in the United States and abroad, both places of publication and both publishers are indicated.

5. *Physical description:* This section provides information about the book's page length and size. A roman numeral indicates the number of pages devoted to front matter (such as a preface, table of contents, and acknowledgments).

6. *Notes:* Any special features such as a bibliography or an index are listed here.

7. *Subject headings:* Assigned by the Library of Congress, these headings indicate how the book is listed in the subject catalog. They also provide useful links for finding other books on the same subject. (For more on the *Library of Congress Subject Headings* [LCSH], see p. 360.)

Finding Periodical Articles

The most up-to-date information on a subject is usually found not in books but in articles published in periodicals. A *periodical* is a publication such as a magazine, newspaper, or journal that is published on an ongoing basis at regular intervals (for instance, daily, weekly, monthly, or annually) and that has different content in each issue. Many periodicals now publish online versions of their print publications. In addition, "webzines" and electronic journals are periodicals published exclusively on the Web. Examples of periodicals include *Sports Illustrated* (magazine), the *New York Times* (newspaper), *Tulsa Studies in Women's Literature* (scholarly journal), *Kairos* (online journal for teachers), and *Slate* (online magazine or "webzine").

Articles in periodicals are usually not listed in the library catalog; to find them, you must use library reference works called *periodical indexes.* Some periodical indexes include *abstracts* or short summaries of articles. Indexes may be available in printed form, in microform, on CD-ROM, through the library's online catalog, or through the campus network. Many indexes and abstracts, including those listed later in this section, are available as computer databases. Regardless of format, periodical indexes all serve the same basic function of leading the user to articles on a specific topic. If you understand how to use one, you will be able to use others.

Distinguishing Scholarly Journals and Popular Magazines

Although they are both called periodicals, *journals* and *magazines* have important differences. Journals publish articles written by experts in a particular field of study, frequently professors or researchers in academic institutions. Journals are usually very specialized in their subject focus, research oriented, and extensively reviewed by specialists prior to publication. They are intended to be read by experts and students conducting research. Magazines, in contrast, usually publish general-interest articles written by journalists. The articles are written to entertain and educate the general public, and they tend to appeal to a much broader audience than journal articles.

Journals contain a great deal of what is called *primary literature,* reporting the results of original research. For example, a scientist might publish an article in a medical journal about the results of a new treatment protocol for breast cancer. *Secondary literature,* published in magazines, is intended to inform the general public about new

Table 13.5   How to Distinguish a Scholarly Journal from a Popular Magazine

Scholarly Journal	Popular Magazine
• The front or back cover lists the contents of the issue.	• The cover features a color picture.
• The title of the publication contains the word *Journal*.	• The title may be catchy as well as descriptive.
• You see the journal only at the library.	• You see the magazine for sale at the grocery store, in an airport, or at a bookstore.
• It does not include advertisements or advertises products such as textbooks, professional books, or scholarly conferences.	• It has lots of colorful advertisements in it.
• The authors of articles have *Ph.D.* or academic affiliations after their names.	• The authors of articles are journalists or reporters.
• Many articles have more than one author.	• Most articles have a single author but may quote experts.
• A short summary (abstract) of an article may appear on the first page.	• A headline or engaging description may precede the article.
• Most articles are fairly long, 5 to 20 pages.	• Most of the articles are fairly short, 1 to 5 pages.
• The articles may include charts, tables, figures, and quotations from other scholarly sources.	• The articles have color pictures and sidebar boxes.
• The articles have a bibliography (list of references to other books and articles) at the end.	• The articles do not include a bibliography.
• You probably would not read it at the beach.	• You might bring it to the beach to read.

and interesting developments in scientific and other areas of research. If a reporter from *Newsweek* wrote an article about the scientist's cancer research, this article would be classified as secondary literature. Table 13.5 above summarizes some of the important differences between scholarly journals and popular magazines.

Selecting an Appropriate Periodical Index or Abstract

Periodical indexes and abstracts are of two types: general and specialized. Both provide you with information that will help you locate articles on a topic.

General Indexes. These indexes are a good place to start your research because they cover a broad range of subjects. Most have separate author and subject listings as well as a list of book reviews. General indexes usually list articles from popular magazines, although some of them may include references to basic scholarly journals. Here is a list of the most common general indexes:

The Readers' Guide to Periodical Literature (1900–; online and CD-ROM, 1983–); updated quarterly. Covers about two hundred popular periodicals and may help you launch your search for sources on general and current topics. Even for general topics, however, you should not rely on it exclusively. Nearly all college libraries house far more than two hundred periodicals, and university research libraries house twenty thousand or more. The *Readers' Guide* does not even attempt to cover the research journals that play such an important role in college writing. Here is an example of an entry for "home education":

> **HOME EDUCATION**
> Home-school kids in public-school activities. D. Brock-
>   ett. *The Education Digest* v61 p67–9 N '95
> Pros and cons of home schooling. il *Parents* v70 p18
>   N '95
> Why homeschooling is important for America [address,
>   August 11, 1995] S. L. Blumenfeld. *Vital Speeches of
>   the Day* v61 p763–6 O 1 '95

Magazine Index. On microfilm (1988–), online (1973–), and on CD-ROM as part of InfoTrac (1973– ; see below). Indexes over four hundred magazines.

InfoTrac. On CD-ROM or online. Time coverage will vary by subscription. Includes three indexes: (1) the *General Periodicals Index,* which covers over twelve hundred general-interest publications, incorporating the *Magazine Index* and including the *New York Times* and the *Wall Street Journal;* (2) the *Academic Index,* which covers four hundred scholarly and general-interest publications, including the *New York Times;* and (3) the *National Newspaper Index,* which covers the *Christian Science Monitor, Los Angeles Times, New York Times, Wall Street Journal,* and *Washington Post.* Some entries also include abstracts of articles. This sample InfoTrac entry is from the *General Periodicals Index:*

AUTHOR(s):	Hawkins, Dana
TITLE(s):	Homeschool battles: clashes grow as some in the movement seek access to public schools.
	illustration photograph
Summary:	An estimated 500,000 students in the US study at home, and there is an increasing tension in some communities as some of the 'homeschoolers' attempt to use the public schools on a limited basis. The parents of one homeschooler in Oklahoma have sued the school district to gain access.
	U.S. News & World Report
	p57(2)
	Feb 12 1996 v120 n6
DESCRIPTORS:	Home schooling_Cases
	Public schools_Cases
	Education_Parent participation

more follows -- press <RETURN>   (Q to quit)

Access: The Supplementary Index to Periodicals (1979–). Indexes magazines not covered by the *Readers' Guide,* such as regional and particular-interest magazines (the environment, women's issues, etc.).

Alternative Press Index (1970–). Indexes alternative and radical publications.

Humanities Index (1974–; online and CD-ROM, 1984–). Covers 330 periodicals in archaeology, history, classics, literature, performing arts, philosophy, and religion.

Social Sciences Index (1974–; online and CD-ROM, 1983–). Covers four hundred periodicals in economics, geography, law, political science, psychology, public administration, and sociology. The complete text of certain articles is available on the CD-ROM.

Public Affairs Information Service Bulletin (PAIS) (1915–; online and CD-ROM, 1972–). Covers articles and other publications by public and private agencies on economic and social conditions, international relations, and public administration. Subject listings only.

Specialized Indexes and Abstracts.   Specialized indexes list or summarize articles devoted to technical or scholarly research. As you learn more about your topic, you will turn to specialized indexes and abstracts to find references to scholarly articles. The following example from *Sociological Abstracts,* which indexes and summarizes articles from a wide range of periodicals that publish sociological research, is typical of entries found in specialized indexes:

> **91X2727**
>
> **Mayberry, Maralee & Knowles, J. Gary** (Dept Sociology U Nevada, Las Vegas 89154), **Family Unity Objectives of Parents Who Teach Their Children: Ideological and Pedagogical Orientations to Home Schooling,** UM *The Urban Review,* 1989, 21, 4, Dec, 209–225.
>
> ¶ The objectives of parents who teach their children at home are examined, using results from 2 qualitative studies: (1) a study conducted in Ore in 1987/88, consisting of interview & questionnaire data (N = 15 & 800 families, respectively); & (2) an ongoing ethnographic study being conducted in Utah (N = 8 families). Analysis suggests that while families have complex motives for teaching their children at home, most respondents felt that establishing a home school would allow them to maintain or further develop unity within the family. It is concluded that a family's decision to home school is often made in an attempt to resist the effects on the family unit of urbanization & modernization. Policy implications are discussed. 36 References. Adapted from the source document. (Copyright 1991, Sociological Abstracts, Inc., all rights reserved.)

When you compare this entry with the previous citations from the *Readers' Guide* and InfoTrac's *General Periodicals Index* (both on p. 370), you will see differences in the following features:

- Format of the citations
- The authors' qualifications
- The titles of the articles
- The titles of the publications where the articles appear
- The length of the articles
- The amount of information given about the content of the articles

Here is a list of specialized periodical indexes that cover various disciplines:

ABI/INFORM (1971–) Online.

Accountant's Index (1944–).

America: History and Life (1954–; CD-ROM, 1964–).

American Statistics Index (1973–).

Applied Science and Technology Index (1958–). Online, CD-ROM.

Art Index (1929–; CD-ROM, 1984–).

Biological and Agricultural Index (1964–). CD-ROM.

Education Index (1929–). Online, CD-ROM.

Engineering Index (1920–).

Historical Abstracts (1955–; CD-ROM, 1982–).

Index Medicus (1961–). Online, CD-ROM (called MEDLINE).

MLA International Bibliography of Books and Articles in the Modern Languages and Literature (1921–). Online, CD-ROM.

Music Index (1949–; CD-ROM, 1981–1989).

Philosopher's Index (1957–). Online.

Psychological Abstracts (1927–). Online (called PsycINFO), CD-ROM (called PsycLIT).

Physics Abstracts (1898–). Online (called INSPEC).

Science Abstracts (1898–).

Sociological Abstracts (1952–). Online, CD-ROM (called Sociofile).

Most periodical indexes and abstracts use their own system of subject headings. *Sociological Abstracts,* for example, has a separate volume for subject headings. Check the opening pages of the index or abstract you are using, or, for online and CD-ROM material, refer to the system documentation to see how it classifies subjects. Then look for periodicals under your most useful subject heading or the heading that seems most similar to it. If you are using the online version of a periodical index, look at information such as the descriptors, thesaurus terms, or subject heading field. Besides telling you what subject headings have been assigned to each reference, the subject headings may function as links to lists of related materials.

Computer Databases.   Most libraries subscribe to online database networks and may own CD-ROM machines that are accessible through the library's computer terminals. Most research databases—like those in the preceding lists—are electronic indexes listing thousands of books and articles.

When you use an online database, check the first screen, which should let you know what information you are accessing. Although you can search a database by author or title, most likely you will use keywords, or descriptors, that describe the subject. Make your descriptors as precise as possible so that your database search results in a manage-able list of sources relevant to your topic. Most databases include a thesaurus of key-words or descriptors and a set of guidelines for using Boolean operators or other combining terms in your search. In addition, many databases include a browse func-tion. When you enter a descriptor, the system automatically lists the terms that are close to it alphabetically. If you enter a very general descriptor, the system provides that general term along with subtopics. Use these subtopics to narrow your search further before you ask the system to retrieve records.

Once you have typed in your descriptors, the computer searches the database and lists every reference to them it finds. If your search is extensive, you can usually print the results or download the records to your own disk. Because online databases contain so much information, you may want to consult with a librarian to develop an efficient search strategy. Also keep in mind that most electronic indexes cover only the last ten to fifteen years; you may need to consult older printed versions of indexes as well.

In addition to the database versions of the indexes listed earlier, many libraries sub-scribe to computer services in particular subject areas that provide abstracts or the full text of articles, either in the database (so you can see them onscreen) or by mail or fax for a fee. The use of computers for scholarly research is becoming more widespread, with new technology being developed all the time, so be sure to check with a librarian about what is available at your library. Some common computer services include the following:

ERIC (Educational Resources Information Center) (CD-ROM, 1969–; online 1966–). Indexes, abstracts, and provides some full texts of articles from 750 education journals.

Business Periodicals Ondisc (1988–) and *ABI/INFORM* (1988–). Provide full-text articles from business periodicals. If your library has a laser printer attached to a terminal, you can print out articles, including illustrations.

PsycBooks (1987–). CD-ROM database that indexes books and book chapters in psychology.

Carl/Uncover (1988–). <http://www.carl.org/carl.html>. An online document delivery service that lists over three million articles from twelve thousand jour-nals. For a fee, you can receive the full text of the article by fax, usually within a few hours.

Interlibrary networks. Known by different names in different regions, these net-works allow you to search in the catalogs of colleges and universities in your area and across the country. In many cases, you can request a book by interlibrary loan. It may take several weeks for you to receive the material. You can also request a copy of an article from a journal to which your own library does not subscribe. Most libraries do not loan their journals but will copy and forward articles for a fee.

Periodicals Representing Particular Viewpoints. Some specialized periodical indexes tend to represent particular viewpoints and may help you identify different positions on an issue.

Index to Black Periodicals (1984–). An author and subject index to general and scholarly articles about African Americans.

Left Index (1982–). An author and subject index to over eighty periodicals with a Marxist, radical, or left perspective. Listings primarily cover topics in the social sciences and humanities.

Chicano Index (1967–). An index to general and scholarly articles about Mexican Americans. Articles are arranged by subject with author and title indexes. (Before 1989, the title was *Chicano Periodical Index.*)

Another useful source for identifying positions is *Editorials on File,* described on p. 376.

Locating Periodicals in the Library. When you identify a promising magazine or journal article in a periodical index, you must go to the library's serial record, online catalog, or periodicals database to learn whether the library subscribes to the periodical and, if so, where you can find the issue you need. Although every library arranges its periodicals differently, recent issues of periodicals are usually arranged alphabetically by title on open shelves. Older issues may be bound like books (shelved by call numbers or alphabetically by title) or filmed and available in microform. Ask a librarian at the reference desk to find out how the periodicals in your library are arranged.

Suppose you want to look up the article on home schooling indexed in *Sociological Abstracts* (see p. 372). Here is a typical record for the *Urban Review* from a library's online catalog or periodicals database. Notice that the title search refers to the title of the journal, *Urban Review,* not the title of the article from the journal.

You searched TITLE   **Urban Review**

— Title of the journal

Title: The Urban Review
Imprint: New York, Agathon Press [etc.] ◄——————— Where the journal is published
                  Library where the journal is located and location of
                      ↓   current (unbound) issues
LOCATION: MAIN-Latest in Curr Per   LC 5101 U75 ◄——— Call number
LIB. HAS: B16-30(1984-98) ◄——— Bound volumes and years the library owns
Latest Received: June 1999 31:2 ◄——— Most recent issue received

---

In this instance, you would learn that the library does subscribe to the *Urban Review* and that you could locate the 1989 article in one of the bound volumes in the library's collection. Remember that no library can subscribe to every periodical, so always copy down references to more articles than you need to look up. This will save you from frustration later when you find out that the library you are using does not subscribe to all the journals you need.

Using Collections of Electronic Journals. Many large libraries subscribe to services that provide electronic access to the text of journals, usually to recent issues. These services tend to be expensive, so they may not be available in smaller college libraries. Ask the reference librarian if any of them are available to you. Table 13.6 lists some services that provide the full text of journals.

Finding Newspaper Articles

Newspapers provide useful information for many research topics in such areas as foreign affairs, economic issues, public opinion, and social trends. Libraries usually miniaturize newspapers and store them on microfilm (reels) or microfiche (cards) that must be placed in viewing machines to be read. Newspaper indexes such as the *Los Angeles Times Index, New York Times Index,* and *London Times Index* help you locate specific articles on your topic. College libraries usually have indexes to local newspapers as well.

Your library may also subscribe to newspaper article and digest services, such as the following:

National Newspaper Index. On microfilm (1989–); online (1979–) and on CD-ROM as part of InfoTrac (see p. 370). Indexes the *Christian Science Monitor, Los Angeles Times, New York Times, Wall Street Journal,* and *Washington Post.*

NewsBank (1970–). On microfiche and CD-ROM. Full-text articles from five hundred U.S. newspapers. A good source of information on local and regional issues and trends.

Table 13.6 Some Collections of Electronic Journals

Service	Subject Areas	Source	Time Coverage
IDEAL Online Library <http://www.idealibrary.com/index.html>	Science, technology, mathematics, and social sciences	250 journals published by Academic Press, Churchill Livingstone, and W. B. Saunders	1997–present
LEXIS-NEXIS Academic Universe <http://www.lexis-nexis.com/lncc/academic>	Legal, news, government information, and statistics	Various academic journals and other sources	Varies by source
JSTOR <http://www.jstor.org>	Humanities and social sciences	117 academic journals	Provides electronic access to older issues
Project Muse <http://muse.jhu.edu>	Humanities, social sciences, and mathematics	Over 40 journals from Johns Hopkins University Press	1996–present
Science Direct <http://www.sciencedirect.com>	Science, technology, medicine, and social sciences	More than 1,000 Elsevier Press journals	1997–present

Newspaper Abstracts (1988 – ; CD-ROM, 1991 –). Indexes and gives brief abstracts of articles from nineteen major regional, national, and international newspapers.

Facts on File (weekly; CD-ROM, 1980 –). A digest of U.S. and international news events arranged by subject, such as foreign affairs, arts, education, religion, and sports.

Editorials on File (twice monthly). A digest of editorials from 150 U.S. and Canadian newspapers. Each entry includes a brief description of an editorial subject followed by fifteen to twenty editorials on the subject, reprinted from different newspapers.

Editorial Research Reports (1924 –). Reports on current and controversial topics, including brief histories, statistics, editorials, journal articles, endnotes, and supplementary reading lists.

African Recorder (1970 –). Articles on African issues from African newspapers.

Asian Recorder (1971 –). Articles on Asian issues from Asian newspapers.

Canadian News Facts (1972 –). On CD-ROM. A digest of current articles from Canadian newspapers such as the *Montreal Star, Toronto Star,* and *Vancouver Sun.* Some articles are available as full text on the CD-ROM.

Foreign Broadcast Information Service (FBIS) (1980 –). A digest of foreign broadcast scripts, newspaper articles, and government statements from Asia, Europe, Latin America, Africa, Russia, and the Middle East.

Keesing's Contemporary Archives (weekly). A digest of events in all countries, compiled from British reporting services. Includes speeches and statistics. Index includes chronological, geographic, and topical sections.

Finding Government and Statistical Information

Federal, state, and local governments are making more of their publications and services available through the World Wide Web. Ask a reference librarian for assistance in locating government sources on the Web. In addition, consider consulting the following sources for information on political subjects and national trends. Although these publications are not always listed in library catalogs or databases, they can usually be found in the reference area or the government documents department of college libraries. If these works are not listed in your library's online catalog, ask for assistance in locating them.

Sources for Researching Political Subjects.   Two publications that report developments in the federal government can be rich sources of information on political issues. Types of material they cover include congressional hearings and debates, presidential proclamations and speeches, Supreme Court decisions and dissenting opinions, and compilations of statistics.

Congressional Quarterly Almanac (annual). A summary of legislation that provides an overview of government policies and trends, including analysis as well as
election results, records of roll-call votes, and the text of significant speeches and
debates.

Congressional Quarterly Weekly Report. A news service that includes up-to-
date summaries of committee actions, votes, and executive branch activities as
well as overviews of current policy discussions and other activities of the federal
government.

Sources for Researching Trends.   Research can help you identify trends to write
about and, most important, provide the statistical evidence you need to demonstrate
the existence of a trend. The following resources can be especially helpful:

Statistical Abstract of the United States (annual). Issued by the Bureau of the
Census, this volume provides a variety of social, economic, and political statistics,
often covering several years. It includes tables, graphs, and charts and gives references to additional sources of information. Selected information is available on
the Web at <http://www.census.gov/statab/www>.

American Statistics Index (1974–; annual with monthly supplements). This
index attempts to cover all federal government publications containing statistical
information of research significance and includes brief descriptions of references.

Statistical Reference Index (1980–). Claiming to be "a selective guide to American statistical publications from sources other than the U.S. government," this
index includes economic, social, and political statistical sources.

World Almanac and Book of Facts (annual). This publication presents information on a variety of subjects drawn from many sources. It includes such things as a
chronology of the year, climatological data, and lists of inventions and awards.

The Gallup Poll: Public Opinion (1935–). This chronological listing of the
results of public opinion polls includes information on social, economic, and
political trends.

In addition to researching the trend itself, you may want to research others' specula-
tions about its causes. If so, the reports of federal government activities described in
the preceding section may be helpful.

Finding Other Library Sources

Libraries hold a vast amount of useful materials other than books, periodicals, and
government documents. Some of the following library sources and services may be
appropriate for your research.

- *Vertical files:* Pamphlets and brochures from government and private agencies
- *Special collections:* Manuscripts, rare books, and materials of local interest

- *Audio collections:* Records, audiotapes, music CDs, readings, and speeches
- *Video collections:* Slides, filmstrips, and videotapes
- *Art collections:* Drawings, paintings, and engravings
- *Interlibrary loans:* Many libraries can arrange to borrow books from other libraries or have copies of journal articles sent from other libraries as part of an inter-library loan program. Ask your librarian how long it will take to get the material you need (usually several weeks) and how to use the loan service (some libraries allow you to send an electronic request to the local interlibrary loan office).
- *Computer resources:* Many libraries house interactive computer programs that combine text, video, and audio resources in history, literature, business, and other disciplines.

■ USING THE INTERNET FOR RESEARCH

The *Internet* is a vast global computer network that enables users to store and share information and resources quickly and easily. The World Wide Web is a network of Web sites, each with its own electronic address (called a URL, or uniform resource locator). You may be able to gain access to the Internet through your library or through a commercial Internet service provider (ISP). To search the Web, you also need a Web browser such as Netscape or Internet Explorer. By now, most of you are familiar with searching the Internet. This section will provide some basic background information about the Net and introduce you to some tools and strategies that will help you use the Internet more efficiently to find information on a topic.

Library catalogs, electronic periodical indexes and abstracts, full-text electronic journal databases, and many government sites are all a part of the Internet. In addition, many other types of resources on the Web can help you with your research topic.

As you use the Internet for conducting research, be sure to keep the following concerns and guidelines in mind.

- *The Internet has no central system of organization.* On the Internet, a vast amount of information is stored on many different networks, on different servers, and in different formats, each with its own system of organization. The Internet has no central catalog, reference librarian, or standard classification system for the vast resources available there.
- *Personal and commercial Internet sources can be less reliable than Internet sources to which your library or campus subscribes or than print sources.* Because it is relatively easy for anyone with a Web page to "publish" on the Internet, judging the reliability of online information is a special concern. Depending on your topic, purpose, and audience, the sources you find on the Internet may not be as credible or authoritative as library sources, and for some topics most of what you find may be written by amateurs. In most cases, you will need to balance or supplement personal or commercial Internet sources with subscription resources from your

library or campus and print sources. When in doubt about the reliability of an online source for a particular assignment, check with your instructor. (See Reading Sources with a Critical Eye later in this chapter for more specific suggestions.)

- *Personal or commercial Internet sources may not be as stable as Internet sources to which the library or campus subscribes.* If you are looking for information on a topic, it is possible that a Web site that existed last week is no longer available today.

- *Internet sources must be documented.* The requirements for documenting source material found on the Internet and source materials found in more traditional sources are the same, though the formats are slightly different. You will need to follow appropriate conventions for quoting, paraphrasing, and documenting the online sources you cite, just as you do for print sources. (Citing Internet sources using MLA style is discussed in Chapter 14, pp. 407–11; APA style is discussed on pp. 418–21.)

- *Keep a working bibliography.* A working bibliography for Internet research serves the same purpose as one for library research. It is an ongoing record of all the sources you discover as you research your subject. (See Figure 13.5 for an example.) The working bibliography becomes the draft for the list of works cited at the end of your essay, even if you do not include all these sources in your final list. The working bibliography will also help you keep track of the addresses (URLs) for the Web sites you visit.

As you locate useful Web sites, record this information in your working bibliography for each site you look up:

Author: _____

Title: _____

Site address: _____

Email address of webmaster: _____

Sponsoring institution: _____

Date of publication: _____

Date of latest update: _____   Date of access: _____

Linkage data: _____

Keywords: _____

Figure 13.5 Information for Working Bibliography—Internet Sources

■ NAVIGATING THE WEB

A *Web browser* is a software program that allows you to display and navigate Web pages on your computer. Web browsers have evolved from basic text-driven browsers such as Lynx into graphical, point-and-click interfaces such as Netscape Navigator and Microsoft Internet Explorer, which support not only text and hypertext links but also sound, images, animation, and video.

Finding Home Pages

A particular Web site usually consists of a home page and pages to which it is linked. A *home page* is the page you most often find first when you access a Web site; it typically provides a title heading, a brief introduction or overview; and a brief table of contents consisting of links to the information available at that site. In this way, it functions like the opening pages of a book. Figure 13.6 shows the home page for the National Home Education Network (NHEN). The bottom of a home page usually includes the name of the person or group responsible for the site and an email address to which you can send requests for further information. Companies, educational institutions, government agencies, organizations, clubs, or individuals can sponsor Web sites.

Using Links

On a World Wide Web page (and in other electronic documents, such as email), *links* to other information are often indicated by underlined text (sometimes with words in bold type or highlighted in another way). For example, the National Home Education Network home page provides a link to the NHEN newsletter, *Voices*. Links can also appear as boxes, buttons, icons, or other graphic images that, when clicked, link to further information. On a color monitor, they are indicated by a different color, and change color once they have been visited. In addition to providing connections to other documents, the links on a home page can perform many other functions—for example, they may open a form to be filled out by the reader, start a video, play music, generate sound, or provide a template for sending an email message to the person responsible for maintaining the Web site.

Understanding URLs

Each Web home page has its own address or *uniform resource locator (URL)*. The URL allows people anywhere in the world to locate a particular Web page. The URL for the National Home Education Network follows the typical pattern: <http://www .nhen.org>.

- The first part of a URL for a Web page usually consists of the abbreviation *http://* (meaning "hypertext transfer protocol"); it tells the sending and receiving computers how to transfer the information being sent.

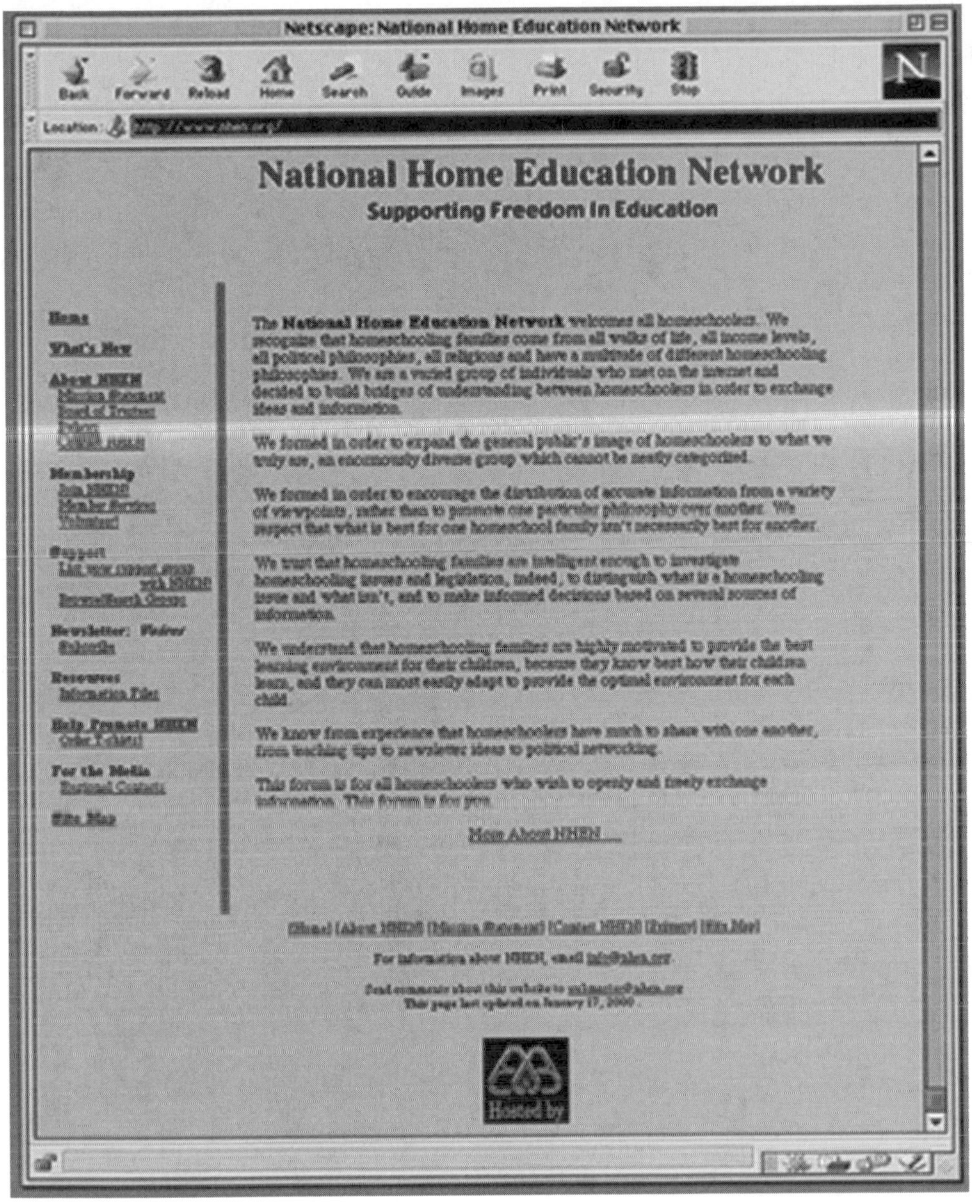

Figure 13.6 Home Page for the National Home Education Network

- The second part of the URL includes the standard *www.*, to establish that the location being accessed is on the World Wide Web, as well as the Internet address of the institution, government agency, corporation, or organization (and the country, if outside of the United States) where the document is located. The three-letter suffix tells the domain of the site; that is, who owns the computer storing the information. *nhen.org* is the address of the National Home Education Network site. The suffix *.org* indicates that it is a site maintained by an organization.

.com = commercial site

.edu = educational institution site

.gov = government site

.org = organization site

.mil = military site

.net = Internet service site

- After a slash, the third part of the URL (which may be quite lengthy) gives the address of the directory and file where the page is found as well as the name of the specific page itself (as in *newsletter/index.html* for the NHEN newsletter, *Voices*).

Creating Bookmarks

When you find a Web page that you may want to visit again, it is a good idea to create a bookmark for that page. For example, in the Netscape program you create a bookmark by choosing Add Bookmark from the Bookmarks menu. The title of the Web page and its URL will be stored in the bookmarks list of the computer you are using. If you are using a computer in a lab, not your own computer at home, you will need to download your bookmarks on to a disk if you want to save them. If you want to return to a site and are unfamiliar with using bookmarks, it is a good idea to write down the URL.

Accessing a Web Site

You may directly access a particular Web site in several ways:

- By typing the URL directly into the location box and then pressing Return or Enter on your keyboard
- By selecting Open Location from the file menu and typing the URL into the dialogue box
- By pasting or copying the URL into the location box from some other source, such as the computer's scrapbook or clipboard
- By selecting the URL from the bookmark menu, if you have previously saved a bookmark for that page

The method you use to access a URL may depend on your Web browser.

■ USING SEARCH ENGINES

Because the World Wide Web does not have a central directory that will point you to specific resources, *search engines* are important resources for searching the Web for information on your topic. Search engines will help you look for information, but in order to use them effectively, you should understand their features, strengths, and limitations. Just as there are many periodical indexes available to help you find articles on your topic, there are many search engines available to help you look for information on the Internet. Table 13.7 lists some popular search engines. However, no *single* search engine searches *every* Web site. In fact, according to an article by Steve Lawrence and C. Lee Giles that appeared in the July 8, 1999, issue of *Nature:*

- No one search engine covers more than 16 percent of the Web.
- Search engine overlap "remains relatively low." (This means that different search engines point you to different Web sites even when you enter the same information.)
- Used together, eleven major search engines (AltaVista, EuroSeek, Excite, Google, HotBot, Infoseek, Lycos, MSN Search, Northern Light, Snap, WebCrawler, and Yahoo!) produce 42-percent coverage of the Web.
- "Popularity" of a Web page (that is, a page with many links, which results in the page being accessed many times) is growing in use as a ranking factor in results lists.

Table 13.7   Commonly Used Search Engines and Meta-Search Engines

Name	*URL*
Search Engines	
AltaVista	http://www.altavista.com
EuroSeek	http://www.euroseek.net
Excite	http://www.excite.com
Google	http://www.google.com
HotBot	http://www.hotbot.com
Infoseek	http://infoseek.go.com
Lycos	http://www.lycos.com
MSN Search	http://search.msn.com
Northern Light	http://www.northernlight.com
Snap	http://www.snap.com
WebCrawler	http://webcrawler.com
Yahoo!	http://www.yahoo.com
Meta-Search Engines (search multiple search engines and directories)	
All-in-One Search Page	http://www.allonesearch.com
Dogpile	http://www.dogpile.com
MetaCrawler	http://www.metacrawler.com
ProFusion	http://www.profusion.com
SavvySearch	http://www.savvysearch.com
WebTaxi SuperSearch	http://www.webtaxi.com/taxi/sswebtop.htm

Always click on the link called "Help," "Hints," or "Tips" on a search engine's Web page to find out more about the recognized commands and advanced search techniques for that specific search engine. Table 13.8 lists some common search engine commands that yield powerful results. These work in most search engines. Double-check the help section if you do not get the results you expect.

Finally, the success of a Web search depends on the keywords you choose; most initial searches yield more sources than any person could look at in a lifetime. Try to narrow your search by using some of the keyword and search techniques described in this chapter (see pp. 359–66). Remember that many different words often describe the same topic. If your topic is ecology, for example, you may find information under the keywords *ecosystem, environment, pollution,* and *endangered species,* as well as a number of other related keywords, depending on the focus of your research. When you find a source that seems promising, be sure to create a bookmark for the Web page so that you can return to it easily later on.

■ READING SOURCES WITH A CRITICAL EYE

From the beginning of your search, you should evaluate potential sources to determine which ones to use in your essay. Obviously, you must decide which sources provide information relevant to the topic. But you must also read sources with a critical eye to decide how credible or trustworthy they are. Just because a book or essay appears in print or online does not necessarily mean that an author's information or opinions are reliable.

Selecting Relevant Sources

Begin your evaluation of sources by narrowing your working bibliography to the most relevant works. Consider them in terms of scope, date of publication, and viewpoint.

Scope and Approach. To decide how relevant a particular source is to your topic, you need to examine the source in depth. Do not depend on title alone, for it may be

---

Table 13.8 Common Search-Engine Commands

+	A plus sign **requires** all the terms to be in any records retrieved or at least pages not having all the terms will appear toward the end of the list. Operation is similar to an AND Boolean operator (see pp. 365–66).
—	A minus sign **excludes** pages that have the identified term or at least the pages retrieved will appear toward the end of the list. Operation is similar to a NOT Boolean operator (see pp. 365–66).
" "	Quotation marks around a set of words cause them to be searched together as a phrase; for example, "home schooling."
*	A **truncation** symbol includes related word variations (see p. 365).
a A	If you want the word you are looking for only if it is capitalized (in a proper noun like *California,* for example), capitalize the word when you enter it into the search engine. This will exclude pages that have only noncapitalized instances of the word.

misleading. If the source is a book, check its table of contents and index to see how many pages are devoted to the precise subject you are exploring. In most cases, you will want an in-depth, not a superficial, treatment of the subject. Read the preface or introduction to a book or the abstract or opening paragraphs of an article and any biographical information given about the author to determine the author's basic approach to the subject or special way of looking at it. As you attend to these elements, consider the following questions:

- Does the source provide a general or specialized view? General sources are helpful early in your research, but then you need the authority or up-to-date coverage of specialized sources. Extremely specialized works, however, may be too technical.
- Is the source long enough to provide adequate detail?
- Is the source written for general readers? Specialists? Advocates? Critics?
- Is the author an expert on the topic? Does the author's way of looking at the topic support or challenge your own views? (The fact that an author's viewpoint challenges your own does not mean that you should reject the author as a source, as you will see from the discussion on multiple viewpoints.)
- Is the information in the source substantiated elsewhere? Does its approach seem to be comparable to, or a significant challenge to, the approaches of other credible sources?

Date of Publication.   Although you should always consult the most up-to-date sources available on your subject, older sources often establish the principles, theories, and data on which later work is based and may provide a useful perspective for evaluating it. If older works are considered authoritative, you may want to become familiar with them. To determine which sources are authoritative, note the ones that are cited most often in encyclopedia articles, bibliographies, and recent works on the subject. If your source is on the Web, consider whether it has been regularly updated.

Viewpoint.   Your sources should represent a variety of viewpoints on the subject. Just as you would not depend on a single author for all of your information, so you do not want to use authors who all belong to the same school of thought. For suggestions on determining authors' viewpoints, see the following Identifying Bias section.

Using sources that represent different viewpoints is especially important when developing an argument for one of the essay assignments in Chapters 5–7. During the invention work in those chapters, you may want to research what others have said about your subject to see what positions have been staked out and what arguments have been made. You will then be able to define the issue more carefully, collect arguments supporting your position, and anticipate arguments opposing it.

Identifying Bias

One of the most important aspects of evaluating a source is identifying any bias in its treatment of the subject. Although the word *bias* may sound accusatory, it simply refers to the fact that most writing is not neutral or objective and does not try or claim to be. Authors come to their subjects with particular viewpoints. In using sources, you must consider carefully how these viewpoints are reflected in the writing and how they affect the way authors present their arguments.

Although the text of the source will give you the most precise indication of the author's viewpoint, you can often get a good idea by looking at the preface or introduction or at the sources the author cites. When you examine a reference, you can often determine the general point of view it represents by considering the following elements.

Title.   Does the title or subtitle indicate the text's bias? Watch for loaded words or confrontational phrasing.

Author.   What is the author's professional title or affiliation? What is the author's perspective? Is the author in favor of something or at odds with it? What has persuaded the author to take this stance? How might the author's professional affiliation affect his or her perspective? What is the author's tone? Information on the author may also be available in the book or article itself, the Web page, or in biographical sources available in the library.

Presentation of Argument.   Almost every written work asserts a point of view or makes an argument for something the author considers important. To determine this position and the reason behind it, look for the main point. What evidence does the author provide as support for this point? Is the evidence from authoritative sources? Is the evidence persuasive? Does the author accommodate or refute opposing arguments?

Publication Information.   Is the book published by a commercial publisher, a corporation, a government agency, or an interest group? Is the Web site sponsored by a business, a professional group, an educational institution, or a government agency? What is that organization's position on the topic? Is the author funded by or affiliated with the organization?

Editorial Slant.   What kind of periodical or online source published the article—popular, academic, alternative? If the article is available on a Web site, is the site maintained by a commercial or academic organization? Does the site provide links to other Web resources? For periodicals, knowing some background about the publisher or periodical can help you determine bias because all periodicals have their own editorial slants. In cases where the publication title does not indicate bias, reference sources may help you determine this information. Two of the most common are the following:

- *Gale Directory of Publications and Broadcast Media* (1990–, updated yearly). A useful source for descriptive information on newspapers and magazines. Entries often include an indication of intended audience and political or other bias.

For example, the *San Diego Union* is described as a "newspaper with a Republican orientation."

- *Magazines for Libraries* (1997). A listing of over 6,500 periodicals arranged by academic discipline. For each discipline, there is a list of basic indexes, abstracts, and periodicals. Each individual listing for a periodical includes its publisher, the date it was founded, the places it is indexed, its intended audience, and an evaluation of its content and editorial focus. Here is an example of one such listing:

> 2605. *Growing Without Schooling.* [ISSN: 0745-5305]
> 1977. bi-m. $25. Susannah Sheffer. Holt Assocs., 2269 Massachusetts Ave., Cambridge, MA 02140. Illus., index, adv. Sample. Circ: 5,000.
> *Bk. rev:* 0–4, 400–600 words, signed. *Aud:* Ga, Sa.
> *GWS* is a journal by and for home schoolers. Parents and students share their views as to why they chose home schooling and what they like about it. While lesson plans or activities are not included, home schoolers could get ideas for interesting activities from articles chronicling their experiences ("Helping Flood Victims," "Legislative Intern"). "News and Reports" offers home schoolers information on legal issues while the "Declassified Ads" suggest resources geared toward home schoolers. This is an important title for public libraries and should be available to students and faculty in teacher preparation programs.

14

Strategies for Using and Acknowledging Sources

In addition to your own firsthand observation and analysis, your writing in college will be expected to include secondary sources — readings, interviews, Web sites, computer bulletin boards, lectures, and other print and nonprint materials.

When you cite material from another source, you need to acknowledge the source, usually by citing the author and page or date (depending on the documentation system) in your text and including a list of works cited or references at the end of your paper. It is necessary to acknowledge sources correctly and accurately in order to avoid *plagiarism*. Plagiarism is the act of using the words and ideas of others as if they were your own. By citing sources correctly, you give credit to the originator of the words and ideas you are using, give your readers the information they need to consult those sources directly, and build your own credibility.

This chapter provides guidelines for using sources effectively and acknowledging them accurately. It includes model citations for both the Modern Language Association (MLA) and American Psychological Association (APA) documentation styles.

■ USING SOURCES

Writers commonly use sources by quoting directly, by paraphrasing, and by summarizing. This section provides guidelines for deciding when to use each of these three methods and how to do so effectively.

Deciding Whether to Quote, Paraphrase, or Summarize

As a general rule, quote only in these situations: (1) when the wording of the source is particularly memorable or vivid or expresses a point so well that you cannot improve it without destroying the meaning, (2) when the words of reliable and respected authorities would lend support to your position, (3) when you wish to highlight the author's opinions, (4) when you wish to cite an author whose opinions challenge or vary greatly from those of other experts, or (5) when you are going to discuss the source's choice of words. Paraphrase passages whose details you wish to note completely but whose language is not particularly striking. Summarize any long passages whose main points you wish to record selectively as background or general support for a point you are making.

Quoting

Quotations should duplicate the source exactly. If the source has an error, copy it and add the notation *sic* (Latin for "thus") in brackets immediately after the error to indicate that it is not your error but your source's:

> According to a recent newspaper article, "Plagirism [sic] is a problem among journalists and scholars as well as students" (Berensen 62).

However, you can change quotations (1) to emphasize particular words by underlining or italicizing them, (2) to omit irrelevant information or to make the quotation conform grammatically to your sentence by using ellipsis marks, and (3) to make the quotation conform grammatically or to insert information by using brackets.

Underlining or Italicizing for Emphasis.   You may underline or italicize any words in the quotation that you want to emphasize, and add the words *emphasis added* (in regular type, not italicized or underlined) in brackets immediately after the words you want to emphasize.

> In his introduction, Studs Terkel (1972) claims that his book is about a search for "daily meaning as well as daily bread, for recognition as well as cash, for astonishment rather than torpor [emphasis added]; in short, for a sort of life rather than a Monday through Friday sort of dying" (p. xi).

Using Ellipsis Marks for Omissions.   Ellipsis marks—three spaced periods (. . .)— signal that something has been left out of a quotation. When you omit words from within a quotation, you must use ellipsis marks in place of the missing words. If you are following the MLA style, place brackets around ellipses you have inserted to distinguish them from any ellipsis marks the author may have used. When the omission occurs within the sentence, include a space before the first bracket and after the closing bracket. There should also be spaces between the three ellipsis marks, but not between the opening bracket and the first ellipsis point or between the closing bracket and the last ellipsis point.

> Hermione Roddice is described in Lawrence's *Women in Love* as a "woman of the new school, full of intellectuality and [. . .] nerve-worn with consciousness" (17).

When the omission falls at the end of a sentence, place a sentence period *directly after* the closing bracket.

> But Grimaldi's recent commentary on Aristotle contends that for Aristotle rhetoric, like dialectic, had "no limited and unique subject matter upon which it must be exercised [. . .]. Instead, rhetoric as an art transcends all specific disciplines and may be brought into play in them" (6).

A period plus ellipsis marks can indicate the omission of the rest of the sentence as well as whole sentences, paragraphs, or even pages.

When a parenthetical reference follows the ellipsis marks at the end of a sentence, place the three spaced periods after the quotation, and place the sentence period after the final parenthesis:

> But Grimaldi's recent commentary on Aristotle contends that for Aristotle rhetoric, like dialectic, had "no limited and unique subject matter upon which it must be exercised [. . .]" (6).

Of course, a writer may decide to leave certain words out of a quotation because they are not relevant to the point being made or because they add information readers will not need in the context in which the quotation is being used. When you quote only single words or phrases, you do not need to use ellipsis marks because it will be obvious that you have left out some of the original.

> More specifically, Wharton's imagery of suffusing brightness transforms Undine before her glass into "some fabled creature whose home was in a beam of light" (21).

Using Brackets for Insertions or Changes.   Use brackets around an insertion or a change needed to make a quotation conform grammatically to your sentence, such as a change in the tense of a verb, in the capitalization of the first letter of the first word of a quotation, or in a pronoun. In this example from an essay on James Joyce's "Araby," the writer adapts Joyce's phrases "we played till our bodies glowed" and "shook music from the buckled harness" to fit the tense of her sentences:

> In the dark, cold streets during the "short days of winter," the boys must generate their own heat by "[playing] till [their] bodies glowed." Music is "[shaken] from the buckled harness" as if it were unnatural, and the singers in the market chant nasally of "the troubles in our native land" (30).

You may also use brackets to add or substitute explanatory material in a quotation:

> Guterson notes that among Native Americans in Florida, "education was in the home; learning by doing was reinforced by the myths and legends which repeated the basic value system of their [the Seminoles'] way of life" (159).

Several kinds of changes necessary to make a quotation conform grammatically to another sentence may be made without any signal to readers: (1) A period at the end of a quotation may be changed to a comma if you are using the quotation within your own sentence, and (2) double quotation marks enclosing a quotation may be changed to single quotation marks when the quotation is enclosed within a longer quotation.

Integrating Quotations

Depending on its length, a quotation may be incorporated into your text by enclosing it in quotation marks or set off from your text in a block without quotation marks. In either case, be sure to blend the quotation into your essay rather than dropping it in without appropriate integration.

In-Text Quotations.   Incorporate brief quotations (no more than four typed lines of prose or three lines of poetry) into your text. You may place the quotation virtually anywhere in your sentence:

At the Beginning

"To live a life is not to cross a field," Sutherland quotes Pasternak at the beginning of her narrative (11).

In the Middle

Woolf begins and ends by speaking of the need of the woman writer to have "money and a room of her own" (4)—an idea that certainly spoke to Plath's condition.

At the End

In *The Second Sex,* Simone de Beauvoir describes such an experience as one in which the girl "becomes as object, and she sees herself as object" (378).

Divided by Your Own Words

"Science usually prefers the literal to the nonliteral term," Kinneavy writes, "—that is, figures of speech are often out of place in science" (177).

When you quote poetry within your text, use a slash (/) with spaces before and after to signal the end of each line of verse:

Alluding to St. Augustine's distinction between the City of God and the Earthly City, Lowell writes that "much against my will / I left the City of God where it belongs" (1–5).

Block Quotations.   In the MLA style, put in block form prose quotations of five or more typed lines and poetry quotations of four or more lines. In the APA style, use block form for quotations of forty words or more. If you are using the MLA style, indent the quotation an inch (ten character spaces) from the left margin, as shown in the following example. If you are using the APA style, indent the block quotation five to seven spaces, keeping your indents consistent throughout your paper.

In a block quotation, double-space between lines just as you do in your text. *Do not* enclose the passage within quotation marks. Use a colon to introduce a block quotation, unless the context calls for another punctuation mark or none at all. When quoting a single paragraph or part of one in the MLA style, do not indent the first line of the quotation more than the rest. In quoting two or more paragraphs, indent the first line of each paragraph an extra quarter inch (three spaces). If you are using the APA style, the first line of subsequent paragraphs in the block quotation indents an additional five to seven spaces from the block quotation indent.

```
In "A Literary Legacy from Dunbar to Baraka," Margaret Walker
says of Paul Lawrence Dunbar's dialect poems:
        He realized that the white world in the United
        States tolerated his literary genius only because
```

> of his "jingles in a broken tongue," and they
> found the old "darky" tales and speech amusing and
> within the vein of folklore into which they wished
> to classify all Negro life. This troubled Dunbar
> because he realized that white America was deni-
> grating him as a writer and as a man. (70)

Punctuating Introductory Statements

Statements that introduce quotations take a range of punctuation marks and lead-in words. Let us look at some examples of ways writers typically introduce quotations.

Introducing a Statement with a Colon

A colon usually follows an independent clause placed before the quotation.

> As George Williams notes, protection of white privilege is critical to patterns of discrimina-
> tion: "Whenever a number of persons within a society have enjoyed for a considerable period
> of time certain opportunities for getting wealth, for exercising power and authority, and for
> successfully claiming prestige and social deference, there is a strong tendency for these
> people to feel that these benefits are theirs 'by right'" (727).

Introducing a Statement with a Comma

A comma usually follows an introduction that incorporates the quotation in its sentence structure.

> Similarly, Duncan Turner asserts, "As matters now stand, it is unwise to talk about communi-
> cation without some understanding of Burke" (259).

Introducing a Statement Using that

No punctuation is generally needed with *that*, and no capital letter is used to begin the quotation.

> Noting this failure, Alice Miller asserts that "the reason for her despair was not her suffering
> but the impossibility of communicating her suffering to another person" (255).

Introducing a Statement Using as . . . said

Using *as* to introduce a quotation places the time of the statement in the past tense, not the present. Without *as*, generally use the present tense to describe authors speaking through their writing. Use the past tense for historical events.

> The token women writers authenticated the male canon without disrupting it, for as Ruth
> Bleier has said, "The last thing society desires of its women has been intellectuality and inde-
> pendence" (73).

Punctuating within Quotations

Although punctuation within a quotation should reproduce the original, some adaptations may be necessary. Use single quotation marks for quotations within the quotation:

Original from Guterson (16–17)

E. D. Hirsch also recognizes the connection between family and learning, suggesting in his discussion of family background and academic achievement "that the significant part of our children's education has been going on outside rather than inside the schools."

Quoted Version

Guterson claims that E. D. Hirsch "also recognizes the connection between family and learning, suggesting in his discussion of family background and academic achievement 'that the significant part of our children's education has been going on outside rather than inside the schools'" (16–17).

If the quotation ends with a question mark or an exclamation point, retain the original punctuation:

"Did you think I loved you?" Edith later asks Dombey (566).

If a quotation ending with a question mark or an exclamation point concludes your sentence, retain the question mark or exclamation point, and put the parenthetical reference and sentence period outside the quotation marks:

Edith later asks Dombey, "Did you think I loved you?" (566).

Avoiding Grammatical Tangles

When you incorporate quotations into your writing, and especially when you omit words from quotations, you run the risk of creating ungrammatical sentences. Three common errors you should try to avoid are verb incompatibility, ungrammatical omissions, and sentence fragments.

Verb Incompatibility.   When this error occurs, the verb form in the introductory statement is grammatically incompatible with the verb form in the quotation. When your quotation has a verb form that does not fit in with your text, it is usually possible to use just part of the quotation, thus avoiding verb incompatibility.

> *he describes seeing himself*
>
> ▶ The narrator suggests his bitter disappointment when "~~I saw myself~~
>
> "as a creature driven and derided by vanity" (35).

As this sentence illustrates, use the present tense when you refer to events in a literary work.

Ungrammatical Omission.   Sometimes omitting text from a quotation leaves you with an ungrammatical sentence. Two ways of correcting the grammar are (1) adapting the quotation (with brackets) so that its parts fit together grammatically and (2) using only one part of the quotation.

▶ From the moment of the boy's arrival in Araby, the bazaar is presented as a

  commercial enterprise: "I could not find any sixpenny entrance and [. . .]

  hand[ed]
  handing a shilling to a weary-looking man" (34).
  ^

▶ From the moment of the boy's arrival in Araby, the bazaar is presented as a

  He
  commercial enterprise: "I could not find any sixpenny entrance" and [. . .]
      ^

  so had to pay a shilling to get in (34).
  handing a shilling to a weary looking man" (34).
  ^

Sentence Fragment.   Sometimes when a quotation is a complete sentence, writers neglect the sentence that introduces the quote—for example, by forgetting to include a verb. It is important to make sure that the quotation is introduced by a complete sentence.

                          leads
▶ The girl's interest in the bazaar leading the narrator to make what amounts

  to a sacred oath: "If I go [. . .] I will bring you something" (32).
                             ^

Paraphrasing and Summarizing

In addition to quoting sources, writers have the option of paraphrasing or summarizing what others have written. In a *paraphrase,* the writer restates primarily in his or her own words all the relevant information from a passage, without any additional comments or elaborations. A paraphrase is useful for recording details of the passage when the order of the details is important but the source's wording is not. Because all the details of the passage are included, a paraphrase is often about the same length as the original passage.

In a *summary,* the writer boils down a long passage—several pages or even a whole chapter or book—to its main ideas. Unlike a paraphrase, a summary conveys the gist of a source, using just enough information to record the points the summarizer chooses to emphasize. In choosing what to include in a summary, be sure not to distort the author's meaning. Whereas a paraphrase may be as long as or even longer than the original, a summary is generally much shorter than the original passage.

To avoid plagiarizing inadvertently, you must use *your own words and sentence structures* when paraphrasing or summarizing. If you include an author's original expressions, enclose them in quotation marks. In the following examples, notice that the names for the two groups—"discovery theorists" and "assimilationist theorists"—are in quotation marks. Even when a paraphrase or a summary is restated in your own words, you still need to include a citation in your text that identifies the original source of the ideas. If you are uncertain about a particular paraphrase or summary, ask your instructor for help while you are still drafting your paper.

Here is a passage from a book on home schooling and an example of a paraphrase:

Original Passage

Bruner and the discovery theorists have also illuminated conditions that apparently pave the way for learning. It is significant that these conditions are unique to each learner, so unique, in fact, that in many cases classrooms can't provide them. Bruner also contends that the more one discovers information in a great variety of circumstances, the more likely one is to develop the inner categories required to organize that information. Yet life at school, which is for the most part generic and predictable, daily keeps many children from the great variety of circumstances they need to learn well.

—David Guterson, *Family Matters: Why Homeschooling Makes Sense,* p. 172

Paraphrase

According to Guterson (172), the "discovery theorists," particularly Bruner, have identified the conditions that allow learning to take place. Because these conditions are specific to each individual, many children are not able to learn in the classroom. According to Bruner, when people can explore information in different situations, they learn to classify and order what they discover. The general routine of the school day, however, does not provide children with the diverse activities and situations that would allow them to learn these skills.

Here is an example of a summary of the longer section that contains the original passage:

Summary

In looking at different theories of learning that discuss individual-based programs (such as home schooling) versus the public school system, Guterson describes the disagreements among "cognitivist" theorists. One group, the "discovery theorists," believes that individual children learn by creating their own ways of sorting the information they take in from their experiences. Schools should help students develop better ways of organizing new material, not just present them with material that is already categorized, as traditional schools do. "Assimilationist theorists," by contrast, believe that children learn by linking what they don't know to information they already know. These theorists claim that traditional schools help students learn when they present information in ways that allow children to fit the new material into categories they have already developed (171–75).

Introducing Cited Material

Notice in the preceding examples that the source is acknowledged by name. Even when you use your own words to present someone else's information, you must acknowledge that you borrowed the information. The only types of information that do not require acknowledgment are common knowledge (John F. Kennedy was assassinated in Dallas), familiar sayings ("Haste makes waste"), and well-known quotations ("To be or not to be. That is the question").

The documentation guidelines later in this chapter present various ways of citing the sources you quote, paraphrase, and summarize; the important thing is that your readers can tell where words or ideas that are not your own begin and end. You can accomplish this most readily by separating your words from those of the source with *signal phrases* such as "According to Smith," "Peters claims," and "As Olmos asserts." When you cite a source for the first time, you may use the author's full name; after that, use just the last name.

Avoiding Plagiarism

Writers—students and professionals alike—occasionally fail to acknowledge sources properly. The word *plagiarism,* which derives from the Latin word for "kidnapping," refers to the unacknowledged use of another's words, ideas, or information. Students sometimes get into trouble because they mistakenly assume that plagiarizing occurs only when another writer's exact words are used without acknowledgment. In fact, plagiarism applies to such diverse forms of expression as musical compositions and visual images as well as ideas and statistics. So keep in mind that you must indicate the source of any information or ideas you use in your essay, whether you have paraphrased, summarized, or quoted directly from the source.

Some people plagiarize simply because they do not know the conventions for using and acknowledging sources. This chapter makes clear how to incorporate sources into your writing and how to acknowledge your use of those sources. Others plagiarize because they keep sloppy notes and thus fail to distinguish between their own and their sources' ideas. Either they neglect to enclose their sources' words in quotation marks, or they fail to indicate when they are paraphrasing or summarizing a source's ideas and information. If you keep a working bibliography and take careful notes (see pp. 354–56), you will not make this serious mistake.

Another reason some people plagiarize is that they doubt their ability to write the essay by themselves. They feel intimidated by the writing task or the deadline or their own and others' expectations. If you experience this same anxiety about your work, speak to your instructor. Do not run the risk of failing a course or being expelled because of plagiarism. If you are confused about what is and what is not plagiarism, be sure to ask your instructor.

■ ACKNOWLEDGING SOURCES

Although there is no universally accepted system for acknowledging sources, there is agreement on both the need for documentation and the details that should be included. Writers should acknowledge sources for three reasons: to give credit to those sources, to enable readers to consult those sources for further information, and to give credibility and authority to the work they produce.

Most documentation styles combine in-text citations keyed to a separate list of works cited or references. The information required in the in-text citations and the order and content of the works-cited entries vary across the disciplines, but two styles predominate: the author-page system, used in the humanities and advocated by the Modern Language Association (MLA), and the author-year system, used in the natural and social sciences and advocated by the American Psychological Association (APA). Check with your instructor about which of these styles to use or whether you should use some other style. A list of common documentation style manuals is provided in Table 14.1.

This section presents the basic features of the MLA and APA documentation styles. In Part One of this book, you can find examples of student essays that follow the MLA style (Linh Kieu Ngo, Chapter 4; Jessica Statsky, Chapter 5; Kristine Potter, Chapter 7) and that use the APA style (Patrick O'Malley, Chapter 6). For more information about these documentation styles, consult the *MLA Handbook for Writers of Research Papers*, Fifth Edition (1999), or the *Publication Manual of the American Psychological Association*, Fifth Edition (2001).

The MLA System of Documentation

Citations in Text

AUTHOR INDICATED IN PARENTHESES

The MLA author-page system requires that in-text citations include the author's last name and the page number of the passage being cited. There is no punctuation between author and page.

> Dr. James is described as a "not-too-skeletal Ichabod Crane" (Simon 68).

Note that the parenthetical citation comes before the final period. With block quotations, however, the citation comes after the final period, preceded by a space (see p. 392 for an example).

AUTHOR INDICATED IN A SIGNAL PHRASE

If the author's name is mentioned in your text, supply the page reference in parentheses following the quoted material as closely as possible without disrupting the flow of the sentence.

> Simon describes Dr. James as a "not-too-skeletal Ichabod Crane" (68).

A WORK WITH MORE THAN ONE AUTHOR

To cite a source by two or three authors, include all the authors' last names; for works with more than three authors, use all the authors' names or just the first author's name followed by *et al.*, meaning "and others," in regular type (not italicized or underlined).

Table 14.1 Some Commonly Used Documentation Style Manuals

Subject	Style Manual	Online Source
General	*The Chicago Manual of Style*, 14th edition. 1993.	http://www.bedfordstmartins.com/online/cite7.html
	A Manual for Writers of Term Papers, Theses, and Dissertations, 6th edition. 1996.	—
Online Sources	*Online! A Reference Guide to Using Internet Sources*. 2000.	http://www.bedfordstmartins.com/online/index.html
	Columbia Guide to Online Style. 1998.	http://www.columbia.edu/cu/cup/cgos/idx_basic.html
	Electronic Styles: A Handbook for Citing Electronic Information. 1996.	—
Biological Sciences	*Scientific Style and Format: The CBE Manual for Authors, Editors, and Publishers*, 6th edition. 1994.	http://www.bedfordstmartins.com/online/cite8.html
Chemistry	*The ACS Style Guide*, 2nd edition. 1997.	—
Government Documents	*The Complete Guide to Citing Government Documents*, rev. edition 1993.	http://www.lib.memphis.edu/gpo/citeweb.htm
Humanities	*MLA Handbook for Writers of Research Papers*, 5th edition. 1999.	http://www.mla.org/style/handbook.htm http://www.bedfordstmartins.com/online/cite5.html
	MLA Style Manual and Guide to Scholarly Publishing, 2nd edition. 1998.	http://www.bedfordstmartins.com/online/cite5.html http://www.uvm.edu/~ncrane/estyles http://www.mla.org/style/manual.htm
Psychology/Social Sciences	*Publication Manual of the American Psychological Association*, 5th edition. 2001.	http://www.apa.org/journals/webref.html http://www.bedfordstmartins.com/online/cite6.html http://www.uvm.edu/~ncrane/estyles

Dyal, Corning, and Willows identify several types of students, including the "Authority-Rebel" (4).

The Authority-Rebel "tends to see himself as superior to other students in the class" (Dyal, Corning, and Willows 4).

The drug AZT has been shown to reduce the risk of transmission from HIV-positive mothers to their infants by as much as two-thirds (Van de Perre et al. 4–5).

TWO OR MORE WORKS BY THE SAME AUTHOR

Include the author's last name, a shortened version of the title, and the page number(s).

When old paint becomes transparent, it sometimes shows the artist's original plans: "a tree will show through a woman's dress" (Hellman, Pentimento 1).

A WORK WITH AN UNKNOWN AUTHOR

Use a shortened version of the title. Begin the shortened version with the word by which the title is alphabetized in the works-cited list,

An international pollution treaty still to be ratified would prohibit all plastic garbage from being dumped at sea ("Awash" 26)

TWO OR MORE AUTHORS WITH THE SAME LAST NAME CITED IN YOUR ESSAY

In addition to the last name, include each author's first initial in the citation. If the first initials are also the same, spell out the authors' first names.

Chaplin's Modern Times provides a good example of montage used to make an editorial statement (E. Roberts 246).

A CORPORATE OR GOVERNMENT AUTHOR

When you use a parenthetical citation, give the full name of a corporate author if it is brief or a shortened version if it is long. When you name the author in your text such as in a signal phrase, give the full name even if it is long.

A tuition increase has been proposed for community and technical colleges to offset budget deficits from Initiative 601 (Washington State Board 4).

According to the Washington State Board for Community and Technical Colleges, a tuition increase . . . from Initiative 601 (4).

A MULTIVOLUME WORK

When you use two or more volumes, include the volume number and the page number(s) for each volume of the work, separated by a colon and one space.

> According to Forster, modernist writers valued experimentation and gradually sought to blur the line between poetry and prose (3: 150).

If you cite only one volume of a multivolume work in your paper, give the volume number in the works-cited entry (see p. 404) and include only the page number(s) in the parenthetical citation.

A LITERARY WORK

For a novel or other prose work available in various editions, provide the page numbers from the edition used as well as other information that will help readers locate the quotation in a different edition, such as the part or chapter number.

> In Hard Times, Tom reveals his utter narcissism by blaming Louisa for his own failure: "You have regularly given me up. You never cared for me" (Dickens 262; bk. 3, ch. 9).

For a play in verse, such as a Shakespearean play, indicate the act, scene, and line numbers instead of the page numbers.

> At the beginning, Regan's fawning rhetoric hides her true attitude toward Lear: "I profess / myself an enemy to all other joys [. . .] / And find that I am alone felicitate / In your dear highness' love" (King Lear I.i.74–75, 77–78).

Note the brackets placed around the ellipsis marks, which the MLA recommends to distinguish them from ellipses the author may have used. In the MLA style, act and scene numbers may instead be given in arabic numerals: (King Lear 1.1.74–75, 77–78).

For a poem, indicate the line numbers and stanzas or sections (if they are numbered), instead of the page numbers. If the source gives only line numbers, use the term *lines* in the first citation and give only the numbers in subsequent citations.

> In "Song of Myself," Whitman finds poetic details in busy urban settings, as when he describes "the blab of the pave, tires of carts [. . .] the driver with his interrogating thumb" (8.153–54).

A RELIGIOUS WORK

For the Bible, indicate the book, chapter, and verse instead of the page numbers. Abbreviate books with names of five or more letters in your parenthetical citation, but spell out full names of books in your text.

> She ignored the admonition "Pride goes before destruction, and a haughty spirit before a fall" (New Oxford Annotated Bible, Prov. 16.18).

A WORK IN AN ANTHOLOGY

Use the name of the author of the work, not the editor of the anthology, but use the page number(s) from the anthology.

In "Six Days: Some Rememberings," Grace Paley recalls that when she was in jail for protesting the Vietnam War, her pen and paper were taken away and she felt "a terrible pain in the area of my heart—a nausea" (191).

A SECONDARY SOURCE

Include the secondary source in your list of works cited. In your parenthetical citation, use the abbreviation *qtd. in* (in regular type, not italicized or underlined) to acknowledge that the original was quoted in a secondary source.

E. M. Forster says "the collapse of all civilization, so realistic for us, sounded in Matthew Arnold's ears like a distant and harmonious cataract" (qtd. in Trilling 11).

AN ENTIRE WORK

Include the reference in the text without any page numbers or parentheses.

In The Structure of Scientific Revolutions, Thomas Kuhn discusses how scientists change their thinking.

A WORK WITHOUT PAGE NUMBERS

If a work has no page numbers or is only one page long, you may omit the page number. If a work uses paragraph numbers instead, use the abbreviation *par(s)*.

The average speed on Montana's interstate highways, for example, has risen by only 2 miles per hour since the repeal of the federal speed limit, with most drivers topping out at 75 (Schmid).

Whitman considered African American speech "a source of a native grand opera" in the words of Ellison (par. 13).

TWO OR MORE WORKS CITED IN THE SAME PARENTHESES

When two or more different sources are used in the same passage of your essay, it may be necessary to cite them in the same parentheses. Separate the citations with a semicolon. Include any specific pages, or omit pages to refer to the whole work.

A few studies have considered differences between oral and written discourse production (Scardamalia, Bereiter, and Goelman; Gould).

MATERIAL FROM THE INTERNET

Give enough information in the citation to enable readers to locate an Internet source in the list of works cited. If the author is not named, give the document title. Include page, section, paragraph, or screen numbers, if available.

In handling livestock, "many people attempt to restrain animals with sheer force instead of using behavioral principles" (Grandin).

List of Works Cited

Providing full information for the citations in the text, the list of works cited identifies all the sources the writer uses. Entries are alphabetized according to the first author's last name or by the title if the author is unknown. Every source cited in the text must refer to an entry in the works-cited list. Conversely, every entry in the works-cited list must correspond to at least one in-text citation.

In the MLA style, multiple works by the same author (or same group of authors) are alphabetized by title. The author's name is given for the first entry only; in subsequent entries, three hyphens and a period are used.

```
Vidal, Gore. Empire. New York: Random, 1987.

---. Lincoln. New York: Random, 1984.
```

The information presented in a works-cited list follows this order: author, title, publication source, year, and (for an article) page range. The MLA style requires a "hanging indent," which means that the first line of a works-cited entry is not indented but subsequent lines of the entry are. The MLA specifies an indent of half an inch or five character spaces.

Books

Here is an example of a basic MLA-style entry for a book:

double-space

author, last name first   *title (and subtitle, if any), underlined*

```
Campbell, Richard. Media and Culture: An Introduction to Mass
    Communication. New York: St. Martin's, 1998.
```

indent one-half inch or 5 typewriter spaces   *publisher's city and name, year of publication*

A BOOK BY A SINGLE AUTHOR

```
Guterson, David. Family Matters: Why Homeschooling Makes Sense.
    San Diego: Harcourt, 1992.
```

A BOOK BY AN AGENCY OR A CORPORATION

```
Association for Research in Nervous and Mental Disease. The
    Circulation of the Brain and Spinal Cord: A Symposium on
    Blood Supply. New York: Hafner, 1966.
```

A BOOK BY MORE THAN ONE AUTHOR

Gottfredson, Stephen G., and Sean McConville. America's Correc-
    tional Crisis. Westport: Greenwood, 1987.

Dyal, James A., William C. Corning, and Dale M. Willows. Read-
    ings in Psychology: The Search for Alternatives. 3rd ed.
    New York: McGraw, 1975.

A WORK BY MORE THAN THREE AUTHORS

The MLA lists all the authors' names *or* the name of the first author followed by *et al.*
(in regular type, not italicized or underlined).

Nielsen, Niels C., Jr., et al. Religions of the World. 3rd ed.
    New York: St. Martin's, 1992.

A BOOK BY AN UNKNOWN AUTHOR

Use the title in place of the author.

Rand McNally Commercial Atlas. Skokie: Rand, 1993.

A BOOK WITH AN AUTHOR AND AN EDITOR

If you refer to the author's text, begin the entry with the author's name.

Arnold, Matthew. Culture and Anarchy. Ed. J. Dover Wilson. Cam-
    bridge: Cambridge UP, 1966.

If you cite the editor in your paper, begin the entry with the editor's name.

Wilson, J. Dover, ed. Culture and Anarchy. By Matthew Arnold.
    1869. Cambridge: Cambridge UP, 1966.

AN EDITED COLLECTION

Carter, Kathryn, and Carole Spitzack, eds. Doing Research on
    Women's Communication. Norwood: Ablex, 1989.

A WORK IN AN ANTHOLOGY OR A COLLECTION

Fairbairn-Dunlop, Peggy. "Women and Agriculture in Western
    Samoa." Different Places, Different Voices. Ed. Janet H.
    Momsen and Vivian Kinnaird. London: Routledge, 1993. 211-26.

TWO OR MORE WORKS FROM THE SAME ANTHOLOGY

To avoid repetition, you may create an entry for the collection and cite the collection's editors to cross-reference individual works to the entry.

> Atwan, Robert, and Jamaica Kincaid, eds. The Best American
> Essays, 1995. New York: Houghton, 1995.
>
> Paley, Grace. "Six Days: Some Rememberings." Atwan and Kincaid
> 187-92.

ONE VOLUME OF A MULTIVOLUME WORK

If only one volume from a multivolume set is used, indicate the volume number after the title.

> Freud, Sigmund. The Complete Psychological Works of Sigmund
> Freud. Vol. 8. Trans. James Strachey. London: Hogarth, 1962.

TWO OR MORE VOLUMES OF A MULTIVOLUME WORK

> Sandburg, Carl. Abraham Lincoln. 6 vols. New York: Scribner's,
> 1939.

A BOOK THAT IS PART OF A SERIES

Include the series title in regular type (not underlined or in quotation marks), followed by the series number and a period. If the word *Series* is part of the name, include *Ser.* before the number. Common abbreviations may be used for selected words in the series title.

> Kirsch, Gesa, and Duane H. Roen. A Sense of Audience in Written
> Communication. Written Communication Annual: An Int. Sur-
> vey of Research and Theory 5. Newbury Park: Sage, 1990.

A REPUBLISHED BOOK

Provide the original year of publication after the title of the book, followed by normal publication information for the edition you are using.

> Takaki, Ronald. Strangers from a Different Shore: A History of
> Asian Americans. 1989. New York: Penguin, 1990.

A LATER EDITION OF A BOOK

> Rottenberg, Annette T. The Structure of Argument. 2nd ed.
> Boston: Bedford, 1997.

A BOOK WITH A TITLE IN ITS TITLE

Do not underline a title normally underlined when it appears within the title of a book.

> Kinney, Arthur F. Go Down Moses: <u>The Miscegenation of Time</u>. New
> York: Twayne, 1996.

> Brooker, Jewel Spears, and Joseph Bentley. <u>Reading</u> The Waste
> Land: <u>Modernism and the Limits of Interpretation</u>. Amherst:
> U of Mass P, 1990.

Use quotation marks around a work normally enclosed in quotation marks when it appears within the title of a book.

> Miller, Edwin Haviland. <u>Walt Whitman's "Song of Myself": A
> Mosaic of Interpretation</u>. Iowa City: U of Iowa P, 1989.

A TRANSLATION

If you refer to the work itself, begin the entry with the author's name.

> Tolstoy, Leo. <u>War and Peace</u>. Trans. Constance Garnett. London:
> Pan, 1972.

If you cite the translator in your text, begin the entry with the translator's name.

> Garnett, Constance, trans. <u>War and Peace</u>. By Leo Tolstoy, 1869.
> London: Pan, 1972.

A DICTIONARY ENTRY OR AN ARTICLE IN A REFERENCE BOOK

> "Tempera." <u>The American Heritage College Dictionary</u>. 3rd ed.
> 1993.

> Suber, Howard. "Motion Picture." <u>The Encyclopedia Americana</u>.
> 1991 ed.

AN INTRODUCTION, PREFACE, FOREWORD, OR AFTERWORD

> Holt, John. Introduction. <u>Better than School</u>. By Nancy Wallace.
> Burnett: Larson, 1983. 9-14.

Articles

Here is an example of a basic MLA-style entry for an article in a journal:

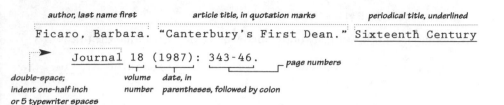

author, last name first   article title, in quotation marks   periodical title, underlined

Ficaro, Barbara. "Canterbury's First Dean." Sixteenth Century

➤   Journal 18 (1987): 343-46.   ┌ page numbers

double-space;   volume   date, in
indent one-half inch   number   parentheses, followed by colon
or 5 typewriter spaces

AN ARTICLE FROM A DAILY NEWSPAPER

Wilford, John Noble. "Corn in the New World: A Relative Late-
    comer." New York Times 7 Mar. 1995, late ed.: C1+.

AN ARTICLE FROM A WEEKLY OR BIWEEKLY MAGAZINE

Bai, Matt. "Ventura's First Round." Newsweek 15 Feb. 1999:
    30-32.

AN ARTICLE FROM A MONTHLY OR BIMONTHLY MAGAZINE

Rohn, Alfie. "Home Schooling." Atlantic Monthly Apr. 1988: 20-25.

AN ARTICLE IN A SCHOLARLY JOURNAL WITH CONTINUOUS ANNUAL PAGINATION

The volume number follows the title of the journal.

Natale, Jo Anna. "Understanding Home Schooling." Education
    Digest 9 (1993): 58-61.

AN ARTICLE IN A SCHOLARLY JOURNAL THAT PAGINATES EACH ISSUE SEPARATELY

The issue number appears after the volume number. A period separates the two numbers.

Epstein, Alexandra. "Teen Parents: What They Need to Know."
    High/Scope Resource 1.2 (1982): 6.

AN ANONYMOUS OR UNSIGNED ARTICLE

Begin with the article title, alphabetizing the entry according to the first word after
any initial *A, An*, or *The*.

"The Odds of March." Time. 15 Apr. 1985: 20+.

AN EDITORIAL

"Stepping Backward." Editorial. <u>Los Angeles Times</u> 4 July 1989:
    B6.

A LETTER TO THE EDITOR

Rissman, Edward M. Letter. <u>Los Angeles Times</u> 29 June 1989: B5.

A REVIEW

Anders, Jaroslaw. "Dogma and Democracy." Rev. of <u>The Church and</u>
    <u>the Left</u>, by Adam Minchik. <u>New Republic</u> 17 May 1993: 42-48.

If the review does not include an author's name, start the entry with the title of the review and alphabetize by that title. If the review is untitled, begin with the words *Rev. of* and alphabetize under the title of the work being reviewed.

Electronic Sources

The range of information available through the worldwide network of computers known as the Internet is astonishing. Setting guidelines for regulating and using this information is an ongoing process. Most of the following guidelines for citing Internet sources are derived from the *MLA Handbook for Writers of Research Papers*, Fifth Edition (1999), and the MLA Web site. Models for citing a few other kinds of Internet sources not covered by the MLA guidelines are based on Andrew Harnack and Eugene Kleppinger, *Online! A Reference Guide to Using Internet Sources* (New York: Bedford/ St. Martin's, 2000). These models will help you incorporate electronic sources of information and data into your own essays. (For more information on using the Internet for research, see Chapter 13, pp. 378–79. For more information on citing Internet sources in the MLA style, go to <http://www.mla.org/style/sources.htm>.)

In-text reference   When citing an Internet source in the body of your text, use the author's name or the document title if the author's name is not given. Do not use the URL (uniform resource locator) for your reference.

List of works cited   For most sources accessed on the Internet, you should provide the following information:

- Name of author or compiler (if available)
- Title of Web site or document (underlined)
- Date of electronic publication or latest update (if available)

- Name of sponsoring institution, if any
- Date of access
- URL (in angle brackets)

PROFESSIONAL OR PERSONAL WEB SITE

```
Meldrum, Ron. Genealogy and History of the Meldrum Family.
     1 Jan. 1996. 19 October 2001 <http://www.royalriver.net/
     meldrum>.
```

If the author's name is not known, begin the citation with the title, underlined.

```
American Horticultural Society. 18 Jan. 2000. AHS. 24 Jan. 2000
     <http://www.ahs.org>.
```

For an untitled professional or personal Web site, put a description such as *Home page* (in regular type, not underlined), followed by a period, in the position a title would normally be cited.

```
Polhemus-Annibell, Wendy. Home page. Jan. 2000. 24 Jan. 2000
     <http://wpannibell.homepage.com>.
```

A BOOK OR POEM AVAILABLE ONLINE

```
Blind, Mathilde. Dramas in Miniature. London: Chatto & Windus,
     1891. Victorian Women Writers Project. Ed. Perry Willett.
     3 Oct. 1997. Indiana U. 13 Oct. 1997 <http://
     www.indiana.edu/~letrs/vwwp/blind/dramas.html>.

Mosko, Marc. "Muir Woods." Home page. 1996. 13 Oct. 1997
     <http://www.tear.com/poems/mosko/muirwoods.html>.
```

AN ONLINE SCHOLARLY PROJECT OR REFERENCE DATABASE

For a complete online scholarly project or reference database, provide the title, underlined, and the name of the editor, if given. Then give the electronic publication information—the version number (if any), the date of electronic publication or latest update, and the name of the sponsoring organization—followed by the date of access and the URL (in angle brackets).

```
The Ovid Project. Ed. Hope Greenberg. 13 Mar. 1996. U of
     Vermont. 13 Oct. 1997 <http://www.uvm.edu/hag/ovid/
     index.html>.
```

For an article within a scholarly project or reference database, begin with the author's name, if known, and the title of the work, enclosed in quotation marks. Follow with the information about the database or project.

> Lee, Vernon. "Limbo." <u>Victorian Women Writers Project</u>. Ed.
> Perry Willett. Aug. 1998. Indiana U. 17 Feb. 2000 <http://
> www.indiana.edu/~letrs/vwwp/lee/limbo.html>.

MATERIAL FROM A DATABASE ON CD-ROM

> Braus, Patricia. "Sex and the Single Spender." <u>American Demo-</u>
> <u>graphics</u> 15.11 (1993): 28-34. <u>ABI/INFORM</u>. CD-ROM. UMI-
> ProQuest. 1993.

If no print version is available, include the author, title, and date (if provided) along with information about the electronic source.

MATERIAL PUBLISHED ON A CD-ROM, MAGNETIC TAPE, OR DISKETTE

> <u>Picasso: The Man, His Works, the Legend</u>. CD-ROM. Danbury:
> Grolier Interactive, 1996.

A WORK FROM AN ONLINE SUBSCRIPTION SERVICE

To cite an article from an online service to which you subscribe personally such as America Online, begin with the author's name, if known, and the title of the work, enclosed in quotation marks. Give the title of the online service provided, underlined, along with the date of publication, the provider's name, the date of access, and the word *Keyword,* followed by the keyword used.

> Weeks, W. William. "Beyond the Ark." <u>Nature Conservancy</u>. Mar.-
> Apr. 1999. America Online. 2 Apr. 1999. Keyword: Ecology.

For a work from an online service to which a library subscribes, first list the information about the work (author, title, publication data). Then give the name of the subscription service, the name of the library, the date of access, and the URL of the service (in angle brackets) if available.

> "Breaking the Dieting Habit: Drug Therapy for Eating Disor-
> ders." <u>Psychology Today</u> Mar. 1995: 12+. Electric Lib. Ohio
> State U Main Lib., Columbus. 31 Mar. 1999 <http://
> www.elibrary.com>.

AN ARTICLE FROM AN ONLINE JOURNAL

MLA includes the volume number and issue number, if given, after the title of the journal. The number of pages, paragraphs, or other sections appears after the colon, if the source gives them. The date of access and the electronic address appear at the end.

```
McIntyre, John. "With So Much Content on the Internet, Why Do
     People Still Read Newspapers?" Writers Write 5.7
     (Aug. 2001): 19 Oct. 2001 <http://www.writerswrite.com/
     journal/aug01/mcintyre.htm>.
```

A NEWSGROUP (USENET) POSTING

Include the author's name (if you know it), the title or subject line of the posting, and the identifying phrase *Online posting*. Follow the posting date with the access date. Enclose the newsgroup's name, preceded by the word *news:* and no space, in angle brackets.

```
Conrad, Ed. "Proof of Life after Death." Online posting. 8 July
     1996. 9 July 1996 <news:sci.archeology>.
```

A LISTSERV POSTING

Include the list's name after the posting date. For a listserv that archives postings at a Web site or listserv address, provide the URL, enclosed in angle brackets.

```
Martin, Francesca Alys. "Wait--Did Somebody Say 'Buffy'?" Online
     posting. 8 Mar. 2000. Cultstud-1. 8 Mar. 2000. <http://
     lists.accomp.usf.edu/cgi-bin/lyris.pl?visit=cultstud-
     1&id=111011221>.
```

For a listserv with no Web site, provide the list moderator's email address in place of a URL.

AN EMAIL MESSAGE

The subject line of the posting is enclosed in quotation marks before its date. Identify the type of message and the person who received it.

```
Somer, Tina. "Medea." Email to the author. 9 Mar. 1996.
```

SYNCHRONOUS COMMUNICATION

For a posting in a forum such as a MOO, MUD, or IRC, provide the name(s) of any specific speaker(s) you are citing; specify the event, and supply its date, the name of the forum, the date of access, and the URL, beginning with *telnet*. (If an archived version of the posting is available, cite the *http* address instead.)

> Patuto, Jeremy, Simon Fennel, and James Goss. Online discussion
> of "The Mytilene Debate." 9 May 1996. MiamiMOO. 28 Mar.
> 1998 <telnet://moo.cas.edu/cgi-bin/moo?look+4085>.

COMPUTER SOFTWARE

> SPSS/PC+ Studentware Plus. Diskette. Chicago: SPSS, 1991.

Other Sources

A LECTURE OR PUBLIC ADDRESS

> Timothy, Kristen. "The Changing Roles of Women's Community
> Organizations in Sustainable Development and in the United
> Nations." UN Assn. of the US. Seattle. 7 May 1997.

A GOVERNMENT DOCUMENT

If the author is known, the author's name may either come first or be placed after the title, introduced with the word *By*.

> United States. Dept. of Health and Human Services. Clinical
> Classifications for Health Policy Research, Version 2:
> Hospital Inpatient Statistics. Rockville: AHCPR Publica-
> tions Clearinghouse, 1996.

A PAMPHLET

> Harborview Injury Prevention and Research Center. A Decade of
> Injury Control. Seattle: Harborview Medical Center, 1995.

PUBLISHED PROCEEDINGS OF A CONFERENCE

If the name of the conference is part of the title of the publication, it need not be repeated. Use the format for a work in an anthology (see p. 403) to cite an individual presentation.

> Duffett, John, ed. Against the Crime of Silence. Proc. of the
> Intl. War Crimes Tribunal, Nov. 1967, Stockholm. New York:
> Clarion-Simon, 1970.

A PUBLISHED DOCTORAL DISSERTATION

If the dissertation was published by University Microfilms International, add *Ann Arbor: UMI,* and the year. List the UMI number at the end of the entry.

> Botts, Roderic C. Influences in the Teaching of English, 1917-
>   1935: An Illusion of Progress. Diss. Northeastern U, 1970.
>   Ann Arbor: UMI, 1971. 71-1799.

AN UNPUBLISHED DOCTORAL DISSERTATION

> Bullock, Barbara. "Basic Needs Fulfillment among Less Developed
>   Countries: Social Progress over Two Decades of Growth."
>   Diss. Vanderbilt U, 1986.

A LETTER

> Hannah, Barry. Letter to the author. 10 May 1990.

A MAP OR CHART

> Mineral King, California. Map. Berkeley: Wilderness P, 1979.

A CARTOON

Provide the cartoon's title (if given) in quotes directly following the artist's name.

> Wilson, Gahan. Cartoon. New Yorker 14 July 1997: 74.

AN ADVERTISEMENT

> Reliance National Employment Practices Liability. Advertise-
>   ment. Wired May 1997: 196.

A WORK OF ART OR MUSICAL COMPOSITION

> De Goya, Francisco. The Sleep of Reason Produces Monsters. Nor-
>   ton Simon Museum, Pasadena.

> Beethoven, Ludwig van. Violin Concerto in D Major, op. 61.

> Gershwin, George. Porgy and Bess.

If a photograph is not part of a collection, identify the subject, the name of the person who photographed it, and when it was photographed.

Washington Square Park, New York. Personal photograph by
    author. 24 June 1995.

A PERFORMANCE

Hamlet. By William Shakespeare. Dir. Jonathan Kent. Perf. Ralph
    Fiennes. Belasco Theatre, New York. 20 June 1995.

A TELEVISION PROGRAM

"The Universe Within." Nova. Narr. Stacy Keach. Writ. Beth
    Hoppe and Bill Lattanzi. Dir. Goro Koide. PBS. WNET, New
    York. 7 Mar. 1995.

A FILM OR VIDEOTAPE

Boyz N the Hood. Writ. and Dir. John Singleton. Perf. Ice Cube,
    Cuba Gooding Jr., and Larry Fishburne. Columbia, 1991.

Casablanca. Dir. Michael Curtiz. Perf. Humphrey Bogart. 1942.
    Videocassette. MGM-UA Home Video, 1992.

A MUSIC RECORDING

Indicate the medium ahead of the name of the manufacturer for an audiocassette,
audiotape, or LP; it is not necessary to indicate the medium for a compact disk.

Beethoven, Ludwig van. Violin Concerto in D Major, op. 61.
    U.S.S.R. State Orchestra. Cond. Alexander Gauk. David
    Oistrikh, violinist. Audiocassette. Allegro, 1980.

Springsteen, Bruce. "Dancing in the Dark." Born in the U.S.A.
    Columbia, 1984.

AN INTERVIEW

Lowell, Robert. "Robert Lowell." Interview with Frederick Sei-
    del. Paris Review 25 (1975): 56-95.

Franklin, Ann. Personal interview. 3 Sept. 1999.

The APA System of Documentation

Citations in Text

AUTHOR INDICATED IN PARENTHESES

The APA author-year system calls for the last name of the author and the year of publication of the original work in the citation. If the cited material is a quotation, you also need to include the page number(s) of the original (for electronic sources without page numbers, use paragraph numbers if they are available). If the cited material is not a quotation, the page or paragraph reference is optional. Use commas to separate author, year, and page in a parenthetical citation. The page number is preceded by *p.* for a single page or *pp.* for a range. Paragraph numbers are preceded by either the ¶ symbol or the abbreviation *para*.

> Dr. James is described as a "not-too-skeletal Ichabod Crane" (Simon, 1982, p. 68).

> Survey results suggest that "unique, high-value, local content is key" for local newspapers (McIntyre, 2001, ¶12).

AUTHOR INDICATED IN SIGNAL PHRASE

If the author's name is mentioned in your text, cite the year in parentheses directly following the author's name, and place the page reference in parentheses before the final sentence period.

> Simon (1982) describes Dr. James as a "not-too-skeletal Ichabod Crane" (p. 68).

> As McIntyre (2001, ¶12) notes, "Unique, high-value, local content is key to the success of numerous free and paid local weekly newspapers."

SOURCE WITH MORE THAN TWO AUTHORS

To cite works with three to five authors, use all the authors' last names the first time the reference occurs and the last name of the first author followed by *et al.* subsequently. If a source has more than six authors, use only the last name of the first author and *et al.* (in regular type, not italicized or underlined) at first and subsequent references.

First Citation in Text

> Dyal, Corning, and Willows (1975) identify several types of students, including the "Authority-Rebel" (p. 4).

Subsequent Citations

> The Authority-Rebel "tends to see himself as superior to other students in the class" (Dyal et al., 1975, p. 4).

TWO OR MORE WORKS BY THE SAME AUTHOR

To cite one of two or more works by the same author or group of authors, use the author's last name plus the year (and the page, if you are citing a quotation). When more than one work being cited was published by an author in the same year, the works are alphabetized by title and then assigned lowercase letters after the date (1973a, 1973b).

> When old paint becomes transparent, it sometimes shows the artist's original plans: "a tree will show through a woman's dress" (Hellman, 1973b, p. 1).

UNKNOWN AUTHOR

To cite a work listed only by its title, the APA uses a shortened version of the title.

> An international pollution treaty still to be ratified would prohibit all plastic garbage from being dumped at sea ("Awash," 1987).

SECONDARY SOURCE

To quote material taken not from the original source but from a secondary source that quotes the original, give the secondary source in the reference list, and in your essay acknowledge that the original was quoted in a secondary source.

> E. M. Forster says "the collapse of all civilization, so realistic for us, sounded in Matthew Arnold's ears like a distant and harmonious cataract" (as cited in Trilling, 1955, p. 11).

List of References

The APA follows this order in the presentation of information for each source listed: author, publication year, title, and publication source; for an article, the page range is given as well.

When the list of references includes several works by the same author, the APA provides the following rules for arranging these entries in the list:

- Same-name single-author entries precede multiple-author entries:

      Aaron, P. (1990).

      Aaron, P., & Zorn, C. R. (1985).

- Entries with the same first author and a different second author are alphabetized under the first author according to the second author's last name:

      Aaron, P., & Charleston, W. (1987).

      Aaron, P., & Zorn, C. R. (1991).

- Entries by the same authors are arranged by year of publication, in chronological order:

Aaron, P., & Charleston, W. (1987).

Aaron, P., & Charleston, W. (1993).

- Entries by the same authors with the same publication year should be arranged alphabetically by title (according to the first word after *A, An*, or *The*), and lower-case letters (*a, b, c*, and so on) are appended to the year in parentheses:

Aaron, P. (1990a). Basic . . .

Aaron, P. (1990b). Elements . . .

The APA recommends that only the first line of each entry be indented five to seven spaces for papers intended for publication, but that student writers may choose instead to use a hanging indent of five to seven spaces. Ask your instructor which format is preferred. The following examples demonstrate a hanging indent of five spaces.

Books

A BOOK BY A SINGLE AUTHOR

Guterson, D. (1992). Family matters: Why homeschooling makes sense. San Diego: Harcourt Brace.

A BOOK BY AN AGENCY OR A CORPORATION

Association for Research in Nervous and Mental Disease. (1966). The circulation of the brain and spinal cord: A symposium on blood supply. New York: Hafner.

A BOOK BY MORE THAN ONE AUTHOR

The APA cites all authors' names regardless of the number.

Gottfredson, S. G., & McConville, S. (1987). America's correctional crisis. Westport, CT: Greenwood.

Dyal, J. A., Corning, W. C., & Willows, D. M. (1975). Readings in psychology: The search for alternatives (3rd ed.). New York: McGraw-Hill.

A BOOK BY AN UNKNOWN AUTHOR

Use the title in place of the author.

Rand McNally commercial atlas. (1993). Skokie, IL: Rand McNally.

When an author is designated as "Anonymous," identify the work as "Anonymous" in the text, and alphabetize it as "Anonymous" in the reference list.

A BOOK WITH AN AUTHOR AND AN EDITOR

Arnold, M. (1966). <u>Culture and anarchy</u> (J. D. Wilson, Ed.). Cambridge: Cambridge University Press. (Original work published 1869)

AN EDITED COLLECTION

Carter, K., & Spitzack, C. (Eds.). (1989). <u>Doing research on women's communication.</u> Norwood, NJ: Ablex.

A WORK IN AN ANTHOLOGY OR A COLLECTION

Fairbairn-Dunlop, P. (1993). Women and agriculture in western Samoa. In J. H. Momsen & V. Kinnaird (Eds.), <u>Different places, different voices</u> (pp. 211-226). London: Routledge.

A TRANSLATION

Tolstoy, L. (1972). War and peace (C. Garnett, Trans.). London: Pan Books. (Original work published 1869)

AN ARTICLE IN A REFERENCE BOOK

Suber, H. (1991). Motion picture. In <u>Encyclopedia Americana</u> (Vol. 19, pp. 505-539). Danbury, CT: Grolier.

AN INTRODUCTION, PREFACE, FOREWORD, OR AFTERWORD

Holt, J. (1983). Introduction. In N. Wallace, <u>Better than school</u> (pp. 9-14). Burnett, NY: Larson.

Articles

AN ARTICLE FROM A DAILY NEWSPAPER

Wilford, J. N. (1995, March 7). Corn in the New World: A relative latecomer. <u>The New York Times,</u> pp. C1, C5.

AN ARTICLE FROM A WEEKLY OR BIWEEKLY MAGAZINE

Bai, M. (1999, February 15). Ventura's first round. Newsweek,
    133, 30-32.

AN ARTICLE FROM A MONTHLY OR BIMONTHLY MAGAZINE

Rohn, A. (1988, April). Home schooling. Atlantic Monthly, 261,
    20-25.

AN ARTICLE IN A SCHOLARLY JOURNAL WITH CONTINUOUS ANNUAL PAGINATION

The volume number follows the title of the journal.

Natale, J. A. (1993). Understanding home schooling. Education
    Digest, 9, 58-61.

AN ARTICLE IN A SCHOLARLY JOURNAL THAT PAGINATES EACH ISSUE SEPARATELY

The issue number appears in parentheses after the volume number.

Epstein, A. (1982). Teen parents: What they need to know.
    High/Scope Resource, 1(2), 6.

AN ANONYMOUS ARTICLE

Awash in garbage. (1987, August 15). The New York Times,
    p. A26.

A REVIEW

Anders, J. (1993, May 17). Dogma and democracy [Review of the
    book The church and the left]. The New Republic, 208,
    42-48.

If the review is untitled, use the bracketed information as the title, retaining the brackets.

Electronic Sources

The APA *Publication Manual* notes that it can be difficult to identify appropriate citation information for many electronic sources, but it recommends that for Internet sources you should at least provide a title or description of the electronic document, the date it was published or most recently updated or on which you retrieved it, and an Internet address (URL). If possible, include the name of the author of the document as well. The APA also recommends that you check the URLs of your Internet sources frequently to make sure that they still provide access to the source and that you update your list of references as necessary.

The following guidelines are derived from the *Publication Manual of the American Psychological Association,* Fifth Edition (2001). Models for citing other kinds of Internet sources not covered by the APA guidelines can be found in Andrew Harnack and Eugene Kleppinger, *Online! A Reference Guide to Using Internet Sources: 2001 Update* (New York: Bedford/St. Martin's, 2001). These models will help you incorporate electronic sources of information into your own essays. (For answers to frequently asked questions on citing Internet sources in the APA style, go to <http://www.apastyle.org/elecref.html>.)

In-text reference When citing an Internet source in the body of your text, use the basic format for citing print sources (see p. 414). If paragraph numbers are not visible, you should cite a division within the document — such as a heading — and the number of the paragraph following it to direct readers to the passage you are quoting. For instance, you might cite a quote from the online version of the preface for this book as follows: Axelrod and Cooper (2001, new to this edition, ¶4). If you are citing an entire Web site, identify it in text instead of in the list of references. You should simply give the name of the site and its Web address in parentheses: for instance, U.S. Census Bureau (www.census.gov).

List of references For most sources accessed on the Internet, you should provide the following information.

- Name of author or compiler (if available)
- Date of publication or most recent update (in parentheses; if unavailable, use the abbreviation *n.d.*)
- Title or description of Web site or electronic document
- Date of retrieval
- URL or path followed to locate the site

AN INTERNET ARTICLE BASED ON A PRINT SOURCE

If you believe the Internet version is the same as the print version:

```
Banker, B. S., & Gaertner, S. L. (1998). Achieving stepfamily
        harmony: An intergroup relations approach. [Electronic
        version]. Journal of Family Psychology, 12, 3, 310-325.
```

If you have reason to believe the Internet version is not the same as the print version:

```
Banker, B. S., & Gaertner, S. L. (1998). Achieving stepfamily
        harmony: An intergroup relations approach. Journal of Fam-
        ily Psychology, 12, 3, 310-325. Retrieved October 4, 2001,
        from http://www.apa.org/journals/fam/998ab.html
```

AN ARTICLE FROM AN INTERNET-ONLY JOURNAL

```
McIntyre, J. (2001, August). With so much content on the Inter-
     net, why do people still read newspapers? Writers Write,
     5(7). Retrieved October 19, 2001 from http://www
     .writerswrite.com/journal/aug01/mcintyre.htm
```

A DOCUMENT ON THE WEB SITE OF A UNIVERSITY PROGRAM OR DEPARTMENT

```
Voight, L. (1999, January). Bridging the gap between language
     and literature. Retrieved October 4, 2001, from Brown Uni-
     versity, Harriet W. Sheridan Center for Teaching and
     Learning Web site: http://sheridan-center.stg.brown.edu/
     teachingexchange/TE_bridgegap.shtml
```

A WEB DOCUMENT WITH NO AUTHOR OR DATE IDENTIFIED

Begin the entry with the title of the document, and put *n.d.* in parentheses where the date of publication or update normally appears.

```
NUA Internet Survey: How many online? (n.d.) Retrieved October
     4, 2001, from http://www.nua.ie/surveys/how_many_online
```

A U.S. GOVERNMENT REPORT AVAILABLE ON A GOVERNMENT AGENCY WEB SITE, NO DATE

```
U.S. Department of Labor Bureau of Labor Statistics. (n.d.)
     Occupational outlook handbook 2000-01. Retrieved October
     4, 2001 from http://stats.bls.gov/ocohome.htm
```

A POSTING TO A NEWSGROUP, ELECTRONIC MAILING LIST, OR OTHER ONLINE FORUM OR DISCUSSION GROUP

Postings to Usenet newsgroups, electronic mailing lists (also called "listservs"), and other online discussion forums should be included in your reference list only if they are archived so that readers can retrieve them. Otherwise, they should be cited only in the text, as personal communications. Include the author's name (use the screen name if the real name is not available), the date of the posting, its subject line or "thread" (followed by any identifying number, in square brackets), and the address of the news or discussion group. For a mailing list, include the name of the list and the address for the archived version of the message.

Sand, P. (1996, April 20). Java disabled by default in Linux
    Netscape. Message posted to news://keokuk.unh.edu,
    archived at http://granite.unh.edu/pasnews/msg00688.html
Crispen, P. (2001, September 2). The Hunger Site/Windows RG/
    WebElements. Message posted to The Internet Tourbus,
    archived at http://www.tourbus.com

AN ABSTRACT RETRIEVED FROM AN ELECTRONIC DATABASE

Natchez, G. (1987). Frida Kahlo and Diego Rivera: The trans-
    formation of catastrophe to creativity. <u>Psychotherapy-
    Patient, 8,</u> 153-174. Abstract retrieved October 4, 2001,
    from PsychLIT database.

A NEWSPAPER ARTICLE RETRIEVED FROM AN ELECTRONIC DATABASE

Kepner, T. (2001, October 17). Suzuki: Made in Japan, Making It
    in America. <u>New York Times.</u> Retrieved October 19, 2001,
    from http://www.nytimes.com

AN EMAIL MESSAGE

In the APA style, do not list personal correspondence, including email, in your reference
list. Simply cite the person's name in your text, and in parentheses give the notation *personal communication* (in regular type, not underlined or italicized) and the date.

COMPUTER SOFTWARE

If an individual has proprietary rights to the software, cite that person's name as you
would for a print text. Otherwise, cite as you would an anonymous print text.

McAfee Office 2000. Version 2.0 [Computer software]. (1999).
    Santa Clara, CA: Network Associates.

Other Sources

A GOVERNMENT DOCUMENT

U.S. Department of Health and Human Services. (1996). <u>Clinical
    classifications for health policy research, version 2:
    Hospital inpatient statistics</u> (AHCPR Publication No.
    HCUP-3). Rockville, MD: Author.

AN UNPUBLISHED DOCTORAL DISSERTATION

```
Bullock, B. (1986). Basic needs fulfillment among less devel-
    oped countries: Social progress over two decades of
    growth. Unpublished doctoral dissertation, Vanderbilt Uni-
    versity, Nashville, TN.
```

A TELEVISION PROGRAM

```
Hoppe, B., & Lattanzi, B. (1995). The universe within (G.
    Koide, Director). In P. Apsell (Producer), Nova. Boston:
    WGBH.
```

A FILM OR VIDEOTAPE

```
Singleton, J. (Writer and Director). (1991). Boyz n the hood
    [Film]. New York: Columbia.
```

A MUSIC RECORDING

If the recording date differs from the copyright date, the APA requires that it should appear in parentheses after the name of the label. If it is necessary to include a number for the recording, use parentheses for the medium; otherwise, use brackets.

```
Beethoven, L. van. (1806). Violin concerto in D major, op. 61
    [Recorded by USSR State Orchestra]. (Cassette Recording
    No. ACS 8044). New York: Allegro. (1980)
```

```
Springsteen, B. (1984). Dancing in the dark. On Born in the
    U.S.A. [CD]. New York: Columbia.
```

AN INTERVIEW

When using the APA style, do not list personal interviews in your references list. Simply cite the person's name (last name and initials) in your text, and in parentheses give the notation *personal communication* (in regular type, not italicized or underlined) followed by a comma and the date of the interview. For published interviews, use the appropriate format for an article.

■ SOME SAMPLE RESEARCH PAPERS

As a writer, you will want or need to use sources on many occasions. You may be assigned to write a research paper, complete with formal documentation of outside sources. Several of the writing assignments in this book present opportunities to do library or field research—in other words, to turn to outside sources. Among the readings in Part One, the essays listed here cite and document sources. (The documentation style each follows is given in parentheses.)

"Cannibalism: It Still Exists," by Linh Kieu Ngo, Chapter 4, pp. 114–18 (MLA)

"Children Need to Play, Not Compete," by Jessica Statsky, Chapter 5, pp. 155–59 (MLA)

"More Testing, More Learning," by Patrick O'Malley, Chapter 6, pp. 200–3 (APA)

"Asthma on the Web," by Kristine Potter, Chapter 7, pp. 236–43 (MLA)

Acknowledgments

Text Credits

David Ansen. "Star Wars: The Phantom Movie." From *Newsweek,* May 17, 1999. Copyright © 1999 by Newsweek, Inc. All rights reserved. Reprinted with permission.

Rick Bragg. "100 Miles per Hour, Upside Down and Sideways." From *All Over but the Shoutin'* by Rick Bragg. Copyright © 1997 by Rick Bragg. Reprinted with the permission of Pantheon, a division of Random House, Inc.

Annie Dillard. "Handed My Own Life." From *An American Childhood* by Annie Dillard. Copyright © 1987 by Annie Dillard. Reprinted with the permission of HarperCollins Publishers, Inc.

Martin Luther King Jr. An annotated sample from "Letter from a Birmingham Jail." Copyright © 1963 by Martin Luther King Jr. Copyright renewed 1991 by The Heirs to the Estate of Martin Luther King Jr. Reprinted by arrangement with the Heirs to the Estate of Martin Luther King Jr., c/o Writers House, Inc. as agent for the proprietor.

Alan I. Leshner. "Why Shouldn't Society Treat Substance Abusers?" From the *Los Angeles Times,* June 11, 1999, p. 7. Copyright © 1999 by Alan I. Leshner, Ph.D., Director, National Institute on Drug Abuse, National Institute of Health. Reprinted with permission of the author.

Mariah Burton Nelson. "Adventures in Equality." Excerpt from *The Stronger Women Get, the More Men Love Football: Sexism and the American Culture of Sports* by Mariah Burton Nelson. Copyright © 1994 by Mariah Burton Nelson. Reprinted with the permission of Harcourt, Inc.

Katherine S. Newman. "Dead-End Jobs: A Way Out?" From *The Brookings Review,* Fall 1995. Copyright © 1995 Katherine S. Newman. Reprinted with permission.

Peggy Orenstein. "The Daily Grind: Lessons in the Hidden Curriculum." From *School Girls: Young Women, Self-Esteem and the Confidence Gap* by Peggy Orenstein. Copyright © 1994 by Peggy Orenstein and American Association of University Women. Reprinted with the permission of Doubleday, a division of Random House, Inc.

Carol Potera. "Internet Addiction." Originally titled "Trapped in the Web." From *Psychology Today,* March/April 1998, vol. 31, #2, p.66. Copyright © 1998 Sussex Publishers, Inc. Reprinted with permission.

Rob Ryder. "Ten Is a Crowd, So Change the Game." From *The New York Times,* March 8, 1998. Copyright © 1998 by The New York Times Company. Reprinted with permission.

"Soup." Originally titled "Slave" from The Talk of the Town section in *The New Yorker* magazine, January 23, 1989. Copyright © 1989 by The New Yorker Magazine, Inc. All rights reserved. Reprinted with permission.

Anastasia Toufexis. "Love: The Right Chemistry." From *Time,* February 15, 1993. Originally titled "The Right Chemistry." Copyright © 1993 Time, Inc. All rights reserved. Reprinted with permission.

Art Credits

"Adventures in Equality" cartoon. © Tim Egan. Reprinted by permission.

"Darth Maul" photo. © Lucasfilm/Photofest.

Index

SUBMITTING PAPERS FOR PUBLICATION

TO STUDENTS AND INSTRUCTORS

We hope that we'll be able to include essays from more colleges and universities in the next edition of *Axelrod & Cooper's Concise Guide to Writing* and our accompanying anthology, *Sticks and Stones and other student essays*. Please let us see essays written using the *Concise Guide* you'd like us to consider. Send them with this Paper Submission Form and the Agreement Form on the back to *Concise Guide*, Bedford/St. Martin's, 33 Irving Place, New York, NY 10003.

PAPER SUBMISSION FORM

Instructor's name _____

School _____

Address _____

Department_____

Student's name _____

Course _____

Writing activity the paper represents _____

This writing activity appears in chapter(s) _____
of *Axelrod & Cooper's Concise Guide to Writing*

AGREEMENT FORM

I hereby transfer to Bedford/St. Martin's all rights to my essay,

(tentative title), subject to final editing by the publisher. These rights include copyright and all other rights of publication and reproduction. I guarantee that this essay is wholly my original work, and that I have not granted rights to it to anyone else.

Student's signature: X _____

Please type

Name: _____

Address: _____

_____

_____

Phone: _____

Please indicate the reader or publication source you assumed for your essay:

_____

Write a few sentences about the purpose or purposes of your essay. What did you hope to achieve with your reader? _____

_____

_____

_____

_____

_____

_____

Bedford/St. Martin's representative: _____